Social Security

Social Security

A Fresh Look at Policy Alternatives

JAGADEESH GOKHALE

THE UNIVERSITY OF CHICAGO PRESS   CHICAGO AND LONDON

JAGADEESH GOKHALE is a senior fellow at the Cato Institute.

The University of Chicago Press, Chicago 60637
The University of Chicago Press, Ltd., London
© 2010 by The University of Chicago
All rights reserved. Published 2010
Printed in the United States of America
19 18 17 16 15 14 13 12 11 10   1 2 3 4 5

ISBN-13: 978-0-226-30033-7   (cloth)
ISBN-10: 0-226-30033-1   (cloth)

♾ The paper used in this publication meets the minimum requirements of the American National Standard for Information Sciences—Permanence of Paper for Printed Library Materials, ANSI z39.48-1992.

Contents

List of Tables   xi

List of Figures   xv

I. Issues in Evaluating Social Security's Finances

CHAPTER 1.   The Simmering Social Security Reform Debate   9

CHAPTER 2.   Simulating U.S. Demographics and Economics:
Beginning in 1970   36

CHAPTER 3.   Forward Motion: Demographic Transition,
1971–2006   47

APPENDIX 3.1.   Mortality Rate Calculations   62

APPENDIX 3.2.   Estimating Fertility Rates by Female Race, Age, and
Education   64

APPENDIX 3.3.   Marriage and Divorce   66

APPENDIX 3.4.   Labor Force Status Transitions   69

APPENDIX 3.5.   Calibration of Immigrants' Characteristics   72

CHAPTER 4.   Peering into the Future   77

CHAPTER 5.   A Framework for Simulating Annual Nominal
Earnings   87

APPENDIX 5.1.   Method for Simulating "Effective Labor Inputs"   105

APPENDIX 5.2.   Simulating Workers' "Effective Labor Inputs"
in 1970   110

APPENDIX 5.3.   Regression for Simulating Life-Cycle "Core Labor
                Input" Trajectories   113

CHAPTER 6.   Simulating Social Security's Finances   116

APPENDIX 6.1.   The Social Security Tax and Benefit Calculator   134

CHAPTER 7.   Micromeasures of Social Security's Financial
                Condition   142

II. Issues in Evaluating Social Security Reform Proposals

CHAPTER 8.   Liberal Proposal 1 by Robert M. Ball: "A Golden
                Opportunity for the New Congress"   173

APPENDIX 8.1.   Estate Tax Revenue Projections for the Robert M. Ball
                Reform Proposal   182

CHAPTER 9.   Liberal Proposal 2 by Peter A. Diamond and Peter R.
                Orszag: "A Balanced Approach"   184

APPENDIX 9.1.   Incorporating Diamond-Orszag Reform Elements into
                DEMSIM   200

CHAPTER 10.   Centrist Proposal 1 by Representatives Jim Kolbe,
                Charles Stenholm, and Allen Boyd: "Bipartisan
                Retirement Security Act"   204

CHAPTER 11.   Centrist Proposal 2 by Jeffrey Liebman, Maya
                MacGuineas, and Andrew Samwick: "A Nonpartisan
                Approach to Reforming Social Security"   229

CHAPTER 12.   Conservative Proposal 1 by the President G. W.
                Bush Commission to Strengthen Social Security:
                Model 2   245

APPENDIX 12.1. Benefit Offset Calculation under G. W. Bush
Commission Model 2   266

CHAPTER 13.   Conservative Proposal 2 by Representative Paul Ryan:
"Social Security Personal Savings Guarantee and
Prosperity Act"   269

APPENDIX 13.1. Progressive CPI Indexing Social Security Benefits under
the Ryan Reform Proposal   292

CHAPTER 14.   Key Conclusions about Social Security's Financial
Condition and Reform Alternatives   294

Acknowledgments   315

Notes   317

References   343

Index   349

Tables

1.1. A brief glimpse of the aggregate effects of alternative Social Security reform proposals   34

2.1. Simulated attributes, attribute values, and conditioning attributes: Family-type: "Non-family"   42

2.2. Simulated attributes, attribute values, and conditioning attributes: Family-type: "Family"   43

2.3. CPS and DEMSIM population characteristics (1970)   46

3.1. Annual attribute transitions and conditioning variables   48

3.2. Share of married adults by race and gender for selected years (%)   55

A3.1. Labor force status transition probabilities   70

4.1. DEMSIM population shares (%) in selected education and labor force participation categories by race, gender, and future year   82

6.1. 75-year and infinite horizon Social Security (OASI) open and closed group imbalances under alternative DEMSIM assumptions   124

7.1. Selected characteristics of DEMSIM adults by birth cohort, gender, race, and present value of lifetime earnings (E)   156

7.2. Social Security wealth as a share of lifetime earnings under DEMSIM baseline assumptions by birth year, gender, race, and present value of earnings (E)   163

8.1. Impact of the Robert M. Ball reform proposal on Social Security's (OASI) finances   179

9.1.   Impact of the Diamond-Orszag reform proposal on Social
       Security's (OASI) finances   190

9.2.   Effects of Diamond-Orszag reform proposal on selected popula-
       tion groups   196

10.1. Impact of the Kolbe-Stenholm-Boyd reform proposal on Social
       Security's (OASI) finances   214

10.2. Effects of Kolbe-Stenholm-Boyd reforms on selected population
       groups   219

11.1. Impact of the Liebman-MacGuineas-Samwick reform proposal on
       Social Security's (OASI) finances   236

11.2. Effects of Liebman-MacGuineas-Samwick reform proposal on
       selected population groups   240

12.1. Impact of the G. W. Bush Commission's Model 2 on Social
       Security's (OASI) finances   255

12.2. Effects of the G.W. Bush Commission's Model 2 on selected
       population groups   260

13.1. Impact of the Ryan proposal on Social Security's (OASI)
       finances   277

13.2. Effects of the Ryan Social Security reform proposal on selected
       population groups   284

13.3. Retirement wealth levels under Ryan guaranteed, Ryan scheduled,
       and current law by 15-year birth cohorts, gender, race, and lifetime
       earnings (E)   288

14.1. Effects of alternative reform proposals on Social Security's
       aggregate finances   303

14.2. Lifetime net tax rates, personal account sizes, and total Social
Security wealth at retirement under various reform
proposals   307

14.3. Reduction in lifetime income uncertainty under DEMSIM
baseline and alternative reform proposals (%)   310

Figures

2.1.   Driver values for the "years of education" attribute: non-white males aged 20–29 in 1970   41

2.2.   Comparing CPS and DEMSIM's simulated population structures (1970)   44

3.1.   CPS and DEMSIM population shares by education category   50

3.2.   Probability of childbirth by female age, race, and education   52

3.3.   CPS and DEMSIM labor force participation rates   57

3.4.   CPS and DEMSIM's simulated population shares by family type and age   60

A3.1.   Mortality rates by race, age, and gender   63

A3.2.   Marriage and divorce rates   67

A3.3-1.   Distributions of immigrants' characteristics   73

A3.3-2.   Distributions of immigrants by age and family size   74

A3.3-3.   Percent of immigrants not participating in the labor force   74

A3.3-4.   Cumulative distributions of immigrants by years-of-education categories   75

4.1.   Projected population shares of simulated family types by age   79

4.2.   Labor force participation rates among 18–75-year-olds and worker/beneficiary ratios for the 18+ population   83

4.3.   Long-term simulation outcomes: population index; crude
        fertility, mortality, and immigration rates; and overall
        population growth rate   85

5.1.   PSID and DEMSIM log labor earnings distributions
        (1970)   91

5.2.   CPS and simulated wage distributions: 1970-2006   94

5.3.   Index of simulated aggregate effective labor inputs:
        2006–2080   99

5.4.   Indices of DEMSIM's inflation-adjusted average labor earnings
        and capital per worker   100

5.5.   Simulated aggregate labor earnings index and its annual
        growth   102

A5.1.   Annual changes in CPI and the nominal composite productivity
        index   109

A5.2.   Variations in DEMSIM's 1970 "core labor inputs" by selected
        worker demographic characteristics   111

A5.3.   Variations in life-cycle "core labor input" trajectories by selected
        worker demographic characteristics   114

6.1.   Projected Social Security (OASI) receipts and benefits for
        2006–2080: 2006 Social Security Trustees' intermediate
        assumptions and DEMSIM baseline   121

6.2.   Social Security's (OASI) financial projections under alternative
        assumptions   127

8.1.   Simulated ratio of taxable-to-total labor earnings under
        DEMSIM's baseline assumptions   176

8.2.   Annual non-interest imbalance ratios: DEMSIM baseline and
        Robert M. Ball reform proposal   180

9.1.   Annual non-interest imbalance ratios: DEMSIM baseline and
        Diamond-Orszag reform proposal   194

10.1.   Annual non-interest imbalance ratios: DEMSIM baseline
        and Kolbe-Stenholm-Boyd reform proposal   217

11.1.   Annual non-interest imbalance ratios: DEMSIM baseline and
        Liebman-MacGuineas-Samwick reform proposal   238

12.1.   Annual non-interest imbalance ratios: DEMSIM baseline and
        G. W. Bush Commission, Model 2   258

13.1.   Indexing NRA to longevity increases under the Ryan reform
        proposal   274

13.2.   Annual non-interest imbalance ratios: DEMSIM baseline and
        Ryan proposal under selected PSA participation rates   281

14.1.   Annual imbalance ratios: DEMSIM baseline and alternative
        reform proposal   305

Issues in Evaluating Social Security's Finances

Social Security—a program that millions of Americans are counting on for a secure retirement—is itself insecure according to its trustees. Publication by the Social Security trustees' of that program's financial outlook each spring triggers habitual posturing by key interest groups. The program's supporters extol its history of support to millions of retirees, their dependents, and survivors. They remind voters of its strong commitment to provide similar benefits in the future. And they claim that the program's financial condition remains sound because its trust fund is not projected to be exhausted for about three more decades. The program's opponents, however, use the opportunity to bemoan its inequities and tax burdens that worsen economic incentives to work and save. They deplore the very low return that the program yields on payroll taxes compared to private market returns, and caution that Social Security will shift from contributing to draining funds from the government's general budget within the decade unless its benefit commitments are brought into line with its dedicated tax receipts.

The trustees' 2009 report shows a significantly worsened financial outlook because rising unemployment has reduced projected payroll taxes and faster-than-expected longevity improvements have increased projected benefit payments. However, when the economy recovers and other favorable events or policies (immigration reform?) transpire, the recent worsening of the program's finances may be partially or even fully offset.

It's not surprising, therefore, that most casual observers have come to view the annual spring Social Security bloviate-fest by various interest groups as just that and nothing more.

Periodic fluctuations in the trustees' estimates of Social Security's finances are only to be expected, but a systematic and significant understatement of the program's financial problems would be much more serious. Unfortunately, the latter appears to be true. The trustees appear to base their conclusions on relatively crude estimation methods—ones that do not take into account important structural features of U.S. demographics, key characteristics of Americans' economic choices, and interrelationships between those two elements. Although the trustees' annual reports contain extensive information on a large number of demographic and economic factors that affect the program's finances, it is very difficult for outside observers to appreciate the factors—even key ones—that may be missing from the trustees' estimation methods and procedures. This book's considerably more detailed, careful, and independent evaluation of the program's finances shows that Social Security's financial problems are much bigger than officially acknowledged.

Information about precisely how and why the trustees' analysis and projections of Social Security's finances may be inadequate can be obtained only through a detailed analysis of all the relevant demographic and economic elements, including their joint evolution in the past and their likely progression through the future. Such an analysis must begin by systematically developing a framework for analyzing and projecting the program's operations from basic building blocks. Fortunately, those building blocks are publicly available in the form of microdata on U.S. demographic and economic features and organization, Americans' behavior patterns, and detailed rules about how Social Security's revenues and benefits are determined.

This book undertakes such an analysis of Social Security by constructing a microsimulation of U.S. demographic and economic features. Microsimulations are useful for understanding how all of those features would interact with each other and evolve over time to determine future characteristics of the U.S. population and economy within which Social Security will operate. The microsimulation developed here is called *D*emographic and *E*conomic *Microsim*ulation or DEMSIM. Although several other microsimulations have been constructed and are regularly used for evaluating various aspects of Social Security's operations, the only evaluations of Social Security's long-term financial condition and of proposals to reform that program are those conducted by government agencies. No private-sector agencies apparently believe it is feasible or desirable to independently check whether those projections adopt the correct methodology and provide reasonable estimates.

Of course, the Social Security Advisory Board convenes a Technical Panel on Assumptions and Methods every four years. This panel, comprised of non-governmental economists and actuaries, makes recommendations on whether and how the Social Security Trustees should revise their key economic and demographic assumptions and how it should improve its methodology. However, many of the panel's key suggestions have appeared to fall on deaf ears: the Social Security Administration (SSA) has moved at a glacial pace in updating its projection methodology. So far, it has not generated any significant capability of using microsimulation methods for analyzing the program's financial conditions and the effects of alternative reforms. Indeed, the latest Technical Panel (Social Security Advisory Board 2007) expresses frustration and impatience about the lack of significant progress in updating and enhancing the SSA's analytical methods and tools—particularly in transitioning to a comprehensive microsimulation approach. Although the Social Security Trustees' financial projections of that program utilize a limited number of microsimulation elements, its methodology is predominantly "cell-based." A cell-based method relies on dividing the population into groups (or cells) based on a particular attribute (such as age) and calculating averages of various other attributes (such as earnings) for each cell. Taxes and benefits are based on average earnings for each cell weighted by the number of members in each cell. Such a method places severe limitations on the types of mutual interactions between relevant variables that can be captured when projecting future demographic, economic, and financial developments for a program such as Social Security.

Most of the competing microsimulations that could be used to evaluate Social Security's finances are also sponsored or influenced by government agencies. Indeed, government budget scoring agencies receive vast amounts of resources for developing capabilities to analyze solvency and effects of reforms for programs such as Social Security. Apart from the Social Security Trustees, the Congressional Budget Office (CBO) also evaluates Social Security's financial condition. Its recent development of a microsimulation for making Social Security's financial projections has been marginally beneficial in generating competition and providing independent evaluations of Social Security's finances. However, those familiar with both methodologies report that the CBO's microsimulation is cali-brated to "agree" on key aspects of underlying demographic projections. For example, the most recent report on CBO's long-term modeling meth-odology states that "CBO adopts the assumptions of the Social Security Trustees—specifically, for this [Social Security] analysis, the assumptions in the 2008 trustees' report on the aggregate fertility rate, the rate of de-cline in mortality, the level of immigration, and the rates of disability inci-dence and termination. CBO's long-term economic assumptions are based on the assumptions used in its baseline budget projections" (Congressio-nal Budget Office 2008, p. 7).

That is, the CBO calibrates its microsimulation to deliver *aggregate demographic outcomes* that are identical to those of the Social Security Trustees. Therefore, depending on how constraints are introduced to de-liver those outcomes, demographic and economic developments that could result from unconstrained mutual interactions between various popula-tion attributes might be distorted under CBO's projections as well, and the limitations of the Social Security Trustees' methodology may creep into CBO's microsimulation-based projections. These considerations make it worthwhile to independently explore whether an unconstrained microsim-ulation—even one that uses the trustees' underlying demographic param-eters—would produce significantly different estimates of Social Security's financial condition and the effects of alternative policy changes.

Other major microsimulations for Social Security analysis are oper-ated by various think tanks and academic consortiums, but their efforts are mostly directed at analyzing special and relatively narrow issues about Social Security's operations. They do not independently and comprehen-sively assess whether government agencies' methods and results provide sufficiently accurate information about the program's future finances and the likely impact of various reform options. Moreover, many of these pri-vate institutions undertake projects on contract for the Social Security Administration and may not be in a position to render independent judg-ments about that agency's methodology and results. Indeed, instead of working as a check on Social Security's official financial projections, most analysts who prepare and use microsimulation-generated Social Security projections first calibrate their baseline results to match official projec-tions as closely as possible.

Given the importance of Social Security—a social insurance program that affects nearly all U.S. residents and is in principle intended to last forever—and given that it exerts significant economic effects, an independent private-sector initiative to construct Social Security's financial projections and analyze reform options seems well worth the effort. This is not to suggest that the Social Security Trustees and CBO officials are inherently biased in some way when scoring the program's finances and reform proposals. But their specific methodologies appear to be incomplete and inadequate to portray reasonably accurately all potential demographic and economic developments that would influence Social Security's future financial trajectory under a given set of Social Security policies.

The key distinction to be emphasized is between simply basing Social Security's financial projections on relatively coarsely specified demographic projections and basing them on a detailed microsimulation of the *interactions* between several demographic and economic variables. Indeed, although DEMSIM's demographic projections closely match those made by the Social Security Trustees in terms of a key population ratio (the number of workers relative to retirees) taking account of the interactions between demographic and economic variables—especially in the projection of labor earnings—under a microsimulation approach yields very different projections of Social Security's prospective finances with important implications for future reforms.

The projections and results described in this book under DEMSIM's baseline assumptions suggest that Social Security's financial condition is significantly worse compared to official projections by the program's trustees. It should not be surprising, therefore, that DEMSIM's results from analyzing six prominent reform proposals paint a significantly different picture compared to their official scoring by Social Security's Office of the Chief Actuary (SSOCACT). Reform proposals that achieve 75-year solvency under official scoring fall far short of that goal under DEMSIM. The chief reason for these results is that DEMSIM's simulation methodology accounts for important interactions between demographic and economic variables going forward—ones that government agency methodologies do not fully consider. Those interactions produce a lower baseline trajectory for future payrolls and payroll taxes. However, the financial imbalance between payroll taxes and benefits, calculated in present value terms, is larger than under official estimates by Social Security's Trustees, implying that the imbalance is also much larger as a share of the present value of payrolls. Moreover, with the base year set at 2006, a significantly larger share of Social Security's total financial imbalance arises during the next 75 years.

Official scoring of Social Security reform options by SSOCACT and CBO also do not provide adequate information about the choices and trade-offs that would be made at the macro and micro levels under different reform proposals. Indeed, under the excuse that social insurance programs involve and require redistributive effects, some analysts support reporting frameworks that restrict information about the Social Security's intra- and intergenerational redistribution through taxes and benefits. This view should be rejected because it fosters policymaking under incomplete information about the effects of alternative reforms on the program's finances and their likely impact on private citizens' budgets.

At the macro level policymakers and the public should be able to judge the impact of current laws on (1) the total size of the Social Security system's financial imbalance—that is, the program's total shortfall of future resources compared to its total future benefit commitments; (2) the timing of when "unfunded" benefit commitments would emerge and become large; and (3) how different population cohorts, broadly defined, would be treated, on net, under the programs current rules—that is, which groups would receive benefits in excess of their payroll taxes and which groups face more payroll taxes compared to benefits over their lifetimes. It should also be possible to assess how these three items would be affected under each reform alternative.

Beginning in 2003, the Social Security Trustees have been publishing new measures of the system's long-term finances that correctly reveal the items listed above under current laws. But the program's trustees and CBO officials have so far not used these measures for evaluating any of the Social Security reforms proposed by lawmakers and others. The program's overall financial baseline and the effects on it under alternative reforms continue to be reported in terms of measures (summary 75-year imbalances and annual cash flows) that do not fully reveal the impact of reforms on the program's future finances and effects on broad subgroups of the current and future population.

At the individual (micro) level, the impact of current laws and alternative reforms are officially evaluated in terms of "income replacement rates" at retirement. As argued in this book, such measures should be complemented with lifetime measures of how the program, and reforms to it, would treat different types of individuals throughout their (adult) lifetimes. Such measures would be useful to inform the public about (1) the Social Security *lifetime net tax rates* that they face—the pure tax portion of their payroll taxes; (2) to what extent the program provides resources for retirement irrespective of taxes paid in the past—a *retirement wealth* measure; and (3) to what extent the program reduces lifetime income uncertainty—that is, protects workers against poor labor market outcomes on a lifetime basis. Such information is crucial for policymakers and practitioners to fully assess the program's current operation and the desirability of alternative reforms.

This book reports results from an independent microsimulation-based evaluation of Social Security's finances and selected reform options. It hopes to convince the reader that independent checks of official reform scoring exercises are useful; that a microsimulation approach has several advantages over the current Social Security Trustees' actuarial practice in making the program's financial projections; and that reform analyses should be based on appropriate aggregate measures of the program's long-term finances and lifetime measures of how various types of individuals fare, on average, under the program's current rules and how they would fare under alternative reforms. Without adopting such comprehensive methods and measures for evaluating Social Security's finances, policymakers and the public would not be sufficiently informed in deciding future policy adjustments for dealing with Social Security's structural shortcomings and financial shortfalls.

CHAPTER ONE

The Simmering Social Security Reform Debate

A Pause and an Opportunity

The Social Security reform debate remains in limbo as of this writing during early 2009. President George W. Bush stopped promoting his preferred approach of introducing Social Security personal accounts after losing Republican majorities in both houses of Congress in the 2006 midterm elections. Although when he assumed office as U.S. treasury secretary, the prime objective of Henry Paulson was to explore broad-based entitlement reforms during the last two years of the Bush administration, a decline in the international value of the dollar compelled greater focus on China-related international trade and finance issues. And when a financial crisis emerged during late 2007, financial, auto, and housing sector bailouts took center stage during the remainder of the G. W. Bush presidency.

The ongoing economic recession is projected to boost annual federal deficits in 2009 and beyond to extraordinary levels. Political pressure to adopt strong countercyclical government spending has prompted Congress and the new Obama administration to propose massive new fiscal stimulus programs financed by government borrowing. In light of already massive entitlement shortfalls, the imperative of reforming Social Security and Medicare with an eye to reducing the federal government's long-term fiscal obligations will only grow more intense.

The 2005 debate on Social Security reform revealed deep ideological and political disagreements on entitlement—especially Social Security—reforms between the two major political parties. However, President Obama has proclaimed the need for "unprecedented" initiatives to meet the nation's long-term economic challenges, and another attempt at reforming Social Security may soon rekindle the debate on policy alternatives. There have also been occasional news reports about behind-the-scenes negotiations on Social Security reform between Republicans and Democrats in Congress.[1] Initiatives by small groups of lawmakers may be useful for refining positions, exploring new options, and maintaining communication channels. However, given the wide ideological rift on approaches to Social Security reform, and because economic interests of large and powerful voter groups are involved, a secretly negotiated "grand bargain" on Social Security appears unlikely to succeed. At the time of this writing, however, one can only guess about how the process of building sufficient political support for implementing a far-reaching Social Security reform will unfold.

The most likely first step would be the appointment of yet another commission to make reform proposals. Past Social Security reform commissions—those appointed by Presidents Bill Clinton and George W. Bush—failed to trigger significant changes to Social Security because no single approach from among the several that were proposed garnered adequate support. However, those two commissions have studied Social Security reform options in considerable detail. In addition, many lawmakers, academicians, and fiscal policy experts from across the political spectrum have proposed a wide variety of alternative approaches for restructuring Social Security.

Collectively, existing Social Security reform proposals seem to exhaust possible approaches for modifying the program, and a new Obama commission on entitlement reforms is likely to simply revisit earlier options and approaches—at least in the case of Social Security. Regardless of how the next Social Security reform effort evolves, one should question whether government scoring agencies employ reasonable methods and measures and whether information obtained from them on the program's finances are reasonably accurate.

Although talk of entitlement reforms may soon be reawakened by the prospective recession-induced buildup of U.S. national debt, the period of relative calm in the Social Security reform debate since 2005 presented an opportunity for assessing Social Security reform options using a fresh perspective. This book reports the results from a microsimulation—

DEMSIM—that was developed after the 2005 Social Security reform debate. It provides a new analytical tool and a new perspective on Social Security's future finances under current laws. The results also provide additional insights into the effects of particular Social Security reform measures from among six selected reform packages.

Another Book on Social Security Reform?

Many analysts and academics find the topic of Social Security reform to be quite riveting. To date, scores of lawmakers, federal budget analysts, university professors, and businessmen have proposed a variety of Social Security reform packages. Social Security's Office of the Chief Actuary (SSOCACT) scores such proposals chiefly, but not exclusively, in response to lawmakers' requests. About thirty Social Security reform packages have been scored by SSOCACT for their effects on the program's overall finances and on various population groups.[2]

Unfortunately, SSOCACT's memoranda are rather terse, and the metrics used for evaluating the proposals' effects have some shortcomings: the evaluation is exclusively in terms of the proposals' impact over a 75-year projection horizon—which means any comparison of alternative proposals based on SSOCACT scoring would not necessarily provide an apples-to-apples comparison. The reason is simply that some proposals may restore 75-year solvency only by pushing the program's costs beyond the 75th year whereas others may not. As a result any conclusions regarding their quality and desirability might be overturned simply because of the passage of a few years as out-year financial shortfalls enter the 75-year projection window. It's not that reporting over finite, even shorter-than-75-year, time horizons is undesirable, but extending the time horizon beyond 75 years to obtain a more comprehensive long-term picture of the program's finances and alternative reforms would be informative and would facilitate proper comparisons across reform alternatives.[3] Indeed, as some analysts have pointed out, focusing on a limited time horizon leads to a bias in policymaking: Lawmakers then have an incentive to favor proposals that minimize short-term imbalances and reject policy alternatives that could place the program's finances on a sounder long-term footing.[4]

Second, SSOCACT and the Social Security Trustees use an actuarial projection methodology that does not allow consideration of important mutual interactions between projected demographic and economic variables. The importance of adopting a rich modeling framework to allow such interactions when projecting future trends will become clearer in later chapters. This book's analysis, which is based on a detailed micro-simulation of future U.S. demographic and economic forces, suggests that such interactions hold significant implications for Social Security's future finances. The 2007 Social Security Technical Panel on Assumptions and Methods makes similar comments about the modeling methodology adopted by SSOCACT and the program's trustees. For example, the report states that "by explicitly accounting for interactions across variables, micro-simulation models increase transparency around key assumptions underlying the cell-based projections. . . . Micro-simulation can improve forecast quality when changes in the cross-section over time affect macroeconomic outcomes and thereby system finances" (Social Security Advisory Board 2007, p. 3).

The phrase "interactions across variables" refers to demographic and economic variables that influence one another. On the one hand, demographic attributes such as mortality, fertility, marriage, divorce, family split-offs (when children become independent adults, for example), racial composition, and so on, govern patterns of family formation and dissolution and influence economic variables such as rates of skill acquisition, working, saving, retirement, labor productivity, earnings, and so on. Consider the hypothetical example of two equally educated adults of the same age: a single female parent with five dependent children and a married male family head with just two dependent children. As microdata surveys confirm, the former is less likely to consistently participate in the workforce and, contingent on participation, earn as much as the latter.

On the other hand, economic variables such as education, labor force participation, and earnings, also affect demographic outcomes. For example, people tend to sort according to age, race, and education when deciding on marriage partners. Similarly, entry into the work force, acquiring education, making fertility and divorce decisions, and so on, trigger differences in family structures, racial composition, migration, and mortality experiences. Without capturing such interactions at the micro level—which is only possible under a microsimulation approach—it is difficult, if not impossible, to properly project the future evolution of labor market outcomes, in particular, to account for the evolution of total "effective labor inputs," which are crucial for determining future earnings distributions and the Social Security payroll tax base.

To provide a relatively simple example, a cell-based approach may project earnings based only on the population's projected age and gender distribution. That is, earnings may not be distinguished by race, education, marital status, family structure, the number of children, and so on, and earnings projections may not be based on the population's evolving cross-sectional distributions of these variables. Such an approach would misestimate future earnings if, conditional on age, "earnings-challenged" demographic groups become dominant in the population over time as in-built demographic and economic forces mutually interact and evolve. Following the earlier hypothetical example, total earnings growth projections based only on the population's projected age and gender distributions may contain large errors if changes in fertility and family formation patterns cause large increases in the share of single adults with many dependent children compared to married household heads with very few children.[5] Indeed, this may occur even if the population's average education level *increases* over time—a seemingly paradoxical result. This is the reason why the Technical Panel—as quoted above—strongly emphasizes the need to track how changes in the population's cross-section over time affect macroeconomic outcomes and thereby Social Security's finances.

Finally, some of the measures used by the Social Security Trustees to describe the impact of reforms are arguably obsolete. In most cases, income replacement rates are reported to asses a reform proposal's effect on specific population groups. However, Social Security is a lifetime program; participants pay taxes and receive benefits for many decades. And longevity increases since Social Security was first introduced in 1935 have made retirement life spans longer, making it especially important to consider lifetime net benefit (or net tax) measures when assessing Social Security's fiscal treatment of various types of individuals.[6] But a cell-based projection methodology permits such calculations only for stylized individuals or household rather than for representative samples of each population subgroup incorporating, for each, its associated demographic and economic attributes. Finally, there appears to be nothing in the literature on Social Security reform or on SSOCACT's Web site that provides a side-by-side and apples-to-apples comparison of different Social Security reform options.

Public Expectations and Government Obligations

Social Security continues to operate because the vast majority of Americans support the current program. In particular, workers acquiesce to payroll tax deductions from their paychecks. They do so because they expect to receive future Social Security benefits upon meeting the program's benefit eligibility terms—which they may be expecting to remain not too dissimilar to current ones. Without such future benefit expectations, it is difficult to imagine why working age voters would continue to support a program that taxes more than a tenth of their hard-won earnings.[7]

Workers' expectations of future benefits commensurate with their payroll taxes are so strongly entrenched that they are generally described as "entitlements"—created by participation in the program by paying payroll taxes during working years. This sense of entitlement to retirement and other benefits is strengthened by the special linkage that has been established under Social Security between worker earnings in occupations covered under Social Security, payroll taxes, benefit eligibility, and the amount of benefits.[8]

Participants' expectations of stability in the program's rules are anchored in the program's objective of enabling participants to maintain a reasonable living standard during retirement. This is the program's so-called social adequacy objective. Moreover, ensuring a *fair* fiscal treatment across different participants, including across different generations—known as the "individual equity" objective—requires that the program's rules remain stable over time. Any changes to the rules must be introduced very gradually and with sufficient lead time to allow participants to adjust their private economic choices—on working, saving, investing, and choosing when to retire—so that their expectations of reasonable living standards during retirement could be realized.

The expectations linking the quid of Social Security payroll taxes to the quo of future Social Security benefits is unique and appreciably stronger than expectations of other public goods and services in return for income taxes and other non-payroll taxes.[9] The stronger linkage of current Social Security payroll taxes with future expected Social Security benefits is created and reinforced by two aspects of the program. First, the Social Security benefit formula incorporates each worker's earnings history in calculating benefits to be awarded. That indirectly but formally links each worker's payroll taxes to future benefits. Second, the Social Security Administration sends annual benefit statements to all non-retired participants (workers) indicating the estimated amounts of various types of benefits that they would receive under current Social Security laws. Although the statements caution recipients that actual future benefits may be different if Congress changes Social Security's rules before they become due and payable, the statements nevertheless strengthen political support for the program by maintaining public confidence in receiving some future benefits. Hence, the statements provide additional political weight against dramatic changes to Social Security's current tax and benefit rules.

These features of Social Security mean that although participation in Social Security via payroll tax payments does not by itself accrue for workers any contractual rights to collect specific future benefits—that is, benefits of given and fixed amounts at particular future dates—such participation creates valid perceptions and expectations of future benefits and promotes the program's continued operation under relatively stable rules. By implication, there exists a corresponding, future payment "obligation" or "commitment" on the part of the federal government to pay benefits as participants become eligible to receive them. This politically supported future payment commitment appears to be quite firm notwithstanding the fact that no formal, contractual, and legally binding agreement for the government to pay benefits exists between the government and any individual participant. And political support for maintaining Social Security benefits close to their current levels is likely to become stronger as members of the baby boom generation enter the ranks of retirees during the next two decades. Yet another reason to believe that the government's future commitment to pay Social Security benefits is quite rigid is that those benefits are indexed to the general price level and, unlike most government bonds, their real value cannot be eroded away via faster inflation.

Social Security's Finances: A Stroll on the Beach or Armageddon?

The number of blogs and opinion columns claiming that Social Security has no financial problems number in the millions. But so do those claiming that Social Security's financial situation is dire.[10] Which perspective is correct? Much of the confusion on display in the public discourse on Social Security arises because of the tendency by some to view the program's operations on an exclusively short-term basis, forgetting that it involves long-term public expectations on taxes and benefits and corresponding government revenue sources and benefit obligations.

The Social Security program is currently generating a surplus of payroll and other dedicated taxes compared to current benefit payments. Indeed, according to the Social Security Trustees' latest projections (Social Security Board of Trustees 2008), the program will continue to accrue a surplus until the year 2017. The federal government will begin to feel the pinch of Social Security's revenue shortfalls after 2017 when the program's non-interest revenues begin to fall short of its benefit payments. However, benefit payments can be continued as scheduled even beyond that date without explicit congressional intervention until the program's trust fund—the repository of Treasury securities representing all accrued surpluses to date—becomes exhausted.

Note that although the trust fund represents past payroll tax surpluses, their mandatory investment in non-marketable Treasury securities makes the surplus payroll taxes available for Congress to spend immediately on other public goods—to the direct benefit of current generations. If beginning in 2017 the trust fund is drawn upon to pay benefits not covered by concurrent Social Security revenues, the costs of redeeming trust fund securities would have to be borne by future taxpayers—either in the form of less federal spending on non–Social Security public goods or by way of higher non-payroll taxes. If the trust fund becomes exhausted as officially projected in the year 2041, explicit legislation by Congress will be required to determine how benefit obligations to retirees in 2041 and later should be financed.

Ongoing payroll tax surpluses mean that Social Security is more than solvent in the short-term—well able to meet its benefit commitments out of current dedicated revenues. However, just taking current annual cash flows into account for evaluating the program's financial condition ignores important aspects of the program's operation. In particular, the cash-flow perspective misses the fact that payroll taxes deducted from workers' paychecks today create "implicit" government commitments to pay retirement and other benefits to them and their dependents and survivors in the future. Such prospective benefit commitments are called "implicit" because they could be reduced through future changes in Social Security laws. But, as discussed above, it is very unlikely that they would be suddenly and completely eliminated. This raises a question: How should future "implicit" benefit commitments be measured?

One possibility is to somehow fix a particular timing and extent of future Social Security tax and benefit changes and incorporate them in financial projections, but this would not be very informative given the vast uncertainty surrounding future changes to Social Security policies. It is more useful to show values of projected Social Security scheduled expenditures, revenues, and net expenditures under today's laws. In fact, reflecting the future financial implications of current laws using such projections is consistent with standard "budget measures" of the future finances of government programs. This approach helps to reveal by how much a program's payment commitments and resources diverge from each other. A simple metric, discussed below, is to calculate "present values" of these items through various time horizons, including in perpetuity because the program is intended to last forever in principle.

A potential hurdle is the interpretation of the term "present value." Although present value calculations are regularly used in financial analysis, some readers may be unfamiliar with how they are implemented or why they are needed. Text box 1 explains the method of finding the present value of a future payment flow and describes why they are useful.

Text Box: 1 Present Value Calculations

Future Social Security shortfalls and other financial flows—such as payrolls, payroll taxes, and future Social Security benefits—must be placed "on par" with each other before comparing them. That's because the time patterns of their accruals under a given Social Security policy may not be identical. This is done by discounting future dollar amounts to make them equivalent to dollars available today—or by calculating their "present values."

Suppose Social Security is projected to face a shortfall of $1 next year. If the government's interest rate equals 3 percent, the present discounted value of each dollar of that shortfall—as of this year—equals $1 / 1.03, or approximately 97 cents. That is, one dollar made available next year is the same as making 97 cents available this year because the latter could be invested at interest to yield $1 next year.

Now suppose Social Security is projected to face a shortfall of $1.20 in 10 years. Discounting it back to the present at a 3 percent interest rate per year would make that amount equal to $1.20 / $(1.03)^{10}$, or 89 cents. Thus, one way to cover the 10th year's projected shortfall is for the government to have 89 cents on hand today, invested at 3 percent per year for 10 years. This makes the sum of all discounted future annual shortfalls minus the value of the Social Security trust fund a key metric—the fund which, if available today and invested at the government's interest rate, would be sufficient to pay for all future shortfalls as they come due.

Social Security's projected annual dollar shortfalls themselves grow over time. Is the total present value of future annual shortfalls calculated in perpetuity a finite sum? Naturally, if the annual dollar shortfalls grow at the same rate or faster than the government's interest rate, their total discounted value would grow larger as the time horizon is extended. If, however, annual dollar shortfalls grow at a slower rate than the government's interest rate, their total discounted value would converge to a finite sum. The latter condition prevails for annual shortfalls and total payrolls under current U.S. economic and demographic projections and Social Security's current financing structure.

The present value of Social Security's future financial shortfalls could be presented in terms of today's dollars, as a ratio of the present value of future payrolls, and as a ratio of the present value of future Social Security benefits. The ratio of the present value of payrolls shows the immediate and permanent percentage point increase in the payroll tax rate that would balance the program's receipts and expenditures. The ratio of the present value of future Social Security benefits shows the immediate and permanent percentage point reduction in benefits that would also balance the system's finances. In either form, the metrics by themselves imply nothing about whether these alternative ways of balancing the system's finances are desirable or politically feasible.

Moving beyond simply evaluating short-term annual cash flows and taking into account net additional future financial commitments accruing over future years makes Social Security's financial condition appear far from secure. Balancing the present value of Social Security's projected resources, which include the value of Treasury securities in its trust fund plus the present value of future Social Security payroll taxes, against the present value of its projected benefit commitments—both evaluated at the government's long-term interest rate—reveals a massive financial imbalance according to Social Security's Trustees. Thus, a long-term perspective points to exactly the opposite conclusion: that Social Security's finances are in a dire state. As discussed below, calculating the *change* in Social Security's present valued financial imbalance from one year to the next also reveals that the program's finances are worsening rapidly.

Projecting Workers' Earnings and Earnings Growth

Apart from underlying demographics, key variables of interest for assessing Social Security's prospective finances are projections of aggregate earnings, the payroll tax base, and Social Security benefits. Payroll taxes are levied on the taxable portion of each individual's labor earnings. And Social Security benefits are based on individual labor earnings histories.

Thus, there is a close relationship between earnings and payroll taxes, and between earnings and (projected) Social Security benefits, even at the aggregate level.

A key objective of DEMSIM is to project future annual earnings and their distributions at both the individual and economy-wide levels. Aggregate labor earnings in each year are simply the sum of individual workers' earnings blown up by a factor of proportionality that depends on the size of the microsimulation relative to that of the total U.S. economy. And labor earnings depend on not just the amount of labor supplied by individuals, but also on overall worker quality. As in the simple example described earlier, both of these factors are influenced by workers' evolving demographic and economic status through time.

In contrast to the Social Security Trustees' approach, DEMSIM's modeling of economic and earnings growth is considerably richer: it specifies a fully articulated "Solow" growth model wherein growth of the economy's inputs—quality-adjusted labor and the capital stock—determines output and earnings growth. The projection of quality-adjusted labor involves projections of total labor quantity (through labor force participation) and each worker's quality (determined by the overall impact of that worker's demographic and economic circumstances). The projected capital stock is also based on the population's demographic attributes—a statistical matching and projection of net wealth ownership by age and gender according to the simulated evolution of the two latter variables.

The Solow growth model enables a detailed specification of earnings growth to capture increases in labor productivity because of (1) the growth in the capital stock and (2) overall technological progress. The standard approach to measuring the contribution of technological progress is by estimating the growth of the economy's total output that is in excess of the growth in labor and capital inputs—based on historical data over many decades. This excess growth is attributed to technological change and summarized by a "multifactor productivity" parameter.[11]

This method of projecting earnings growth is much more firmly grounded and consistent with the population's projected economic and demographic attributes: Each future year's growth rate is influenced by the evolution through that year of interacting demographic and economic attributes—which determine total quality-adjusted labor and capital inputs. The growth in inputs, combined with historically determined multifactor productivity growth, determine total output growth. Finally, applying another historically determined parameter to capture labor's share of total output yields projected annual rates of labor earnings growth. In essence, the Social Security Trustees assume future productivity growth to be a constant based on its historical average, whereas DEMSIM allows future productivity to vary in response to simulated demographic and economic developments.

The Open Group Unfunded Obligation Measure

If future benefit commitments must be included when evaluating Social Security's finances, how far into the future should we peer? The Social Security Trustees report the program's financial condition over several horizons—10, 25, 50, 75 years, and in perpetuity. At first glance, evaluating the program's finances in perpetuity or even over another 75 years seems rather long. Note, however, that the argument made earlier applies here as well: under a 10-year horizon, benefit commitments payable after the 10th year created from payroll taxes before the 10th year would be ignored. Not taking those post-horizon benefit commitments into account would understate the program's financial shortfall.

Logically speaking, this argument can be applied to any finite projection horizon. By implication, Social Security's financial condition would be comprehensively reflected only under a perpetuity, or infinite horizon, present value calculation of its future resources and benefit commitments under current rules. Note the infinite horizon present value calculation of future shortfalls is meaningful because it is not based on hypothetical future policies—that is, it is not a forecast of future shortfalls—but is based on the assumption that the program's current laws would be maintained. Thus, no matter how long the projection horizon is, the attempt is to project the future implications of the program's current laws, not to forecast future laws. Under this construction, it does not matter that the likelihood that Congress will alter the program's laws increases with the time horizon.[12]

To maintain comparability with official projections and reform analyses, this book reports annual imbalance ratios—the ratio of annual financial shortfalls and annual payrolls—extended through the 75-year horizon. The time series of annual imbalance ratios provides information on the time profile of future imbalances—when they are projected to emerge and grow rapidly. But this book also makes extensive use of the 75-year and infinite horizon present value ("summary") measures of

Social Security's financial condition under current laws. Under this approach, the program's total unfunded obligations can be calculated as the present value of projected benefits minus the present value of future tax receipts and minus the value of Treasury securities in its trust fund. This measure is called Social Security's *open group unfunded obligation* (open group measure, or "fiscal imbalance" for short). The last item in its calculation represents the federal government's commitment, again under current laws, to raise additional resources in the future (over and above payroll and other dedicated taxes) to return the accumulated value of past surpluses to the Social Security Trust Fund. The latest official estimate of Social Security's fiscal imbalances over 75 years and in perpetuity equal $4.3 trillion and $13.6 trillion, respectively (Social Security Board of Trustees 2008).

The open group measure has a simple and intuitive meaning: It represents the total net benefit in present value that Social Security would provide to *all* generations—past, present, and future—under indefinite continuation of the program's current policies. A *positive* net Social Security benefit for all generations must be paid for somehow. The standard assumption would be that the federal government's general account would provide the necessary resources. Thus, the open group measure indicates the net charge on general government resources that Social Security would impose were its current laws maintained in the future.

Another interpretation of the open group measure is that it represents the amount of additional funds that the government needs to have on hand—invested at interest—to offset all Social Security financial shortfalls as they arise in the future. Were this amount somehow available, the government would never have to adjust the program's current laws—that is, the additional fund would make current laws sustainable. Not having such a fund means that an equivalent amount must be raised by changing future federal policies—Social Security benefit reductions, payroll tax increases, or transfers from the general government budget—individually or in combination.

Reporting the open group measure for 75 years and in perpetuity also reveals the share of the program's total (infinite horizon) financial shortfall that accrues beyond the 75th year.[13] Under the Social Security Administration's official projections (as reported above), about two-thirds of the program's overall financial imbalance arises after the 75th year. Again, this suggests that restricting the measure to the next 75 years—seemingly, a very long period—would result in a substantial understatement of the program's total financial imbalance.[14]

Pay-as-You-Go

A debate before Social Security was enacted about how to finance the program was temporarily won by those wishing to pre-fund retirement benefits through payroll taxes.[15] Had such pre-funding persisted, the Social Security Trust Fund would have grown to more than $22 billion by 1955—a sizable amount in those times. However, arguments against pre-funding benefits eventually won the day on grounds that it would reduce spending discipline by providing the Treasury and the Congress with free access to funds and would eventually result in larger tax burdens on future generations. In addition, pre-funding future benefits would immediately withdraw investible resources from the economy leading to job losses.

To avoid a large accumulation of funds with the government, Congress amended the program in 1939, and retirement benefit payments began two years earlier (1940 instead of 1942). Congress also introduced new benefits for dependent spouses and survivors of covered workers. Those amendments reduced projected trust fund accumulations to just under $7 billion by 1955 and converted Social Security's financing to a fully "pay-as-you-go" system.

Under a pay-as-you-go financial structure, each year's payroll taxes are fully used to pay benefits. None of the revenues are saved and invested for meeting future benefit obligations to current workers.[16] Although the 1983 Social Security reforms resulted in larger trust fund accumulations, the reasoning of those who argued against pre-funding Social Security benefits appears to have been vindicated. Limited to accumulating just non-marketable Treasury securities in its portfolio, the Social Security Trust Fund is simply a conduit for the Treasury and the Congress to divert Social Security's surpluses for funding other current government expenditures—those that, perhaps, would not be undertaken in the absence of such surpluses.[17] That means current generations directly benefit from additional current government spending on public goods, the cost of which must be borne by future generations when the loaned funds are returned to Social Security by the U.S. Treasury by imposing additional costs on future taxpayers.

The early conversion of the program's financing structure from pre-funding to pay-as-you-go caused a massive transfer of resources to the initial generation of retirees. Those generations received benefits despite having paid little in payroll taxes when they were working. The payroll taxes of workers who funded the initial retiree cohort's benefits created implicit obligations for the system—to be financed out of payroll taxes from the next generation of workers, and from the next generation after that, and so on, throughout the future. Indeed, as the program was expanded to broader segments of the population and as its benefits were made more generous, payroll taxes had to be increased periodically to maintain annual pay-as-you-go solvency. As a result, several generations of early Social Security participants received very high returns on their previous payroll taxes by way of retirement and other benefits.

The program maintained pay-as-you-go solvency until 1983—that is, each year's payroll taxes were just sufficient to cover that year's Social Security benefits and no significant surpluses accumulated in its trust fund. The 1983 amendments to Social Security introduced "partial prefunding" by increasing payroll taxes, subjecting the benefits of high-income retirees to income taxes (revenues from which are also dedicated to Social Security), and scheduling increases in Social Security's normal retirement age—the age at which just-retiring workers become eligible to full retirement benefits. As a result of these changes since 1983, the Social Security Trust Fund has accumulated a cumulative surplus of $2.2 trillion today, all of it invested in non-marketable Treasury securities.

But the 1983 amendments did not reverse the cumulative historical evolution of Social Security's benefit formula toward increasing generosity. Neither did it put in place sufficient additional revenues to pay for the program's prospective benefit commitments to today's generations: the program's *future* benefit commitments to today's retirees and workers, net of their *future* payroll taxes, total $17.4 trillion according to official estimates. That's many times larger than the $2.2 trillion commitment to raise future resources as embodied in the program's trust fund.

The Closed Group Unfunded Obligation Measure

Social Security's net benefit commitment to current generations over their entire *lifetimes* (as opposed to just in *future* years) is difficult to isolate. That's because the net surplus/deficit of their past payroll taxes and benefits is embedded in the trust fund, which also incorporates the net surplus/deficit from past generations' payroll taxes and Social Security benefits. The two cannot be disentangled without full information on the entire history of Social Security's transactions with each birth cohort of participants. But it is possible to cleanly estimate the lifetime net benefits, including future commitments, to *past and current* generations together. This involves estimating the present value of projected benefits to current retirees and workers, subtracting their projected Social Security taxes (payroll taxes and income taxes on their future benefits), and subtracting the current value of the trust fund. This measure of the total net benefit commitment to past and current generations is called the *closed group unfunded obligation* ("closed group measure" for short).[18] The Social Security Trustees estimate this amount at $15.2 trillion (see Social Security Board of Trustees 2008).

The closed group measure reveals how much past and current workers would receive by way of net benefits in present value if current Social Security laws are maintained through their lifetimes. Recall that the open group measure encompasses the net present value of benefits of all generations—past, current, and future. Therefore, subtracting the closed group measure from the open group measure reveals the present value of net benefits of future generations under current Social Security policies. Thus, under official projections, future generations would receive –$1.5 trillion ($13.6 trillion minus $15.2 trillion).[19] That is, the present value of future generations' payroll taxes would be larger than the present value of their future Social Security benefits under current policies.

The closed group measure has yet another interpretation: it is the amount of Social Security's financial burden that current generations would bequeath to future ones if current policies are maintained—not indefinitely, but only throughout the lifetimes of current generations. That's because, if the closed group Social Security commitment were fulfilled by granting current generations excess net benefits of $15.2 trillion dollars—as under current Social Security laws—future generations must bear the burden of the debt created as a result. They must pay it off either by increasing payroll taxes, reducing their Social Security benefits, or transferring funds from the general government account (or by implementing a combination of these policies).[20]

Policy Calculus Using Open and Closed Group Measures

Any evaluation of Social Security reforms must enable policymakers and the public to understand how they would change the program's overall financial condition. The key questions that must be addressed are whether and by how much a proposed policy change improves or worsens the program's financial condition—both over 75 years and in perpetuity—and how the costs of that policy change are distributed across broad population groups—especially across those alive today and those who will inherit the program's obligations. The infinite horizon open group and the closed group measures taken together can answer these questions. However, although the Social Security Trustees report these measures under Social Security's current laws, none of its evaluations of Social Security reforms use them to provide these answers. The Congressional Budget Office reports these measures only partially and, again, does not use them to evaluate Social Security reform options.

The open group measure—estimated by the Social Security Trustees to be $13.6 trillion—tells us how far current policy is from balancing the program's revenues and expenditures taking past, present, and future generations' transactions into account. The *change* in the open group measure in response to a change in Social Security's policies indicates how much closer to balance that policy would bring the program's finances. Obviously, there are myriad combinations of changes in Social Security taxes and benefits that could reduce the open group measure by a given amount, each potentially corresponding to a different distribution of the total change in net payments on current and future generations.

Correspondingly, the closed group measure—estimated by the trustees to be $15.2 trillion—tells us Social Security's financial shortfall on account of just past and current generations. Again, a *change* in the closed group measure from a Social Security reform would show the extent to which the new policy changes the net benefits of current generations; obviously, past generations' net benefits cannot be changed. Hence, the change in the open group measure minus the change in the closed group measure shows the change in the net payment burden of future generations—which is currently estimated at $1.5 trillion.

Thus, open and closed group measures used in tandem enable an assessment of (1) whether and by how much any proposed policy change improves the program's financial condition (reduces its open group financial imbalance) and (2) how the costs of the policy change are distributed across current and future generations in terms of changes to their prospective excess benefits from the program or net payments to it.

A Slippery Slope

According to the 2007 Social Security Trustees annual report, Social Security's beginning-of-year shortfall of $13.6 trillion would accrue interest amounting to $700 billion during 2007. That means Social Security's total shortfall by the beginning of 2008 would be bigger by $700 billion if financial projections remain unchanged and no policy changes are undertaken in 2007 to reduce its size.

The fact that Social Security's shortfall grows larger by accruing interest costs over time would not matter if the U.S. economy's capacity to pay it also grows at the same or faster pace. However, under normal circumstances—especially for a modern economy such as the United States—national economic output generally grows at a slower pace. Under normal economic conditions, U.S. gross domestic product (GDP)—the total amount of goods and services produced, which amounted to $13.8 trillion in 2007—grows more slowly than the rate at which interest accrues on Social Security's financial shortfall. An interest cost of about $700 billion on a total Social Security shortfall of $13.6 trillion implies a nominal interest rate of 5.1 percent per year. However, according to the Congressional Budget Office, the nation's nominal GDP grew by 4.9 percent during 2007. The long-term wedge projected by the Social Security Administration between the average annual interest rate of 5.7 percent and annual GDP growth of 4.9 percent is even larger (Social Security Board of Trustees 2008).

Some analysts suggest that Social Security need not be reformed any time soon. They point to the still-growing trust fund that extends the program's financial integrity through the 2040s without need of overt government intervention. However, the fact that program's financial imbalance is growing at the rate of several hundred billion dollars per year—and at a rate that is faster than the growth of the nation's GDP—should give pause to supporters of that view. Delaying adjustments to Social Security's current laws will allow current workers and retirees to escape some of the adjustment burden—implying a larger adjustment burden on younger and future Social Security participants. Thus, delays will only increase costs, relative to available resources, for balancing the program's revenues and expenditures over time.[21]

Social Security's Fiscal Treatment of Population Subgroups

Social Security systematically treats different population groups differently with respect to their lifetime taxes and benefits. This is the result of systematic interactions between Social Security's rules regarding payroll taxes, determination of benefit eligibility, the benefit formula, the form in which benefits are paid, and the population's demographic and economic attributes. Those interactions result in a dissimilar—some would say in-equitable—lifetime fiscal treatment of various population subgroups. The differences in lifetime fiscal treatment—including treatment relative to lifetime earnings levels—can be measured by using the *lifetime net tax rate* metric. This metric is simply the difference between the present value of lifetime Social Security taxes and benefits as a ratio of the present value of lifetime earnings. It shows the fraction of lifetime earnings surrendered to Social Security as a "premium charge" for participating in its provision of social insurance.

For example, ineligibility to retirement benefits before age 62 implies that groups with shorter life expectancies receive fewer benefits during their lifetimes, which increases their lifetime net tax rates. Dependent and survivor benefits also imply smaller lifetime net tax rates for longer-lived individuals (women, for example) and larger ones for single as opposed to married individuals. These systematic differences potentially introduce economic inefficiencies making appropriate structural reforms of Social Security quite desirable. Indeed, many reform proposals explicitly target such effects produced under current Social Security rules. The lifetime net tax rate metric is one way of measuring whether and by how much alternative reform proposals succeed in redressing the program's micro-level inequities.

A Look Ahead

This book develops a microsimulation—called the Demographic and Economic Micro Simulation or DEMSIM—calibrated to microdata on the U.S. economy with the objective of analyzing Social Security's finan-cial outlook and the financial implications of alternative Social Security reforms. DEMSIM is quite detailed in its modeling of the many relevant demographic and economic variables that will influence Social Security's financial future. The exercise shows that when one takes account of how those variables will evolve going forward and, most importantly, how forces built into them under their current configuration would interact with each other in the future, the program's financial outlook appears far worse than official projections lead us to believe. As a result, most of the reforms that have been proposed to restore the program to financial health are likely to fall well short of achieving that objective.

Chapters 2–5 develop the demographic elements of DEMSIM: chapter 2 describes the development of its initial population of individuals and families as of the year 1970. It describes how the simulation controls the construction of the initial population in detail to match the U.S. population structure during the late 1960s and early 1970s. The controls and matching procedures are based on information from microdata surveys that are statistically closely representative of the U.S. population—mainly the Current Population Survey (CPS; Census Bureau and Bureau of Labor Statitistics, various years). The construction is validated against the entire sample of the CPS to convince the reader that this part of the simulation "works." In particular,

- DEMSIM closely matches the CPS population by family structure, distinguishing between single individuals and single and dual parent families by age and gender.
- It also matches other demographic and economic attributes of the initial population such as race, age, gender, family size, labor force participation, education, and so on.
- It simulates earnings in 1970 based on microdata from the Panel Survey of Income Dynamics (PSID) to derive cross-section earnings profiles by age, gender, and other demographic and economic attributes for each simulated individual. The simulated earnings distribution is closely matched to that of the PSID in 1970.

Chapter 3 takes the simulation forward in time from 1970 through 2006. This is the "historical simulation." Constructing the historical simulation involves incorporation of annual "transition rules" for each of many population characteristics—race, age, gender, education, labor force participation, and so on. These rules are derived from PSID microdata during the corresponding years using population weights as appropriate to ensure their representativeness vis-à-vis the U.S. population. Again, the simulated distributions of demographic and economic variables are compared with corresponding distributions from the CPS to ensure that DEMSIM accurately captures the momentum of interacting forces embedded in those variables through 2006. Details about how the historical simulation is calibrated are provided in several appendices.

Chapter 4 describes forward motion of DEMSIM beyond 2006—the "projected simulation." If the demographic and economic forces that drive the historical simulation through 2006 capture reasonably accurately the

historical evolution of the U.S. population and economy for all key variables, carrying those forces forward should capture the future evolution
of those variables and provide a foundation for analyzing the financial
outlook for a program such as Social Security—whose finances are closely
influenced by the characteristics of the population that it serves. Chapter
4 describes the findings for the population's structure and other variables
from continuing DEMSIM beyond 2006.

One key variable that must be incorporated into DEMSIM is labor
earnings because it is the basis for determining Social Security's payroll
taxes and benefits. Chapter 5 discusses how the labor earnings process is
modeled and fused into DEMSIM. Individual labor earnings are likely to
be influenced by many attributes, such as a person's age, gender, level of
education, family type, and so on. The evolution of these factors—that
govern people's participation and performance in the work force—is projected for future years in a manner that captures their interactions with
each other conditional on their past states, including past earnings. In
turn, this enables the projection over future years of their impact on total
work effort, and especially on labor quality, both of which influence future
earnings. The simulation of future earnings also accounts for growth in
labor productivity from general technological changes and the evolution
of the economy's capital stock. The results show that

- Future growth of aggregate "effective labor inputs" will be diminished significantly because of declining labor quality. That is, total labor inputs are likely
  to be much smaller in future years when measured in terms of "effective labor
  units" rather than simply by total numbers of workers or hours of work as is
  done conventionally. The projected decline in effective labor inputs results from
  the interactions of demographic and economic forces over time.
- Because of small but positive growth in the population and population aging,
  the overall capital stock continues to grow larger.
- Because of a growing capital stock and positive overall (capital-cum-labor, or
  multifactor) productivity growth, labor productivity continues to grow over
  time, but the growth is quite slow, on average. That means, total labor earnings
  and payroll tax revenues continue to grow, but at a slower rate compared to
  official projections.

Having incorporated and validated all relevant demographic and economic variables, chapter 6 describes the simulation of Social Security's
future finances. This part of DEMSIM makes use of a Social Security Tax

and Benefit Calculator to calculate payroll taxes, benefit eligibility, and the amount of benefits for each of DEMSIM's simulated individuals in each period beginning in 2006. The calculations include retirement benefits, dependent and surviving spouse and child benefits, divorced spouse benefits, benefits for young parents with children in care, and so on. They also incorporate many details of the Social Security benefit formula, including reductions for early retirement, credits for late retirement, reductions in dependents' and survivors' benefits for early retirement, earnings tests applicable at specific ages after early retirement, and so on. The calculations are validated by comparing them with those from the official Social Security Administration calculator across a wide range of stylized cases—for individuals distinguished by year of birth, lifetime earnings, and ages of retirement and benefit collection.

Chapter 6 describes the calculations of Social Security's aggregate finances under current laws (called DEMSIM baseline) and compares them with official projections from the Social Security's Trustees' Report for 2006. Chapter 6 also describes the sensitivity of the results under alternative assumptions about productivity, discount rates, immigration, mortality and fertility rates, future labor force participation and education acquisition transitions, and so on. The results show that

- Social Security's projected receipts and expenditures are smaller than their official estimates—chiefly because of the projected decline in aggregate effective labor inputs.
- The time profile of Social Security's expenditures displays a much larger bulge during the retirement of the baby boomers relative to the official time profile.
- The larger bulge in the early net-benefit time profile implies that a large share—52 percent—of the open group shortfall emerges before the 75-year time horizon under DEMSIM.[22]

Social Security's aggregate finances are reported in terms of the open group measure—calculated over 75 years and in perpetuity—and the closed group measure. These measures are also reported as "actuarial imbalances"—as ratios of the present value of payrolls calculated over corresponding time horizons.

- DEMSIM's estimate of Social Security's 75-year open group measure as a ratio of the present value of payrolls over 75 years is 3.4 percent—twice as large as the trustees' estimate of 1.7 percent.

- DEMSIM's estimate of Social Security's infinite horizon open group imbalance is \$13.4 trillion. The actuarial imbalance ratio when the present values of the open group measure and payrolls are calculated in perpetuity under DEMSIM equals 4.8 percent.
- DEMSIM's closed group imbalance equals \$14.2 trillion, implying that under baseline assumptions, future generations face a net payment burden of \$0.8 trillion.
- Under optimistic and pessimistic demographic and economic assumptions, DEMSIM's infinite horizon actuarial imbalance ratios range between 2.0 and 8.5 percent, respectively. No corresponding range is published by the Social Security Trustees.

DEMSIM's microsimulation provides the means for evaluating the impact of Social Security's current rules and alternative reforms in terms of their effects on particular population groups—distinguished by race, gender, birth cohort, and earnings level. Chapter 7 describes these "micromeasures" of how different types of Social Security participants would be fiscally treated, on average, under the program's rules and changes to them. Evaluating an individual's "fiscal treatment" under Social Security amounts to comparing lifetime payroll taxes relative to lifetime benefits received, where the evaluation is related to that person's lifetime earnings. The key measure of "fiscal treatment" used is the *lifetime net tax rate:* The difference between the present value of lifetime payroll taxes and the present value of lifetime benefits divided by the present value of lifetime labor earnings. All of these present values are evaluated as of the person's entry into adulthood—assumed to be age 18 in DEMSIM. This measure shows the excess taxes paid during the person's lifetime relative to lifetime labor earnings.[23]

The lifetime net tax rate measure focuses on the effects of payroll taxes and benefits relative to earnings over individuals' entire lifetimes—rather than on the more popular measure of the program's *income replacement rate* at the time of retirement. The former measure emphasizes Social Security's increasing role as a substitute for personal retirement saving rather than its originally conceived role as an insurer to protect against income loss from old age. The rationale for adopting the lifetime net tax rate measure in preference to the replacement rate measure is described in chapter 7. Lifetime net tax rates are shown as averages across 15-year birth cohorts: 1946–60 through 2036–50.[24] Results under DEMSIM's baseline assumptions show several interesting features—for example:

- Across all races, genders, and lifetime earners, lifetime net tax rates are relatively small for the baby boomers —averaging 5.1 percent and ranging between 3.9 and 6.6 percent.

- Average lifetime net tax rates (across all race, gender, and earnings level for a given 15-year birth cohort) peak at 6.1 percent for the 1991–2005 birth cohort. They decline gradually for later birth cohorts because of their longer projected life and retirement spans.

- Women—within given lifetime earnings and race categories—bear smaller lifetime net tax rates from participating in Social Security than do men, simply because they outlive men and collect more by way of dependent benefits based on their male spouses' earnings.

- High lifetime earners generally have *smaller* lifetime net tax rates compared to low lifetime earners, partly because of high-earners' greater longevity and benefit collection life spans, but also because of their higher lifetime earnings relative to their lifetime payroll taxes because of Social Security's taxable earnings ceiling.

Chapters 8–13 explore the financial implications of six selected Social Security reform proposals from across the political spectrum. The two liberal proposals selected are those by Robert M. Ball (chapter 8) and by Peter Diamond and Peter R. Orszag (chapter 9). These proposals generally adhere to liberal political tenets on Social Security reforms—to maintain the program's current structure and benefits as far as possible and increase the program's revenues in various ways.

The two centrist proposals are by lawmakers—Representatives Jim Kolbe (R-AZ), Charles Stenholm (D-TX), and Allen Boyd (D-FL) (chapter 10)—and by academicians and think-tank experts on budget policy— Jeffrey Liebman, Maya MacGuineas, and Andrew Samwick (chapter 11). These two proposals are popularly viewed as centrist because they borrow features from both conservative and liberal proposals. Both include the creation of Social Security personal accounts.

The final two proposals selected are Model 2 of the G. W. Bush Commission to Strengthen Social Security (chapter 12) and the proposal by Representative Paul Ryan (R-WI). These two proposals are popularly labeled as conservative because of their heavy emphasis on "carve-out" financed Social Security personal accounts: A portion of each individual's existing Social Security payroll taxes are (voluntarily) redirected into personal accounts with the costs offset from reductions in future traditional Social Security benefits on a person-by-person basis.

Table 1.1 provides a summary of the aggregate results from all six reform proposals under the open and closed group measures described earlier. The results of table 1.1 show that

- The Ball proposal changes Social Security's open and closed group measures by
  very small amounts. Were the goal to leave Social Security's current structure
  undisturbed, this proposal would deliver it very well. Were the goal to resolve
  the program's outstanding financial imbalance and eliminate its other shortcomings, the Ball proposal would be ineffective.
- The Diamond-Orszag (DO) proposal reduces the open group measure by about
  90 percent and about 42 percent of the total required change (the baseline open
  group imbalance) is accomplished within the first 75 years. However the imbalance on account of today's generations—the closed group imbalance—is
  reduced by only 23 percent. Hence, much of the adjustment cost is imposed on
  future generations.
- The Kolbe-Stenholm-Boyd (KSB) proposal reduces the infinite horizon open
  group measure by 86 percent, and 27 percent of the total required adjustment is
  achieved within the first 75 years.
- The Liebman-MacGuineas-Samwick (LMS) proposal reduces the infinite horizon open group measure by 82 percent and imposes more than one third of
  the required adjustment cost on current generations. The LMS proposal also
  achieves about 36 percent of the required adjustment within the first 75 years.
- In terms of its effect on the open group measure, the G. W. Bush Model 2 reform proposal is weaker compared to the DO proposal and both centrist (KSB
  and LMS) proposals. And it imposes a very small fraction of the adjustment
  cost on current generations.
- The Ryan proposal is the strongest in terms of its reduction of Social Security's
  open and closed group imbalances. However, a very small percent of the required adjustment is achieved within the first 75 years.
- The DO and Ryan proposals reduce the open group measure by large amounts.
  However, the two proposals are far from similar in how they achieve this result—
  as described in later chapters.

Each reform proposal includes several reform elements, each of which
is evaluated separately before implementing all elements together, including interactions among them, to examine each proposal's total impact on
Social Security's aggregate finances and distributions of adjustment costs
on population subgroups. The evaluation using DEMSIM's demographic
and economic projections turns up some surprising results: Some reform

TABLE 1.1 **A Brief Glimpse of the Aggregate Effects of Alternative Social Security Reform Proposals**

	75-year open group imbalance	Infinite horizon open group imbalance	Closed group imbalance	75-year	∞-horizon	Closed group imbalance	Reduction in ∞-horizon open group imbalance from baseline	Reduction in 75-year imbalance as a percent of baseline ∞-horizon imbalance	Reduction in closed group imbalance as a percent of baseline closed group imbalance
	Trillions of constant 2006 dollars			Percent of present value of payrolls			Percent		
DEMSIM baseline	6,985	13,364	14,172	3.4	4.8	9.7	...	...	...
Liberal Ball	5,832	11,415	14,046	2.8	4.1	9.6	14.6	8.7	0.9
DO	1,386	1,610	10,889	0.7	0.6	7.5	88.0	41.9	23.2
Centrist KSB	3,369	1,841	10,498	1.6	0.7	7.2	86.2	27.1	25.9
LMS	2,120	2,446	9,364	1.0	0.9	6.4	81.7	36.4	33.9
Conservative Model 2	7,851	5,247	12,233	3.8	1.9	8.4	60.7	-6.5	13.7
Ryan	4,661	-983	9,152	2.2	-0.3	6.3	107.4	17.4	35.4
Present value of payrolls	208,495	281,064	145,572	...	...	...	...	...	...

Source: Author's calculations.

elements are rendered almost fully ineffective. Others have much stronger effects than might be expected at first glance.

One so-called centrist proposal has weak revenue effects and strong benefit-side elements and might be better labeled as a conservative proposal. The other is true to its word about being "balanced" even on the basis of neutral distributional metrics including tax- and benefit-side effects and the cross-generational distribution of the adjustments that it would impose.

Among the conservative proposals, one has relatively weak reform elements and Social Security's finances are worsened during the first 75 years and improved only slightly overall. The other is true to its conservative label and imposes large reductions in traditional benefits and large increases in personal accounts to ensure adequate retirement wealth for most cohorts even when personal account accumulations are estimated very conservatively—that is, without any "free lunches."

Chapter 14 concludes the book by summarizing the macro-financial and distributional trade-offs that the six proposals provide. That chapter also presents results on Social Security's role in reducing lifetime income uncertainty. It discusses how each of the five proposals considered would improve or degrade this function—keeping in mind the costs of doing so.

CHAPTER TWO

Simulating U.S. Demographics and Economics

Beginning in 1970

Overview

Analyzing Social Security's finances and the impact of reforms requires a model of both the program itself and of the population that it will affect. Most studies of Social Security use highly stylized mathematical models of the economy and highly stylized Social Security rules. Here, we develop a very detailed computer laboratory—a program that simulates a mini economy of individuals and families that tracks the U.S. economy quite closely along relevant demographic and economic attributes. The development of such a laboratory—called DEMSIM for demographic and economic microsimulation—is described in this and the next four chapters.

DEMSIM has two parts—historical and projected. It begins with the construction of an initial population as of the year 1970 by using information on family structures and other demographic attributes of the U.S. population during the late 1960s and early 1970s. Next, DEMSIM "grows" the initial population through time using rules based on microdata information on the U.S. economy after 1970. These data tell us how the U.S. population evolved in terms of several key characteristics such as family structure, family formation and dissolution, mortality, fertility, the acquisition of education (or skills), labor force participation, and so on. DEMSIM captures that evolution by applying a detailed set of conditional distributions of the characteristics being simulated.[1]

Such conditional distributions of population characteristics are derived from various publicly available and nationally representative data sets on individuals and families such as the Current Population Survey, the Panel Study of Income Dynamics, various U.S. decennial censuses, and data on U.S. demographics provided by the U.S. Social Security Administration.

The historical simulation begins in 1970 and runs through 2006. The projected simulation begins in the year 2007 and can be carried as far forward as required. The projected simulation uses year-to-year transition rules that are applicable in the last few years of the historical simulation—2006.[2] The projected simulation carries forward the momentum of forces built into the U.S. population and economic features. Trends in the population's age structure are driven by past fertility, mortality, and immigration rates, each of which varies according to population characteristics such as race, gender, education level, and so on. Economic trends such as the rates of acquisition of education, labor force participation, and earnings growth will interact with demographic forces. The interplay of these forces will determine the population's characteristics in the future. These interactions are likely to play a large role in determining the population's evolving structure and would, therefore, influence Social Security's finances in future years given the program's current rules. As such, DEMSIM will provide a laboratory to study the implications of current programmatic features of Social Security and to analyze the implications of alternative Social Security reforms.[3]

Demographics

The demographic features that are simulated include several attributes of the U.S. population as they evolve through time. Given that much of Social Security's prospective financial shortfalls will arise from the ongoing aging of the U.S. population—because of both increasing longevity and the impending retirement of the baby boom generation—the evolution of the population's age structure and its transition through time must be captured with adequate precision. Moreover, because Social Security pays auxiliary benefits to dependents and survivors, the simulated population must track each individual's family affiliations. In each year of the historical simulation, those affiliations must evolve collectively to deliver changes in the population shares of different family types that closely match those calculated from nationally representative microdata surveys—such as the

Current Population Survey.[4] Only if the historical simulation closely reflects the actual evolution of U.S. population's characteristics—as measured by the Current Population Survey (CPS) microdata—could one have confidence in its ability to adequately portray the likely future path of U.S. demographic and economic characteristics.

Economics

The economic aspects of the historical simulation (between 1970 and 2006) mainly include labor force participation, acquisition of additional education, and the conditional evolution of labor earnings in terms of their nominal level and distribution. Projections of future labor earnings are based on a regression calibrated using data from the Panel Survey of Income Dynamics. This approach captures each simulated individual's life-cycle variation in labor earnings according to changes over the life cycle in that individual's demographic and economic attributes. Projected growth in nominal earnings after 2006 is determined by parametric assumptions on rates of future productivity growth, capital intensity, and general price inflation.[5]

Simulating the Initial (1970) Population

A simulation, as distinct from a calculation, involves the use of random numbers. This statement may lead readers to wonder whether the demographic and economic laboratory being constructed is a random collection of individuals with a random set of attributes. If so, it would appear incapable of delivering a tool suitable for approximating the demographic structure of the U.S. population, much less for analyzing Social Security's finances and the impact of reforms to it.

That first impression is incorrect, however, because although the creation (or "simulation") of each family and non-family unit and each individual within such units is, indeed, determined with the use of random numbers, the entire process is controlled by "drivers" or parameters derived from microdata surveys of the demographic and economic characteristics of the U.S. population. When a large number of individuals and families are created in this manner, the features of the simulated population can be made to closely resemble those of the actual U.S. population—

as is demonstrated later in this chapter. Using additional driver parameters, the evolution of the initial population over time can also be matched closely with the actual pattern of demographic and economic developments of any particular nation.

Such a simulation-based analysis has several advantages, particularly the ability to observe the collective operation and interaction of different demographic and economic "drivers" to build a financial baseline for a program—such as Social Security—whose finances are highly dependent on future demographic developments. A financial baseline built upon simulated demographics reflects the joint operation of demographic and economic developments and programmatic rules that can be projected into the future to analyze their financial implications. In addition, such a simulation allows its users to assess the impact of changing one or more demographic, economic, or programmatic drivers that influence future financial outcomes.

Information on individual and family characteristics from the Current Population Surveys between 1968 and 1972 is used to calibrate the simulated population's base-year (1970) demographic features. Multiple CPS years are used in order to obtain a sufficiently robust representation of the U.S. population's demographic features around the year 1970.[6] The procedure involves first deriving averages of individual characteristics from microdata surveys that serve as DEMSIM's demographic "drivers." For example, the first structural element that is simulated is whether a unit is of "family" or a "non-family" type. A "family" is defined to include two or more people (two spouses with or without children or a single family head with at least one child), whereas a "non-family" unit includes only one individual with no relationship (as observed in CPS microdata) to anyone else in the population.

A very simple example of the basic simulation technique would probably help at this stage. Consider the aggregate share of "families." According to data from the Current Population Surveys between 1968 and 1972, that share was found to be 0.688 (or 68.8 percent), with the rest of the population being of "non-family" type.

The initial simulated population is designed to contain 15,000 such units (family and non-family units). For the first unit, a random number is drawn to decide whether it will be of family or non-family type.[7] A computerized random number generator is used to obtain a real (decimal) number between zero and one. Let's suppose it equals 0.452, which falls below the threshold value 0.688. Hence, the first unit is designated to be a "family" unit. Suppose that the next random number generated equals 0.794—which is larger than the threshold of 0.688. Hence, the second unit is designated to be a "non-family" unit, and so on.

This procedure generates a "family" or a "non-family" designation for all 15,000 units. If the random number generation process operates correctly—that is, each real number drawn between the bounds of 0.0 and 1.0 is equally likely to occur—about 68.8 percent of units should receive the "family" designation. Note that because the process is random, the simulated fraction of "family" units will not be exactly 68.8 percent. But the statistical "law of large numbers" applies here: the larger is the total number of units that is simulated, the closer the simulated fraction of "family" units is likely to be to the CPS-derived share of "family"-type units of 68.8 percent.

In this example, the "driver" parameter for share of "family" units describes the distribution of the population according to a family-type characteristic. In the example described here, the characteristic of family type can assume either one of two possible values—"family" and "non-family." Other demographic and economic characteristics may involve multiple values: for example, the attribute "years of education attained" has 19 values ranging from 0 through 17 and "18 or more" (18+). Hence, there would be 19 driver parameters for that attribute describing the distribution of individuals across the 19 values (0 through 18+) for the "years of education attained" characteristic.

Moreover, the drivers of some characteristics may be "conditional" on the values of other attributes. For example, the driver parameters for "years of education attained" (as observed from microdata surveys) may vary systematically based on individuals' race, gender, and age. To capture such systematic variation of some attributes with others, the drivers for "years of education attained" are derived separately (conditionally) for each combination of values involving race, gender, and age. And the simulation of "years of education attained" is implemented only after simulating each individual's race, gender, and age attributes.

No matter how many conditioning variables are selected for a particular demographic attribute, and no matter how many driver parameters are required to describe the distribution of that attribute, DEMSIM's procedure is the same as that described earlier: a random decimal number within the range of 0.0 and 1.0 is drawn, and its value is compared with the range of the appropriate (conditional) driver parameters of the characteristic to be simulated. The characteristic value designated for the individual

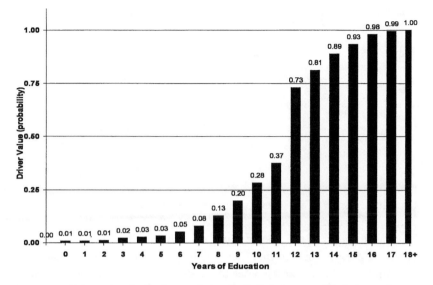

FIGURE 2.1. Driver values for the "years of education" attribute: non-white males aged 20–29 in 1970. Source: Author's calculations.

being considered is that associated with the driver parameter just above the random number drawn. For example, figure 2.1 shows driver parameters for years of education ranging between 0 and 18+ for people who are male, non-white, and aged between 20 and 29 in 1970. From figure 2.1 it is easy to see that if the random number drawn equals 0.228, the "years of education" designation would equal 10—because the driver parameter immediately above the random number, 0.28, corresponds to 10 years of education.[8] Similarly, if the random number falls just above 0.99 but below or equal to 1.00, the "years of education" value that is assigned to the simulated individual under consideration is "18 or more" (or 18+).

The Scope of the Demographic Simulation for 1970

Tables 2.1 and 2.2 show the characteristics that are simulated for "non-family" and "family" units, respectively. Also listed are the values of each simulated characteristic and the list of conditioning characteristics used for deriving driver parameters for each characteristic value.

The simulation implemented to generate the initial 1970 population considers several variables, especially those relevant for analyzing Social

TABLE 2.1 **Simulated Attributes, Attribute Values, and Conditioning Attributes: Family-type: "Non-family"**

Attribute	Values	Conditioning attributes
Race	White, non-white	Family type
Sex	Male, female	Family type, race
Age	0–99	Family type, race, sex
Years of education	0–18+	Family type, race, sex, age
Disability status	Disabled, non-disabled	Family type, race, sex, age
Labor force status	Full time, part time, NILF*	Family type, race, sex, age, education

* NILF = not in labor force.

Security. Together, they are capable of adequately capturing the rich set of demographic and economic characteristics of the U.S. population in 1970. The variables for which distributions of both "family" and "non-family" types are derived include race, gender, age of adults, number of children in "families," the age and gender of children, disability status for adults, years of education, labor force status, and labor earnings.

Many of these attributes are simulated conditional on other attributes. For example, the labor force status of adults in "families" is conditional on single- or dual-headed (married) family status, race, own age, spouse's age, own education, and spouse's education. And married females' (spouses') labor force status is conditional on their race, own age, age of husband, own education, and husband's education.

Finally, what is the result of performing such a demographic simulation of the 1970 U.S. population? Figure 2.2 shows the results. The first chart in figure 2.2 is derived from the 1970 CPS. It shows the population at each age as a share of the total population in 1970 (labeled "total" in the charts). The corresponding line in the second chart of figure 2.2 shows the same statistic but for the simulated population of 15,000 family and non-family units (comprising approximately 39,000 individuals). As is evident from comparing the two charts, the "total" line of the simulated population tracks the corresponding CPS line quite closely.

In both the simulated and CPS distributions of figure 2.2, the total population shares of individuals at very young ages—younger than age 25—are quite high relative to the shares of older individuals. Children and young adults between the ages of 6 and 24 in 1970 are the baby boomers—those who were born between the years 1964 and 1946, respectively. Because mortality rates are much higher for middle-aged and older individuals, the shares of those older than age 50 decline with age. Thus, the

TABLE 2.2 **Simulated Attributes, Attribute Values, and Conditioning Attributes: Family-type: "Family"**

Attribute	Values	Conditioning attributes
Marital status	Married, single-headed family	Family type
Race of head	White, non-white	Family type, marital status
Race of spouse*	White, non-white	Race of head
Age of head	0–99 years	Family type, marital status, race of head, race of spouse*
Age of spouse*	0–99 years	Family type, marital status, race of head, race of spouse,* age of head
Number of children	1–14	Family type, marital status, race of head, race of spouse,* age of head, age of spouse
Age of child	0–17 years	Family type, marital status, race of head, race of spouse, age of head, age of spouse*
Sex of child	Male, female	Allocated as male with probability 0.52; as female with probability 0.48
Education of head	0–18+	Family type, marital status, race of head, age of head, age of spouse*
Education of spouse*	0–18+	Family type, marital status, race of head, age of head, age of spouse,** education of head
Disability status head	Disabled, non-disabled	Family type, marital status, race of head, age of head, age of spouse*
Disability status spouse*	Disabled, non-disabled	Family type, marital status, race of head, age of head, age of spouse,* physical status of head
Labor force status—head	Full time, part time, NILF**	Family type, marital status, race of head, age of head, age of spouse,* education of head, education of spouse
Labor force status— spouse*	Full time, part time, NILF**	Family type, marital status, race of head, age of head, age of spouse,* education of head, education of spouse, labor force status of head
Education of kids	0–12 years	Family type, marital status, age of kid

* Spousal variables are not applicable to single-headed (non-married) families.
** NILF = not in the labor force.

overall structure of the simulated 1970 population is very similar to that observed in CPS microdata for 1970.

The simulated and CPS population distributions of figure 2.2 contain other features that also match each other quite closely. In both figures, the lines labeled "Non-Family" represent populations of single "non-family" individuals. The positions of the "Non-Family" lines indicate that their

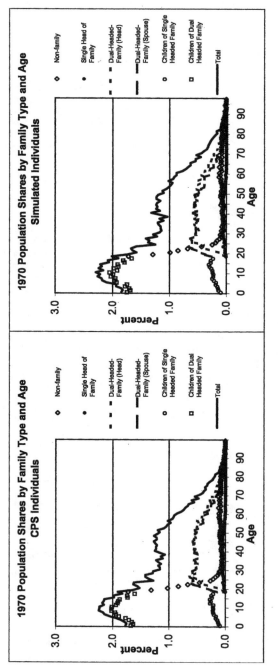

FIGURE 2.2. Comparing CPS and DEMSIM's simulated population structures 1970. Source: Author's calculations.

shares in the simulated 1970 population closely track those of the 1968–70 CPS population. As expected, the share of "non-family" individuals is very high among younger adults, a large number of whom are as yet unmarried and have no children. The population of "non-families" declines rapidly between the ages of 18 and 25 in both the CPS and simulated populations.

The label "Single-Head of Family" represents shares of single-headed families—adults with one or more children. Very few single-headed families existed in the late 1960s and early 1970s. The simulated distribution is, again, quite similar to that observed in the CPS. Both distributions have positive values between the ages of 18 and 60 (approximately). That's because children leave home after attaining adulthood (age 18 in DEMSIM) and older adults are unlikely to bear children.

The populations of individuals labeled "Dual-Headed Family (Head)" and "Dual-Headed Family (Spouse)" show the shares of such adult family members by age in 1970.[9] Because adults married early during the early 1970s, the modal ages of married family heads and spouses occurs in the mid-twenties. In both charts, the distribution of "Dual-Headed Family (Spouse)" begins at younger ages—as expected since females marry at younger ages than males—and the locations (level and age range) of both distributions are similar in both charts. Likewise, the locations of simulated and CPS distributions labeled "Children of Single-Headed Family" and "Children of Dual-Headed Family" are also quite similar. Finally, very few people survived into their nineties during the early 1970s.

In order to use demographic simulation for analyzing a program such as Social Security, the distributions of several other variables need to be considered and validated against microdata information on the U.S. population and economy from 1970. Table 2.3 shows simulated and CPS population averages for several demographic variables such as race, gender, age, and economic variables such as education, disability status, and labor force participation.[10] It also shows the simulated and CPS distributions of "families" by number of children (younger than age 18). The table's averages and distributions for the simulated population's attributes match closely with those derived from the CPS for 1968–72.

These results show that the simulation of the 1970 population "works"—it generates a simulated population of families and individuals that matches the CPS population around that year (1968 through 1972) in terms of its overall demographic structure and economic attributes. The next chapter describes transition rules calibrated according to microdata

TABLE 2.3 **CPS and DEMSIM Population Characteristics (1970)**

	CPS	DEMSIM
Whites (%)	87.7	88.8
Males (%)	48.4	49.7
Average age of population	31.4	29.8
Education (%)		
Less than high school diploma	40.9	39.7
High school diploma but no college degree	48.8	49.9
College degree or more	10.3	10.4
Disability (%)	4.4	3.4
Labor force participation (%)		
Non-participants	36.9	38.1
Full-time workers	37.0	36.7
Part-time workers	26.1	25.2
Number of children (%)		
0	42.6	40.3
1	18.9	19.2
2	17.8	18.6
3	10.7	11.8
4	5.5	5.6
5	2.4	2.7
6	1.1	1.1
7+	0.9	0.8

Source: Author's calculations.

information on the U.S. economy. DEMSIM applies these rules to drive the evolution of the simulated 1970 population forward through time. Chapter 3 compares the evolution of DEMSIM's simulated population structure with that observed in the CPS along several dimensions, which serves to validate the simulation.

CHAPTER THREE

Forward Motion

Demographic Transition, 1971–2006

Annual Transitions

Matching the features of the simulated initial population to those of the Current Population Survey (CPS) from 1968 to 1972 is relatively easy. If the driver parameters are accurate and are defined in sufficient detail to capture all of the important demographic characteristics of the 1970 U.S. population, the simulation procedure described earlier is almost guaranteed to work correctly. The law of large numbers implies that one could generate as close a match between the features of the simulated and actual U.S. populations for the year 1970—by generating a sufficiently large sample of simulated family and non-family units. Although according to the U.S. Statistical Abstract for 1972, the U.S. economy was made up of 63 million families and more than 200 million individuals, simulating just 15,000 family and non-family units for that year (involving about 39,000 individuals) appears to be sufficient to adequately capture the population's essential features.

The next step of "growing" the 1970 simulated population—that is, transitioning from the 1970 features of the simulated population to those pertaining to 1971—is more difficult because the rules for migrating from the set of attribute values applicable in 1970 (each individual's "state" in 1970) to a new set of attribute values for 1971 ("state" in 1971) involves a considerably more complicated set of rules.

TABLE 3.1 **Annual Attribute Transitions and Conditioning Variables**

Attribute	Result	Conditioning attributes
Mortality	Survival or death	Race, gender, age(t–1)*
Age	Advances by 1 year	Survival
Marital status	Marriage/divorce	Non-married→married: age, race, education
		Married→non-married: age, race
Child split-off	New family	Become age 18
Fertility	New child in family	Female age 14–49, race, education
Disability	Disability↔ Non-disability	Race, age
Education	Acquire additional year of education	Race, gender, age, prior education years
Labor force status	Not-in-labor force; part-time; full time	Race, gender, age, years of education, prior labor force status

* Newborns are assigned the race of their father and gender = male with probability 52 percent. Race and gender are fixed throughout a person's lifetime.

The annual transitions implemented here are based on as simple a set of rules as possible—preserving only the most important conditioning variables for each attribute. Table 3.1 provides a summary of the transitions that are implemented and the conditioning variables underlying each transition. A description of the different elements involved in implementing the transition is given in the following subsections.

Aging and Mortality

The simplest transition rules pertain to aging and mortality. A person alive in 1970 must either die at the end of that year or, if (s)he survives, must become older by a year in 1971. Mortality probabilities by year, race, gender, and age are used to first simulate whether an individual survives for an additional year and, if (s)he does, the person's age is increased by one year.[1] Historical mortality rates by year, race, gender, and age are taken from the National Center for Health Statistics (NCHS, various years).

NCHS mortality rates are available through the year 2003. For later years, those rates are projected by benchmarking against the Social Security Administration's mortality rate projections. Thus, the projected simulation's mortality rate drivers are *not* those applied in the terminal year of the historical simulation. Rather they continue the observed historical trend in mortality declines at the same rates by age and gender as under the Social Security Administration's projections. The latter are available only by future year, age, and gender and not by race. To decompose them by race, observed differences in the average mortality of whites and non-whites in the last five years (1999 through 2003) of available NCHS mortality data are preserved in the benchmarking procedure.[2] Appendix 3.1 provides details about how mortality rates are projected for future years.[3]

Education

Education is a key variable because it enters as a conditional attribute in several other variables. Table 3.1 shows that the distribution of "years of education attained" affects marriage and divorce, fertility, education acquisition rates, and labor force status transition rates. For example, the transition rules for education determine whether any individual (aged six and older) acquires an additional year of education in the current year. A person's race, gender, age, and prior years of education are important determinants of the likelihood of advancing education by an additional year. PSID data, however, are very sparse and the computed average rates of advancing education by one year for each individual type are extremely volatile from year to year. Hence, the data are smoothed and calibrated based on matching aggregate shares of individuals in three education categories—"less than high-school," "high-school diploma but no college degree," and "college graduate or more."

These three education categories correspond to CPS years of education responses between 0–11, 12–15, and 16 or more (16+), respectively. The education transition probabilities are thus a combination of survey averages across years beginning in 1970, a regression smoothing algorithm, and additional adjustment factors that deliver a reasonable overall match of the fraction of individuals in the three education categories mentioned earlier.

Figure 3.1 shows the match between CPS and simulated shares of the population by the three "years of education" groups between 1970 and 2006. It shows that for white males and females, the share of those with a high school diploma or more but without a college degree increased through the late 1970s and then stabilized at about 60 percent. However, the share of those with less than a college degree declined continuously during this period while the share of those with a college degree or more increased slowly. The share of whites with college degrees or more education has reached almost 30 percent by 2006.

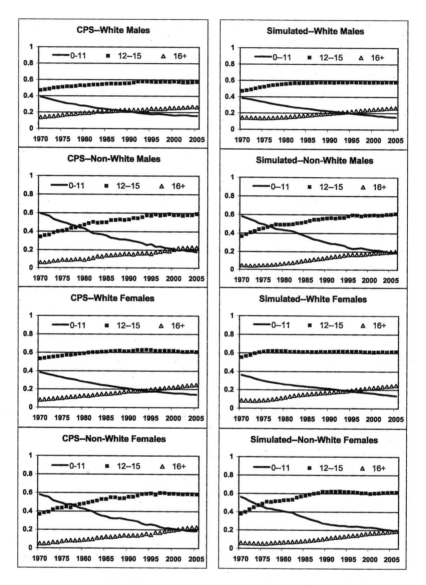

FIGURE 3.1. CPS and DEMSIM population shares by education category. Source: Author's calculations based on DEMSIM and Current Population Survey.

A similar story is true for non-white individuals, except that the share of those with a high school diploma but no college degree begins at a much lower level in 1970 compared to that for whites and does not reach 60 percent until the mid-1990s. Moreover, although the share of those with a college degree or more also increases continuously for non-whites, it remains several percentage points lower than the corresponding share for whites in 2006.

The projected simulation takes the terminal probabilities of acquiring an additional year of education as given. Note, that the population's educational attainment would be determined by the evolution of its demographic characteristics—that is, its age, race, and gender distributions over time. Obviously, momentum from the historical simulation of rising educational attainment will affect characteristics such as fertility rates, labor force participation, earnings, and marital status. It must be kept in mind, however, that the interaction between many of these variables is mutual and that the population's overall attributes are not solely dictated by the evolution of any one variable. Thus, although educational rates for all population groups may increase over time, changes in the population weights of different population groups will also determine the population's average educational attainment in future years. Thus, although future rates of education acquisition conditional on age, race, and gender are maintained at their 2006 values, and although that implies increasing educational attainment by all gender-race groups, the evolution of other demographic characteristics also influences the direction of the population's overall educational attainment as well as other outcomes—such as labor force participation rates and earnings.

Fertility

Once survivors from the 1970 simulated population "arrive" into 1971, several other transitions are implemented: children who become 18 years old split off from their families to establish their own family types—"non-families" or "families." They could establish a "family" either by marrying (only adults aged 18 and older participate in the marriage market) or, if the split-off is a woman, by giving birth to a child. Women aged between 14 and 49 may give birth. A woman aged 14 through 17 (a child in a family) who gives birth is split off immediately and forms her own single-parent family. But she enters the marriage market only after attaining age 18. Childbirth is calibrated using fertility rates by year, race, age, and education

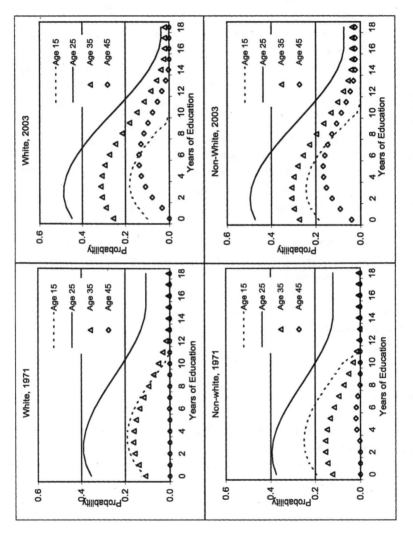

FIGURE 3.2. Probability of childbirth by female age, race, and education. Source: Author's calculations.

of the mother. These data are not directly available and must be con-structed from information available from the Census Bureau—as de-scribed in appendix 3.2.

An important feature of U.S. fertility rates is their secular decline over time. However, fertility rates during the early 2000s ("today") are higher than the lows they attained during the post–baby boom years of the late 1960 and early 1970s—as figure 3.2 shows. That figure shows other inter-esting features of the evolution of fertility rates during the last three de-cades. The likelihood of childbirth is higher for non-whites than for whites, especially at younger ages. The likelihood of childbirth declines with fe-male age after women reach their mid-20s. It also declines with education, and is especially low for those with more than high school education.

It is interesting to note that if the share of women with less than high school education continues to trend downward—as shown in figure 3.1—the shares of those with more than high school education must increase. To the extent that being more educated "causes" lower fertility rates, overall fertility rates may decline in the future. However, figures 3.2 also shows that the likelihood of childbirth among relatively older women (within the fertile age range) has increased during the last three decades, including among those with more educational attainment. The trend toward higher fertility at later ages suggests that acquiring higher education may lead to postponement of childbirth, which would counteract the overall decline in fertility rates by age.

Projected fertility rates are derived using a procedure similar to that used for mortality rates. That is, fertility rate projections from the Social Security Administration are used to benchmark Census Bureau's fertility rates after the year 2003. The Social Security Trustees' fertility rates are distinguished only by female age, not by race and education. Hence, in each year after 2004, the benchmarking process distributes the trustees' fertility rates across race and education categories (using female popula-tion weights) to preserve average differences in rates across those attri-butes as observed in the five years prior to the terminal year (2003) of the Census Bureau's fertility data.

Marriage and Divorce

Single persons (non-families and single-headed family heads) are entered into the marriage market each year. A mate-matching function is used to determine pairings of males and females depending on age, education, and race. The function has a complicated mathematical representation (see appendix 3.3), but its intuition is quite simple. People of disparate age and education levels have a smaller chance of being paired together. In addition, the likelihood of marrying is much smaller for potential mates of different race than for mates of the same race.

The match-making process considers pairing each male 20 times with randomly selected females until the marriage pairing succeeds. Following the procedure described in chapter 2, the marriage function provides a "driver" probability of matching the two selected individuals, and a random number drawn between 0.0 and 1.0 determines whether the pair will be married. If so, they are segregated into the pool of "dual-headed families." If the male remains unmarried after 20 attempts, he is returned to the category of "non-family" or "single-headed" family depending on whether there are any children in the family or not.

The marriage rate function used in the projected simulation retains the parameters used in the terminal year of the historical simulation. However, the interaction of the function with changing age, race, and education distributions imply that overall marriage rates would be influenced by ongoing demographic changes in several other attributes, including, labor force participation, earnings, and so on—variables that mutually interact with the three variables upon which marriage rates are directly conditioned.

Adults who enter a period as members of a "dual-headed family" (head and spouse) are potential divorcees. Divorce probabilities are estimated from the PSID based on age and race. In each case, the probability is compared against a random number drawn between 0.0 and 1.0 to determine whether each couple would be divorced within the year. If they become divorced, the family splits into two parts: the divorced male becomes a "non-family" unit. Any children in the family are attached to the divorced mother to form a new "single-headed family." Appendix 3.3 provides details about how potential partners are married and how divorce probabilities are calculated from the Panel Study of Income Dynamics.

Rates of marriage have been declining in the United States during the last several decades. More than 70 percent of adults were married in 1970 but that share declined to about 60 by 1990. The share of married adults has continued to decline gradually during the 1990 and 2000s.[4] The fraction of married adults in any given year is mainly the result of the joint influence of marriage and divorce rates—along with the entry of new 18-year-olds in the population and mortality among married and single adults. Hence, both

TABLE 3.2 **Share of Married Adults by Race and Gender for Selected Years (%)**

		Non-white		White	
		Females	Males	Females	Males
1975	CPS	45	55	65	72
	Simulated	51	57	74	78
1985	CPS	40	48	61	67
	Simulated	42	48	64	68
1995	CPS	36	43	58	62
	Simulated	36	40	56	61
2005	CPS	39	45	56	59
	Simulated	35	37	53	58

Source: Author's calculations.

processes could be validated by comparing the simulated and CPS shares of married adults over time. Table 3.2 does just that for selected years in percentage terms. It shows that the simulated shares of married adults are quite similar in magnitude to the CPS shares in each of the years shown. A smaller share of non-white adults are married compared to whites, and the shares of married adults for both whites and non-whites decline over time. However, table 3.2 shows that the rate of decline is quite slow after 1995.

Labor Force Status

All adults are classified according to three labor force participation categories: The "Not-in-Labor-Force" (NLF) status could apply to individuals of any age—that is, for young students, non-working wives, unemployed adults, and retired individuals. Alternatively, individuals may be working "full-time" (FT) or "part-time" (PT). In general young adults are more likely to be non-participants in the labor market but are likely to have high probabilities of moving from non-participation to part- or full-time participation.

Middle-aged men, and to a lesser extent middle-aged women, have high rates of full-time participation but also high rates of staying in full-time jobs. Older adults are more likely to switch from full- and part-time jobs to non-participation, and the very old are likely to stay retired. The likelihoods of switching labor force status at different ages and genders are likely to vary by educational status as well. Workers with college-plus education are more likely remain in full-time jobs than those with fewer years of education.

These patterns of labor force status transitions by race, age, gender, and education are described in greater detail in appendix 3.4. The application of these transition rules to the simulated population generates life-cycle patterns of labor force affiliations for each simulated adult. The simulated labor force transitions can be compared with those observed in the CPS for 1975 and 2005. Figure 3.3 performs these comparisons. The first four charts show the results for females in 1975 and 2005 and the second set of four charts show the results for males in 1975 and 2005.

For both the years shown (and for intervening years), the general patterns of simulated labor force affiliations match those calculated from the CPS quite closely. In both CPS and simulated histograms, the share of young and middle-aged women not participating in the labor force declines from around 40 percent in the mid-1970s to about 30 percent or less by the mid-2000s. During the same period, the share of part-time female workers remained fairly stable, implying that the share of those working full-time increased. For women older than age 65, the rate of non-participation—reflecting retirement—was well above 80 percent during the 1980s and 1990s (not shown), but has declined back to levels that prevailed during the mid 1970s.

Comparing men and women reveals much smaller rates of non-participation and part-time work among younger men than among younger women. Like women, men in the 60s and older have high rates of non-participation due to retirement. The rates of non-participation for men are considerably lower and have held steady during the decades since the 1970s. Again, the patterns of the simulated shares of labor force affiliation are quite similar to those calculated from the CPS.

Annual time series of labor force affiliation show steady shares of full-time work for men but an increasing share of full-time work for women and declining share of non-participation and part-time work. The retirement of the baby boom generation, however, portends higher shares of non-participation overall for both men and women.

The labor force status transition probabilities in the projected simulation are the same as those used in the terminal year of the historical simulation. In general, the labor force behavior of future populations would be determined by many factors, including technological changes. The tremendous improvements in "home-production" technology, for example, provided the impetus for increasing women's participation in the work force during the 1970s and 1980s. That transition, however, is unlikely to be reversed in the future because improvements in home production technologies are likely to continue. Hence, current labor force affiliation

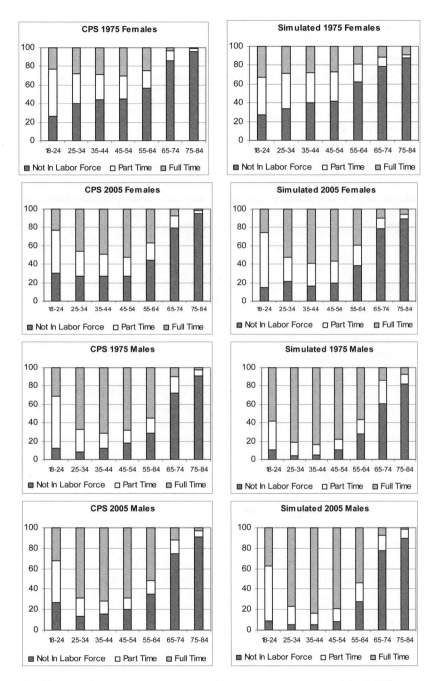

FIGURE 3.3. CPS and DEMSIM labor force participation rates. Source: Author's calculations.

patterns by gender over individuals' life cycles are likely to persist and current labor force transitions across individual life cycles may be a good approximation to future patterns, subject to their mutual interaction with other evolving demographic and economic features of the population.[5]

Immigration

Although new immigrants constitute a relatively small fraction of the overall population in any given year, the American population's overall characteristics today are essentially shaped by those of immigrants who entered during past decades. The historical simulation incorporates the effects of net immigration by adding to the existing population a number of new "family" and "non-family" individuals calibrated according to Census information on the characteristics of immigrants in each decade. New individuals representing immigrants are added to the simulated population in each year beginning in 1971 after the transitions for all other variables have been implemented.

The number of total (legal and other) net immigrants to be added to the simulated population is determined by annual ratio of net immigrants to the United States to the total resident population taken from the Social Security's Trustees' 2006 annual report. This ratio is applied to the simulated population of each year prior to 2007 to determine the total number of immigrants. The number of net immigrants in the projected simulation is based on the ratio of net immigrants to the total population as projected by the Social Security trustees. For years beyond the terminal year of the trustees' projections, an annual rate of change is applied to the net immigration ratio based on the average rate of change during the last two decades of the official projections.[6]

The simulation of immigrant characteristics proceeds similarly to that of the resident population—one "family" (or "non-family") at a time. Appendix 3.5 describes the procedures and cumulative distributions ("drivers") used to assign various characteristics to immigrant populations.

Validating Demographic Transitions: 1971–2006

Earlier sections validated the distributions of specific attributes within the simulated population by comparing them with corresponding CPS distributions. The overall performance of the historical simulation, however, requires assessing the overall evolution of its demographic structure through 2006 against those of the U.S. economy as measured by CPS microdata. Figure 3.4 helps compare CPS and simulated population shares of individuals by family type and age for selected years between 1975 and 2006 (the corresponding population shares for 1970 are shown in figure 2.2 in chapter 2). In Figure 3.4, the charts on the left show the age-distribution by family type from the CPS for selected years. Those on the right show the same distributions for corresponding years as simulated under DEMSIM. An important thing to note is that in both cases, the population shares are constructed by always using the total 1970 populations in the denominators—the CPS 1970 population for the charts on the left and the simulated 1970 population for the charts on the right. Using the 1970 total populations in the denominators preserves relative population shares by family types in each chart and preserves information about changing age structure and family composition of the population over time. But, in addition, the total area under each curve also provides a visual clue about how rapidly the population is growing—for each family type and for the overall population. The CPS and simulated charts for corresponding years show that DEMSIM tracks past U.S. demographic changes quite closely in terms of the overall population and its component family structures, and the growth of the components and the overall population over time.[7]

Figure 3.4 shows how the simulated baby boom generation moves through the age distribution of the total population in a manner similar to its movement as observed in the CPS. In addition, the population share of simulated single-headed families—labeled "sing-hd" in the figures—increases over time, as does the share of simulated older "non-family" individuals—again in a manner similar to that observed in the CPS. The increasing share of "non-family" households at older ages exhibits an interesting pattern.

During the 1970s, high marriage rates and low divorce rates meant that the share of "non-family" households was concentrated among very young adults—aged approximately between 18 and 25 years. However, the decline in marriage rates and increase in divorce rates through the years since 1970 resulted in larger shares of adults in their late twenties and early thirties remaining single. That explains why the "non-family" curve is steep during the early 1970s but becomes flatter during later years. It also explains why modal values of married adults' ages increase over time. The larger incidence of divorce and out-of-wedlock births also explains why the share of single-headed ("sing-hd") families increases among young and middle-aged adults. The share of "non-family" adults also increases

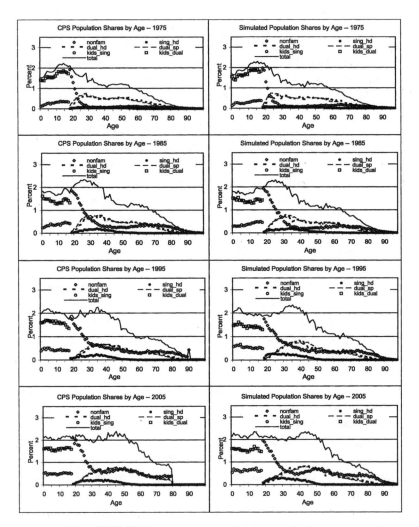

FIGURE 3.4. CPS and DEMSIM's simulated population shares by family type and age. Source: Author's calculations.

among older individuals over time as children in the now more numerous single headed families split off and form their own families.

Furthermore, the share of children as a whole in the total population declines over time, as members of the "echo boom" (children of baby boomers) move into adulthood. However, the population share of children in married families declines even more rapidly over the years since 1970. And the population share of children in single-headed families increases slightly—again the result of the greater prevalence of such families because of declining marriage rates and increasing divorce rates during those decades. Also notable is the rapid increase in the population share of older adults—a trend that will only accelerate during coming decades as the baby boom generation enters retirement and human longevity increases. Taken together, these demographic changes exhibit and portend a gradual but persistent dissolution of family structures in the United States.

Some Remarks on DEMSIM's Demographic Projections

The 2007 Technical Panel on Assumption's and Methods suggests that with greater computing power and new data sources, it should be possible to construct detailed models of the population and economy to provide a proper foundation for analyzing Social Security's finances. By its nature, Social Security's future operation and finances will be governed by the dynamic evolution of the population that it serves. Hence, any model that purports to project and analyze that program's future financial condition must demonstrate that it is based on a fundamentally sound demographic model—one that has been vetted in detail with reference to available information on the demographic composition and dynamics of the U.S. population.

Matching DEMSIM's past demographic evolution in terms of population subcomponents with historical data on the U.S. population's subcomponents and demonstrating that the transition rules adopted deliver accurate population dynamics in terms of those subcomponents—as demonstrated in this chapter—will hopefully convince readers that DEMSIM provides an adequate demographic foundation for the task at hand. Of course, more work is required to advance the demographic framework: to carry it forward in time—as described in chapter 4—and augment it with additional variables that are key determinants of Social Security's operations and financial condition. One such variable is labor earnings, which is modeled and fused into DEMSIM's demographic structure—as described in chapter 5.

Mortality Rate Calculations

The mortality rates used in DEMSIM from year 1971 onward are derived from raw death counts provided by the NCHS. Combining these data with data on the U.S. population from the National Cancer Institute (NCI) enables construction of morality rates for the years 1971–2003 conditional on race, gender, and age. Mortality rates by race, gender, and age after 2003 are derived using the Social Security Trustees' projected mortality rates by gender and age. For each future year, gender, and age, the percentage change in the trustees' mortality rates are calculated and applied to the 2003 values of the NCHS generated death rates for each year, sex, and age.

For each year t (>2003), race, r (w/nw), age, j $(0–99)$, and sex, s (m/f), let $\xi_{(t,r,j,s)}$ represent NCHS mortality rates. For each year t (>2003), age, j $(0–99)$, and sex, s (m/f), let $\emptyset_{(t,j,s)}$ be the trustees' death rates. Then the mortality rate by race, gender, and age in a future year t, $\xi_{t,r,j,s}$, is calculated as $\xi_{t,r,j,s} = \xi_{2003,r,j,s}[1 + (\emptyset_{t,j,s} - \emptyset_{2003,j,s}) / \emptyset_{2003,j,s}]$. That is, the same change in mortality is assumed to occur for both white and non-white individuals. Figure A3.1 shows mortality rates by race and gender for selected years beginning in 1971.

As expected, mortality rates increase with age for everyone. On average, mortality rates are higher for non-white individuals compared to white individuals. However, mortality is projected to decline gradually over time. The rates of decline incorporated in the rates used in DEMSIM are the same as those of the Social Security Administration.

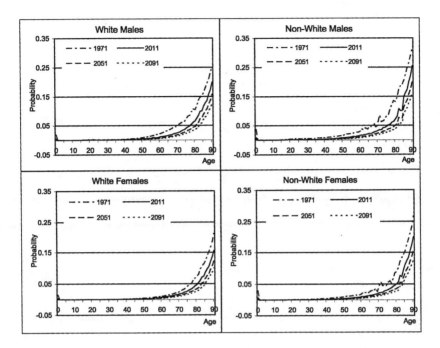

FIGURE A3.1. Mortality rates by race, age, and gender. Source: Author's calculations.

Estimating Fertility Rates by Female Race, Age, and Education

Following standard conventions in fertility measurement and reporting, females aged 14–49 are assumed to have positive fertility. Unfortunately, publicly available data on female fertility rates is not differentiated by year, age, race, and education and must be derived using related data that is available. Luckily, data on the distribution of new mothers by age, race, and education is publicly available from the Census Bureau. Also available are fertility rates by year, age, and race.

Let $f(\varepsilon \mid b, t, a, r)$ be the conditional probability density function over education (ε) given that a birth (b) has occurred for a new mother of age a and race r in year t. Also let $f(b \mid t, a, r)$ represent the probability of a birth conditional only on year, age, and race, where the female age range considered is 14–49. By applying Bayes's law, one can obtain the conditional density function $f(b \mid \varepsilon, t, a, r)$. Bayes's law, in this case, can be specified in two ways:

$$f(\varepsilon \mid b, t, a, r) \times f(b \mid t, a, r) = f(\varepsilon \bullet b \mid t, a, r) \tag{1}$$

and

$$f(b \mid \varepsilon, t, a, r) \times f(\varepsilon \mid t, a, r) = f(\varepsilon \bullet b \mid t, a, r), \tag{2}$$

where "$\varepsilon \bullet b$" indicates the joint event of a birth (denoted by b) for a new mother with a particular education level (denoted by ε).

Equations (1) and (2) can be used to obtain the required values for the probability of a birth conditional on education, age, race, and year as

$$f\,(b\,|\,\varepsilon,\,t,\,a,\,r) = f\,(\varepsilon\,|\,b,\,t,\,a,\,r) \times f\,(b\,|\,t,\,a,\,r)\,/\,f\,(\varepsilon\,|\,t,\,a,\,r). \qquad (3)$$

Implementing this calculation requires data on all the terms on the right-hand side of equation (3).

As noted above, data on the distribution of females by education, race, and age conditional on a new birth—the first term, $f\,(\varepsilon\,|\,b,\,t,\,a,\,r)$, on the right-hand side of equation (3)—is available from the Census Bureau. The distribution of females by education conditional on age and race is obtained from the Current Population Survey's June supplements between 1970 and 2003. These data provide the component $f\,(\varepsilon\,|\,t,\,a,\,r)$ on the right-hand side of equation (3). These data show that very few of both white and non-white females had more than a high school diploma during the early 1970s. They also show that during years close to 2003, the proportion of women with more than a high school diploma had increased considerably for both races and across the entire range of fertile age.

Data on the distribution of live births, $f\,(b\,|\,t,\,a,\,r)$, for white and non-white women of fertile ages between 1970 and 2003 are also obtained from the Census Bureau. These data show that birth rates peak for non-white women in their early 20s and for white women in their late 20s. They also show a rapid surge after 1975 in birth rates for white women in their early 30s. Very few fertile women had education higher than a high school diploma during the early 1970s. By 2003 however, those with some college or more than a college degree were the most numerous, especially among older new mothers.

Marriage and Divorce

Marriage

In every year of the simulation, adults in non-family units and single (non-orphan) family heads (including those just divorced) are entered into the marriage pool, one for each gender. Marriages are implemented by considering all entrants in the male marriage pool. Each male is paired with up to 20 eligible females in succession until a marriage occurs.[8] If no marriage occurs after 20 attempts, the male (and any accompanying children) is returned to the main population without being married. After a marriage occurs, the resulting family is also returned to the main population.

Marriage probabilities are based on marriage rates per 1,000 males provided by the National Center for Health Statistics from 1970 to 1988.[9] The problem of missing data for the older age groups is corrected by use of a log-linear regression to smooth the data and generate predicted male marriage rates per 100 males. This regression is used to project marriage rates through the year 2005. The first chart in figure A3.2 shows predicted marriage rates by male age. It shows that young males had much higher marriage rates in the early 1970s compared to more recent years. Males in their 20s and 30s marry at higher rates than those in their 40s and 50s. The age of peak marriage rates has increased over the years since 1970.

The marriage regression projects marriage rates approaching zero over time. But an assumption of zero marriages in future years seems less

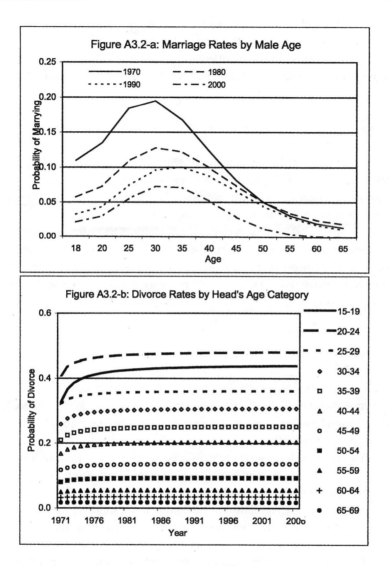

FIGURE A3.2. Marriage and divorce rates. Source: Author's calculations based on the Panel Survey of Income Dynamics.

defensible than one that assumes a low constant marriage rate prevailing in the future. Hence, the 2005 estimated marriage rates by male age are used for years after 2005. Year specific marriage rates, selected values of which are shown in the first chart of figure A3.2, are used to create an index normalized to the rate for year 1971 and the first age category (age

18). The product of this index and a marriage parameter is applied to a mate-matching function so that the age and year specific marriage rates are consistent with those used in creating the index—such as those shown in the figure. Marriage probabilities based on age and education are calculated as:

$$P(marriage) = marr\_param * marr\_index * \left(e^{-0.2\sqrt{[(Age_m - Age_f)^2 + (Edu_m - Edu_f)^2]}} \right). \quad (1)$$

This function delivers smaller probabilities of marriage the larger the differences in potential partners' ages and years of education are. For each male in the marriage market, a female is selected at random from the population of eligible females. The pairing is rejected if the total number of children in both mates' families exceeds 14. The pair is married if a random number drawn from a uniform [0, 1] distribution is less than that pair's marriage probability. The probability of interracial marriages is discounted to just 5 percent of the probability specified by the function given in equation (1).[10]

Divorce

Head's and spouses in each dual-headed family are potential divorcees. The probabilities of divorcing are calculated by using data from NCHS on male and female divorce and annulment rates between 1970, 1980, and 1982–90. For years after 1990, divorce rates are estimated by implementing an asymptotic time-series regressions on prior years' probabilities for each age category for family heads ranging from 15–19 through 65–59. The results are shown in the second chart of figure A3.2.

Family heads are simulated to be divorced if a uniform random number draw is less than the applicable divorce probability for the age of the (male) family head. Upon divorce, males split off to form a "non-family" unit; females form a "non-family" if there are no children and a "single-headed family" by acquiring custody of all children aged 17 or younger.

The second chart of figure A3.2 shows that families with younger heads tend to have higher divorce probabilities. And over time, the rates increase through the early 1990s. The asymptotic regressions provide stable divorce rates by age of head for later years.

Labor Force Status Transitions

A dults are assumed to be in one of three labor force statuses: Not-in-Labor-Force (NLF), part-time (PT) worker, or full-time (FT) worker. Appendix table A3.1 shows the probabilities of shifting to a given state in the current year (column values) given the individual's labor force status in the previous year (row values). The table shows such probabilities for two periods, the 1970s and the 2000s. Similar tables are computed for intervening year groupings.

The probabilities shown in appendix table A3.1 are calculated from the Panel Survey of Economic Dynamics, which tracks the same households, families, and individuals over many years. Each individual is assigned the full-time status if (s)he worked in a formal job for more than 1,700 hours during the year; part-time status if (s)he worked between 50 and 1,700 hours; and NLF status if (s)he worked less than 50 hours. All adults are classified as belonging to one of these three states in each year of the survey. Individuals participating in the survey in each pair of consecutive years are used to derive average rates of switching labor force participation status. The transition probabilities are calculated as fractions of those who are observed to transit from each given state in year $t - 1$ to each of the three states in year t.

The table can be read as follows: Each square block of nine numbers represents the transition table for the corresponding population group as labeled in row and column headings. The rows in each block represent

TABLE A3.1 **Labor Force Status Transition Probabilities**

Age / Status	1970s												2000s											
	Not a high school graduate						College graduate plus						Not a high school graduate						College graduate plus					
	Males			Females			Males			Females			Males			Females			Males			Females		
	NLF	FT	PT	NLF	FT	PT	NLF	FT	PT	NLF	FT	PT	NLF	FT	PT	NLF	FT	PT	NLF	FT	PT	NLF	FT	PT
Whites																								
Young (18–22) NLF	0.61	0.12	0.27	0.62	0.06	0.31	0.37	0.35	0.28	0.20	0.12	0.68	0.65	0.10	0.25	0.65	0.05	0.30	0.00	0.42	0.58	0.00	0.15	0.85
Young (18–22) FT	0.05	0.75	0.20	0.12	0.62	0.25	0.00	0.85	0.15	0.00	0.57	0.43	0.02	0.75	0.23	0.06	0.34	0.60	0.13	0.76	0.11	0.12	0.80	0.09
Young (18–22) PT	0.16	0.27	0.57	0.21	0.21	0.57	0.17	0.53	0.30	0.03	0.45	0.52	0.11	0.18	0.70	0.14	0.09	0.77	0.08	0.30	0.62	0.15	0.44	0.41
Middle aged (38–42) NLF	0.84	0.06	0.10	0.83	0.04	0.13	1.00	0.00	0.00	0.89	0.00	0.11	0.79	0.00	0.21	0.79	0.00	0.21	0.26	0.27	0.46	0.76	0.00	0.24
Middle aged (38–42) FT	0.00	0.94	0.05	0.16	0.66	0.18	0.00	0.97	0.03	0.00	0.69	0.31	0.01	0.90	0.09	0.02	0.80	0.18	0.00	0.96	0.04	0.01	0.82	0.17
Middle aged (38–42) PT	0.09	0.53	0.38	0.15	0.23	0.62	0.00	0.48	0.52	0.10	0.22	0.68	0.20	0.48	0.32	0.22	0.33	0.45	0.01	0.54	0.46	0.04	0.20	0.76
Old (58–62) NLF	0.90	0.02	0.08	0.92	0.05	0.03	1.00	0.00	0.00	0.89	0.00	0.11	0.97	0.00	0.03	0.97	0.00	0.03	0.93	0.00	0.07	0.89	0.02	0.09
Old (58–62) FT	0.06	0.81	0.14	0.18	0.67	0.16	0.02	0.79	0.19	0.00	0.69	0.31	0.02	0.78	0.21	0.06	0.73	0.21	0.01	0.85	0.14	0.00	0.81	0.19
Old (58–62) PT	0.28	0.25	0.47	0.21	0.25	0.54	0.15	0.37	0.48	0.21	0.15	0.63	0.33	0.37	0.31	0.31	0.11	0.58	0.31	0.09	0.59	0.19	0.11	0.70
Non-whites																								
Young (18–22) NLF	0.68	0.10	0.21	0.67	0.08	0.25	0.94	0.04	0.02	0.06	0.41	0.53	0.74	0.09	0.17	0.72	0.01	0.27	0.46	0.14	0.40	0.33	0.00	0.67
Young (18–22) FT	0.08	0.63	0.29	0.16	0.58	0.25	0.82	0.18	0.00	0.46	0.31	0.23	0.03	0.61	0.36	0.04	0.60	0.36	0.00	0.80	0.20	0.02	0.58	0.40
Young (18–22) PT	0.26	0.32	0.42	0.28	0.24	0.49	0.00	0.05	0.95	0.33	0.20	0.47	0.21	0.19	0.60	0.30	0.12	0.58	0.28	0.22	0.49	0.21	0.36	0.43
Middle aged (38–42) NLF	0.88	0.08	0.03	0.72	0.11	0.17	1.00	0.00	0.00	0.50	0.00	0.50	0.94	0.02	0.04	0.76	0.08	0.16	1.00	0.00	0.00	1.00	0.00	0.00
Middle aged (38–42) FT	0.01	0.92	0.08	0.14	0.68	0.18	0.00	0.99	0.01	0.00	0.26	0.74	0.01	0.92	0.08	0.05	0.71	0.24	0.00	0.87	0.13	0.01	0.74	0.24
Middle aged (38–42) PT	0.12	0.48	0.41	0.16	0.31	0.52	0.00	1.00	0.00	0.00	0.00	1.00	0.12	0.27	0.61	0.45	0.26	0.29	0.00	0.46	0.54	0.01	0.43	0.56
Old (58–62) NLF	0.90	0.03	0.06	0.90	0.07	0.03	1.00	0.00	0.00	1.00	0.00	0.00	0.99	0.00	0.01	0.93	0.01	0.06	1.00	0.00	0.00	1.00	0.00	0.00
Old (58–62) FT	0.07	0.78	0.15	0.23	0.57	0.20	0.00	1.00	0.00	0.10	0.43	0.47	0.01	0.76	0.22	0.03	0.73	0.24	0.00	0.68	0.32	0.00	0.38	0.62
Old (58–62) PT	0.18	0.32	0.50	0.16	0.20	0.64	0.00	0.00	1.00	0.00	0.00	1.00	0.14	0.48	0.38	0.27	0.13	0.60	0.00	0.00	1.00	0.01	0.04	0.96

Source: Authors' calculations based on the Panel Survey of Income Dynamics (various years).

labor force status in year $t - 1$ and columns represent the same three states in year t. For example, the position (row = FT, column = FT) in each block shows the probability that a person who worked full-time in year $t - 1$ (row position) also works full time in year t (column position). The position (row 1, column 3) represents the probability that a person who was NLF in the previous year would work part-time this year, and so on.

Appendix table A3.1 shows several interesting features. For example, comparing the (row 2, column 2) positions of males and females in the 1970s, shows that females at all ages were much less likely to remain in full-time jobs. The corresponding probabilities during the 2000s are generally much higher for females retaining full-time jobs, both absolutely, and also relative to the corresponding probabilities for males.

Older males who are NLF to begin with (row 1) are much more likely to remain NLF compared to younger ones in all groups. Young white men having at least a college education are more likely to assume full-time jobs this year, no matter which labor force status they had last year—compared to those with less education. The same is true for non-whites in the 2000s, but was not true in the 1970s (the latter result is most likely the result of sparse data on young and educated non-white men during the 1970s). Finally, the NLF status exhibits greater persistence in general for non-whites compared to whites.

Calibration of Immigrants' Characteristics

Immigrant's simulated characteristics are governed by cumulative distributions of their demographic and economic attributes obtained from the Census Bureau. Appendix figure A3.3-1 shows decade-wise unconditional cumulative distributions of immigrants by "family" and "non-family" status and race, and conditional cumulative distributions of gender for "non-family" immigrants, and single- versus dual-headed status for immigrants in "families."

The figure shows that most immigrants arrived as "families" during the decades since 1970; that more than 50 percent of immigrants are non-white; that immigrants' gender distribution was equal across the two sexes during 1970–79 but has skewed of late in favor of male immigrants. Finally, the figure shows that most immigrant "families" are dual headed (with married spouses) rather than single headed.

Figure A3.3-2 shows the decade-wise cumulative distributions of immigrant family sizes. Note that these distributions are not applicable in DEMSIM if the simulated immigrant is a "non-family" individual. If the immigrant head is of "family" type and is married, the distribution of family size determines how many children there would be in the family—ranging from zero if there are only two individuals simulated for this family or five if there are seven individuals simulated.

If the simulated immigrant is of "single-headed" type, then the number of children range from one through six depending on the family size simulated using the distributions shown in figure A3.3-2.

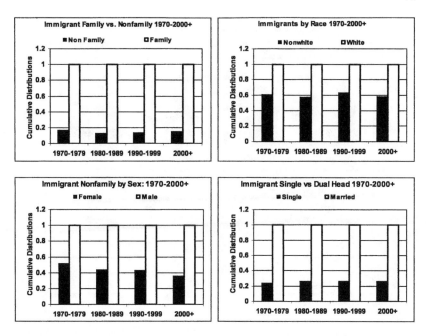

FIGURE A3.3-1. Distributions of immigrants' characteristics. Source: Author's calculations based on Census Bureau data.

The two lower charts in figure 3.3-2 depict decade-wise cumulative age distributions of adult immigrant males and females. The distributions are according to 15 age categories ranging from 18–19, 20–24, 25–29, . . . 80–84, and 85+. Conditional on gender, once the age category is determined via random simulation using the appropriate distribution, the specific age within each age category is randomly assigned using a uniform distribution across ages within the relevant age category. The cumulative age-category distributions of figure 3.3-2 show that immigrants to the United States today are considerably younger compared to the 1970s.

Figure A3.3-3 shows the decade-wise occupational status of male and female immigrants. They indicate that the percent of new male immigrants who have been out of the labor force has remained steady at about 6 percent through the decades since 1970. However, the share of non-working females has increased over time from about 5.5 percent in the 1970s to almost 10 percent today.

Figure A3.3-4 shows cumulative distributions of new immigrants' years of education. These distributions show very little change over the decades since 1970. The only subtle but discernible pattern is that the number of

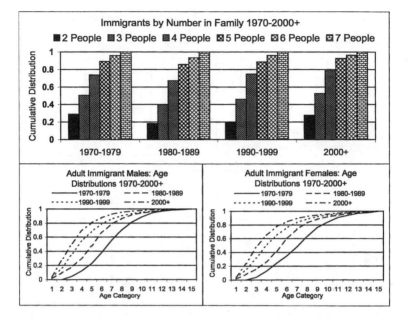

FIGURE A3.3-2. Distributions of immigrants by age and family size. Source: Author's calculations based on Census Bureau data.

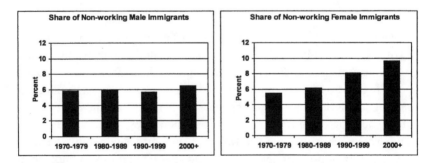

FIGURE A3.3-3. Percent of immigrants not participating in the labor force. Source: Author's calculations based on Census Bureau data.

immigrants with a high school diploma (12 years of education) or less declined after the 1980s, implying that today's immigrants are slightly better educated.

Cumulative distributions of nominal wages—available from the Census Bureau by "family" and "non-family" status and gender—are used to assign earnings to new immigrant adults. The earnings distributions are,

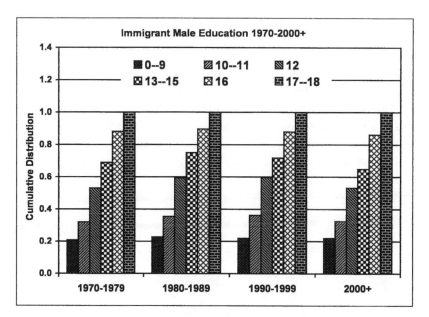

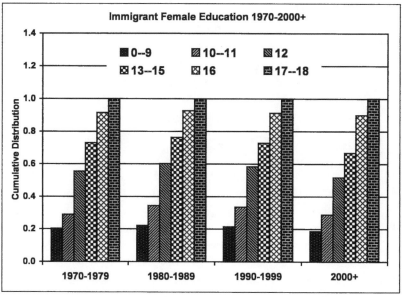

FIGURE A3.3-4. Cumulative distributions of immigrants by years-of-education categories. Source: Author's calculations based on Census Bureau data.

again, available decade-wise. Hence, the Census Bureau's nominal earnings values are assumed to apply to the middle of each relevant decade.
Nominal earnings for other years are calculated by inflating the mid-decade
values by the applicable year's GDP deflator relative to its value in the
mid-decade year. Historical GDP deflator values are those reported by
the Bureau of Economic Analysis. Similarly, the Census Bureau provides
distributions of child ages in immigrant families that are used to assign
ages to children in immigrant families. Gender assignment for immigrant
children is implemented randomly with a 50 percent chance for each sex.

CHAPTER FOUR

Peering into the Future

Projecting DEMSIM Forward in Time

Maintaining the transition rules that are operational in 2006 and executing DEMSIM for years thereafter provides clues about how the U.S. population's demographic and economic attributes might evolve in future years. Of course, this assumes that the built-in momentum of those forces remains unaffected by any significant and permanent changes in productivity, technology, and public policies. Based on the historical evolution between 1970 and the mid-2000s, what should one expect to see in the future?

Chapter 3 showed the progression of the baby boom generation through the population age distribution during the historical transition between 1970 and 2006. In 2006, the boomers spanned the ages of 42 through 60. Few women give birth or care for young children at these ages. Indeed, for most families with middle-aged household heads, children have left home, and both spouses are likely working and earning at the highest levels during their lifetimes. By 2020, however, the baby boomers would be aged between 56 and 74. By then, about one half of the boomers would have retired, and their numbers will begin to decline as they begin to experience higher mortality at older ages.

As the boomer generation of workers is replaced by their children, the demographic and economic profile of the population, and especially of workers, will undergo significant changes. The description in chapter 3 provides clues to additional patterns of demographic evolution that are likely to occur.

Future Evolution of the U.S. Population's Age Distribution by Family Type

Figure 4.1 shows the result of carrying DEMSIM forward beyond 2006. It shows the age distribution of the total population as well as age distributions of subcomponent shares of various family types for the year 2020 and for every 15th year thereafter through the year 2125. The charts show that the shape of the total population's age distribution stabilizes after 2050, once the baby boom generation has passed away. Indeed, the share of children in the total population and the shares of various family types also stabilize over time.

Figure 4.1 shows other interesting features as well: until they stabilize, the shares of married individuals in the total population decline over time, and those of single-headed families increase. The latter change is especially clear when compared to the chart for 2005 in figure 3.4. The share of "non-family" individuals increases over time—especially among older individuals. DEMSIM assumes that marriage and divorce rates would remain stable after 2006. However, because the likelihood of getting married declines with age, population aging implies a declining overall rate of marriage. In addition, the continued greater longevity of females implicit in projected mortality rates means that the older population would be increasingly comprised of single individuals—especially widows.

The projected simulation shows that the fraction of older individuals would be permanently higher compared to today—that is an "aged population" will be a lasting feature of the future U.S. demographic landscape with a much larger fraction of the population surviving through their 100th birthdays. Moreover, a larger fraction of the older population would belong to "non-families." DEMSIM makes no explicit assumptions about living arrangements. However, historical trends in living arrangements show that joint living by the elderly with their adult children has been declining during past decades.[1] If that trend continues into the future, a larger share of "non-family" individuals will likely imply that a greater fraction of the older population would be living alone (which includes living in old-age homes) in the future.

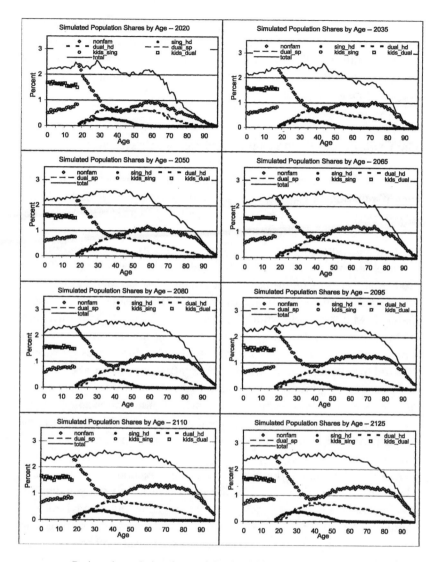

FIGURE 4.1. Projected population shares of simulated family types by age. Source: Author's calculations.

An increasing fragmentation of family structures in the future that figure 4.1 suggests may contribute to declining provision of goods and services within families and a greater demand for market provision of services such as health care, entertainment, elder housing, financial and estate planning, and so on.

The Evolution of Demographic and Economic Attributes

The future evolution of demographic and economic attributes of the simulated population carries forward the momentum of forces built into the current population structure. It is modified slightly each year by the demographic attributes assigned to immigrants. Thus, historical trends in mortality, fertility, education acquisition, labor force participation and earnings, and marital rates and patterns, along with assumed rates of labor productivity growth, determine the future population's characteristics.[2]

One important determinant of those characteristics is the relative shares of white and non-white populations in the total. As it turns out, DEMSIM's transition rules—calibrated using microdata on the U.S. economy through 2006—incorporate systematic differences by race in most of the demographic and economic attributes listed above. As is well known, non-white females exhibit higher fertility rates, especially at younger ages. In addition, because the share of non-whites among immigrants is assumed to be about 60 percent going forward, the demographic characteristics of immigrant populations are, on balance, more similar to those of non-whites.

Extending the simulation beyond 2006 suggests that the share of non-whites in the U.S. population would grow larger, and the population's characteristics and average demographic and economic behavioral propensities (education acquisition, labor force entry, rates of labor force participation, earnings, fertility, retirement ages, survival, and so on), would gradually evolve to become closer to those of non-whites.

This is not to say that behavioral characteristics of whites and non-whites will remain exactly as they are today. Evolution toward greater diversity in the population may lead to behavioral changes in both racial groups, and it is difficult to predict whether those changes would imply greater or lesser need for providing economic security via programs such as Social Security. Recent studies by Dora Costa and others suggest that social cohesion, friendship, community participation, and willingness to

sacrifice personal interests for achieving greater social benefits deterio-
rate with greater social and ethnic diversity. That means the willingness to
support tax-financed Social Security and other social safety net programs
could become weaker in the future.[3]

But such adjustments are likely to be very gradual. In general, projecting the implications of currently observed differences in demographic and
economic behaviors among different population groups and their interactions and inferring their implications for a program such as Social Security is meant to be suggestive rather than incontrovertible proof about
the future environment within which the program would operate and its
prospective financial condition.

Keeping these considerations in mind, however, the simulation and projection exercise conducted using DEMSIM points to a sustained increase
in population diversity. Cumulatively, immigration at current counts and
higher fertility among non-whites lead DEMSIM to project that the population's share of non-whites would grow from 17 percent in 2006 to 29
percent by the end of the 21st century. Correspondingly the population
share of white individuals declines from 83 percent to 71 percent. Under
DEMSIM's assumptions, these trends would continue well beyond the
year 2100.[4]

Key Demographic Statistics for Social Security's Finances

Table 4.1 shows education achievement and labor force participation rates
for men and women for selected years through the year 2100. It shows that
by the end of this century non-whites would gradually achieve parity with
whites in educational achievement. The table shows that full-time labor
force participation rates are similar among female whites and non-whites
and that both rates decline slightly over time. More white females work
part-time compared to non-white females and, again, those participation
rates decline over time. For males, the full-time participation rate among
non-whites is considerably smaller compared to whites and the difference
is not fully offset by non-whites' higher part-time participation rate, implying that a larger fraction of non-whites remain out of the labor force.
Among both males and females, overall rates of labor force participation
rates are projected to decline gradually over time.[5]

The different population shares of labor force attachments for non-
whites compared to whites implies that, with a growing population share

TABLE 4.1 **DEMSIM Population Shares (%) in Selected Education and Labor Force Participation Categories by Race, Gender, and Future Year**

Year	Education						Labor force participation					
	Less than high school			College plus			Full time			Part time		
	Non-white	White	All	Non-white	White	All	Non-white	White	All	Non-white	White	All
	Females											
2006	20.9	13.1	14.3	18.5	25.3	24.2	40.2	42.6	42.2	18.5	21.6	21.1
2010	18.6	11.7	12.9	19.8	26.0	24.9	38.8	40.3	40.0	19.5	22.4	21.9
2025	12.8	7.2	8.3	24.5	31.4	30.1	38.4	41.3	40.7	19.2	21.1	20.7
2040	10.0	6.4	7.2	27.7	34.4	32.9	38.1	42.5	41.5	17.8	20.9	20.2
2055	8.4	6.1	6.7	30.7	35.6	34.4	39.8	40.9	40.7	18.5	21.0	20.4
2070	6.5	6.2	6.3	32.2	36.0	35.0	40.4	41.7	41.3	16.1	21.4	19.9
2085	6.0	5.9	5.9	33.3	36.7	35.7	39.0	41.6	40.8	16.4	20.5	19.3
2100	5.4	6.2	6.0	35.4	36.2	36.0	38.5	41.4	40.5	17.6	20.4	19.5
	Males											
2006	21.2	14.6	15.6	20.0	27.5	26.3	48.4	62.8	60.4	20.6	17.2	17.8
2010	18.2	12.5	13.4	20.3	27.7	26.5	46.7	63.4	60.5	19.8	16.3	16.9
2025	11.8	8.6	9.2	22.7	31.2	29.6	47.3	61.5	58.6	20.5	16.7	17.5
2040	9.1	7.7	8.0	25.5	33.2	31.6	48.3	63.8	60.2	18.0	14.3	15.2
2055	7.6	7.5	7.5	30.0	34.8	33.7	48.8	63.6	59.9	16.8	14.3	15.0
2070	6.5	7.8	7.5	32.1	35.5	34.6	48.2	64.8	60.2	16.5	14.6	15.1
2085	5.8	7.2	6.8	34.4	35.9	35.5	45.7	62.6	57.6	19.9	15.6	16.8
2100	5.3	7.3	6.7	34.5	35.9	35.5	46.8	62.4	57.5	17.7	14.8	15.8

Source: Author's calculations.

of non-whites, the overall rate of labor force participation under full- and part-time status would decline over time. Figure 4.2 shows the overall labor force participation rate for several decades beginning in 2006. It shows that the overall labor force participation rate—the ratio of full-time and part-time workers to the total population aged between 18 and 75—declines rapidly until about 2025. The one important factor governing this decline is the retirement of the baby boomers. For about 20 years after 2025, as the oldest boomers move past age 80 and experience higher mortality, the overall labor force participation rate remains stable. After about 2040, however, the rate declines consistently—reflecting the increasing impact of a larger share of non-whites in the overall population.

A key determinant of Social Security's finances is the ratio of covered workers to retirees. In calculating this ratio for the Old Age and Survivors Insurance (OASI) program, DEMSIM applies the official Social Security

Administration's ratio of covered workers to total workers to its total sim-ulated worker population—with the latter defined as those working either full-time or part-time each year.

DEMSIM's beneficiary population equals those older than age 18 receiving OASI benefits as determined by the Social Security Tax and Benefit Calculator (SSTBC) described in chapter 6. SSTBC assumes that individuals begin to collect Social Security benefits sometime between the ages of 62 and 70.[6] For those whose last year of earnings occurs before age 62, Social Security benefit collection is assumed to begin at age 62. For those whose last working year falls between the ages of 62 and 70, benefit collection is assumed to begin at the first year of retirement. And for those who continue to earn at age 70 and later, benefit collection is assumed to begin at age 70.

Taking the ratio of beneficiaries to covered workers yields a ratio of 3.3 for 2006—which matches the official ratio almost exactly.[7] Figure 4.2 shows that the DEMSIM population's worker-beneficiary ratio declines from 3.3 in 2006 to 2.0 by 2040; the latter value is again very close to the official ratio of 2.1. In the long term, DEMSIM's ratio declines faster be-cause of a lower projected labor force participation. For example, figure

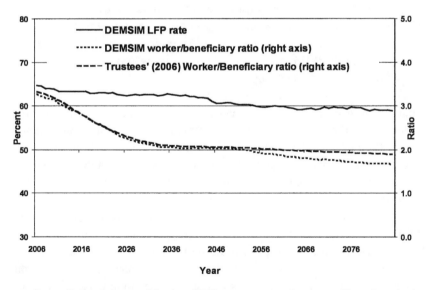

FIGURE 4.2. Labor force participation (LFP) rates among 18–75-year-olds and worker/beneficiary ratios for the 18+ population. Source: Author's calculations based on DEMSIM and data from the Social Security Administration.

4.2 shows that DEMSIM's worker-to-beneficiary ratio equals 1.7 in 2085, whereas the official ratio equals 1.9 in that year. Overall, however, figure 4.2 shows that DEMSIM's projections are quite close to those of the Social Security Administration over the medium term for this key demographic determinant of Social Security's finances. And the simulated ratio deviates slightly over the long term from official projections because of understandable projected changes in the demographic composition of the population.

Outcomes from DEMSIM's Long-Range Demographic Simulation

Figure 4.3 depicts outcomes from projecting DEMSIM forward for 500 years after 1970 (through 2469) in terms of the population's size, crude fertility, mortality, and immigration rates, and the population's growth rate.[8]

Panel A of figure 4.3 shows the total population index—the ratio of the population in a future year to that of 1970. Applying historical fertility, mortality, and immigration rates between 1970 and 2006 produces a population index of 1.470 for 2006. This value is quite close to the index value of 1.454 calculated using the Census Bureau's population data.[9] Continuing DEMSIM forward through the next 500 years (beginning in 1970) yields a final population index of 4.811. That is, under the baseline projected simulation, DEMSIM's population in the year 2469 is a little more than three times as large as in 2006.

The population index profile shown in figure 4.3 shows a mildly wavy pattern, indicating the long-term ebb and flow in the population growth rate. This is the result of changes in several factors over time, but primarily of the periodic change in the proportion of women within the fertile age range relative to the total population. Such a pattern may be expected from the propagation of a population wave generated by the baby boom during the latter half of the 20th century.

Panels B through D of figure 4.3 show crude fertility, mortality, and immigration rates, respectively, for the 500-year forward simulation. The crude fertility rate (the number of newborns divided by the total population) declines in the projected simulation from its current value of about 15 per 1,000 individuals fluctuates within a narrow bound around 10.4 per 1,000 individuals toward the end of the simulation horizon.[10] The crude death rate initially increases as the baby boomers die off. Once they have

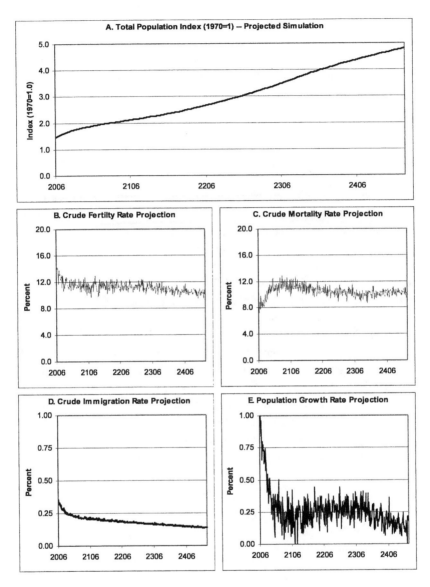

FIGURE 4.3 Long-term simulation outcomes: population index; crude fertility, mortality, and immigration rates; and overall population growth rate. Source: Author's calculations.

passed away, the mortality rate also stabilizes at about 10.3 per thousand. Panel D of figure 4.3 shows that the crude immigration rate declines over time but remains positive. The small difference between the fertility and mortality rates and the positive immigration rate means that the total population continues to grow as shown by the increasing population index in the figure's panel A.

Next Steps

The demographic and economic simulation based on microdata surveys of U.S. households—as described in this chapter—is intended for developing a forward-looking analysis of Social Security's finances. That requires first assigning earnings levels to adult workers in the simulated population and calculating Social Security taxes and benefits through each person's adult lifetime as a participant in the Social Security program. The method used for assigning earnings for each adult in each year of DEMSIM's simulation is described in chapter 5.

DEMSIM's detailed simulation of the U.S. population's demographic and economic attributes, including labor earnings, provides a tool for evaluating Social Security's future finances. Social Security taxes and benefits are calculated for the OASI program using a detailed Social Security Tax and Benefit Calculator.[11] Details about the operation of SSTBC are provided in chapter 7. Subsequent chapters describe the measures used for evaluating Social Security's finances and the impact of alternative reforms on the programs financial solvency and long-term sustainability.

CHAPTER FIVE

A Framework for Simulating Annual Nominal Earnings

Labor Earnings—Key Determinant of Social Security Finances

To be useful for analyzing Social Security's finances, the demographic and economic simulation developed so far must include a method of assigning labor earnings to each simulated adult over his or her lifetime. This is a crucial step because Social Security's revenues in each period are based on the labor earnings of workers in occupations covered under the program and benefits are based on the history of labor earnings during each retiree's working lifetime. The methodology used in DEMSIM for estimating and projecting labor earnings is the topic of this chapter.

The framework for simulating labor earnings developed here neatly incorporates the impact of the population's demographic and economic attributes as they evolve through the historical period of 1970–2006 and beyond. The interacting set of demographic and economic attributes are used to first determine each worker's "core labor input." Each individual's "core labor input" is then adjusted to capture the full extent of cross-sectional and longitudinal labor earnings volatility as observed in U.S. microdata. Finally, each worker's earnings level is determined by applying projected parameters for general price inflation, productivity growth, and the share of labor earnings in total output.

Simulated *demographic* attributes of mortality, fertility, immigration (distinguished by race, gender, age, and so on) affects the number of workers and worker-to-beneficiary ratios over time—both of which are key determinants of Social Security's financial status. The previous chapter showed that DEMSIM's simulated trajectory of these variables for future decades—especially the worker-to-beneficiary ratio—closely approximates official projections. However, the influence of the population's *economic* attributes must also be taken into account—variables such as educational attainment, participation in the work force, and the joint influence of demographic and economic attributes on workers' "earning ability," or "labor quality."

As will become clear in this chapter, the momentum of interacting demographic and economic attributes determines workers' "effective labor inputs," which, in turn, determine their labor earnings over time. As shown below, the measurement and projection of "effective labor inputs" is necessary because they constitute key determinants of aggregate payrolls, Social Security taxes, and benefits—in addition to the key demographic ratios described earlier. Although there is a fair amount of literature on the measurement of labor quality, this element is usually absent in most standard approaches for projecting Social Security's finances.[1]

The University of Michigan's Panel Study of Income Dynamics (PSID) rather than the Current Population Survey (CPS) is used to obtain the initial (1970) distribution of labor earnings. That's because the panel feature of the PSID—wherein it follows the same individuals over time—is exploited to obtain life-cycle earnings profiles along annual transitions of the population through time, as described below. This feature of the PSID makes it a robust source for calibrating earnings distributions during year-to-year transitions after 1970. However, as demonstrated later, using the CPS's annual earnings distributions to validate DEMSIM's post-1970 earnings assignments generates a very good match.

General Methodology for Simulating Labor Earnings

The method of simulating labor earnings incorporates the demographic and economic evolution of the population to project worker earnings taking into account their contributions of both labor quantity and labor quality. Appendix 5.1 provides a detailed description of how the standard Solow growth model framework is used to capture the impact of labor quantity and quality on total national output—a share of which is allocated to each worker based on that worker's contribution of quality-adjusted work effort.

Under the Solow growth model, national output is determined by the joint operation of physical and human capital under a certain production technology. That output is distributed to the owners of physical capital and to workers based on their marginal contributions to the economy's total production. The human capital input is composed of labor quantity and labor quality. The latter is dependent on the demographic and economic attributes of the working population.

Obviously, those who don't participate in the work force in any given period have zero "labor quality" and zero hours of work and, therefore, zero earnings in that period. The variables used for determining each worker's labor quantity are their choices between working full- or part-time. Each work-force participant's labor quality is determined by that individual's demographic and economic attributes. Workers' "core labor inputs" (or core labor quality) are estimated using historical microdata from the PSID: wage-growth-adjusted earnings of labor force participants in the PSID are regressed on their demographic and economic characteristics (see appendices 5.2 and 5.3 for details).

The coefficients obtained from that regression are applied to each worker's *simulated* characteristics under DEMSIM to derive that worker's simulated "core labor inputs." Estimating just "core labor inputs" is not sufficient, however, because those do not incorporate the influence of unobserved worker characteristics on workers' labor quality—characteristics responsible for the high cross-sectional and longitudinal variability in earnings across workers and through time. To simulate that volatility realistically as "effective labor inputs," simulated "core labor inputs" are adjusted using random draws from the distribution of errors taken from the PSID-based regression described earlier.

The next step is to estimate the economy's stock of physical capital in each period. The historical capital stock index is taken from a study by Jorgenson et al. (2007). For future years, the capital stock index is projected based on average net wealth holdings by age and gender. This calibration of the capital stock to demographics uses microdata from the Federal Reserve's Survey of Consumer Finances for 2004 (Board of Governors 2004). Simulated population distributions according to these two demographic attributes determine the evolution of the physical capital stock index in future years.

To complete the Solow growth model framework, the human (labor quantity × quality) and physical capital inputs are combined to yield total nominal output in each year of DEMSIM's historical and projected simulations. The combination of these two inputs is calibrated using three historically determined parameters: (1) multifactor productivity, (2) the share of labor in total output, and (3) annual (historical and projected) inflation rates. The first two parameters are also taken from the afore-mentioned study by Jorgenson et al., and the historical inflation series is taken from the Bureau of Labor Statistics—the Consumer Price Index for urban wage earners and clerical workers (CPI-W). The future growth of general prices is assumed to remain equal to its historical average since 1982.

The particular values of the first two parameters used in DEMSIM's baseline assumptions are discussed below and in the appendices to this chapter. Here, it is sufficient to note that the "multifactor" productivity parameter captures how efficient each unit of combined human and physical capital is in each year of the simulation. The growth rate of multifactor productivity is assumed to equal its observed historical rate since 1982. The labor share parameter determines how total output is distributed between owners of physical capital and workers. For future years, this parameter is also assumed to remain at its historically observed rate.

Thus the process of determining labor earnings under DEMSIM can be summarized as follows: Physical and human capital combine each year under the parametric assumptions described earlier to determine total output in each year. Annual output growth depends on simulated growth in human and physical capital inputs and the assumed parametric growth rate of multifactor productivity. The growth of the two inputs is determined by the simulated evolution of the population's demographic and economic attributes. Note that human capital growth is the product of growth in labor quantity and "effective labor inputs" (or labor quality). Each year's output is allocated between owners of human and physical capital. Hence, overall output growth each year determines that year's growth of workers' earnings—the sum total of the marginal returns to each worker's quality-adjusted provision of labor effort (see appendix 5.1 for a more detailed and technical description).

The key item of note here is that each worker's earnings over his or her working life span are determined by the simulated evolution of that worker's economic and demographic characteristics. In addition the aggregate capital stock depends on the population's demographic characteristics. Hence, the growth of physical capital, growth of worker productivity, labor quality, and workers' earnings are all fully grounded in the population's projected demographic and economic attributes. This method of projecting labor earnings by incorporating the population's projected characteristics into a Solow growth framework provides a far more consistent projection of future earnings. It enables DEMSIM to capture the implications of the population's built-in demographic and economic forces for the growth of the economy's future payroll base, payroll taxes, Social Security benefits, and Social Security's financial condition.

Simulating Labor Earnings for 1970

Following the general methodology described above, 1970 labor earnings are assigned by first implementing the above-described PSID regression for 1970—a cross-sectional regression as described in equation (6) of appendix 5.1: the logarithms of PSID individual wage-growth-adjusted earnings are regressed on individual 1970 PSID demographic and economic variables (including fixed effects for different birth cohorts).[2] The regression's explanatory variables selected from the PSID correspond to

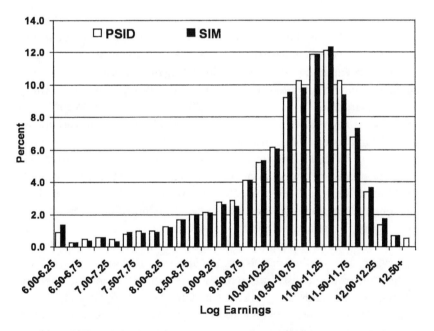

FIGURE 5.1. PSID and simulated log labor earnings distributions (1970). Source: Author's calculations.

the demographic and economic attributes developed for DEMSIM's 1970 population as described in earlier chapters.

Next, the cross-sectional regression's coefficients are applied to the DEMSIM population's simulated demographic and economic attributes to obtain "core labor inputs." The latter are converted into "effective labor inputs" by applying a randomly drawn perturbation term from the distribution of regression errors. Finally, 1970 values of the general price index, multifactor productivity, and the capital stock index are applied to obtain the wage assignment for each DEMSIM adult in 1970.

To validate the calculations, the simulated 1970 earnings distribution is compared with that calculated from the PSID for 1970. As figure 5.1 shows, the two distributions match each other quite closely. Appendix 5.2 provides details of the cross-section labor input regression and shows how "core labor input" levels vary with selected worker demographic and economic attributes.

Simulating Labor Earnings Transitions after 1970

The next step is to assign labor earnings for years after 1970. That means each DEMSIM-simulated individual would be assigned labor earnings over his or her remaining working life span. Beginning in 1971, "core labor inputs" are simulated for each year and for each individual using a longitudinal earnings regression. This time around, data on individual earnings and demographics from 1971 to 1993 PSID surveys are used for implementing the regression of wage-growth-adjusted earnings on workers' demographic and economic attributes. This regression also includes labor earnings from the previous year among the explanatory variables to capture the dependence of a person's current earning on his or her past earnings.[3]

Simulated earnings for years after 1970 are, again, obtained by applying the longitudinal regression's coefficients to each individual's demographic and economic characteristics as applicable in the year in question. As before, this yields each worker's simulated "core labor input" profile over his or her working life span. Next, the application of a randomly drawn error value from the distribution of regression errors (from the longitudinal regression) yields that worker's simulated "effective labor inputs" for various years. Finally, the application of historical or projected values, as appropriate, of the price index, multifactor productivity, and capital stock index completes the simulation of each of DEMSIM's workers' life-cycle labor earnings. Appendix 5.3 provides details of DEMSIM's longitudinal PSID regression and describes how longitudinal "core labor inputs" vary with workers' underlying demographic and economic attributes.

It should be noted that DEMSIM's simulation of demographic and economic attributes between 1970 and 2006 are based on the CPS. Nevertheless, because both PSID and CPS microdata pertain to the same underlying economy (the United States), a close match of the two wage distributions would indirectly confirm that the underlying distributions of simulated demographic and economic attributes closely approximate those underlying the PSID as well. As shown below, simulated labor earnings distributions match those calculated from the CPS quite closely. This indicates that the former distributions provide a good representation of the features of the U.S. population and economy during the decades since 1970.

Validating Labor Earnings Distributions during Transition Years

The final validation exercise examines whether the post-1970 simulated earnings distributions conform to those observed for the U.S. economy. The estimation process for wage earnings described earlier generates *nominal* earnings for each adult individual in the simulated population. Figure 5.2 compares quantiles of simulated and CPS earnings between 1970 and 2006 for corresponding population subgroups of DEMSIM's simulated populations and the CPS sample populations. Each chart shows time series of the first through the ninth deciles of each year's nominal earnings distribution.

The charts of figure 5.2 show that the simulated and CPS earnings distributions are quite similar when compared for specific demographic attributes such as race and gender. The slopes and positions of the decile curves are similar in both charts. For example, the dark solid line in the center of the simulated earnings distributions—which shows the evolution of DEMSIM's median earnings between 1970 and 2006—is positioned similarly to the corresponding curve in the CPS distribution. The same remark applies to the other charts in figure 5.2, each pair of which compares the CPS and simulated earnings distributions for a specific population group. The match is also quite good for other population groupings not shown here because of space constraints—for example, young, middle-aged, and old individuals, those with low and high education, and those for simulated and CPS populations overall.

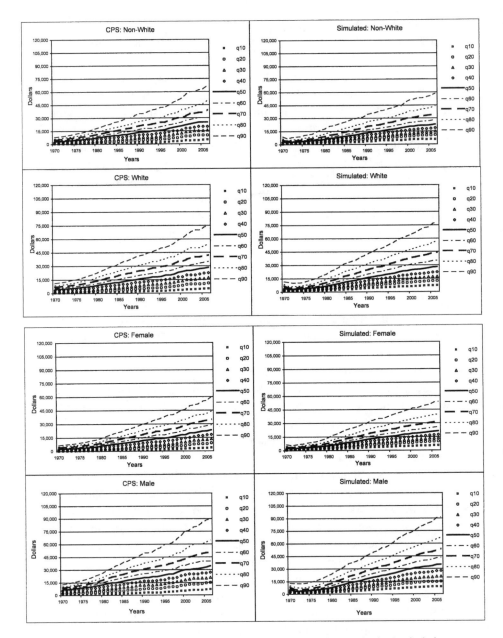

FIGURE 5.2. CPS and simulated wage distributions: 1970–2006. Source: Author's calculations.

The fact that simulated nominal earnings distributions between 1970 and 2006 are so similar to their CPS counterparts indirectly validates the underlying demographic and economic simulations—that is, the entire collection of population characteristics simulated for 1970 and the transition rules used to calibrate their evolution through 2006.

There is one additional adjustment that must be implemented in the calibration of labor earnings to make them suitable for estimating Social Security's financial condition. It concerns the match between aggregate labor earnings derived from the CPS and economy-wide labor earnings (total wages excluding fringe benefits that are not subject to payroll taxes and excluding employer-paid social insurance taxes) as reported by the Bureau of Economic Analysis as part of the National Income and Product Accounts (Bureau of Economic Analysis 2007). The weighted sum of CPS wages and salaries underestimates NIPA aggregate wages in each year between 1970 and 2006.[4] On average, the degree of underestimation for years included in the earnings regression is 13 percent. Thus labor earnings assigned to each individual between 1970 and 2006 are increased by an annual adjustment factor so that aggregate simulated labor earnings would closely approximate those reported for the U.S. economy between 1970 and 2006. The average adjustment factor of 13 percent is also applied to labor earnings for the projected simulation—for years beyond 2006.

Whither Effective Labor Inputs?

Each individual's simulated nominal wage earnings can be decomposed into three parts: an inflation component, a composite productivity component (from the combined effect of multifactor productivity and the size of the physical capital stock), and an "effective labor input" component. In turn, the "effective labor inputs" are the product of labor quantity and labor quality, both of which depend upon each worker's demographic and economic attributes.

The multifactor productivity component used for calibrating the wage simulation for transition years through 2006 is provided by the Jorgenson et al. (2007) study of U.S. output growth decomposition. Annual inflation rates are set using the CPI-W. An exponential regression of the product of multifactor productivity and inflation indices against a polynomial of the time (year) variable yields an annual growth rate estimate of 3.86 percent per year.[5] The estimated average inflation rate from BLS's historical CPI-W

series between 1982 and 2005 equals 2.99 percent. That implies a real productivity growth impact of 0.85 percent per year.[6] This means that if "effective labor inputs" and the stock of capital were to remain constant, total
output would grow at the rate of 0.85 percent per year.

Simulated future "effective labor inputs," however, would be determined by the momentum of demographic and economic characteristics
built into the U.S. population as described in chapter 4. Moreover, growth
in total wages would be determined by the evolution of the capital stock.
Consider, first, the future evolution of the "effective labor input" per
worker: for each future year, applying the PSID longitudinal regression
coefficients to each person's simulated demographic and economic attributes and aggregating across all workers (those working full- or part-time)
and dividing by the number of workers yields a future time path of simulated aggregate "effective labor input" per worker. What does the time
series look like?

Before answering this question, it would be useful to examine how demographic and economic attributes influence "core labor inputs." Appendix 5.3 describes the details about how longitudinal "core labor inputs"
vary with workers' underlying demographic and economic attributes. To
summarize those results, future overall "effective labor input" per worker
would be smaller if more people work part-time or withdraw from the
work force rather than work full-time if more of them belong to "non-
families," if a larger fraction of the population is non-white, if people have
more children in the future relative to the mean number of children per
family today, and so on, because each of these features is associated with
a lower life-cycle trajectory of a worker's "core labor input." On the other
hand, future "effective labor input" per worker would increase if workers'
have more education, if more workers were married (were in "families"
rather than "non-family" individuals), more worked full-time, and so on.
How "effective labor inputs" (per worker and in the aggregate) change
over time depends on the relative strengths of these demographic and economic attributes as they jointly evolve in future years.

Note that earlier chapters revealed that the family as a social institution
is undergoing a gradual dissolution in America—with increasing prevalence of single-parent families and "non-families" from low marriage rates
and high divorce rates. Moreover, the population's diversity is increasing
as the share of non-whites increases through the years. That implies that
the population's features would generally shift closer to those associated
with lower longitudinal "core labor input" trajectories. The one attribute

expected to shift in the opposite direction is the population's average educational achievement. As shown in table 4.1, the proportion of those with less than high school education will decline in the future, and a larger share of the population would have at least a college education.[7] As described in greater detail below, the effect of the former trend—that depresses labor earnings—dominates the earnings-increasing effect of higher average educational attainment.

Such a finding is subject to several strong qualifications, most importantly, that the underlying regression coefficients ("labor input aggregators") that determine each simulated adult's "core labor input" would remain stable over time and that DEMSIM's projected demographic and economic attributes represent, sufficiently accurately, the determinants of labor quantity and quality in future years.

There is little evidence that despite significant changes in labor force participation rates among specific demographic groups, relative productivity, and compensation levels across worker types —by race, gender, labor force status, and so on, have changed significantly during past decades. That suggests that labor input aggregators estimated via the regression described earlier are likely to remain stable in the future. The salient exception is the sizable growth of wage premiums for more educated persons during the past three decades.

There have been a number of studies pointing to stagnation in the skill level of the U.S. work force (Kirkegaard 2007).[8] Recent evidence suggests that the education wage differential has varied considerably in the past and remains on a rising trend (Goldin and Katz 2007).[9] A persistent increase in the educational wage differential since 1980 through today indicates a persistent shortfall in the supply of educated workers relative to demand. However, another study by Dupuy and Marey (2008) documents that the skill premium appears to be stabilizing. The latter study suggests that an assumption of a constant skill premium may not be unreasonable going forward, especially in light of the result of chapter 4, which shows a falling share of less-than-high-school attainment and an increasing share of those with a college degree or more years of education (see table 4.1).

The assumption that the population's future demographic and economic features will remain close to those implied by continuing their built-in momentum over time also implies that there would be no dramatic *behavioral* changes in labor force participation rates across groups with different demographic characteristics. Such changes have occurred in the past, for sure. For example, women's labor force participation rates relative to men's increased considerably during the 1960s, 1970s, and 1980s. Those increases resulted from labor saving innovations in household production activities—innovations that spurred the provision of previously home-produced goods and services via formal markets and enabled women to devote more time to market work. But female participation rates have stabilized since the 1990s, and there appears little likelihood that they would increase by even more or decline back to pre-1960 rates in future years.[10]

Another potential future change is a significant postponement of retirement by the baby boomers. Recent evidence suggests increasing average ages of retirement among those in their sixties—which should increase the quantity of workers for some time. However, if younger entering cohorts' skill levels do not grow sufficiently rapidly in the future, postponement of retirement ages by the boomers won't increase the population's average skill level; it will only delay by a few years the day when total "effective labor inputs" begin to decline.

Obviously, little can be done to "prove" that the post-2005 evolution of DEMSIM's population in terms of its demographic and economic features closely captures the likely future evolution of the U.S. population's features. The only reassuring element in this regard is the close approximation of DEMSIM's historical simulation against U.S. microdata surveys—the "success" of the validation exercises reported earlier. The quality of the match between the two suggests that the transition rules built into DEMSIM are sufficiently accurate and that the momentum of interacting transition rules are likely to provide a good approximation of future trends in the U.S. population's demographic features and economic characteristics that would determine future "effective labor inputs." Finally, even if the projections under DEMSIM's assumptions as discussed so far contain (hopefully minor) errors, taking account of the potential impact of interacting demographic and economic forces on "effective labor inputs" appears to be better than ignoring them when making future financial projections of programs such as Social Security.

Now to answer the question posed earlier: an index of "effective labor input" per worker is constructed by dividing each future year's value by its value for 2006 (see equation [11] in appendix 5.1).

Figure 5.3 shows simulated index values of the aggregate (economy-wide) "effective labor input" generated by DEMSIM. It shows that the total "effective labor input" is projected to decline through time. The average annual rate of decline over the next 75 years (through 2080) equals

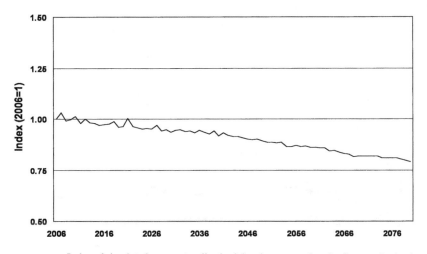

FIGURE 5.3. Index of simulated aggregate effective labor inputs: 2006–2080. Source: Author's calculations based on DEMSIM.

0.31 percent. Thus, whereas the extrapolation of historical real multifactor productivity growth contributes 0.85 percentage points to real annual growth of future labor earnings, DEMSIM's projected decline in effective labor inputs subtracts a large chunk from that growth.

Thankfully, that's not the end of the story because future wage growth would also be affected by the evolution of the economy's real capital stock. Estimating the future capital stock by extrapolating past rates of capital accumulation won't suffice, however. Total capital accumulation depends on net saving out of family incomes—the sum total of net assets accumulated by private individuals.[11]

One alternative is to assume that future capital per worker would remain constant. However, there is considerable evidence that private individuals' net asset holdings vary systematically with age because people accumulate assets during their working lifetimes to attain peak net worth around retirement age. Wealth holdings are subsequently drawn down to finance retirement consumption and bequests to the next generation.[12] DEMSIM adopts a special method to estimate the aggregate real capital stock during the projected simulation—one designed to account for the effects of the population's age structure and productivity growth on the total capital stock.[13]

On the one hand, as the baby boomers approach retirement, their collective saving before retiring and subsequent dissaving after retirement

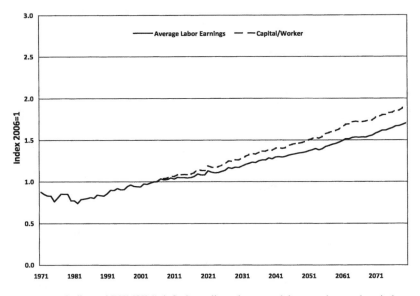

FIGURE 5.4. Indices of DEMSIM's inflation-adjusted average labor earnings and capital per worker. Source: Author's calculations.

could generate a boom-and-bust cycle in the amount of capital per worker during the next several decades. Thus, although retired boomers will no longer contribute to economic output via their labor efforts, they would nevertheless contribute by providing a sizable amount of capital to boost the amount of capital per worker. On the other hand, a major determinant of capital accumulation is annual output growth, which is likely to slow as the boomers leave the labor force and that will likely impart a drag on capital accumulation.

Indeed, during the next decade or two, DEMSIM suggests that the impact of slower output growth on capital accumulation will be quite significant: As the boomers (having already accumulated their savings) depart from the work force they will begin drawing down their assets. In addition, their gradual departure from the workforce will reduce "effective labor input" growth and stall earnings and output growth to slow capital accumulation by those still in the workforce.[14] The latter effect appears strong enough to stall growth in the amount of capital per worker during the next two decades. This is evident from figure 5.4, which shows indexes of simulated labor earnings per worker and capital per worker during 2006–80 averaged over three DEMSIM runs. It indicates a relatively flat trajectory for average labor earnings and the capital stock through the early 2020s. DEMSIM suggests that the capital-to-worker ratio won't resume a strong upward trend until after the baby boomers are retired.

DEMSIM projects the capital stock to grow at 1.19 percent per year on average through the next 75 years: Under positive population growth, saving by the young slightly exceeds capital draw down's by retirees, leading to slow secular growth in the economy's aggregate capital stock. Note that although the capital stock grows during the next few decades, its impact on output and wage growth will be relatively small under the assumed responsiveness of output to an additional dollar of capital (the output elasticity of capital) of 0.42 cents. Hence, capital growth of 1.19 percent per year would enhance output by just $1.19 \times 0.42 = \$0.50$ cents per year (see appendix 5.1, equation [10]). Thus, total wages would grow by ($1.0085 \times 1.0050) / 1.0031 = 1.0104$, or 1.04 percent per year. Wages *per worker*, however, would grow slower because DEMSIM projects labor force growth to average 0.32 percent per year through 2080. That is, labor productivity and labor earnings growth per worker would average $1.0104 / 1.0032 = 0.71$ percent per year.[15]

As figure 5.5 shows, notwithstanding the negative average annual growth of "effective labor inputs," inflation-adjusted total labor earnings exhibit secular growth because of multifactor productivity growth (0.85 percent) and growth in the output-share-adjusted capital stock (0.50 percent).[16] However, the decline in "effective labor inputs"—essentially, a decline in overall labor quality—imposes a considerable drag on real wage growth.

The long-term growth rate of inflation-adjusted wages per worker of 0.71 percent per year estimated under DEMSIM is considerably smaller than the annual "real wage differential" of 1.1 percentage points assumed by the Social Security Administration for making that program's financial projections. Most of the difference is accounted for by DEMSIM's simulation of a secular decline in the "effective labor input." This decline in labor quality reduces growth-promoting effects of technological change and capital accumulation—a feature that official projections do not explicitly take into account.

Japan's experience with repeated Social Security reforms during the 1990s and 2000s is instructive. Despite enacting several round of reforms to Social Security taxes and benefits, subsequent financial projections revealed higher prospective Social Security deficits because unanticipated developments forced revisions of demographic and economic projections (Kabe 2007). A similar experience may be repeated in the United States if

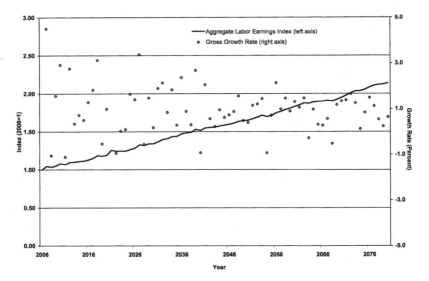

FIGURE 5.5. Simulated aggregate labor earnings index and its annual growth. Source: Author's calculations.

Social Security reforms are based on financial projections that ignore key determinants of long-term payroll growth.

Assigning Pre-1970 Labor Earnings

Because DEMSIM begins in 1970 and only adults aged 18 and older are assigned earnings in each year thereafter, full lifetime earnings are simulated only for those born in 1952 and later—that is, for those aged 18 and younger in 1970. Only a part and possibly none of earnings histories are simulated for those among the 1970 population cross-section who are born before 1952—those older than age 18 in 1970. It is important, however, to obtain pre-1970 earnings for those born before 1952 in order to estimate aggregate benefits beginning in 2006.

A special method for imputing pre-1970 earnings is developed using a sample of actual earnings histories provided by the Social Security Administration—the Benefit and Earnings Public-Use File (2004 version). This file contains a 1 percent representative sample of beneficiary records drawn from the OASDI program as of December 2004. That is, it has approximately 470,000 records with information on Social Security participants' years of births and annual earnings over their careers. According to the file's documentation, "because information on the internal . . . file is used to administer the OASDI program, these data are validated and kept current. As a result, the quality of the data in this public-use file is extremely high."

For those born before 1952, earnings histories are made up of two parts: post-1970 ("late career") earnings simulated via DEMSIM, and pre-1970 ("early career") earnings, imputed from the Social Security Administration's Benefits and Earnings Public-Use file (hereafter referred to as "public-use file"). Data from the public-use file are used to obtain the "early career" earnings segment for DEMSIM individuals born before 1952.

For those aged 62 and older in 1970, an entire life trajectory of earnings from the Social Security Administration's public-use file is used. For each worker, the earnings history is drawn at random from among the public-use file's sample of individuals born in the same year. Where simulated earnings are available for part of a simulated individual's career (for those born between 1908 and 1952), "early career" earnings are selected by first randomly drawing an earnings record from among the public-use file of those born in the same year. Next, to avoid splicing a high- (low-)earner's early career earnings record from the public-use file with that of a low-(high-)earner's late career earnings trajectory in DEMSIM's simulated population, a level-shift factor is estimated using corresponding early and late career segments of mean simulated life-cycle earnings (shown in the charts of figure A5.3). This factor is applied to the early career earnings segment to adjust its level in conformity with the life-cycle trajectory of DEMSIM's late career simulated earnings.[17] This "benchmarking" procedure ensures conformity of early career (pre-1970) earnings levels drawn from the public-use file with simulated earnings levels during late career (post-1970), where the levels are profiled to track the simulated earnings profile for a person with mean characteristics as closely as possible. It also preserves the temporal pattern of earnings volatility that may be associated with business cycle fluctuations in particular years before 1970.

Next Steps

A slower rate of growth of average wages and the economy's payroll base would generate lower trajectories of Social Security payroll taxes and benefits. The next chapter describes the application of a Social Security tax and benefit calculator for making that program's financial projections using DEMSIM's projected simulation. It also shows how those projections can be used to evaluate that program's overall financial condition and its impact on different population subgroups.

Method for Simulating "Effective Labor Inputs"

The assignment of labor earnings to DEMSIM's simulated adults is sufficiently important to warrant a detailed description of its methodology. Labor earnings assignments—in the initial year (1970) and during annual transitions of historical (1971–2006) and projected (post-2006) simulations—are based on the standard Solow growth model framework. The framework envisions that in each year, each simulated labor force participant works in an economy with a certain amount of (economywide) capital. Each worker's annual wage equals the marginal return to work effort that the worker contributes to the economy's production, and that the marginal return is influenced by the labor quality provided by the worker.

Annual nominal output produced by a worker is represented by the Cobb-Douglas production function:

$$Y_{it} = P_t A_t K_t^{\alpha} (q_{it} h_{it})^{1-\alpha}. \tag{1}$$

This function relates the ith worker's nominal output in period t, Y_{it}, to labor and capital inputs in the worker's production process. Two parameters govern the conversion of inputs into output: A_t specifies the productivity of the composite input of capital and labor in year t ("multifactor productivity" attributed to technological change), and α governs how real output responds to an increase in the amount of capital per worker. The parameter, α, which is calibrated to positive but less than one, can also be interpreted as the share of capital in output when capital and labor are compensated according to their marginal contributions to output—as they would be in a competitive economy.[18]

Inputs into the production process include the economy-wide real capital stock in period t, K_t, and the "effective labor input" of the ith worker in year t, $q_{it}h_{it}$—measured as the product of the worker's labor quantity, h_{it}, and "effective labor input," q_{it}. Finally, the price index, P_t, converts real output into its nominal value in year t.

Worker i's annual wage in period t, W_{it}, equals his or her labor supply, h_{it}, times the wage rate, w_{it}. Note that $h_{it} = 1$ for those who work and $h_{it} = 0$ for those who don't. Conditional on $h_{it} = 1$, the choice about whether to work full-time or part-time is considered to be one of the determinants of the worker's "effective labor input," q_{it}. Equating the wage rate with the marginal product of working, dY_{it} / dh_{it}, yields

$$W_{it} = h_{it} w_{it} = h_{it} \frac{dY_{it}}{dh_{it}} = (1 - \alpha) P_t A_t K_t^{\alpha} (q_{it} h_{it})^{1-\alpha}.$$

Taking logarithms when $h_{it} = 1$ yields the equation

$$\ln W_{it} = \ln(1 - \alpha) + \ln P_t + \ln A_t + \alpha \ln K_t + (1-\alpha)\ln q_{it}. \qquad (2)$$

Labor quality is modeled as:

$$q_{it} = e^{\sum_{j=1}^{m} \theta_j X_{jit}}, \qquad (3)$$

where the explanatory variables in matrix X_{it} include m demographic and economic determinants of labor quality of worker i in year t—such as a birth year (a birth cohort fixed effect), race, gender, age, marital status, number of dependent children, disability status, education, type of family unit, whether head of family, and the difference between head's and spouse's ages. DEMSIM simulates all of the variables corresponding to those used in constructing the matrix X_{it}. X_{it} also includes square and cubic orders of these variables and accounts for interactions between the worker's demographic and economic attributes.

Taking logarithms of both sides of equation (3) yields

$$\ln q_{it} = \sum_{j=1}^{m} \theta_j X_{jit}. \qquad (4)$$

Equation (4) relates the logarithm of worker quality to m worker attributes. Substituting equation (4) into equation (2) and rearranging yields

$$\ln W_{it} - \ln P_t - \ln A_t - \alpha \ln K_t = \ln(1 - \alpha) + (1 - \alpha) \sum_{j=1}^{m} \theta_j X_{jit}. \quad (5)$$

This relationship motivates a regression model for estimating workers' "effective labor inputs" (or labor quality) as the impact of k observed worker attributes on adjusted wages—that is,[19]

$$\ln Z_{it} = f(X_{it};\theta) + u_{it} = \ln(1 - \alpha) + (1 - \alpha) \sum_{j=1}^{k} \theta_j X_{jit} + u_{it}. \qquad k < m \quad (6)$$

An estimate of each worker's "core labor input" is obtained by first implementing the regression of equation (6) and applying the estimated coefficients to the worker's *simulated* demographic and economic attributes.[20] Thus, the worker's "core labor input" equals

$$\tilde{Z}_{it}^{C} = e^{f(\tilde{X}_{it};\hat{\theta})}. \quad (7)$$

In equation (7), the qualifier ~ represents simulated values and the qualifier ^ indicates estimated values of equation (6)'s regression parameters. The term $\tilde{Z}_{it}^{C}$ represents the ith worker's simulated "core labor input" in year t.

Note, however, that "core labor input" values do not account for the full cross-cohort variability of "effective labor inputs" because the regression parameters do not account for the influence of $m - k$ unobserved worker attributes—those summarized in the distribution of estimated errors from implementing the regression of equation (6). To capture that variability fully, each worker's simulated "core labor input" is perturbed by a random error term drawn from the estimated distribution of regression errors. Thus, the simulated "effective labor input," $\tilde{Z}_{it}^{E}$ is calculated as

$$\tilde{Z}_{it}^{E} = e^{f(\tilde{X}_{it};\hat{\theta}) + \hat{e}_{it}}, \quad (8)$$

where $\hat{e}_{it}$ is a random draw from the distribution of estimated regression errors $\hat{u}_{it}$. $\tilde{Z}_{it}^{E}$ accounts for all sources of labor input variation not captured in each worker's observed demographic and economic attributes.[21]

Finally, a worker's simulated annual labor earnings are obtained by applying equation (5):

$$\tilde{W}_{it} = P_t \times A_t \times K_t^{\alpha} \times \tilde{Z}_{it}^{E}. \tag{9}$$

Equation (9) shows that each worker's simulated nominal labor earnings in year t can be decomposed into three parts: The price level, P_t, the aggregate productivity level in period t, which depends upon multifactor technological change and the quantity of capital, $A_t K_t^{\alpha}$, and the ith worker's simulated "effective labor input" in year t, $\tilde{Z}_{it}^{E}$. Finally, economy-wide wages and salaries equal

$$\sum_i \tilde{W}_{it} = P_t A_t K_t^{\alpha} \sum_i \tilde{Z}_{it}^{E}, \tag{10}$$

and average earnings per worker in year t equal $(1 / N_t) \sum_i \tilde{W}_{it}$, where N_t is the number of workers in full- and part-time jobs.

The calculation of equation (9) is implemented using the U.S. Bureau of Economic Analysis indices for the price level, P_t, for years between 1970 and 2006 (the CPI-W). The indices for A_t and K_t are taken from the time series of multifactor productivity and aggregate capital constructed by Jorgenson et al. (2007).[22] That study suggests that capital's output share, α, has remained steady at 0.42 since 1959. Hence, the value of α is set to 0.42 for all (past and future) periods of the simulation.

Figure A5.1 shows growth rates of the real composite index, $A_t K_t^{\alpha}$ and the inflation component, P_t, separately for the period 1970–2006. It shows that inflation was not truly brought under control—to consistently be in the low single digits—until the early 1990s. It also shows that the nominal composite productivity factor has averaged about 4 percent per year since the early 1990s, of which inflation accounted for roughly 3 percentage points.

Finally, figure 5.3 in the main text, which shows the index of "effective labor inputs" per worker, is calculated as

$$Q_t = \frac{\sum_i \tilde{Z}_{it}^{E}/N_t}{\sum_i \tilde{Z}_{i,2006}^{E}/N_{2006}} = \frac{\left(\sum_i e^{f(\tilde{X}_{it};\theta) + \hat{e}_{it}}\right)/N_t}{\left(\sum_i e^{f(\tilde{X}_{i,2006};\theta) + \hat{e}_{i,2006}}\right)/N_{2006}}, \quad t \geq 2006, \tag{11}$$

where N_t stands for the number of workers (those working full- and part-time) in year t.

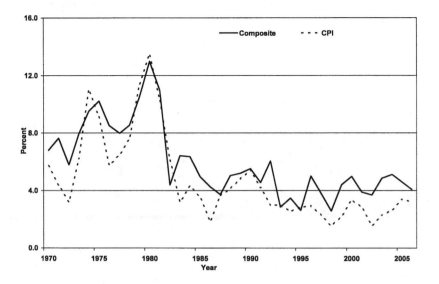

FIGURE A5.1. Annual changes in the CPI and in the nominal composite labor productivity index. Source: Author's calculations.

Simulating Workers' "Effective Labor Inputs" in 1970

A worker's "effective labor input" is defined as the product of labor quantity and labor quality. Thus, even though a person may work for the same number of hours each year, that person's overall demographic and economic characteristics such as age, gender, education, labor force status, number of children, marital status, race, and so on, are associated with his or her productivity as a worker. This appendix describes how each worker's "effective labor input" is simulated by DEMSIM.

Data from the PSID for survey years 1968–72 are used to simulate "effective labor input" levels for family heads and spouses in DEMSIM's initial year (1970). The logarithm of individual wages is regressed on a set of demographic variables.

Regressor variables include a cubic in age, sex, race, education, number of children, whether individual is in a "family" or "non-family" (see description at the beginning of chapter 2), whether head of family, employment status, and difference in ages between head and spouse in a two-headed family. Interaction terms between these variables and birth cohort fixed effects are also included.

The charts in figure A5.2 show cross-section labor input profiles by age derived by applying the regression coefficients to *simulated* demographic characteristics. In these figures, "mean" cross-section "effective labor input" profiles show their values at mean (PSID) values of all demographic characteristics other than age and birth cohort fixed effects. The jagged appearance of the profiles results from the application of each birth co-

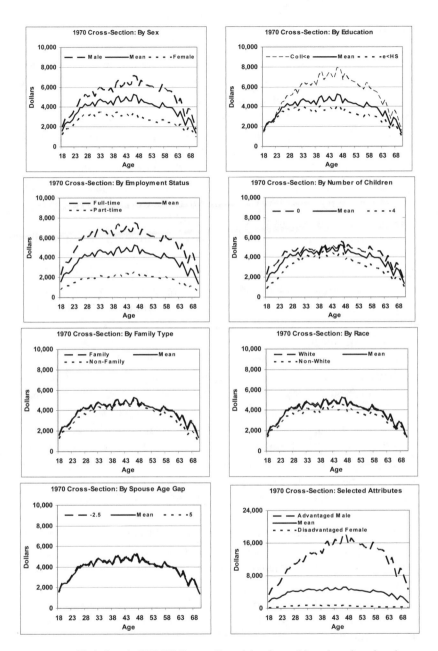

FIGURE A5.2. Variations in DEMSIM's 1970 "core labor inputs" by selected worker demographic characteristics. Source: Author's calculation.

hort's fixed effect when calculating the 1970 cross-section "effective labor input" levels shown in figure A5.2.

Each chart in figure A5.2 shows the amount by which the "core labor input" level would deviate from its corresponding mean level in response to variations in selected demographic characteristics. For example, the first chart in figure A5.2 shows that for 25-year-olds, being male (rather than of "mean gender") would, on average, result in a higher 1970 simulated labor input and being female would reduce it.

As another example, consider varying the person's employment status. The corresponding chart in figure A5.2 shows that full-time workers have a higher labor input level compared to those working part-time. Nonworking individuals are assigned zero wages.

As another example, consider the chart in figure A5.2 that shows how initial labor input levels vary in response to differences in the number of children in the family. Those with fewer children are assigned higher labor input levels at all ages, on average. This regression-driven pattern of initial labor input assignments suggests that those with more children have a higher opportunity cost of time and may work fewer hours, or may spend less time acquiring human capital.

The charts in figure A5.2 show that the patterns of association between demographic variables and variations in "core labor inputs" for 1970 conform to generally accepted (or defensible) notions about how earning abilities differed across individuals during the late 1960s and early 1970s. The last chart in figure A5.2 shows that 1970 simulated labor qualities are much larger for "advantaged individuals" at different ages (a full-time working white male head-of-married-family with one child and with more than a college education) compared to "disadvantaged individuals" at corresponding ages (a part-time working high school dropout non-white female with five children).

The actual labor qualities used in assigning earnings to each individual would differ from the "core labor input" levels shown in figure A5.2 by an error term (see the discussion in the text). The perturbation term is derived by employing a bootstrap on the regression's sampling distribution of residuals. These perturbations generate a more realistic distribution of simulated labor qualities and earnings across the 1970 population of simulated adults.

Figure 5.1 in the main text shows the resulting distribution of simulated log wages for the initial population and the log-wage distribution of predicted values from the underlying PSID data used to implement the regression described in this appendix.

Regression for Simulating Life-Cycle "Core Labor Input" Trajectories

Lifetime labor input trajectories are modeled beginning in 1970 or the year of attaining age 18, whichever occurs later. A first order autocorrelation regression in log annual wages using PSID survey years after 1970 is used to simulate labor quality over each adult's life cycle. Individual life-cycle "core labor input" trajectories conditional on individual demographic and economic characteristics are shown in figure A5.3. The "mean" longitudinal profile by age shows the average labor input trajectory over the life cycle for a worker with mean demographic and economic characteristics (except for age) and 1970 mean labor input at age 18 as described in appendix 5.2. Much like figure A5.2, each chart in figure A5.3 shows the amount by which simulated life-cycle labor input trajectories would deviate from the mean trajectory in response to a change in a particular demographic or economic characteristic.

For example, figure A5.3 shows that the labor input trajectory during his or her life cycle is much lower for an individual with less than a high school education than for one with a college diploma. The shifts in labor quality trajectories in response to shifts in underlying demographic and economic attributes shown in figure A5.3 conform to normally expected outcomes of how life-cycle earnings abilities differ across individuals with different characteristics. For example, the last chart in figure A5.3 shows that an "advantaged individual" (a full-time working white male head-of-family with one child and with more than a college education) has a much higher labor input path compared to that of a "disadvantaged individual"

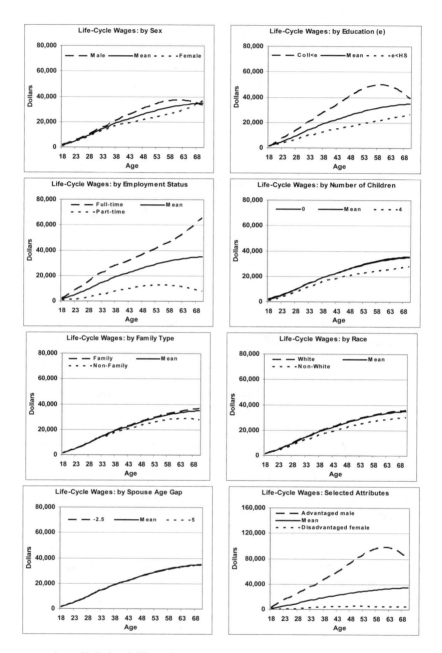

FIGURE A5.3. Variations in life-cycle "core labor input" trajectories by selected worker demographic characteristics. Source: Author's calculations.

(a part-time working high school dropout non-white female spouse with five children).

Of course, the characteristics of each individual would not remain fixed over the life cycle. The particular course of demographic and economic transitions simulated for each individual would determine the progression of labor input and, therefore, wage earnings over his or her working life, including years with zero earnings corresponding to years of non-participation or "unemployment." Thus, the actual trajectories of labor input and wages assigned to an individual over his or her life cycle would not be as smooth as those shown in each chart of figure A5.3. Moreover, figure A5.3 shows only the "core labor input" values based on the regression described in herein. Those values are perturbed (as in the simulation of 1970 wages described in the main text) by an error term that is bootstrapped from the distribution of regression errors. However, the usefulness of figures A5.3 lies in indicating how much higher or lower core labor input levels are for individuals with different demographic and economic attributes—that is, before perturbation term is applied to derive the simulated labor input levels in each year of their life cycles.

CHAPTER SIX

Simulating Social Security's Finances

First Steps

S ocial Security's arithmetic creates deep disagreements in part because people use different metrics for evaluating its financial condition. Most often, those metrics are focused on particular aspects of the program—such as the value of securities in its trust fund or its current cash flows—which do not fully reflect the program's financial condition. This book adopts particular measures aimed at comprehensively evaluating the program's financial condition at the aggregate level and providing information about how it affects different population subgroups—the micro level. Indeed, the recent report released by Social Security's Technical Panel recommends placing "higher priority on comprehensive estimation techniques and . . . allow[ing] more thorough analysis of outcomes on particular populations."[1] This chapter discusses the rationale underlying aggregative measures used to evaluate Social Security's financial condition. The next chapter will discuss the rationale for micro- or individual level measures that are used in this book.

The Social Security program includes three subprograms: a retirement or "old age" portion, a "survivors' " portion, and the "disability" portion. The term "Social Security" is generally understood to include all three programs and is called the "Old Age, Survivors, and Disability Insurance" (OASDI) program. However, the disability portion has a separate Disability

Insurance (DI) trust fund and a specific portion of Social Security's payroll taxes is dedicated to it. Most Social Security reform proposals do not include changes to the DI portion of Social Security. Accordingly, only reform elements relevant to the Old Age and Survivor Insurance (OASI) portion are evaluated in this book, and the term "Social Security" will henceforth be used interchangeably with the acronym OASI.

Evaluating Social Security's reform options requires combining the simulated demographic and earnings attributes with a Social Security tax and benefit calculator. Many Social Security calculators are available online, the most prominent being that provided by the Social Security Administration called ANYPIA. Unfortunately, it proved impossible to merge ANYPIA's computer code with that of DEMSIM. However, an alternative and also quite detailed calculator is available and could be dovetailed with DEMSIM. This calculator is called the Social Security Tax and Benefit Calculator (SSTBC).

Social Security benefits are triggered and influenced by several life events—retirement, child and spousal dependency, divorce, widowhood, and so on. SSTBC is a unique program that calculates each type of benefit depending on the demographic and economic status of the person in question, including changes in family relationships that could trigger benefits at various life stages. Appendix 6.1 provides a description of SSTBC's calculations of Social Security benefits.

SSTBC is used to calculate Social Security payroll taxes and various types of Social Security benefits—for retirees, dependent spouses and children, surviving spouses and children, divorcees, parents with children in care, and so on. The following sections provide an overview of these calculations and describe their implications for Social Security's aggregate future finances.

Social Security (OASI) Tax Calculations

OASI tax and benefit calculations begin in the year 2006. Calculating Social Security taxes is relatively straightforward: it involves applying the payroll tax rate—10.6 percent under current Social Security rules—to individuals' earnings subject to Social Security's ceiling on taxable payrolls.[2] For the years 2006–8, payroll taxes are calculated by applying the taxable earnings ceilings as already specified in the law. The ceiling levels for those years, available at the Social Security Administration's Web site, are

$94,200, $97,500, and $102,000, respectively. Current laws schedule future growth in Social Security's taxable earnings ceiling at the rate of growth of the national average wage.

DEMSIM calculates the national average wage for each future year by averaging labor earnings across all simulated workers in a given year and dividing by the number of labor force participants. Since labor earnings are simulated for each of DEMSIM's labor force participants in each year after 1970, this series is called the "simulated national average wage." Annual growth rates derived from the simulated national average wage are used to determine annual growth in the taxable earnings ceiling. Indeed, the simulated national average wage is used to construct simulated average wage indexes for calculating the average indexed monthly earnings (AIME) and other key elements of Social Security's benefit formula as described in appendix 6.1.

Aggregating payroll taxes across all individuals in a given year yields total Social Security payroll tax revenues. An adjustment factor is applied to account for the fact that not all taxpaying individuals in the population may be covered under Social Security.[3]

Social Security (OASI) Benefit Calculations

After implementing DEMSIM and recovering earnings histories for the simulated population, simulating Social Security's benefit projections is simply a matter of applying the SSTBC to those earnings histories, recovering Social Security benefit histories, and aggregating taxes and benefits across all individuals in each year.

Before applying SSTBC to DEMSIM's earnings histories to calculate each person's benefit trajectory, however, SSTBC is tested to ensure its proper operation. The test involves comparing its calculations of two variables—the Primary Insurance Amount (upon which all auxiliary benefits are based) and the final retirement benefit—against the calculations of the Social Security Administration's ANYPIA calculator, which is available on the Social Security Administration's Web site. Both calculations are tested under various assumptions: artificial cases are constructed of individuals born in different years, having different nominal earnings histories, retiring at different ages, and collecting benefits at yet different ages (including before and after retiring from the labor force). In all of the cases and for both variables, the results from the two calculators match very closely.[4] That means, using SSTBC for calculating taxes and benefits for DEMSIM's simulated population should yield sufficiently accurate payroll tax and benefit allocations to DEMSIM's simulated individuals. Moreover, given that DEMSIM is calibrated using representative microdata survey samples of the U.S. population, aggregating across all taxes and benefits in a given year should yield reasonably accurate projections of OASI's future financial status under current laws and DEMSIM's demographic and economic calibrations.

Applying the SSTBC for calculating a person's Social Security benefits requires first collecting each simulated person's entire history of earnings since 1951 and aggregate pre-1951 earnings, if any. Next, it requires identifying the earnings history of the person's spouse. That is easy to do if the person under consideration is married in the year of benefit collection. If the person is not married in that year, the earnings history of the latest divorced spouse is used, if such a spouse is present, is fully insured, and is age-eligible to receive Social Security benefits.[5] If no spouse is present, only retirement and—if any children are present and eligible—child dependent benefits are calculated based on the person's own earnings history. If a spouse or divorced spouse is present, the calculation is extended to include spousal dependent and survivor benefits for the person under consideration—and child dependent benefits are updated if the spouse's record would provide larger benefits subject to the limit on total family benefits as stipulated in the benefit formula. Calculations of the spouse's benefits are implemented symmetrically. All child benefits calculated in this process are stored separately and assigned to the child when the child's future retirement benefits are calculated.

Baseline Simulation of Aggregate OASI Receipts and Expenditures

The Social Security Administration projects OASI finances under three alternative assumptions labeled "low-cost," "intermediate-cost," and "high-cost." As described in chapter 1, Social Security's revenues are projected to fall short of benefits under intermediate assumptions. The low-cost projections involve higher fertility, mortality, immigration, productivity, and real wage growth rates, compared to intermediate assumptions. Each of these alternatives improves the program's finances. For instance, higher fertility, productivity, and wage growth rates imply more workers and higher wages in the near term relative to the number of retirees and, therefore, higher payroll tax revenues relative to benefit outlays. Higher mortality rates imply a smaller number of future beneficiaries and therefore smaller benefit costs. Because all of the assumptions are applied together, the low-cost scenario would deliver a substantial improvement in Social Security's finances compared to intermediate assumptions—as shown below. High-cost assumptions, on the other hand, worsen Social Security's financial projections—that is, they increase its projected revenue shortfalls.

Projections under intermediate assumptions represent Social Security Administration officials' best guess about the future course of Social Security's finances under current program rules. Under the low-cost (high-cost) alternative, all key assumptions are changed simultaneously for deriving an improvement (worsening) of financial projections. The alternatives represent best official guesses about how much better (worse) Social Security's finances could turn out to be.[6]

To distinguish between DEMSIM and Social Security Trustees' projections, the labels used for the corresponding scenarios under DEMSIM are "optimistic," "baseline," and "pessimistic." Under baseline assumptions, immigration, fertility, mortality, productivity, wage growth, labor force participation rates, and education acquisition rates are those described in earlier chapters. As described in chapter 5, real productivity growth factors (including the influences of multifactor productivity growth and capital stock growth) and inflation together contribute 4.38 percent per year to growth in total nominal economy-wide wages. Inflation accounts for 2.99 percentage points of this annual nominal growth, implying that, after adjusting for inflation, productivity growth factors contribute 1.35 percentage points per year to growth in total real wages. However, DEMSIM's simulations indicate that the aggregate "effective labor input" is projected to decline by 0.31 percent per year, on average, through the year 2080 and the worker population is projected to grow at 0.32 percent per year. That implies average annual growth of real labor earnings per worker of just 0.71 percent per year.

These parameters—the results from combining demographic and economic variables for projecting effective labor inputs—provide the baseline scenario for computing total annual labor earnings and aggregate Social Security taxes and benefits. The lower net earnings growth arising from declining "effective labor inputs" will likely result in substantially smaller aggregate payrolls, OASI taxes, and future OASI benefits compared to official estimates of these items. This result obtains despite the close match between DEMSIM's and the Social Security Administration's worker-to-beneficiary ratios under baseline assumptions—as shown in figure 4.2.

DEMSIM's Baseline Results

Figure 6.1 compares DEMSIM's baseline estimates of OASI revenues to those of the Social Security Administration's intermediate assumptions. In both cases, nominal values are converted to constant 2006 dollars using a projected inflation rate of 2.99 percent per year.

Figure 6.1 shows aggregate OASI revenues and expenditures to be quite close to those of the Social Security Administration in the year 2006—the first year of DEMSIM projections.[7] However, DEMSIM's financial projections deviate from official ones thereafter. Recall from chapter 4 (figure 4.2) that DEMSIM's baseline projection of the worker-to-beneficiary ratio tracks the Social Security Trustees' projection quite closely. If the worker-to-beneficiary ratio were the only key determinant of Social Security's finances, DEMSIM's total payrolls, payroll taxes, and Social Security benefits would also match the trustees' projections closely. However, the projected

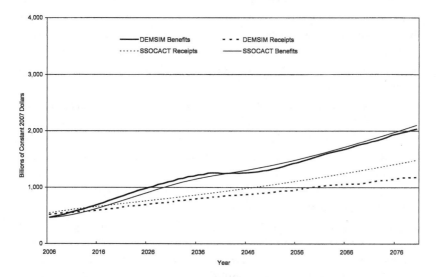

FIGURE 6.1. Projected Social Security (OASI) receipts and benefits for 2006–2080: 2006 Social Security Trustees' intermediate assumptions and DEMSIM baseline. Source: Social Security Administration and author's calculations.

decline in "effective labor inputs" prevents a close match between the two projections of Social Security's revenues and expenditures: DEMSIM's long-term trajectories of payroll taxes and Social Security benefits are lower than the corresponding trustees' trajectories.

By the 75th and final year of the trustees' projections, DEMSIM's revenues are just 80 percent of the trustees' estimate. As would be expected, lower future earnings arising from lower "effective labor inputs" lead to smaller projected OASI benefit expenditures. Figure 6.1 shows that DEMSIM's 2006 benefit outlays are also quite close to the trustees' estimates. However, they exceed the trustees' estimates slightly during the next three decades (through 2042) and are smaller thereafter. By the end of the 75-year time horizon, DEMSIM's benefits are 97 percent as large as the trustees' estimate in the year 2080. DEMSIM's detailed accounting of U.S. demographics and future demographic changes suggests a much larger early bulge in benefits relative to payroll taxes during the next three decades.

Comparing the two projections during the first 75 years after 2005, DEMSIM's total benefits fall short of the trustees' total benefits by a smaller percentage compared to DEMSIM's revenues relative to the trustees' revenues. Given the progressivity of Social Security benefits, whereby low lifetime earners receive more generous benefits relative to their payroll taxes, this result suggests that labor earnings distributions shift over time—toward larger concentrations at low earnings levels. Such a shift is consistent with the prospective retirement of the baby boom generation that currently occupies the middle of the population age distribution—a life-cycle phase when labor earnings are at a life-cycle peak. The significance of such a shift in the labor earnings distributions in future years for policy reforms is described in subsequent chapters.

Under DEMSIM, Social Security's receipts and benefit expenditures are smaller and grow less rapidly than under the trustees' projections because of the projected decline in the "effective labor input" per worker under the former. One question that arises is whether there could be offsetting factors that are not being considered. If "effective labor inputs" are projected to decline, productivity and the capital stock might grow faster than implied by the 4.38 percent annual nominal growth of composite productivity factors assumed under DEMSIM's baseline assumptions. But it is difficult to think about how that could happen: little can be inferred about future multifactor productivity growth—that is, in the development, adoption, and diffusion of productive technologies—beyond simply observing the past trend in the average rate of technological growth and extrapolating it forward in time.

As for the capital stock, evidence from the 1980s and 1990s suggests that foreign capital inflows are unlikely to fully offset low and declining domestic saving. In order to fully offset the decline in "effective labor inputs," the capital stock would have to grow by more than 60 percent faster than its projected rate of 1.19 percent per year during the next 75 years.[8] Furthermore, the impact of population growth in offsetting the drag from declining labor inputs and national output has already been accounted for under the method used under DEMSIM for projecting capital accumulation.

The only remaining item is changes in the population's attributes that slow the projected decline in "effective labor inputs." One possibility is for the baby boomers to postpone retirement and for more of them to remain in full-time work. Such changes may come about as a result of a feedback effects of wages and interest rates that are not modeled in DEMSIM. For example, the retirement of the baby boomers is likely to cause a worker shortage at all skill levels that might push wages upward and induce some of the boomers to postpone retirement and continue full-time rather than part-time work, encourage more immigration, induce more women to enter the work force, and so on. However, to the extent that retirements are motivated by non-wage considerations—such as poor health, skill obsolescence, declining salaries, needs for additional home production, and so on, such changes appear unlikely to fully offset the impact of the rather sizable projected decline in "effective labor inputs" per worker under DEMSIM's baseline assumptions.

An important feature of the comparison between DEMSIM's and the trustees' results shown in figure 6.1 is the pronounced bulge in DEMSIM's time profile of aggregate benefits compared to the trustees' time profile. DEMSIM's benefit estimates based on a detailed simulation of the U.S. population's age structure through time yields a larger bulge in benefit outlays during the next three decades compared to the trustees' estimates. No significant bulge is visible in both DEMSIM's and the trustees' time profiles of Social Security's payroll tax revenues.

Comparing DEMSIM's and the trustees' financial projections, as shown in figure 6.1, clearly suggests that the gap between revenues and expenditures is larger under DEMSIM. However, the more pronounced early bulge in DEMSIM benefits relative to revenues makes the gap even larger in present value terms—especially during the first 75 years. In addition, because the present value of payrolls is smaller under DEMSIM, its

TABLE 6.1 **75-year and Infinite Horizon Social Security (OASI) Open and Closed Group Imbalances Under Alternative DEMSIM Assumptions**

	DEMSIM			SSA
	Optimistic	Baseline	Pessimistic	Intermediate[1]
Long-term discount rate assumption (%)[1]	3.6	2.9	2.1	2.9
OASI total future imbalance ($ billions)[2]				
75-year	2,341	8,395	14,966	5,481
Infinite horizon	9,228	15,027	22,235	15,100
Trust fund value ($ billions)[3]	1,663	1,663	1,663	1,663
Present value of trust fund at end-year 2080	290	253	375	298
OASI open group imbalance ($ billions)[2]				
75-year	968	6,985	13,678	4,116
Infinite horizon	7,565	13,364	20,572	NA
Taxable payrolls ($ billions)[2]				
75-year	232,434	208,495	195,096	244,670
Infinite horizon	378,682	281,064	242,943	366,600
OASI open group imbalance/taxable payrolls (%)				
75-year	0.42	3.35	7.01	1.7
Infinite horizon	2.00	4.75	8.47	3.7
Closed group unfunded obligation ($ billions)[2]	9,540	14,172	20,179	13,300
Closed group taxable payrolls ($ billions)[2]	221,106	135,492	103,494	NA
Closed group / taxable payrolls (%)	4.3	10.5	19.5	NA

[1] Assumptions based on the 2006 Annual Report of the Social Security Trustees. NA = not available.
[2] Present discounted value as of the beginning of 2006 in constant 2006 dollars.
[3] Assumed to equal beginning-of-2006 value reported in the 2006 Social Security Trustees' Annual Report.
Source: Author's calculations.

75-year "actuarial balance ratio" is larger than that estimated by the Social Security Trustees.

The actuarial balance is a key summary measure used by the Social Security Trustees to characterize the program's projected finances. It refers to the present value of revenues over the next 75 years minus the present value of benefits over the same period; plus the value of the existing OASI trust fund; and minus the present value of one year's benefit expenditures in the 75th year. Taking this amount as a ratio to the present value of taxable payrolls over the next 75 years yields the actuarial balance, which tells us how big Social Security's financial surplus is to ensure that the program can pay benefits for 75 years and have a reserve equal to one year's benefit expenditures on hand in the 75th year.

Because the numerator of the actuarial balance is negative (future benefits and the terminal-year reserve provision exceed the trust fund's current value plus the present value of future revenues), the actuarial balance is a negative number. In this book, however, revenues and the trust fund are subtracted from benefits to generate the actuarial *im*balance ratio—a positive number—that shows Social Security's projected shortfall relative to its payment obligation over the next 75 year (or, alternatively, in perpetuity as discussed below).

The bulge in benefits relative to revenues during the early years under DEMSIM's baseline financial projections makes its actuarial imbalance larger than under the trustees' projections. Table 6.1 shows that the DEMSIM's estimate of the actuarial balance is 3.4 percent—twice as large as the trustees' estimate of 1.7 percent.[9]

Results under DEMSIM's Alternative Assumptions

Under the optimistic scenario, the assumed value of annual multifactor productivity growth is increased from 0.85 percent per year to 1.35 percent, and inflation is reduced from 2.99 to 1.99 percent—yielding a joint growth impact of 3.36 percent. Other demographic assumptions are also changed to slow the future decline in "effective labor inputs." Specifically, the rates of immigration, fertility, mortality, education acquisition, and full-time labor force participation are increased slightly.[10] Because these changes interact with each other, it is difficult to calibrate the changes collectively to generate specific overall changes in the annual growth rates of the population and "effective labor inputs." Taken together, the alternative assumptions increase the average 75-year population growth rate to

0.67 percent—instead of 0.32 percent under baseline assumptions. These alternative assumptions eliminate the decline in total "effective labor inputs" from −0.31 under DEMSIM's baseline assumptions to zero percent per year through 2080. This is not surprising because the decline in total "effective labor inputs" during the next few decades is primarily the result of baby boomer retirements. Faster population growth implies that retiring baby boomers will be replaced by larger cohorts of post-boomer generations. However, that change will be gradual—taking full effect only after several decades beyond 2006.

Because capital accumulation is linked to population growth, faster population growth increases the pace of capital accumulation to 2.10 percent per year during the next 75 years—up from 1.19 percent per year under baseline assumptions. As a result of faster capital accumulation and the implied boost to labor productivity and earnings, total payroll growth is also faster. On a per-worker basis, these assumptions generate a 75-year average growth rate of labor earnings per worker of 1.58 percent per year—considerably larger than the baseline growth rate of 0.71 percent per year.

Under the pessimistic scenario, the contributions of inflation and real multifactor productivity growth on nominal wages are assumed to be 3.99 percent and 0.35 percent, respectively—yielding a joint growth impact of 4.35 percent. Correspondingly, immigration, fertility, mortality, education acquisition, and full-time labor force participation rates are each changed by the same percentage as under the optimistic scenario but in the opposite direction. All of these changes induce a decline in the growth of total effective labor inputs—making it even more negative: −0.62 percent instead of −0.31 percent per year under baseline assumptions. Slower population growth, however, also reduces the pace of capital accumulation to zero. The net result of the pessimistic assumptions is to make the growth rate of labor earnings per worker negative—averaging −0.24 percent per year—through the next 75 years.

Figure 6.2 shows several key charts. It shows that worker-to-beneficiary ratios decline over time under all sets of assumptions. Under optimistic assumptions, individuals remain in and transit into full-time labor force status with higher probabilities. This change implies that the worker-to-beneficiary ratio increases considerably immediately after 2006 as many among the still-working baby boomers work more and remain in the work force for longer than under baseline assumptions. The increase in labor force participation lasts for only a few years, however. Because the baby boomers will eventually retire, the worker-to-beneficiary ratio begins to

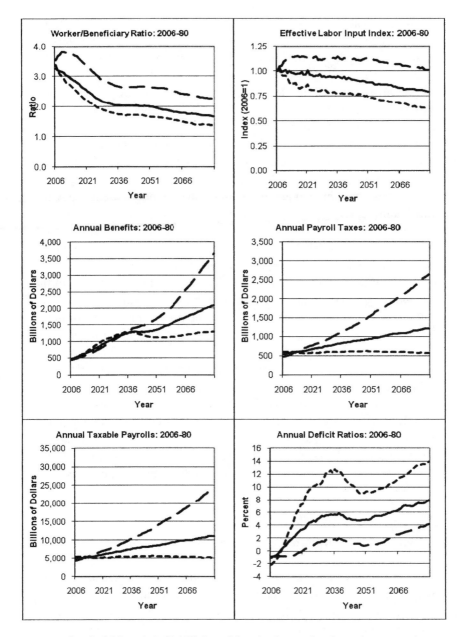

FIGURE 6.2. Social Security's (OASI) financial projections under alternative assumptions. Long dashes = optimistic; short dashes = pessimistic; solid line = baseline. Source: Author's calculations.

decline again in just a few years after 2006. Under pessimistic assumptions, where the likelihood of remaining in and transiting to full-time working status is reduced, the worker-to-beneficiary ratio declines rapidly after 2006 and remains below the baseline level throughout the 75-year projection horizon shown in figure 6.2. The second chart in figure 6.2 show 75-year projections of aggregate "effective labor inputs"—which decline consistently under all three assumption sets.

Figure 6.2 also shows projected taxable payrolls, Social Security taxes and benefits, and the "annual deficit ratio"—the excess of benefits over payroll taxes during a given year as a ratio of taxable payrolls for that year—under the three assumption alternatives. Under baseline assumptions, annual deficit ratios increase rapidly through the mid-2030s—by which year all of the baby boomers are projected to be fully retired. Thereafter, annual deficit ratios decline for a few years as the boomers pass away in increasing numbers. The decline continues through the late 2040s but then reverses and continues to increase through the end of the 75-year projection horizon. The post-2040s increase in annual deficit ratios reflects the continued long-term aging of the population arising from the increase in longevity assumed under all three assumption alternatives. The terminal (year 2080) annual deficit ratio equals 8.0 percent under baseline assumptions—significantly larger than the trustees' official estimate of 4.8 percent under intermediate assumptions.[11]

The differences between DEMSIM's and the trustees' estimates stem mainly from the former's projected decline in "effective labor inputs." Under the optimistic and pessimistic alternatives, DEMSIM's annual deficit ratio estimates are 4.1 percent and 14.8 percent, respectively, in the year 2080. The official ratios under low- and high-cost assumptions equal 0.5 and 11.5, respectively.

Social Security's Infinite Horizon Open Group Imbalance

Many economists have argued for the adoption of a projection horizon longer than 75 years for evaluating Social Security's finances. The case for a longer horizon rests on the so-called moving window problem: under a finite projection horizon, Social Security's measured financial condition worsens with each passing year as deficits in the out-years (beyond the 75th year) are gradually included in the 75-year projection window. A second problem is that projections under a limited time horizon implicitly assume balanced finances beyond the 75th year, thereby making the program's finances appear to be better than they really are. A third criticism of adopting a finite projection horizon is that it introduces a "short-term policy bias": that is, by focusing exclusively on shorter horizon Social Security deficits, policymakers may tend to favor policies that reduce short-term deficits in preference to those that may increase near-term deficits but would reduce them by much more over the long term. Policymakers may choose the former policies even though the latter ones would be financially sounder for the program and, possibly, might be preferred by citizens. A fourth problem with adopting a finite projection horizon is that such measures potentially exhibit perverse responses to changes in underlying assumptions.[12, 13]

There is no limit, in principle, to the number of future years for which DEMSIM's demographic and economic simulation can be implemented, which makes it feasible to construct infinite horizon estimates of Social Security's finances under the three assumption alternatives specified earlier. Infinite horizon estimates of the present values of total and taxable annual payrolls and Social Security revenues and benefits are calculated under those three alternatives to derive open and closed group measures of the program's finances.[14] These results are shown in table 6.1.[15] The table shows that DEMSIM's infinite horizon open group imbalance equals $13.4 trillion. Unfortunately, the trustees do not report this measure of the OASI program, but one would conjecture that DEMSIM's estimate is larger than the trustees' estimate.[16]

Overall, DEMSIM's 75-year imbalance is larger, and its infinite horizon imbalance is also larger than the official imbalance but not in the same proportion. This is the result of slower longevity improvement in the distant future incorporated in DEMSIM's forward simulation. One key element of this transition is a rising share of non-white individuals in the population. Because non-whites have higher mortality rates compared to whites, an increase in their population share lowers the rate of mortality decline in the long term.[17] Those slower mortality declines reduce Social Security's long-term excess of benefits relative to revenues.

Nevertheless, because declining future labor quality reduces future payrolls, DEMSIM's infinite horizon open group imbalance as a ratio of the infinite horizon present value of taxable payrolls is estimated to be 4.8 percent—*larger* than the trustees' 3.7 percent estimate in their 2006 annual report—if a very small imbalance on account of the Disability Insurance program is assumed.

Social Security's Closed Group Imbalance

Table 6.1 also shows Social Security's closed group imbalance. The closed group imbalance conveys how much more past and current generations are slated to receive over and above their past payroll taxes were today's policies continued during their lifetimes. As would be expected, DEMSIM simulates very few individuals in their mid-sixties and older in 2006 to be working and earning. Their net benefits account for the largest portion of the closed group unfunded obligation. Among younger workers, net benefits are negative because very few between the ages of 18 and 60 qualify for Social Security benefits (the exceptions are survivors aged 50 and older with a child in care), but many work part- or full-time and pay OASI payroll taxes. Moreover, only a few children qualify as dependents and survivors. Table 6.1 shows DEMSIM's estimate of OASI's closed group imbalance to be $14.2 trillion under baseline assumptions—larger than the infinite horizon open group imbalance of $13.4 trillion.

The closed group measure has been criticized as inappropriate for a public pension program such as Social Security.[18] The main criticism is that net costs on account of past and current generations do not fully reflect the program's financial condition. For example, the closed group unfunded obligation may be positive, implying excess benefits for past and living generations, but the open group value may be zero, implying offsetting net contributions by future generations. In such a case, focusing on the closed group measure would suggest, incorrectly, that the program is unsustainable. However, that is precisely the purpose of the closed group measure: to point out that despite the seeming overall sustainability of the program's current rules as reflected in a zero open group imbalance, an excessively large closed group imbalance—implying gradual accumulation of a massive financial burden on future generations under existing laws—may not be consistent with the program's financial sustainability. Far from being irrelevant or misleading in the context of a public pension program like Social Security, the closed group imbalance provides complementary and policy-relevant information about how the program's net benefits are distributed across current and future generations.

When calculated under alternative policies, changes in the closed group imbalance reveal the extent to which current generations' net benefits would be changed—important information for understanding whether policy changes would financially harm or benefit current citizens and, indirectly, whether they may stimulate or reduce current consumer expenditure and labor supply. And the closed group imbalance measure would prove useful for individuals—to form expectations about their own future resources. Thus, from an economic policy perspective, reporting *both* open and closed group imbalances under current policies and under alternative reforms is necessary for a full view of the program's financial condition, for judging the distributional effects of alternative reforms, and assessing their potential effects on the broader economy.

The closed group imbalance is also useful for calibrating Social Security reforms. The entire open group imbalance of $13.4 trillion must be paid for by current and future generations together. Hypothetically current generations would receive $14.2 trillion more than the present value of their payroll taxes if current policies are continued until those generations pass away. Furthermore, were those policies continued thereafter, future generations would be slated to pay $0.8 trillion ($13.4 trillion minus $14.2 trillion) more in payroll taxes than the present value of their Social Security benefits. The two net payments add up to the open group imbalance of $13.4 trillion.

Since current policies must be changed to prevent Social Security from running out of funds, the closed and open group imbalances show the implications of alternative ways of coming up with the required amount from living and future generations. Suppose policymakers agreed that future generations, as a whole, should "pay their way but no more." In that case, current generations would have to surrender resources equal to the present value to their entire closed group imbalance of $14.2 trillion—in effect paying their way as well and, thus, eliminating the open group imbalance of $13.4 trillion. In doing so, they would reduce to zero the financial burden on future generations that, under current policies, amounts to $0.8 trillion.

Alternatively, policymakers may view an even split in the total adjustment cost between current and future generations as the appropriate policy. That would require current generations to surrender $6.7 trillion (50 percent of $13.4 trillion)—and reduce the closed group imbalance from $14.2 trillion to $7.5 trillion. In turn, the total financial cost on future generations would become $7.5 trillion ($0.8 trillion under existing Social Security rules and an additional $6.7 trillion toward paying off the remaining open group imbalance).

Appreciating such trade-offs and conducting an informed debate about reform alternatives would become feasible only when both open and closed group imbalance measures are reported regularly and used for scoring reform alternatives. Their advantage lies in imposing strict financial discipline in broadly tracking the costs and benefits imposed on living versus future generations. The Social Security Trustees already report these two measures regularly in their annual reports. The logical next step is for the Social Security actuaries to use them to evaluate Social Security reform options.

The reform proposals analyzed in later chapters of this book will be evaluated in terms of their impact on OASI's baseline open and closed group imbalances as reported above under DEMSIM. However, DEMSIM's detailed simulation approach also makes it possible to examine the impact of reforms more precisely across various population subgroups—distinguished by race, gender, birth cohorts, earnings levels, and so on. Whereas the open and closed group measures provide information on Social Security's aggregate financial condition and broad generational trade-offs, delving deeper requires the development of micromeasures of the impact of reform options on specific population groups. Such individual-level measures are described in the next chapter.

Chapter Summary

Utilizing DEMSIM together with SSTBC enables the construction of (simulated) individual Social Security payroll taxes and benefits. The key feature of this approach is the projection and incorporation of "effective labor inputs" as implied by the momentum of demographic and economic forces that are built into the U.S. population and economy. The evolution of "effective labor inputs" is determined by the balance of forces between those that worsen it, such as low labor force participation, family fragmentation, and the age and racial composition of the population, and others which improve it, such as an increasingly educated population. The approach also allows for a full set of interactions between demographic and economic forces that affect overall mortality, fertility, labor force participation, and family formation rates, which also potentially exert significant effects on Social Security's future finances.

DEMSIM projects a significant decline in future "effective labor inputs" per worker, which has important implications for Social Security's future financial condition. Measured over the next 75 years, Social Security's financial shortfalls are about the same as the trustees' estimates in present value terms, but as ratios to the present value of payrolls, they are twice as large as the trustees' actuarial balance estimates. DEMSIM's infinite horizon open group measure also shows a large shortfall relative to future taxable payrolls—4.8 percent. Similar to the trustees' assumptions, DEMSIM's closed group measure shows that past and living generations account for more than Social Security's open group liability, implying that under current policies, future generations as a whole would pay $0.8 trillion more in payroll taxes than they would receive by way of OASI benefits in present value as of 2006.

The Social Security Tax and Benefit Calculator

The Social Security (OASI) tax formula is quite simple: Wages in covered occupations (including self-employment in those occupations) are subject to employer and employee payroll taxes at a common rate.[19] Historical payroll tax rates are used in SSTBC as applicable for various years between 1970 and 2005. The rate applicable for the projected simulation is 5.3 percent on covered wages. Covered wages equal gross employee wages and salaries except for certain worker benefits—such as employer premium payments for employee health insurance coverage—that are exempted from payroll taxes. Almost all private and public sector occupations are included except for a limited number of occupations that are not covered by Social Security.[20]

Social Security's benefit eligibility rules and formulas are quite complicated, with numerous elements applicable to beneficiaries with different demographic and economic histories and under different current circumstances. And the applicable rules change as beneficiaries' circumstances change over time. The Social Security Handbook contains definitions, descriptions, and examples of eligibility and benefit computation rules.[21] This appendix describes the features of the benefit formula that are incorporated into SSTBC.

Insured Status under Social Security

Individuals must be *fully insured* to become eligible to receive any type of Social Security benefit—retirement, dependent, for survivors, and so on. This status is determined using the person's past labor earnings. Becoming fully insured requires sufficient earnings from a job (including self-employment) covered under Social Security. Fully insured status is conferred once a person has acquired 40 *credits* prior to retirement. Total earnings between 1937 and 1977 are aggregated and divided by $400, and the result (rounded down to an integer number) equals pre-1978 credits. These are added to credits earned after 1977 to determine insured status. During 1978 and later, workers earn one credit for each quarter of the year they work in Social Security–covered employment and earn above a specified minimum amount. The year of *first eligibility* for retirement benefits is the year in which the individual becomes age 62. The individual is *entitled* to retirement benefits after an application for benefits is submitted, but never before age 62.

The Primary Insurance Amount (PIA)

The PIA is the basis for all benefit payments made on a worker's earnings record. There are several steps in computing the PIA. *Base years* are computed as the years after 1950 up to the first month of entitlement to retirement benefits begins. For survivor benefits, base years include the year of the worker's death. *Elapsed years* are computed as those years after 1950 (or after attainment of age 21, whichever occurs later) up to (but not including) the year of first eligibility. The maximum number of elapsed years for an earnings record is 40 (it could be shorter, for purposes of calculating survivor benefits if the person dies prior to age 62). *Computation years* are calculated as the number of elapsed years less five or two, whichever is greater. Earnings in base years (up to the maximum taxable limit in each year, and through age 60 or two years prior to death, whichever occurs earlier) are wage-indexed according to economy-wide average wages. Of these, the highest earnings in years equaling the number of computation years are added together, and the sum is divided by the number of months in computation years to yield the AIME. The AIME is converted into a PIA using a formula that involves *bend points*. The bend point formula adds together 90 percent of the first X dollars of AIME, 32 percent of the next Y dollars of AIME, and 15 percent of the AIME in excess of Y dollars. The dollar amounts X and Y are also wage indexed and are different for different eligibility years. The dollar amounts pertaining to the year of attaining age 60 (or, for survivor benefits, the second year before death, whichever is earlier) are applied in computing the PIA.

Retirement Benefits

A person who begins to collect benefits at his or her "normal retirement age" receives the PIA as the monthly retirement benefit. In subsequent years, the monthly benefit is adjusted based on the Consumer Price Index for urban wage earners and clerical workers (CPI-W) to maintain its purchasing power. Beginning in 2003, the applicable normal retirement age is being increased by two months for every year that a person's 65th birthday occurs later than the year 2003. For example, those becoming 65 years old in 2004 have a normal retirement age of 65 years and two months; those achieving age 65 in 2005 have a normal retirement age of 65 years and four months, and so on. This progressive increase in the normal retirement age for those born later is scheduled to pause between the years 2008 through 2020; those attaining age 65 in these years have a normal retirement age of 66. The increase in the normal retirement age—at the rate of two month per year of later attainment of age 65—resumes after 2020: those attaining age 65 in 2025 or later have a normal retirement age of 67.

Actuarial Reduction for Early Retirement

The normal retirement age determines the amount of retirement and other benefits payable on a worker's earnings record. A person who begins to collect retirement benefits earlier than the applicable normal retirement age receives a reduced benefit. The benefit reduction factor equals 5/9 of 1 percent for each month of entitlement prior to the normal retirement age. The reduced benefit rate (except for the inflation adjustment) continues throughout the person's remaining lifetime. If the number of months of reduction exceeds 36 months (for example, in case of entitlement at age 62 when the normal retirement age is 67), then the reduction factor equals 5/12 of 1 percent for every additional month of early entitlement beyond 36 months.

Delayed Retirement Credits

Those who choose to wait before applying for (and thereby becoming entitled to) Social Security benefits until after their normal retirement age (but not later than age 70) are awarded larger benefits. The benefit increment per month of delayed entitlement depends on the year in which a person attains normal retirement age. For example, those attaining age 65 in 1997 receive an additional 5 percent in monthly benefits for each year of delay in entitlement. However, those attaining age 65 in the year 2008 will receive an additional 8 percent in benefits for each year of delayed entitlement.

The Earnings Test

If a person continues to work and earn after the month of entitlement, benefits are reduced relative to the PIA. Beneficiaries under the normal retirement age, lose $1 for each $2 earned above an earnings limit. However, if the year of extra earnings falls in the same year as when the worker attains normal retirement age, the reduction applies only during months prior to the attainment of normal retirement age. During these months, the earnings threshold is higher and the rate of benefit reduction is smaller ($1 in reduced benefits for each $3 of earnings above the new threshold). Both earning thresholds are scheduled to grow with average wages in future years. All benefits payable on a worker's earnings record, including the worker's own retirement benefits and spousal and child dependent benefits are proportionally subject to reduction under the earnings test.

Benefit Recomputations

Earnings in any year after entitlement to benefits has been established are included in a recomputation of the PIA and benefit levels for the subsequent year. However, post–age 60 earnings are not indexed before inclusion in the AIME calculation. If such earnings are higher than a prior year's earnings (indexed earnings through age 60 or unindexed earnings after age 60) , they result in an increase in the PIA and payable benefits. If they are smaller than those taken into account in the previous year's computation of the PIA, they are not included in the AIME calculation and would not reduce the worker's PIA or benefits (the highest earnings in base years that are included in the calculations are no different this year compared to last year).

Spousal and Child Dependent Benefits

Wives and husbands of insured workers (including divorced spouses) are entitled to dependent benefits if the couple was married for at least 10 years at the time of application for spousal benefits, the spouse is older than age 62 or has in care a child under age 16 entitled to benefits under the insured worker's record, and the insured worker is collecting retirement benefits. Children of insured workers under age 16 are entitled to dependent children's benefits if the child is unmarried and the worker is collecting retirement benefits.

Spousal and child benefits equal 50 percent of the insured worker's PIA (each). Child dependent benefits may be lower only if the *family maximum* applies. Spousal benefits may be smaller due to the family maximum, a reduction for the spouse's age, the application of the earnings test, or the spouse's receipt of retirement benefits based or her or his own earnings record.

All benefits paid under a worker's record (except retirement benefits or divorced spousal benefits) are reduced proportionately to bring them within the family maximum benefit level. The maximum benefit payable on a worker's earnings record is determined by applying a bend point formula to the PIA similar to that applied to the AIME in calculating the PIA itself. For example, the family maximum equals 150 percent of the first $X of PIA plus 272 percent of the next $Y of the PIA plus 134 percent of the next $Z of the PIA plus 175 percent of the PIA greater than $X + $Y + $Z. The values X, Y, and Z are scheduled to grow at the rate of economy-wide average wages. In case the spousal benefit is eliminated for any reason, the remaining benefits payable on the insured worker's record are subjected to the family maximum test again, treating the spouse as though he/she were not eligible for spousal benefits. This could result in higher benefits for children who may be eligible for dependent benefits under the worker's record.

Adjustments to Spousal Benefits

A person may elect to receive (may become entitled to) spousal dependent benefits before attaining normal retirement age. In this case the spousal benefit is reduced by 25/36 of 1 percent for each month of entitlement prior to normal retirement age. If the number of months of reduction exceeds 36 months (for example, in case of entitlement at age 62 when the normal retirement age is 67), then the reduction factor is 5/12 of 1 percent for every additional month of early entitlement. If a spouse is earning above the amount allowed by the earnings test, the spousal benefits he or she is eligible to receive will be earnings tested according to the pre- and post-normal retirement schedule described above. If a spouse is already collecting retirement benefits, the spousal benefit is redefined as the greater of the excess of the spousal benefit over the spouse's own retirement benefit or zero.

Survivor Benefits: Widow(er), Father/Mother, and Children

The surviving spouse of a deceased worker is eligible for widow(er) benefits if the widow(er) is at least age 60, is entitled (has applied for widow[er] benefits), the worker died fully insured, and the widow(er) was married to the deceased worker for at least nine months. The widow(er) of a deceased worker is eligible for father/mother benefits if the widow(er) is entitled to benefits (has applied), the worker died fully insured, the widower has in care a child of the worker. A surviving child is eligible for child survivor benefits on the deceased worker's record if the child is under age 18 and is entitled (an application has been filed) and the worker was fully insured.

Survivor Benefits

Monthly benefits equal 100 percent of the worker's PIA for a widow(er); they equal 75 percent of the PIA for father/mother and child survivor benefits. Widow(er) and child survivor benefits may be lower only if the family maximum applies. Widow(er)s may become entitled to (elect to receive) survivor benefits earlier than normal retirement age, but not earlier than age 60. In this case the reduction is 19/40 of 1 percent for each month of entitlement prior to normal retirement age. After the widow(er) is 62 or older, he or she is may become entitled to (elect to receive) retirement benefits based on own past covered earnings. In this case widow(er) benefits are redefined as the excess over own retirement benefits or zero, whichever is larger. Finally, widow(er) and own retirement benefits are also subject to the earnings test. If the deceased worker was already collecting a reduced retirement insurance benefit, the widow(er)'s benefit cannot be larger than the reduced widow(er) benefit or the larger of 82.5 percent of the worker's PIA and the worker's own retirement benefit. If the deceased worker is already collecting a retirement insurance benefit larger than the PIA because of delayed retirement, the widow(er) is granted the full dollar amount of the delayed retirement credit over and above the (reduced) widow(er) benefit. Father/mother benefits are not similarly augmented by delayed retirement credits that the deceased worker may have been receiving.

Father/Mother Benefits

These benefits may be reduced if the family maximum applies or if the father or mother is entitled to their own retirement benefit. In this case the father/mother benefit is redefined as the excess over the father's or mother's own retirement benefit or zero, whichever is greater. Father/mother benefits are also subject to the earnings test. On the other hand, they are not reduced for age. For those eligible to receive both widow(er) and father/mother benefits, the program calculates both and takes the larger benefit.

Calculation of a Deceased Worker's PIA

The calculation of survivor benefits in the case of a widow(er) benefits uses the larger of two alternative calculation's of the deceased worker's PIA. These are the "wage indexing" method and the "re-indexing" method. Moreover, the year up to which the worker's wages are indexed may be different depending upon whether the deceased worker would have become age 62 before or after the widow(er) attains age 60.

The Wage-Indexing Method

The last year for indexing earnings is the earlier of a) the year the worker dies minus 2 years or b) the year worker would have attained age 60. Bend point formula dollar amounts are taken from the earlier of the year the worker dies or the year the worker would have attained age 62. The PIA thus calculated is inflated by the CPI up to the year the widow(er) turns age 60 (if later) to obtain the PIA value on which widower benefits would be based. Where applicable, these benefits are then adjusted for the family maximum, reduction for age, delayed retirement credits, and the earnings test.

The Re-indexing Method

The worker's original earnings are indexed up to the earlier of the year the widow(er) attains age 58 or b) the year the worker attains age 60. The elapsed years are computed as the number of years from 1951 (or the worker's age 22 if later) through the year the widow(er) attains age 60. The computation years equal elapsed years minus five years (computation years cannot be less than two). Bend point formula dollar values are applied from the year the widow(er) attains age 60. There is no subsequent indexing of the PIA for inflation.

The Sequencing of Widow(er) Benefit Calculations

Widow(er) benefit reductions proceed in a particular sequence: First, the widow(er) plus children's benefits are subjected to the family maximum. Second, the widow(er) benefit is reduced for early entitlement (of the widow[er] prior to normal retirement age). Third, the widow(er) benefit is compared to the widow(er) own retirement benefit if entitled to the latter. Fourth, the widow(er) benefit is redefined as the excess over own benefit if own benefit is positive. Finally, the earning's test is applied, first to the widow(er)'s own benefit and then to the widow(er) benefit that is in excess of own benefit. If the widow(er) benefit is eliminated as a result of these tests, the benefits payable on the insured worker's record are subjected to the family maximum test again, treating the widow(er) as though he/she were not eligible for the widow(er) benefit. This procedure can potentially increase children's benefits if the family maximum limit was binding the first time through.

CHAPTER SEVEN

Micromeasures of Social Security's Financial Condition

Focus on Retirement Saving Rather than Insurance

A key objective that motivated the creation of Social Security during the mid-1930s was to insure workers against loss of income from old age. Although additional benefits were introduced in subsequent years, the program's main focus continues to be on providing a basic level of protection against loss of earnings because of old age. Given this objective, the standard yardstick used by analysts to assess how individuals fare under the program has been the "replacement rate." For any participant, this rate is simply the ratio of Social Security's monthly retirement benefit to monthly earnings during their working lifetime (pre-retirement earnings). The replacement rate communicates the extent to which Social Security benefits replace earnings lost as workers retire upon becoming old. As such, the replacement rate is a measure of the insurance protection against income loss from old age that Social Security provides. However, demographic developments during many decades since Social Security was established in 1935 have made the replacement rate measure less useful today.

When the program was started, the age of qualifying for old-age benefits was set at 65.[1] During the 1920s and 1930s, however, survival through and beyond age 65 was considerably less likely compared to today. The average life span given that a person reached age 20 did not extend much beyond age 65.[2] Under those conditions, it was reasonable to interpret Social Security's retirement benefits as insurance against the loss of labor earnings from old age. Some analysts describe the program's operation in this regard as a *social response* to prevent destitution and poverty among those who happen to survive to old age but lose their ability to earn and support themselves and their families because of old age.

The continual extension of the human life span that has occurred since after Social Security was established means that most of today's young adults may expect to live in good health through their late seventies and beyond. Surviving to Social Security's early and normal retirement ages and qualifying for its retirement and other benefits is no longer the "accident" that it used to be during the 1930s and earlier. Rather, it is the normal and expected outcome for most workers today. Moreover, the expansion of service sector employment during the last several decades means that many workers could remain gainfully employed well beyond their mid-60s if they choose to: most jobs are not as physically taxing today as was the case when Social Security was introduced. Under such longevity and health expectations and employment possibilities, it is no longer appropriate to consider Social Security benefits under current program rules—which include eligibility to full retirement benefits soon after achieving age 65—as a social response to the fluke of survival with insufficient means through one's mid-sixties and beyond. An alternative interpretation supported by some analysts is that the encouragement to retire provided via Social Security serves to expand employment opportunities for younger workers. However, a recent multicountry study by Gruber et al. (2009) shows the opposite to be true: more retirements among older workers fostered by generous public pension benefits tend to hurt employment among the young.

Most workers today probably believe that Social Security's eligibility and benefit rules would remain relatively stable during their lifetimes. It would be rational for them to consider those rules among economic and other constraints that they must weigh for deciding about when to retire and begin to collect Social Security benefits. The "retirement phenomenon" of the late 20th century—the view that after a career through age 65, even younger of late, one should retire to a life of leisure supported by personal savings and public and private pensions—is very likely a consequence of early retirement incentives built into private and public pension systems. Retirement soon after age 62 (Social Security's earliest retirement eligibility age) is the most often preferred choice—one promoted by

Social Security's (and Medicare's) age-eligibility thresholds and earnings tests.[3]

The decision to "retire and lose one's income" is now an induced, *private response* of workers—one that is elicited by Social Security's relatively inflexible early and normal retirement age and other eligibility rules that most workers take as given.[4] And worker expectations of Social Security (and Medicare) benefits after retirement very likely influence how much they personally save for retirement during their working careers. Thus the tables are now turned on how Social Security policies and private behavior are juxtaposed under today's demographic and economic realities: What was earlier considered to be a social response of insurance provision to demographic constraints in an uncertain economic environment has been transformed into a system wherein ossified Social Security program rules induce a private response of low saving and early departure from the workforce.[5]

Continued improvement in human longevity during the latter half of the 20th century means that the program's operation under decades-old rules has drifted far from its original objective as a social insurance program to protect the elderly from income loss. The replacement rate is not as good or as appropriate an indicator of Social Security's impact when survival in good health through Social Security's normal retirement age and beyond is a relatively sure bet for most people. Under current demographic realities, Social Security's taxes and benefits are less similar to "insurance" protection and more similar to (or substitutes for) personal saving for retirement. In the absence of a government commitment to provide retirement benefits via Social Security, most people would work longer and save more out of their post-tax incomes under today's expectations of longevity and health.[6]

It now appears more appropriate to treat and evaluate Social Security as a public retirement savings program rather than as a purely social insurance program. An evaluation in terms of taxes and benefits during participants' entire lifetimes is more relevant now when survival well beyond the normal retirement age is highly likely and expected. In addition, because policymakers are concerned about the extent to which the program supports retirees, supplementary measures that indicate how much the program contributes toward retirement wealth among different segments of the population would be useful.

Yet another feature of the retirement-survival calculus that supports using saving and wealth accumulation measures in favor of income replacement rates is that the latter measure is blind to systematic differences in retirement ages, ages of collecting Social Security benefits, mortality rates, family structures across individuals and groups, their lengths of working lifetimes and unemployment spells, and so on. For example, although Social Security's replacement rates are more generous for low-earners—that is, low-wage workers receive larger annual retirement benefits per dollar of yearly pre-retirement wages than high-wage workers—it does not necessarily imply a proportionally better overall fiscal (tax and benefit) treatment under Social Security for low-wage workers' during their lifetimes: less educated workers, low-earners, and members of minority groups generally experience higher mortality rates on average and, therefore, expect to enjoy fewer years of retirement and Social Security benefit collection, on average. Measuring such differences requires actuarial measures of fiscal treatment under Social Security and Social Security wealth measures to properly reflect the program's effect on different types of participants.

Because lifetime measures of fiscal treatment under Social Security's are more relevant under today's economic and demographic circumstances, such measures should receive greater emphasis compared to traditional measures for judging the program's finances and for understanding how different population groups would fare under the program's current rules and alternative reforms. Although several micromeasures could be constructed to satisfy this objective, only a couple are used in this book—the Social Security lifetime net tax rate and the Social Security retirement wealth as a ratio of lifetime earnings—for reasons discussed later in this chapter.

Lifetime net tax rates and Social Security wealth ratios averaged over members of various DEMSIM population subgroups, including current and future birth cohorts distinguished by race, gender, and other demographic characteristics are used to examine the implications of continuing Social Security's current tax and benefit rules for those groups. Furthermore, the implications of alternative Social Security reforms can be analyzed using such micro-level measures and the aggregative measures of the program's finances that are described in chapter 6.

Measures of Individuals' Treatment under Social Security

DEMSIM's detailed simulation of the U.S. population's future economic and demographic evolution and the Social Security Tax and Benefit

Calculator's (SSTBC's) detailed Social Security tax and benefit calculations means that the treatment of specific population subgroups under the program's current tax and benefit laws can be tracked. It is quite straightforward to calculate how each simulated individual's lifetime benefits—including those received as a dependent or surviving child or spouse, retiree, divorcee, parent with child in care, and so on—stack up against payroll taxes paid while working.

There are various ways of making such a comparison. For example, one could calculate the "internal rate of return" that benefits provide over the "investment" of payroll taxes by each participant. This requires calculating an interest rate that would make the actuarial present value of benefits—say as of the person's 18th birthday—equal to the actuarial present value of payroll taxes.[7] The solution provides the rate of return that the worker implicitly receives on past payroll taxes by way of Social Security benefits.

A less well known method is to calculate the "wealth tax rate" that Social Security imposes on each participant. The wealth tax rate equals the fraction of the actuarially accumulated value of Social Security payroll taxes at retirement (accumulated at a private market rate of return) that is lost through participation in the program. The loss occurs because the actuarial present value at retirement of post-retirement benefits (discounted at the same rate) is generally much smaller. Like the internal rate of return, the wealth tax rate metric involves a comparison of just Social Security payroll taxes and benefits.

Metrics that involve just the present values of payroll taxes and benefits are insufficient because of the way Social Security is designed: to serve the twin functions of "social adequacy" and "equity." That means a proper metric must also reflect how progressive or regressive the Social Security's taxes and benefits are relative to workers' lifetime labor earnings.[8]

Thus, the selected metric should compare lifetime payroll taxes and benefits with each other within the context of lifetime earnings. The measure that achieves both tasks is the lifetime net tax rate.

In the term "lifetime net tax rate," "lifetime" indicates present discounted values of all three financial flows spanning the person's entire working and retirement life span, evaluated as of a specific time point in that span. In this book, the present values of inflation-adjusted labor earnings, Social Security benefits, and payroll taxes used in the lifetime net tax rate formula are calculated as of each worker's year of attaining age 18. The term "net tax" indicates that lifetime benefits are subtracted from lifetime payroll taxes to measure net taxes paid over the lifetime in present value terms. And "rate" indicates division by lifetime labor earnings.[9] In summary, lifetime net tax rate shows the excess of lifetime taxes over lifetime benefits as a ratio of lifetime labor earnings.

An important consideration in the lifetime net tax rate calculation is the choice of an appropriate discount rate. First, since the transactions — payroll taxes and benefits — occur over many decades during a person's lifetime, the rate used should be consistent with long-term interest rates. Second, one could choose to use a long-term inflation-adjusted (and riskless) government rate interest rate, say 3.0 percent, but that would not be appropriate because Social Security benefits and payroll taxes are subject to future changes — arising from events in people's lives as well as changes in Social Security policies — and are, therefore, risky payment streams. Using a market rate of return on risky investments — such as stocks that have returned about 7 percent in inflation-adjusted terms over the long term — would also be inappropriate because Social Security taxes and benefit payments do not exhibit comparable volatility and have been more predictable than returns on private capital investments. The intermediate variability of payroll taxes and Social Security benefits suggests using an intermediate rate of return for calculating present values. A 5 percent inflation-adjusted annual rate of discount is used — which splits the difference between the government interest rate and private market rates or return on stocks.[10]

Suppose that applying a 5 percent discount rate produces an average lifetime net tax rate of 6.0 percent for a particular population group. What's the meaning of this number? It's simply that out of total Old Age and Survivor Insurance (OASI) payroll and benefits taxes paid each year, 6.0 percent of lifetime earnings is surrendered to the government as a pure tax from participating in Social Security. The rest of payroll taxes above 6.0 percent of labor earnings could be interpreted as "saving" by the government on behalf of that participant — which it returns to the participant by way of Social Security benefits. Those benefits provide a 5 percent inflation-adjusted return per year on the payroll taxes above 6.0 percent of taxable earnings.

It is easy to see that the lifetime net tax rate splits total Social Security taxes into two parts — a pure-tax component and a government-saving portion. The latter earns an intermediate-risk market rate of return by way of benefits under the current system. It seems as though the latter portion could alternatively be invested in private capital markets — in securities with a moderate risk level to provide the same moderate rate of return on average. But doing so under a fully pay-as-you-go system generates an off-setting cost—usually called a "transition cost"—of additional government borrowing, higher taxes, or lower government spending on non–Social Security items in order to continue meeting Social Security's benefit obligations to current retirees. Thus, the lifetime net tax rate metric is useful only for learning about how the pure-tax component of Social Security lifetime payroll taxes varies across different demographic groups. And changes in this component under alternative reforms show how different population groups would fare under them.

If the 5 percent discount rate were replaced with a different one—say a lower rate of 4 percent per year—calculated lifetime net tax rates would be smaller because the present value of benefits that are received much later would increase by more relative to the increase in the present value payroll taxes. Consequently, a larger share of total Social Security taxes would be deemed equivalent to retirement savings, but it would be associated with (or earn) the now lower discount rate by way of future Social Security benefits.

Admittedly, the 5 percent real rate of return used as the discount rate is based on a rough guess about the riskiness of Social Security taxes and benefits. But the exercise here is not to establish an "indisputably correct" breakdown of payroll taxes into its "pure tax" and "saving" components, but to generate a metric for evaluating the impact of Social Security reforms at the micro level—on various population subgroups.

The standard interpretation of the Social Security lifetime net tax rate is that it is the share of lifetime earnings surrendered to the government by participating in the program. It could alternatively be interpreted as an insurance premium: the fraction of lifetime (taxable) labor earnings that Social Security participants surrender to the government to purchase income insurance—(partial) replacement of earnings lost because of old age. However, because under today's conditions, the program appears to be more like a substitute for retirement saving, it appears more appropriate to interpret it as a "load" factor that the government charges each worker to save funds on their behalf for financing consumption during retirement. Because all three items—career earnings and Social Security taxes and benefits—depend on myriad economic and demographic events during people's lives, the load would be expected to vary across various population groups according to systematic and predictable differences in their demographic and economic attributes.

As shown below, key demographic characteristics and behavioral economic propensities—such as survival, the propensity to marry, procreate, acquire education, hold a job, and retire early or late—vary systematically (and potentially predictably) across different population subgroups. Such systematic variations may be expected to continue in the future—carried forward by the momentum of demographic and economic forces built into the population's current structure. Those systematic variations imply systematic differences in lifetime net tax rates under Social Security—differences that can be evaluated using a simulation technique such as DEMSIM's. They imply that mandatory participation in Social Security implies systematically different loads charged ex ante on a lifetime basis for different population subgroups.

The predictable and systematic differences in tax treatment under current Social Security laws should serve as the baseline for evaluating the impact of future reform options. Lifetime net tax rate calculations—under the assumed discount factor of 5 percent per year—shows how different population groups would be treated if current laws were continued through their lifetimes. Even if those laws cannot be continued because the program's scheduled revenues are insufficient to cover scheduled benefits under current laws, the lifetime net tax rates under current laws are useful as guidelines for evaluating the effects of alternative reforms proposed to make the program financially sustainable.

Obviously, payroll tax increases and reductions in scheduled benefits would both cause lifetime net tax rates to increase, but the increases are unlikely to be uniform or proportional across different cohorts. Calculating lifetime net tax rates under current Social Security laws would help in evaluating how changes to current Social Security policies would increase and redistribute the program's loads across different population subgroups.

Measuring the Size and Distribution of Personal Accounts

Four of the reform proposals analyzed in this book introduce individual Social Security accounts. All four proposals include provisions for carve-out individual accounts—created by partially diverting payroll taxes into the accounts as investment contributions. One of the proposals also introduces add-on financed contributions—by mandating additional individual contributions over and above existing payroll taxes.

Introducing carve-out financed individual accounts reduces lifetime net tax rates under the existing ("traditional") Social Security program. As mentioned earlier, however, under the mostly pay-as-you-go U.S. Social Security program, contributions carved out of existing payroll taxes must be made up somehow—either via benefit cuts or via general revenue transfers—implying potential changes to the government's non–Social Security budget. To the extent that the former option is used to offset Social Security's revenue loss from carved-out payroll taxes, lifetime net tax rates calculated for the traditional Social Security system would correctly reflect distributional effects. However, if the carve-out revenue loss is mostly made up from general revenue transfers—a provision also contained in some of the reform proposals evaluated herein—the distributional effects would depend on how those transfers are financed. Whatever the manner of financing them, DEMSIM has no way of evaluating their distributional implications. Luckily, all of the individual account proposals considered in this book include substantial Social Security benefit offsets against benefits derived from personal accounts, so that the loss of distributional information should be relatively small.

Under reform proposals that introduce individual accounts, whether add-on or carve-out, contributions into them when working and future benefits from them in the form of withdrawals and annuities offset each other in present value. All individual account accumulations are considered to be eventually spent by their owners including by way of involuntary bequests upon death. Despite this, it is important to recognize and compare how large individual accounts are and how their size is distributed across different population groups under alternative reform proposals. To show this information, lifetime net tax rate tables are augmented with tables showing lifetime retirement wealth ratios and the share contributed by traditional Social Security benefits—the rest coming from personal accounts.

Social Security's Contribution to Retirement Wealth

Lawmakers and practitioners of Social Security policy are concerned about citizens' financial vulnerability during retirement. Social Security's formal objective—replacing income lost because of old age—is consistent with the program's goal of providing a basic level of retirement support. But because of the constancy of Social Security's benefit eligibility rules and benefit calculations, different population groups are able to extract systematically more or less retirement wealth from Social Security depending on their demographic and economic characteristics. That is, because Social Security benefits depend on demographic and economic events—employment and wages, marriage and divorce, having children, retirement choices, mortality, and so on—the program's contribution to retirement wealth differs for different population groups. Under a view of the program as a substitute for private retirement saving, a simple but useful metric for assessing the impact of current laws and alternative Social Security policies would be the measure of Social Security retirement wealth as a share of lifetime earnings—where both Social Security wealth and lifetime earnings are measured as of each person's first benefit collection year in inflation-adjusted dollars.

The retirement wealth metric requires just two of the three components involved in the lifetime net tax rate calculation—the present value of benefits divided by the present value of earnings, where both present values are calculated using a 5 percent inflation-adjusted discount rate and the calculation is as of the person's benefit collection year. This calculation is analogous to the traditional "replacement rate" measure but takes account of earnings and benefits during a person's entire lifetime.

The interest here is to devise a metric for evaluating how retirement wealth is affected under alternative reforms. Under reform proposals that introduce Social Security individual accounts, this metric is easily adapted by including in the numerator the accumulated value of individual account contributions using a 3.0 percent rate of return to reflect investment in very low-risk financial securities.[11] Values of retirement wealth ratios and their distribution across different population groups are reported later in this chapter. Changes under alternative reforms are reported in subsequent chapters.

Additional Considerations

Obviously, pre- and post-reform lifetime net tax rates and total Social Security wealth are "static" measures. By presenting such calculations, it is not meant to imply that people's future economic and social choices would remain fixed and immutable when Social Security reforms are implemented. Indeed, most people would likely adjust their behavior in response to changes in Social Security taxes and benefit policies. Estimating those "feedback" effects, however, is quite difficult, and the issue of "dynamic scoring" is as yet unsettled among economists and budget analysts. Such "feedback" calculations are, therefore, excluded from this book.[12] The impact of Social Security's current policies and alternative reforms are evaluated under given "baseline" evolution and interaction of demographic and economic characteristics, including unchanged individual economic choices, during future decades as described in earlier chapters.

Later chapters show results from a "static scoring" of alternative Social Security reform proposals. Specifically, the Social Security program's aggregate financial status and lifetime net tax rates of selected population subgroups are first calculated under current Social Security tax and benefit rules. These provide "baseline" estimates. Next, Social Security's tax and benefit rules are changed according to the specifications of a proposed Social Security reform while keeping the projected demographic and economic simulation unchanged. The impact of implementing the reform is evaluated by comparing the new estimates of Social Security's aggregate micrometrics with their values under baseline assumptions.

Results under baseline and alternative assumptions on Social Security's aggregate financial status were described in chapter 6. The remainder of this chapter discusses the characteristics of key selected population subgroups and baseline calculations of lifetime net tax rates and retirement wealth ratios. Before presenting those results, however, the next section describes how Social Security taxes and benefits are allocated among members in DEMSIM's simulated families.

Allocation of Social Security Payroll Taxes and Benefits

In developing the lifetime net tax rate metric, it is necessary to specify how payroll taxes and the many benefits paid under OASI are allocated among family members. Payroll taxes are relatively easy to deal with. For each worker, total employee plus employer payroll taxes are used to measure the present discounted value of lifetime OASI payroll taxes. The standard rationale is followed: if all payroll taxes were paid by the employee— rather than split between employee and employer—the forces of supply and demand in the labor market would establish a different gross wage level inclusive of the employer's share of payroll taxes.

Social Security benefits used in calculating individuals' lifetime net tax rates include only those that the person in question receives directly. Thus, dependent benefits paid to a husband based on the past earnings of his spouse are counted as the husband's benefits to be netted from his payroll taxes. An alternative and more difficult method would be to assign all benefits to the primary worker whose past labor earnings generate them— regardless of whether or not that worker receives the benefits directly. This method would not fully reveal the redistributive implications of Social Security because, for example, survivors' benefits would be assigned to primary workers during years when they are already deceased.

Demographic and Economic Attributes of Selected Population Groups under DEMSIM

Table 7.1 shows a averages for a number of variables that determine a person's lifetime net tax treatment under OASI: the averages are shown for various birth cohorts in 15-year groups ranging from 1946–60 and 2036–50. Each birth cohort is further subdivided according to gender, race, and two lifetime earnings categories demarcated by median lifetime earnings for the entire 15-year birth cohort.

An "analysis sample" is obtained by first calculating lifetime net tax rates for each person and excluding outlier observations: 5 percent of the observations are eliminated from the top and bottom of the lifetime net tax rate distribution for each subgroup distinguished by birth year, gender, race, and lifetime earnings category.

As the first panel of table 7.1 shows, each 15-year birth cohort includes between 10,000 and 15,000 DEMSIM individuals. As expected, the subgroup with the smallest number of observations (110) is non-white women born during 1946–60 with more than median lifetime earnings for that birth cohort—a minority group with few labor market participants and sparse presence in high-wage occupations. Again as expected, the subgroup with the largest number of observations (4,057) is of white males born during 1991–2005 with more than median lifetime earnings—majority-race baby boomer children at the beginning of adulthood. The other panels of table 7.1 explore systematic differences in key demographic and economic dimensions that correlate with how individuals are treated under Social Security—as simulated under DEMSIM's baseline assumptions.

The second panel of table 7.1 shows rising longevity for later-born DEMSIM cohorts. Average ages at death increase from 78.8 years for the baby boomers (the majority of whom are in the oldest birth cohort) to

83.5 years for those born toward the middle of this century.[13] It shows that for both males and females, whites and non-whites, those with higher-than-median lifetime earnings outlive those with below-median lifetime earnings, on average, with the differences being most pronounced for white males. This result of the simulation, although consistent with prior expectations (for example, because the well-off can access better health care services), is rather striking because DEMSIM's calibrations of earnings and longevity are formally independent of each other. Indeed, to the author's knowledge, there are no official, publicly available data that associate longevity with lifetime earnings. However, because the earnings simulation module takes account of many demographic and economic attributes and the mortality module also distinguishes death rates by year of birth, race, gender, and age, the factors that promote both longevity and higher earnings are, apparently, captured consistently in both modules. The feature that high-earners enjoy longer lifetimes is an important motivating element for some reform proposals (such as Diamond and Orszag 2004), and failure to capture it would disqualify DEMSIM as an appropriate tool for evaluating that and similar reform proposals (and, perhaps, any reform proposals in general).

Comparing within earnings and gender categories, white individuals tend to outlive non-whites, in general—as expected given that underlying mortality rates are distinguished by race and incorporate higher mortality rates for non-whites. Finally, as is well known, DEMSIM's females, especially whites, have much longer life spans on average compared to males, although gender differences within most earnings and race categories narrow for later-born cohorts. Again, this feature is consistent with information on relative mortality rates from several independent sources.[14]

The third panel of table 7.1 shows each birth cohort's average age at retirement. Quite understandably, high-earners retire much later compared to low-earners within each gender and race group. Keeping gender and earnings fixed, non-whites retire earlier than whites among women. Among men, however, the opposite is true—both low- and high-earning white men retire earlier than their counterparts among non-white men.

The fourth panel of table 7.1 shows the average number of years spent in retirement for members of each subgroup. The retirement lifetime extends from the year when labor earnings become zero (and are never positive thereafter) to the last year of the person's life span.[15] First, as is clear from table 7.1, high-earning cohorts spend fewer years in retirement despite the fact that they enjoy longer average life spans. This, of course, is not surprising: individuals are grouped according to whether their lifetime earnings are higher or lower than median lifetime earnings across their entire birth cohort—and the chief way of becoming included in the high lifetime earner group, especially for non-whites who are disadvantaged in the labor market (as suggested by the earnings regressions described in chapter 5), is to work for more years. Given non-whites' shorter life spans, it directly implies that high-earners among them spend fewer years in retirement compared to whites.[16]

This feature of table 7.1 is especially important from the perspective of Social Security reforms. Policies that penalize high-earners by, say, increasing payroll taxes or increasing the limit on taxable payrolls, would provide work disincentives to those who would otherwise choose long working careers. Some Social Security reform proposals hope to incentivize participants to extend their working careers (for example, by increasing the penalties for earlier retirement and benefit collection). The close association between high lifetime earnings and long careers suggests that increasing taxes on high lifetime earners as a way of improving Social Security's financial condition would result in the opposite incentives and offset the impact on Social Security's financial condition by inducing earlier retirements and benefit collection.

Second, comparing differences by gender within each earnings and race category shows that non-white women spend many more years in retirement compared to non-white men. This is because non-white women retire earlier and live longer compared to non-white men. White women, however, spend slightly less time in retirement compared to white men— the former offset their longer life spans by working through older ages than white men, on average. From a reform perspective, one interpretation of these features may be that non-white women face higher risks of financial vulnerability during old age. But another interpretation could be that Social Security's generosity toward those with lower average earnings induces earlier labor force exits and longer retirements among non-white women. The nature of DEMSIM's exercise, however, is not suitable for distinguishing between these alternative views.

The fifth panel of table 7.1 shows the number of years for which DEMSIM individuals collect Social Security benefits. Unlike the impact of longer retirement life spans, a longer benefit collection period unambiguously implies a smaller lifetime net tax rate, all else equal. Of course, retirement and benefit collection spans do not fully determine lifetime net tax rates because the latter also depend on the size of labor earnings and

TABLE 7.1 **Selected Characteristics of DEMSIM Adults by Birth Cohort, Gender, Race, and Lifetime Earnings (E)**

Birth Cohort	All	Female				Male			
		Non-White		White		Non-White		White	
		E≤Med	E>Med	E≤Med	E>Med	E≤Med	E>Med	E≤Med	E>Med
Panel 1	Number of Observations								
1946–1960	10,564	718	110	3,277	1300	488	325	798	3,548
1961–1975	11,851	946	170	3,147	1,559	676	464	1,154	3,735
1976–1990	12,132	1,053	261	3,160	1,559	755	514	1,187	3,643
1991–2005	14,043	1,243	327	3,639	1,813	921	636	1,407	4,057
2006–2020	13,746	1,428	342	3,306	1,756	1,037	778	1,287	3,812
2021–2035	14,032	1,470	400	3,171	1,804	1,102	810	1,378	3,897
2036–2050	14,062	1,572	512	3,039	1,707	1,169	938	1,355	3,770
Panel 2	Average Age at Death								
1946–1960	78.8	77.6	80.0	80.5	82.1	70.9	76.7	72.6	78.9
1961–1975	79.6	78.5	81.8	81.5	84.2	71.9	77.7	73.0	79.8
1976–1990	80.1	79.7	81.5	81.5	84.9	73.6	79.8	72.2	80.9
1991–2005	80.9	79.7	83.5	82.2	85.6	73.7	80.1	73.7	81.9
2006–2020	82.1	80.7	86.1	83.2	86.5	75.0	81.8	76.2	83.3
2021–2035	82.8	82.2	85.4	84.6	87.1	76.0	81.8	76.6	83.6
2036–2050	83.5	82.7	85.2	85.8	87.5	76.7	82.5	78.0	84.1
Panel 3	Average Age at Retirement								
1946–1960	61.7	59.2	65.2	62.1	67.0	59.1	68.7	52.7	61.6
1961–1975	61.7	57.5	65.7	62.1	67.2	60.4	70.0	52.9	61.9
1976–1990	61.6	57.3	64.0	61.5	67.3	60.9	70.8	52.7	62.1
1991–2005	61.9	56.7	64.4	61.9	67.8	61.6	71.1	52.5	62.6
2006–2020	62.3	56.6	65.4	62.0	67.7	62.7	72.3	53.3	62.7
2021–2035	62.5	56.9	65.8	62.6	67.9	63.0	72.6	53.3	62.7
2036–2050	63.1	57.6	67.0	63.4	68.5	64.4	72.5	53.9	62.8
Panel 4	Years Spent in Retirement								
1946–1960	18.1	19.4	15.8	19.4	16.1	12.8	9.0	20.9	18.2
1961–1975	18.9	21.9	17.1	20.5	18.0	12.5	8.7	21.1	19.0
1976–1990	19.5	23.3	18.4	21.1	18.6	13.7	10.1	20.5	19.8
1991–2005	19.9	24.1	20.1	21.3	18.8	13.1	10.0	22.2	20.3
2006–2020	20.8	25.1	21.7	22.2	19.8	13.3	10.6	23.9	21.5
2021–2035	21.3	26.3	20.6	23.0	20.2	14.0	10.2	24.4	21.9
2036–2050	21.4	26.1	19.3	23.4	20.0	13.3	11.0	25.2	22.4
Panel 5	Years of Benefit Collection								
1946–1960	15.1	14.1	15.1	16.8	17.1	6.4	10.5	10.7	15.6
1961–1975	15.8	15.0	16.8	17.7	19.2	7.1	11.1	11.2	16.5
1976–1990	16.3	16.2	17.1	17.7	20.0	8.6	12.9	10.2	17.5
1991–2005	16.9	16.3	19.0	18.3	20.5	8.5	13.1	11.9	18.4
2006–2020	18.1	17.3	21.4	19.4	21.5	9.4	14.5	14.2	19.8
2021–2035	18.7	18.8	20.6	20.7	22.0	10.4	14.4	14.7	20.1
2036–2050	19.2	19.0	20.2	21.8	22.3	10.7	15.1	16.0	20.6

TABLE 7.1 (*continued*)

Birth Cohort	All	Female				Male			
		Non-White		White		Non-White		White	
		E≤Med	E>Med	E≤Med	E>Med	E≤Med	E>Med	E≤Med	E>Med
Panel 6	Working-Lifespan								
1946–1960	43.2	37.8	47.1	43.5	49.1	35.6	50.7	33.8	44.2
1961–1975	42.5	35.2	47.0	42.9	49.2	36.8	51.7	32.6	44.0
1976–1990	42.5	35.2	45.7	42.3	49.4	38.0	52.5	32.6	44.4
1991–2005	43.2	35.6	46.1	43.3	49.9	40.0	53.0	33.0	45.0
2006–2020	43.6	36.0	47.3	43.2	49.9	42.1	54.3	33.8	45.2
2021–2035	43.8	36.2	47.7	43.9	50.1	41.4	54.6	34.1	45.2
2036–2050	44.5	37.1	48.9	44.7	50.5	43.5	54.7	34.7	45.2
Panel 7	Years of Non-Participation in the Labor Force								
1946–1960	10.0	13.9	8.2	14.9	10.4	13.7	10.1	7.8	4.6
1961–1975	10.3	13.5	8.3	15.4	11.0	14.2	10.7	7.7	5.0
1976–1990	10.6	13.7	9.0	15.5	11.8	15.0	11.7	7.5	5.2
1991–2005	11.0	13.9	8.7	15.8	12.0	16.1	11.3	7.4	5.5
2006–2020	11.4	14.5	9.8	16.2	11.9	17.6	12.2	7.5	5.3
2021–2035	11.3	14.0	10.3	16.3	12.1	17.9	12.5	7.5	5.2
2036–2050	11.9	14.7	11.3	16.8	12.8	18.9	12.9	7.7	5.4
Panel 8	Lifetime Educational Achievement (Years of Education—0 through 18+)								
1946–1960	15.5	14.1	16.1	15.6	16.5	13.3	15.5	13.9	16.0
1961–1975	15.2	13.9	16.2	15.1	16.2	13.2	15.4	13.7	15.8
1976–1990	15.0	13.5	16.2	14.9	16.2	12.9	15.2	13.4	15.8
1991–2005	15.4	14.6	16.3	15.4	16.3	14.0	15.7	13.9	16.1
2006–2020	15.4	14.6	16.2	15.2	16.3	14.5	15.8	14.2	16.0
2021–2035	15.5	14.7	16.1	15.4	16.3	14.3	15.8	14.2	16.1
2036–2050	15.5	14.9	16.2	15.4	16.2	14.6	15.8	14.3	16.0
Panel 9	Percent "Married"								
1946–1960	47.3	29.9	16.4	51.2	46.4	28.1	27.1	44.6	53.5
1961–1975	43.8	26.0	26.5	48.3	45.9	24.9	24.1	43.8	50.3
1976–1990	40.8	26.7	22.2	44.6	44.1	25.8	24.7	40.4	47.1
1991–2005	41.0	27.6	27.2	44.7	43.5	29.0	27.4	40.9	46.7
2006–2020	41.2	27.3	29.5	45.8	45.9	25.6	28.5	40.2	48.5
2021–2035	41.8	30.2	27.5	47.5	43.5	31.2	28.8	43.5	47.3
2036–2050	41.7	31.0	31.4	48.2	45.2	31.2	28.8	42.8	46.6
Panel 10	Lifetime Earnings (Thousands of constant 2006 dollars)								
1946–1960	515.4	219.4	551.7	282.6	595.3	233.4	628.5	317.1	832.0
1961–1975	506.1	239.8	588.0	292.2	607.0	262.5	657.4	326.5	785.1
1976–1990	588.8	285.0	691.6	348.8	726.5	310.8	762.0	379.3	916.6
1991–2005	676.3	353.0	800.2	412.4	835.3	381.0	887.8	442.6	1,049.1
2006–2020	758.3	413.4	919.2	465.2	954.0	442.3	987.0	507.1	1,161.7
2021–2035	860.0	465.1	1,063.1	539.7	1,073.5	512.0	1,152.1	599.5	1,291.8
2036–2050	981.1	539.9	1,208.0	632.4	1,220.8	590.2	1,310.1	677.8	1,457.7

TABLE 7.1 (*continued*)

| Birth Cohort | All | Female | | | | Male | | | |
| | | Non-White | | White | | Non-White | | White | |
		E≤Med	E>Med	E≤Med	E>Med	E≤Med	E>Med	E≤Med	E>Med
Panel 11	Lifetime Net Tax Rates								
1946–1960	5.08	4.6	5.4	3.9	4.9	6.5	6.6	6.3	5.7
1961–1975	6.10	5.9	6.3	5.1	5.9	7.3	7.1	6.9	6.5
1976–1990	6.11	6.1	6.1	5.2	5.8	7.4	6.7	6.7	6.5
1991–2005	6.14	6.2	6.1	5.3	5.8	7.5	6.6	6.9	6.4
2006–2020	6.06	6.1	6.1	5.3	5.6	7.1	6.6	6.8	6.3
2021–2035	5.93	6.1	5.8	5.2	5.5	7.0	6.3	6.4	6.2
2036–2050	5.78	5.9	5.7	4.8	5.5	6.7	6.2	6.4	6.1

Note: E = present value of lifetime earnings; Med = median value of E.
Source: Author's calculations.

other demographic factors. High lifetime earners, whites, and women (each attribute considered while keeping the other two fixed) collect benefits over longer periods during their lifetimes—mostly because of their greater longevity—compared to members in the opposite group within each attribute. For comparisons across lifetime earnings, the largest differences are for white males (as expected), whereas for comparisons across gender, the largest differences are for non-white low-earners—because those women live longer, stop working earlier and, therefore, collect Social Security benefits for more years than their male counterparts.

The sixth panel of table 7.1 shows the average number of years in a person's working lifetime—that is, the number of years between the first and last years with positive earnings *including* years spent out of the labor force—as a young adult, perhaps acquiring more education, during unemployment spells, and when voluntarily out of the work force. The average number of non-working years within the working life span is shown in the seventh panel of table 7.1.[17] These panels show that DEMSIM individuals—and, by implication, U.S. workers—spend just over 30 years participating in the work force, on average.

Furthermore, the two panels show that low lifetime earners work during many fewer years—the chief reason that they have below-median earnings among their birth cohort. Comparing across race—with the other two attributes fixed—non-white women work fewer years compared to white women in both lifetime earnings groups. Among men, however, low-earning non-whites work fewer years compared to low-earning whites, whereas high-earning non-whites work for more years compared to high-earning whites. Again, this shows that for "disadvantaged" non-white men, achieving higher-than-cohort-median lifetime earnings requires a rather long working career. Finally, comparing across gender while keeping earnings levels and race fixed, shows that women spend fewer years in the work force compared to men. The exception here is white low-earning women who work for more years than white low-earning men—although the differences are small and declining for later-born cohorts.

The eighth panel of table 7.1 shows highest years of education achieved during the lifetime, where the year categories include 0 through 17 and 18 or more. Overall (the "all" column), average educational achievement increases initially, and then stabilizes at about 15.5 years—just a little less than college-degree level.[18] This panel shows higher educational achievement for higher lifetime earners—as expected. Moreover, the lifetime educational achievement of non-whites improves slightly, whereas that of whites remains mostly steady. Because of the much larger fraction of whites in the population, overall education levels remain more or less steady, especially for those born during the 1990s and later.[19] A comparison across race indicates that whites have more education than non-whites—an important reason for the former's higher lifetime earnings as discussed below. A comparison across genders reveals that women achieve more years of education than men—which probably mitigates somewhat the gender gap in lifetime earnings from fewer years of labor force participation by women.

The ninth panel of table 7.1 shows average marriage rates. In constructing this statistic, DEMSIM individuals are classified as "married" if the person's benefit calculation is implemented with reference to the earnings history of a current or former divorced spouse—that is, the person is either married at the time of benefit collection or, if not, was married in the past for at least 10 years to a now-benefit-eligible spouse. This panel shows that early-born baby boomers have slightly higher marriage rates and that overall marriage rates are generally stable for later-born cohorts. Across gender—men versus women for given lifetime earnings and race—marriage rates are roughly similar overall. Across race—given lifetime earnings and gender—whites enjoy Social Security spousal and survivor benefits with much greater frequency than non-whites, by more than 25 percentage points in some earnings and gender groups.

One interesting feature of marriage rates is seen by comparing across high and low lifetime earners. Among non-whites, high lifetime earners generally have lower marriage rates compared to low lifetime earners. High lifetime earners among some white women also have lower marriage rates compared to low-earning white women. For white men, however, high lifetime earners have higher marriage rates compared to low lifetime earners. These results suggest that achieving high lifetime earnings requires sacrificing family life if one is otherwise "disadvantaged" in the labor market—that is, if one is either non-white or female, both of whom have lower career earnings trajectories, on average, compared to white males according to the longitudinal earnings regression described in chapter 5.

The tenth panel of table 7.1 shows average present value at birth of lifetime earnings in constant 2006 dollars. This is the average of the denominator of the lifetime net tax rate metric for each DEMSIM individual. Lifetime earnings averages reflect the impact of all demographic and economic attributes, some of which vary systematically across population groups as described earlier. The panel shows that the lifetime earnings of successive cohorts grow larger: recall from chapter 5 that even after accounting for the secular decline in effective labor input per worker, DEMSIM's real earnings per worker grow at the rate of 0.71 percent per year under baseline assumptions.

An interesting feature of table 7.1 is that lifetime earnings are depressed for members of the 1961–75 birth cohort relative to those born earlier. As is well known, members of this birth cohort entered the work force at a time when productivity and output growth underwent a two-decade slowdown—from the early 1970s through the mid-1990s. That slowdown—which is included in the calibration of DEMSIM's historical earnings simulation—occurs when those born between 1961 and 1975 enter the DEMSIM labor force (during years 1979–93). The other columns of the fifth panel of table 7.1 show, as expected, that non-whites earn less than whites and women earn less than men during their working lifetimes.

The eleventh panel of table 7.1 shows one of the key micrometrics used in this book: the OASI lifetime net tax rate—the difference between lifetime payroll taxes and benefits divided by lifetime earnings. Across all races, genders, and lifetime earners, lifetime net tax rates are relatively small for the baby boomers. They peak at 6.14 percent for the 1991–2005 birth cohort and decline gradually for succeeding ones. The decline occurs chiefly because of the expanding longevity of those born later in time who, therefore, spend more time in retirement and benefit collection as shown in panels 4 and 5 of table 7.1.

As expected, women, within given lifetime earnings and race catego-ries, bear smaller lifetime net tax rates from participating in Social Secu-rity than do men—simply because women outlive men on average and collect more in survivor benefits based on their spouses' earnings. Because their lifetime earnings are generally smaller than men's, women also col-lect dependent benefits more often than men.

Comparing across race keeping gender and earnings categories fixed shows that non-whites face larger lifetime net tax rates compared to whites. This is as expected given non-white individuals' shorter average lifetimes and benefit collection spans.

Finally, comparing across earnings categories keeping race and gen-der fixed shows that high-earning males face *smaller* lifetime net tax rates compared to low-earning males. Moreover, high-earning non-white women among today's working aged and older birth cohorts (those born before 1990) face *larger* Social Security lifetime net tax rates compared to their low-earning counterparts. This is as expected because the Social Security benefit formula is progressive and because low-earning women draw dependent and survivor benefits with greater frequency than high-earning ones. Non-white high-earning women born after 1990, however, enjoy longer retirement and benefit collection life spans because of espe-cially rapid projected longevity improvements.

For men, however, high lifetime earners of both races have *smaller* life-time net tax rates compared to low-earners. Part of the explanation here is high-earners' greater longevity and benefit collection life spans. But part of the reason is on the tax side: high lifetime earnings increase the denomi-nator of the lifetime net tax rate but do not increase payroll taxes in the numerator proportionately because many participants' annual earnings in this group are above the taxable ceiling for a significant number of years during their work span.

These examples suggest that the conventional view of Social Security's progressivity, even when evaluated using the standard lifetime net tax rate measure, does not apply to the highest earners in the population or to those disadvantaged in the labor force—who comprise about one third of the overall population.[20] This observation does not necessarily imply, how-ever, that the right approach to reforming Social Security is to make the system more progressive on the tax side by increasing the taxable earning ceiling at a faster rate. That is because such a policy could subvert workers' incentives to remain in the work force during late career years—the key means of achieving higher lifetime earnings and living standards.

Estimating Social Security's Contribution to Retirement Wealth

The first two panels of table 7.2 show Social Security wealth levels based on scheduled and payable benefits, respectively, under current laws in constant 2006 dollars. Each person's payable Social Security benefits are calculated by applying an across the board reduction to scheduled benefits each year so that total benefits do not exceed the program's total receipts under current laws. Such across the board benefit reductions are applied beginning in the year when the Social Security Trust Fund is exhausted under DEMSIM's baseline assumptions and projections—2027.

The third and fourth panels of the table show the retirement wealth metric as described earlier in this chapter—the contribution of Social Security to retirement resources as a share of lifetime earnings under the two alternative benefit definitions. This measure is calculated as the present value of Social Security benefits evaluated at each person's benefit collection year divided by lifetime earnings accumulated to the same year. The numerator and denominator are both calculated using a 5 percent real annual discount rate. And the ratios are averaged across members of selected population groups as shown in the table.

It should be reiterated that the Social Security retirement wealth metric *does not consider* payroll taxes. Nor does it consider any changes to the non–Social Security federal budget required to offset transition costs when introducing individual accounts—as will become clear later. It is motivated by key aspects of the Social Security program—of providing an "adequate" base level of retirement support to workers during old age. From the perspective of the program as a substitute for personal saving, the amount of resources "transferred" from the working to the retirement phase is of independent interest apart from considerations of lifetime fiscal treatment across population groups wherein the tax side must be also be considered.[21] Table 7.2 shows the metric in two ways. The third panel shows the metric based on Social Security's scheduled benefits under current laws, and the fourth panel shows the metric based on payable benefits as defined earlier.[22]

Table 7.2 shows that under the payable benefits calculation, Social Security provides between 2.0 and 4.0 percent of lifetime earnings, on average, by way of retirement benefits for most population groups. The percentage levels themselves are arbitrary because the denominator is evaluated using an arbitrary (5.0 percent) interest rate. Nevertheless, table 7.2 shows interesting differences among population subgroups. First, among almost

TABLE 7.2 **Social Security Wealth as a Share of Lifetime Earnings Under DEMSIM Baseline Assumptions by Birth Year, Gender, Race, and Present Value of Earnings (E) in Thousands of Constant 2006 Dollars**

Years of Birth	All	Female				Male			
		Non-White		White		Non-White		White	
		E≤Med	E>Med	E≤Med	E>Med	E≤Med	E>Med	E≤Med	E>Med
Panel 1	Present Value of traditional Social Securiy benefits *scheduled* under current laws								
1946–1960	178.2	116.8	204.4	158.3	241.8	89.4	183.0	102.4	213.5
1961–1975	181.9	113.7	214.9	156.2	245.5	101.2	213.6	108.3	226.0
1976–1990	212.9	128.1	259.7	181.0	295.1	115.9	265.9	135.0	264.3
1991–2005	245.0	153.3	288.7	209.9	331.8	137.6	312.8	150.7	309.5
2006–2020	280.8	181.0	329.2	237.0	386.4	179.1	346.5	169.1	355.8
2021–2035	324.5	202.2	391.4	274.8	433.2	208.0	428.7	220.3	405.6
2036–2050	375.6	239.1	431.8	335.7	492.7	240.1	490.8	245.4	464.1
Panel 2	Present Value of traditional Social Security benefits *payable* under current laws								
1946–1960	147.4	95.7	167.2	129.6	195.5	71.7	143.3	87.4	180.2
1961–1975	124.3	77.6	146.5	106.7	167.5	68.9	145.3	74.4	154.6
1976–1990	140.6	84.7	170.6	119.3	193.2	76.4	174.2	90.2	175.3
1991–2005	148.8	93.0	174.2	127.2	200.4	83.0	187.5	92.9	189.1
2006–2020	159.9	103.2	187.0	134.7	219.0	101.5	195.9	97.3	203.3
2021–2035	177.9	110.9	214.4	150.7	237.3	113.7	234.2	121.2	222.6
2036–2050	205.4	130.7	236.1	183.6	269.5	131.3	268.4	134.1	253.7
Panel 3	Current law *scheduled* Social Security wealth as a share of lifetime earnings								
1946–1960	4.08	5.19	3.54	5.64	3.99	3.25	2.55	3.47	2.85
1961–1975	3.93	4.51	3.60	5.26	3.92	3.08	2.83	3.53	3.08
1976–1990	3.85	4.21	3.71	5.07	3.93	2.93	2.97	3.64	3.09
1991–2005	3.77	4.02	3.52	4.91	3.88	2.77	3.00	3.41	3.12
2006–2020	3.81	4.08	3.50	4.91	3.90	3.10	2.97	3.45	3.23
2021–2035	3.86	4.04	3.60	4.94	3.90	3.14	3.17	3.80	3.28
2036–2050	3.92	4.12	3.48	5.20	3.88	3.25	3.17	3.74	3.34
Panel 4	Current law *payable* Social Security wealth as a share of lifetime earnings								
1946–1960	3.41	4.32	2.93	4.69	3.26	2.65	2.01	2.99	2.42
1961–1975	2.69	3.08	2.46	3.60	2.68	2.10	1.93	2.43	2.11
1976–1990	2.55	2.79	2.44	3.35	2.58	1.94	1.95	2.44	2.06
1991–2005	2.30	2.45	2.13	2.99	2.35	1.68	1.80	2.11	1.91
2006–2020	2.18	2.33	1.99	2.80	2.22	1.76	1.68	1.99	1.85
2021–2035	2.12	2.21	1.97	2.71	2.14	1.72	1.73	2.09	1.80
2036–2050	2.14	2.25	1.90	2.84	2.12	1.78	1.73	2.04	1.82
Panel 5	Current law payable benefits as a percent of current law scheduled benefits								
1946–1960	82.7	81.9	81.8	81.9	80.8	80.2	78.3	85.3	84.4
1961–1975	68.3	68.2	68.2	68.3	68.2	68.1	68.0	68.7	68.4
1976–1990	66.0	66.1	65.7	65.9	65.5	66.0	65.5	66.8	66.3
1991–2005	60.7	60.6	60.3	60.6	60.4	60.3	60.0	61.6	61.1
2006–2020	56.9	57.0	56.8	56.8	56.7	56.7	56.6	57.5	57.2
2021–2035	54.8	54.8	54.8	54.8	54.8	54.7	54.6	55.0	54.9
2036–2050	54.7	54.7	54.7	54.7	54.7	54.7	54.7	54.6	54.7

Source: Author's calculations.

all groups, lower-than-median lifetime earners receive larger Social Security retirement support as a share of their lifetime earnings than higher-than-median earners. This observation is barely true for lower-earning non-white males because of their significantly shorter average benefit collection life spans. Also as expected, females receive more retirement support compared to males. However, non-whites' retirement wealth under Social Security is smaller compared to that of whites.

Some readers may complain that these differences only reflect Social Security's intended operation as an insurance program—those with shorter life spans have relatively smaller Social Security wealth relative to lifetime earnings because they don't "need" benefits for as long. However, low values of the retirement wealth metric could also be interpreted as reflecting inflexible retirement eligibility rules under current Social Security laws that disallow earlier benefit collection by those with shorter expected total life spans—and especially for groups predominantly employed in physically taxing occupations who may be forced to quit working earlier during their careers. Such groups are forced into shorter benefit collection periods under Social Security's age eligibility rules, thereby reducing their advantage from the program's existence and operation.

These considerations suggest that normative judgments about the program's operation based on this metric are best avoided—especially when the focus is on retirement wealth. Judging whether current Social Security laws provide *adequate* retirement wealth for various groups is beyond the scope of this book. The estimates of table 7.2 should be viewed only as benchmarks—useful for evaluating changes in Social Security's contribution to retirement wealth under alternative reforms. The direction and percentage change in this metric will convey the extent to which retirement wealth is enhanced or worsened under liberal and conservative reform proposals.

Next Steps

Table 7.1's analytical sample, with demographic and economic features derived from DEMSIM's baseline assumptions, will form the backbone for analyzing the micro-level impact of various Social Security reforms in the next few chapters. Reforms will be analyzed in terms of both macro- and micrometrics described in this and earlier chapters. The objective will be to assess how alternative reforms would affect the system's overall financing over 75 years and in perpetuity; how they would affect the lifetime net tax treatment of various population subgroups; and how they would alter the retirement wealth of different population groups—those alive today and in the future as projected through the lens of DEMSIM's baseline simulations.

PART II

Issues in Evaluating Social Security Reform Proposals

Social Security is considered by many as a bulwark of the nation's social programs. Although it is not intended to be the sole source of retirement resources, its provision of retirement annuities is considered to be the bedrock upon which to build retirement support through additional private saving and employer pensions. However, about a third of retirees depend on Social Security benefits almost exclusively to cover their living expenses. As the "first pillar" of the retirement system Social Security is credited with having protected successive generations from falling into poverty during old age in a rough-and-tumble free-market economy by extending support to workers' dependents and survivors. According to Robert M. Ball, erstwhile Social Security commissioner, Social Security is "America's most successful and—deservedly—most popular social program. . . . No other program so clearly makes the United States a better and safer place."

The program's critics have focused attention on the bad deal that it provides to younger and future generations, who are projected to receive much smaller returns on their payroll taxes compared to returns they could otherwise obtain by investing the same funds in private capital market. Although this observation is correct, the pay-as-you-go nature of current Social Security's financing does not permit the unhampered diversion of payroll taxes into private capital investments without also proposing compensating changes to the program's benefits or taxes. Thus, the observation (and fact) that it provides a poor rate of return to workers is impotent as a first line of criticism. Instead, emphasizing that the program's current rules and operation—which have remained quite close to their original construction—now yield considerably diluted social protections and that its current financing structure and structural features significantly damage the nation's long-term economic prospects may be more persuasive.

Current Social Security's capacity to fulfill its original intent and goals has been undercut by cumulative changes in the economic and demographic environment during the last several decades. Under now significantly longer life spans compared to Social Security's statutory retirement age thresholds, it functions increasingly as a substitute for retirement saving. According to the 2007 Annual Statistical Supplement, less than 20 percent of Old Age and Survivor Insurance (OASI) benefits are awarded to survivors. The vast majority of benefits are for retirees and their dependents—replicating withdrawals and annuities out of personal savings that individuals and families might undertake in the program's absence. And such saving would generate "second round" positive effects on economic growth by boosting national saving, reducing the nation's trade deficits, and increasing future worker productivity.

In contrast, rather than protecting workers' retirements during periods of unexpected longevity, the current Social Security program subsidizes expected survival beyond statutory retirement ages—and encourages many participants to work less, retire earlier, and reduce personal saving for future consumption needs. The result is a continual erosion of domestic output, capital formation, and productivity. The difference in this scenario compared to the potential as outlined in the previous paragraph makes Social Security (OASI) a highly expensive way of providing social insurance.

No matter one's perspective, however, this book's limited aim is to evaluate the program's finances and fiscal treatment of various population groups. Given the relatively static approach—one that does not allow for feedback effects of changes in future policies, wages, and interest rates on capital formation and work effort—the book only explores the direct "first round" impact of reform alternatives on the program's financial condition.

Based on the results described in previous chapters, Social Security faces earlier and considerably more serious financial jeopardy than is appreciated and acknowledged under its official financial projections. Under DEMSIM's projections, a much larger proportion of the program's total shortfall occurs during the first 75 years. Moreover, Social Security's financial shortfall over the next 75 years, measured as a share of the present value of payrolls over 75 years, is much larger than is estimated by the program's trustees. The trustees do not take into account important factors in the momentum of forces built into today's population and economy that imply a smaller present value of future total and taxable payrolls.

Concerns about the program's solvency and long-term sustainability have prompted many policymakers, financial experts, and academicians to propose Social Security policy reforms—to bolster the program's receipts, curtail its benefit expenditures, introduce alternative retirement saving systems in the form of personal accounts, and so on. Indeed, proposing reforms to Social Security constitutes a minor industry in Washington, DC, with adherents of liberal and conservative political persuasions continually touting the advantages of their favorite reform ideas.

Naturally, armed with a new approach and tools for estimating Social Security's finances under U.S. economic and demographic conditions, the logical next step is to evaluate how alternative reforms would fare in "fixing" Social Security—making it solvent over a finite horizon or sustainable in perpetuity—and to analyze how those policies would affect current and future population groups.

One problem in evaluating Social Security reform proposals is the fact that they were designed with the prior knowledge of the trustees' financial projections. The reform proposals would likely have been very different if official projections had also reflected DEMSIM's considerably more dire outlook on the program's finances. But speculating about how the proposals would have been different under alternative baseline projections would be inappropriate. Here, the approach adopted is quite straightforward— of examining their effects as originally proposed but under DEMSIM's assumptions and projections.

Given the multitude of reform proposals available, selecting which ones to analyze is a difficult task. In order to cover as wide a range of reform elements as possible under limited time and resources, it was decided to examine just six proposals—two liberal, two centrist, and two conservative. The forthcoming chapters discuss the proposals and describe the findings from implementing each of their reform elements within DEMSIM's environment. Luckily, the Social Security Administration's Office of the Chief Actuary provides ready summaries of these proposals and an evaluation using a 75-year cash-flow accounting framework.

This book's analysis is conducted in terms of the proposals' impact on (a) 75-year and infinite horizon open group imbalances and the closed group imbalance; (b) 75-year annual imbalance ratios—the ratios of annual financial shortfalls to annual taxable earnings; (c) lifetime net tax rates of participants grouped by 15-year birth cohorts and by gender, race, and lifetime earning level; and (d) Social Security retirement wealth by the same population groupings. Each of these measures has a unique role in communicating the impact of reforms. Changes to annual imbalance ratios show the extent to which the proposal under consideration brings Social Security's baseline annual deficits closer to financial solvency—to a balanced or surplus position. If deficits persist despite full implementation of the reform proposal in question, the annual imbalance ratios reveal each year's gap in revenues relative to post-reform scheduled benefits— expressed as a share of annual taxable payrolls. Changes to the infinite horizon open group imbalance show the progress that a reform makes toward making the program sustainable. Changes to the 75-year open group show the share of the total adjustment in perpetuity that is accomplished within the first 75 years. It should be noted that comparing alternative reform proposals on an apples-to-apples basis requires infinite horizon open and closed group measures.[1] Changes to the closed group imbalance show how large are the adjustments imposed on those currently alive. Changes to lifetime net tax rates show how each proposal's costs are distributed on a lifetime basis among members of different population groups, and the retirement wealth metric shows the extent to which each reform increases or reduces the share of lifetime resources devoted to retirement consumption—irrespective of past payroll tax payments.

It should be clear that because Social Security is a pay-as-you-go financed transfer program, changes to its earmarked revenue and benefit rules would have a direct impact on the federal government's or private individuals' non–Social Security budgets. For example, if additional general revenue financing were proposed, the improvement in Social Security's finances would be matched by a worsening of the federal government's non–Social Security budget, other things equal. If higher payroll taxes are proposed, the improvement in Social Security's finances would be matched by a worsening in the finances of those private individuals who are to bear the additional taxes. The same remark goes for proposals to cut benefits or increase statutory early or normal retirement age thresholds, and so on. In addition, it should be noted that switching portfolios of the trust fund from government bonds to private securities or redirecting payroll taxes to personal accounts financed by additional issuance of government debt would alter portfolio holding patterns of other reciprocal public and private entities. That would rearrange the pattern of securities holdings given the available collection of government and privately issued securities. Such reciprocal changes in non–Social Security budgets and portfolios are usually described as the "no free lunch" constraint involved in making the Social Security program financially solvent and sustainable.

Appreciation of such reciprocal changes in Social Security and non–Social Security budgets is important because the Social Security metrics described earlier for evaluating the impact of reforms on Social Security's budget do not reflect such reciprocal changes in non–Social Security budgets and portfolios. Ideally, the impact of each reform proposal on Social Security's financial measures and on non–Social Security budgets (private and government) should both be displayed—through a sort of double-entry bookkeeping approach. Unfortunately, such reciprocal impacts of policy changes cannot be shown for all reforms under DEMSIM—for example, those that bring new revenues to Social Security.

The fact that compensating changes in non–Social Security budgets are always involved does not mean that reforms that improve Social Security's finances by imposing costs on other budgets are not worth undertaking. It may be desirable to pay for Social Security's promised benefits by reducing government spending in some areas that are wasteful or less valuable. It may also be feasible to improve Social Security's finances via mandatory or voluntary mechanisms that would repair economic disincentives created under current program rules. Other changes may also improve choices for workers in saving, investing, and disposing of their retirement wealth that would improve citizen's well-being, whether or not they improve the traditional Social Security program's financial status.

Another issue worth noting is that the analysis in this book is based on a static evaluation of proposed Social Security policy changes. It shows only the first order effects of those changes on the program's finances. But second order effects would also arise from most reforms: In general, second order effects could reinforce or offset first order effects. For example, a reduction in future benefit commitments would bring the program's finances closer into balance directly—a first order effect. But if such reductions induce workers to postpone retirement, payroll tax revenues would increase and move Social Security's finances even closer toward balance or into a surplus.

As another example, consider an increase in payroll tax rates, which would directly improve the program's finances. However, if workers decided to take longer vacations and retire earlier in response to higher payroll taxes, the direct impact would be offset and Social Security's finances would improve by less. An evaluation of the second-order effects arising from changing prices—and private economic responses to those price changes—is beyond the scope of DEMSIM's framework. However, predicting the sign and measuring the size of the second order feedback effects is a controversial topic and generally excluded from official projections and analyses of policy proposals.[2] In most cases, however, second order effects are likely to be smaller than the direct, first order effects, and evaluating just the latter remains useful for understanding each reform's potential impact on Social Security's financial condition.

CHAPTER EIGHT

Liberal Proposal 1 by Robert M. Ball

"A Golden Opportunity for the New Congress"

It's the essence of responsibility, in my view, to insist on no benefit cuts.—Robert M. Ball

As the quotes provided earlier suggest, Robert M. Ball, was a staunch defender of the Social Security program.[1] He made several proposals to return the program to financial balance, two of which have been evaluated by the Social Security Administration's Office of the Chief Actuary.[2] Earlier proposals by Ball recommended preserving current benefits while increasing the program's revenues through various measures—expanding the payroll tax base, increasing payroll tax rates, and dedicating new revenue sources to the program. The only benefit-side reform that ex-commissioner Ball recommended is to revise the cost-of-living index that is applied to keep nominal benefits growing with inflation.

In a more recent publication (Ball 2007), however, ex-commissioner Robert M. Ball retains just three "non-burdensome changes that are desirable in any event." In "Golden Opportunity for the New Congress," the goal is to reduce Social Security's then officially estimated long-term shortfall of 2 percentage points of payrolls to within a range consistent with balanced finances through the next 75 years and beyond.[3] The proposal aims to build up the trust funds continually "so that future earnings on the invested reserve will contribute to financing the system beyond the current 75-year estimating period." The Ball proposal is motivated by the observation that without such a reserve, payroll tax rates would have to be increased from today's 12.4 percent to 17.8 percent by 2080 and by even more thereafter.

Key Elements of the Ball Reform Proposal

The three components of the Ball proposal are:

1. Collect Social Security taxes on 90 percent of earnings in covered employment: This element of the proposal is motivated by the much faster earnings growth at the top of the earnings distribution during the 1980s and 1990s, which reduced the share of Social Security taxable payrolls in total payrolls. That share was originally set to be 90 percent of total earnings, but stood at just 83.3 percent in 2006, according to the 2008 Social Security Trustees' Annual Report. A gradual increase in the taxable earnings ceiling at a rate faster than scheduled—the rate of growth of average wages—would be "virtually painless," according to the proposal, but it would reduce Social Security's 2 percentage point actuarial deficit by about one third or about 0.7 percentage points.

2. Earmark estate tax revenues for Social Security: According to the Ball proposal, starting the Social Security program involved a "legacy cost"—the award of benefits to the first retiree generation despite small or zero payroll tax payments by them when they were working.

    The original intent of Social Security's founders was to create a "contributory" system with the benefits of successive worker cohorts fully paid for out of their own previous payroll taxes. But, according to the Ball proposal, the cost of *starting* the program need not be exclusively contributory: that cost should be borne by everyone alive then and in the future, and not just by workers earning below a certain threshold. Such a financing of start-up costs justifies, according to ex-commissioner Ball, eventual general revenue financing. Given that the estate tax is to expire in 2010, and is to be reinstated in 2011 at year 2000 estate tax rules, those revenues should, instead, be dedicated to Social Security as a means of achieving general revenue financing of legacy costs and balancing the program's future expenditures with revenues. Under official projections, this change is expected to reduce the 2 percentage point imbalance during the next 75 years by another one quarter or 0.5 percentage points.

3. Invest the trust fund in equities: According to the Ball proposal, there is no good reason for continuing the current practice of exclusively purchasing Treasury securities with Social Security's trust fund surpluses. Diversification into equities is routine among other public and private pension funds, and this step would further strengthen Social Security's finances. The Ball proposal accordingly recommends a gradual diversification—by 1 percent of trust fund securities in the first year, 2 percent in the second year, and so on. Such a progressive increase in portfolio diversification would continue until 20 percent of the trust

becomes invested in private equities. Such investments are to be restricted to a well-diversified index fund (such as the Wilshire 5000), and the Social Security Trust Fund would not be allowed to own more than 15 percent of outstanding equities of any broad private index. A board of managers protected from political influence would be appointed with long and staggered terms to select index funds and portfolios, but board members would not have any stock voting rights on private company boards. This step would enable the trust fund to create a reserve to meet future costs. Overall, it would account for another one quarter of the projected 2 percentage point 75-year shortfall.

According to the Ball proposal, these three changes together would reduce the official 75-year present discounted Social Security shortfall of 2 percentage points of present valued payrolls to within 0.5 percentage points—thereby eliminating the need to increase payroll tax rates significantly or resort to future benefit cuts. The remaining shortfall would be well within the forecasting uncertainties inherent in making long-term financial projections.

Implementing the Ball Reforms under DEMSIM's Baseline Assumptions

The first item—Social Security's ratio of taxable-to-total payrolls—is likely to be sensitive to future demographic and economic changes. Indeed, based on the chapter 5's charts showing core effective labor inputs (figure A5.3) and chapter 3's charts showing the population age distributions through time (figure 3.4), the past observed decline in the ratio of taxable to total earnings is not surprising at all: it is the outcome of the baby boomers' transition into the ages of highest life-cycle earnings during the 1970s, 1980s, and 1990s.[4] Currently, the boomers are either in or are approaching their highest earning years. However, as they retire in the future, the proportion of individuals in the highest earning ages will decline and cause the ratio of taxable-to-total payrolls to reverse course—at least until the boomer retirement process is completed by the late 2020s. Thereafter, this ratio is likely to remain stable for a many years as boomers' children—who also constitute a relatively large birth cohort, but not as large as the boomer cohort itself—begin to enter ages of highest life-cycle earnings.

DEMSIM's calibration does not include explicitly targeting the taxable-to-total earnings ratio series. Nevertheless, DEMSIM's demographic and

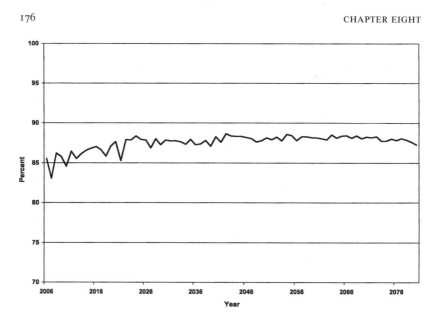

FIGURE 8.1. Simulated ratio of taxable-to-total labor earnings under DEMSIM's baseline assumptions. Source: Authors' calculations.

earnings estimation produces a very close match of this ratio for 2006. Its estimate of the 2006 ratio of 85.6 percent is quite close to the official ratio of 83.3 percent according to the 2008 annual report of the Social Security Trustees. This provides another indication of DEMSIM's success in capturing key features of the earnings distribution. And DEMSIM shows that the taxable-to-total payrolls ratio is likely to increase substantially in the future. Figure 8.1 shows taxable-to-total earnings ratios through 2080 projected under DEMSIM's baseline assumptions.

The ratio increases from 85.6 percent in the year 2006 to attain peak values above 88.0 percent beginning in the mid-2020s. It remains between 87 and 89 percent through the late 2060s, after which it declines slowly through the remainder of the 75-year horizon. Its value in the year 2080 equals 87.3 percent. The ratio continues to decline gradually beyond 2080—the result of rising earnings inequality in the long term under DEMSIM and because the fraction of individuals at high-earning ages relative to low earning ages would continually increase with ongoing, gradual population aging.[5]

The clear objective of the Ball proposal is to gradually approach and attain the taxable-to-total payrolls ratio of 90 percent by 2036, but that goal is already almost fully achieved under DEMSIM's baseline assumptions. Most of its major revenue impact, therefore, would emerge from maintaining the ratio at 90 percent after the 2060s instead of allowing it to decline as projected under baseline assumptions.

This reform is implemented in DEMSIM by following the procedure outlined in the Ball proposal: to increase the taxable payroll ceiling by more each year than scheduled under current law—that is, faster than annual increases in average wages. The additional increase required to achieve the 90 percent ratio, however, is only 0.2 percent per year beginning immediately (in 2006) and continuing through 2038. To prevent the ratio from declining after 2070, the taxable ceiling's growth rate is augmented by 0.25 percent each year permanently.

Although this procedure succeeds in maintaining the taxable-to-total earnings ratio at 90 percent beyond 2038 permanently, it contributes very little toward bringing the program closer to 75-year solvency or sustainability. The 75-year open group imbalance improves by just $237 billion, putting hardly any dent in DEMSIM's baseline estimate of $7.0 trillion—as shown in table 8.1. And the open group imbalance in perpetuity is reduced by just $758 billion, which is also quite small compared to the baseline open group imbalance of $13.4 trillion.

As would be expected, this reform element contributes very little even as a percent of the present value of taxable payrolls. Taking DEMSIM's pre-reform taxable payrolls as the base, the improvement over the next 75 years is about 0.1 percentage points—an order of magnitude smaller than the official estimate of 0.7 percentage points reported in Ball (2007). The small contribution by this particular element under DEMSIM's baseline projections is not surprising because bringing the taxable-to-total payrolls ratio to the proposal's target value involves very small increments to the growth rate of the taxable earnings ceiling.[6]

The second reform element under Mr. Ball's 2007 proposal would devote estate tax revenues to Social Security beginning in 2010. Currently, estate taxes are repealed only during the year 2010, after which the applicable laws revert to those from the year 2000—imposing a 55 percent tax rate on taxable estates larger than $1 million. The Ball reform proposes a freeze on the rules after 2009 at their 2009 thresholds—which involve taxing estates larger than $3.5 million at the rate of 45 percent. Thus, the Ball proposal eliminates the estate tax repeal for the year 2010, but reinstates a less draconian estate tax compared to the year 2000 laws. Revenues from year 2009 estate tax laws are permanently dedicated to Social Security beginning in 2010.

Appendix 8.1 describes how estate tax revenues are estimated under DEMSIM's baseline assumptions using the distribution of net worth by age, race, and gender taken from the Federal Reserve Board's Survey of Consumer Finances. That exercise reveals smaller estate tax collection after 2010 under the Ball proposal than under current law applicable after that year because of the former's higher exemption limit of $3.5 million per decedent (instead of $1 million) and smaller tax rate of 45 percent (instead of 55 percent). For example, 2006 estate tax collections were $24.2 billion (in constant 2006 dollars). Under current estate tax laws, projected revenues for 2011 under the method described in appendix 8.1 would be $40.1 billion in constant 2006 dollars. However, under the Ball proposal, 2011 revenues are projected at just $24.2 billion.

Calculations show that this element of the Ball proposal would boost the program's resources in present value by almost $814 billion through the year 2080 and by $1,081 billion in perpetuity. These changes amount to about 0.4 percent of the present value of taxable payrolls both through 2080 and in perpetuity—see table 8.1—a bit smaller than the 0.5 percentage point change reported in Ball (2007).

The third item under Mr. Ball's proposal is to shift a part of the trust fund's portfolio from investing in Treasury securities to private equities. Clearly, this element would crowd out private holders of equities, forcing them to hold government bonds instead: investing some portion of the trust fund in equities—where the portion devoted is gradually increased as described earlier—would mean that the equivalent portion of current Social Security surpluses would not be deposited with the Treasury in exchanges for special-issue non-marketable Treasury bonds. The federal government could accommodate smaller Treasury net receipts from Social Security by reducing non–Social Security expenditures or by increasing non–Social Security taxes. If it does neither (as is normally assumed), the Treasury must issue more bonds to the public to cover its now larger overall deficit. The net result would be that the Social Security Trust Fund and the public would swap equities for bonds—the public holding more government bonds, and the Social Security Trust Fund holding more equities. Such an exchange also transfers the risks associated with the swapped assets: the Social Security Trust Fund's portfolio would become more volatile, and the public's portfolio less volatile because equity prices are generally more volatile than Treasury bond prices.

The Ball proposal aims to provide Social Security a means of earning more income from interest, dividends, and capital appreciation by this

TABLE 8.1 **Impact of the Robert M. Ball Reform Proposal on Social Security's (OASI) Finances**

Horizon	DEMSIM baseline	Ball reform elements			Remaining imbalance	Difference from DEMSIM baseline
		Increase the taxable ceiling to 90 percent of payrolls	Earmark estate tax revenues after 2009	Invest 20 percent of the trust fund into equities		
		Present value in billions of constant 2006 dollars				
75 years	6,985	237	814	110	5,823	1,161
Infinite	13,364	758	1,081	110	11,415	1,949
		As shares of the present value of baseline taxable payrolls (%)*				
75 years	3.35	0.11	0.39	0.05	2.71	0.64
Infinite	4.75	0.27	0.39	0.04	3.95	0.67

* The present value of baseline taxable payrolls under DEMSIM's as of 2006 in constant 2006 dollars equals $208.5 trillion over 75 years and $281.1 trillion in perpetuity. See table 6.1.
Note: Dollar figures and percentages may not add up because of rounding.
Source: Author's calculations.

portfolio swap with the public, even if that makes the trust fund a little riskier. Such a portfolio swap would extend Social Security's ability to continue paying scheduled benefits under current laws.

However, this element also does not contribute much toward making Social Security financially solvent. Assuming a 6.45 percent average rate of return per year on equities net of management costs, the schedule of equity purchases suggested by the Ball proposal provides only an additional $110 billion over the next 75 years and in perpetuity. The estimate is the same for both time horizons because, even after including the effects of the other two elements, the Social Security trust fund is exhausted by the year 2029 under DEMSIM's projections—including the interacting effects of the two Ball reform elements discussed above.

Overall, as table 8.1 shows, the Ball proposal reduces the 75-year imbalance by only about 0.6 percentage points of the present value of pre-reform taxable payrolls, bringing the overall 75-year imbalance from $6.8 trillion under DEMSIM's baseline to $5.8 trillion. The general failure of the Ball proposal under DEMSIM is evident in figure 8.2. This figure shows that annual imbalance ratios under the Ball proposal would not be very different from that under DEMSIM's baseline—which incorporates Social Security's current tax and benefit rules. It shows that the overall effect of the Ball proposals is quite small—much smaller than would be

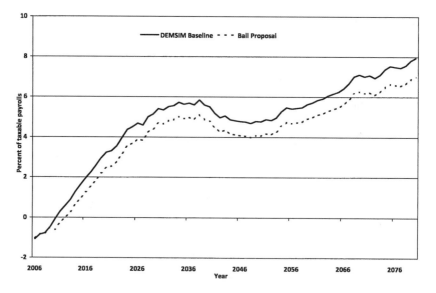

FIGURE 8.2. Annual non-interest imbalance ratios: DEMSIM baseline and Robert M. Ball reform proposal. Source: Authors' calculations.

necessary to place Social Security's finances on a sound footing through the 75-year time horizon.

Final Remarks

DEMSIM's framework for projecting Social Security's finances includes a detailed simulation of the labor earnings process incorporating differences in life-cycle earnings patterns according to several demographic and economic characteristics of labor force participants. Age-earnings profiles and the evolving demographic profile of the population suggest that the recent decline in the ratio of taxable-to-total payrolls is the natural result of the transition of the baby boomer generation across life-cycle age-earnings distributions. Life-cycle age-earnings patterns involve increasing annual wages through workers' middle ages followed by slower wage growth or even wage declines during late career stages. That means the proportion of workers earning more than Social Security's taxable limit grows larger and the share of taxable-to-total wages grows correspondingly smaller as the baby boomers enter their late forties and fifties in DEMSIM's simulation.

In the future, the taxable-to-total earnings ratio is likely to reverse course—eventually to almost 90 percent—as the boomers gradually leave the work force. That means reforms that specify an increase in the ratio from its current value in the low 80 percents to 90 percent in a few years won't fetch much additional revenue for Social Security because such an increase is already built into the processes governing U.S. demographics and earnings—as reflected in DEMSIM's baseline projections. The virtual elimination of the effectiveness of this reform option is also evident in other reform proposals—as described in later chapters.

Earmarking estate tax revenues generates by far the largest additional revenue under the Ball proposal as projected via DEMSIM. But estate tax projections based on the distribution of decedents' estates calibrated to information from the Survey of Consumer Finances shows that even here the contribution is likely to be small relative to Social Security's overall financial imbalances as projected under DEMSIM.

The smallest contribution arises from investing the Old Age and Survivor Insurance (OASI) trust fund in equities. Indeed, far from becoming a permanent source for funding future Social Security benefits—even beyond the 75-year horizon as claimed in Ball (2007)—this source dries up once the trust fund is exhausted in 2029, just 2 years beyond DEMSIM's baseline exhaustion date of 2027. The operation of this Ball reform element is clearly dependent on substantial additional revenue generation from the other two elements—which would have allowed a trust fund buildup for many additional years. However, failure of those two elements to contribute substantial additional revenues means that trust fund investments in equities are also short-lived as a financial solution.

All three elements of the Ball proposal are intended to generate revenues from higher-earners by increasing the taxable earnings ceiling and from wealthier individuals and families who mostly hold riskier equities and leave bequests. Unfortunately, DEMSIM's current framework does not include estimation of personal family budgets. Because all three of the Ball reform elements generate financial effects that lie outside the purview of Social Security's payroll tax and benefit rules, they cannot be represented as changes to Social Security's lifetime net tax rates.

Estate Tax Revenue Projections for the Robert M. Ball Reform Proposal

The first step for simulating federal estate taxes under DEMSIM's baseline assumptions is to impute a value of *gross taxable estate* for each person who dies in the base year—2006. The imputation is based on the 2004 Survey of Consumer Finances: random assignments of estates for those who die in each simulation year after 2005 are based on percentile distributions of SCF net worth distinguished by race, sex, and age category. Age categories are in five-year age groups of adults—18–22, 23–27, . . . 93–97, and 98–99. For the year 2006, the 2004 SCF net worth values are increased by the ratio of the economy-wide household net worth for 2006 to that in 2004 (1.16). For subsequent years, the 2006 values are increased by an index of nominal wage growth calculated within DEMSIM.

The next step is to adjust gross estates for various deductions allowed by law. These include items such as the decedent's debts, attorney and executor fees, court costs, costs of last illness, death and burial, costs of property sales, and marital and charitable deductions. Obviously, DEMSIM cannot derive any except the marital deduction—only the estates of decedents with no surviving spouse ("non-family" individuals) are subject to the estate tax since the marital deduction equals 100 percent.

The potential (non-marital) deductions, however, provide a way to calibrate the estate tax simulation: the gross estate of each DEMSIM "non-family" decedent in 2006, ε_{2006}, is multiplied by a (non-marital) deductions-factor, α, to obtain the *gross taxable estate,* $\eta = \varepsilon(1 - \alpha)$. The value of α—the fraction of the estate that is deducted—is selected so that when the 2006 estate tax rate of 46 percent is applied to each decedent's *net taxable estate* (see below) the total estate tax flow for 2006 equals that reported in the National Income and Product Accounts (NIPA) of the Bureau of Economic Analysis—$24.2 billion (in constant 2006 dollars). The latter value is derived from the $25.7 billion reported value under estate and gift taxes in NIPA's table 5.10 (also converted to constant 2006 dollars), after applying an adjustment to remove the gift tax share. The gift tax adjustment is implemented by applying a factor derived from data from the Statistics of Income division of the Internal Revenue Service (Internal Revenue Service 2007).

The gross taxable estate of each 2006 decedent whose estate is subject to the tax is further reduced by the 2006 exemption amount of $2 million to derive the net taxable estate. Applying the tax rate to this amount yields the tax liability calibrated as described above.

For years beyond 2006, the value of α is kept fixed at the 2006 level, but each year's scheduled exemption amount and estate tax rate is applied to calculate that year's individual and aggregate estate taxes. The year-specific federal estate tax exemption amounts are $2 million between 2006 and 2008, $3.5 million in 2009, and $1 million after 2011. Under current law, the estate tax is repealed only for the year 2010. The tax rates applicable are 46 percent for 2006, 45 percent for 2007 through 2009, zero for 2010, and 55 percent for 2011 and later.

Because DEMSIM's sample size is much smaller relative to the U.S. population, the estate tax revenue projections are quite volatile. The volatility arises from the considerably skewed net worth distributions derived from the SCF. A calculation of the impact of a larger sample size on the temporal volatility of estate tax revenues suggests that smoothing the projected values would be appropriate. Hence, a third degree polynomial regression of projected revenues on a time index is used to derive smoothed estimates of future estate tax revenues under the current-law baseline and under assumptions of the Ball policy proposal.

CHAPTER NINE

Liberal Proposal 2 by
Peter A. Diamond and Peter R. Orszag

"A Balanced Approach"

Social Security can be designed so that the need for legislation is infrequent.
—Peter A Diamond and Peter R. Orszag

Peter A. Diamond, economics professor at MIT, and Peter R. Orszag, currently director of the Office of Management and Budget, are both prominent and highly respected economists.[1] Both have made wide-ranging contributions in the areas of fiscal policy and social insurance including, in particular, to the Social Security reform debate. Diamond was awarded the Robert M. Ball Award by the National Academy of Social Insurance in 2008 for outstanding achievements in social insurance. The two economists collaborated to produce a detailed Social Security reform proposal in the year 2003. Their proposal was scored by the Social Security's Office of the Chief Actuary in October 2003. The evaluation of their proposal here is based on details provided in their book entitled *Saving Social Security: A Balanced Approach* (Diamond and Orszag 2005).

Notwithstanding the term "balanced" in the subtitle to their book, the Diamond-Orszag reform proposal is classified as a liberal proposal because of its emphasis on revenue-side reforms. However, its authors are motivated by two observations that are not generally accepted by political liberals: First, they explicitly acknowledge that the program faces long-term financial shortfalls and that a resolution of its future financial problems would be easier if actions are taken earlier rather than later. This is unlike many on the political left who continue to deny or ignore Social Security's structural financial imbalance. Second, Diamond and Orszag believe that changes in socioeconomic conditions since the last major Social Security reforms in 1983 have made many of the program's features obsolete and in need of adaptation. This view is consistent with the position taken in this book, but, again, it is not a widely supported belief among liberals.

It is noteworthy, however, that Diamond and Orszag suggest that pre-1983 reforms were simply an adaption of Social Security to evolving issues. An unvarnished statement would have acknowledged that those changes to Social Security were mostly for expanding the program's benefits—by introducing new types of benefits, extending coverage to newer population groups, and increasing benefit generosity—partly because of electoral calculation by politicians and *despite* ongoing gains in human longevity. Pre-1983 reforms did not address the latter, rather important, development with negative implications for Social Security's financial cost and longer term viability. As a result, the program now provides massive consumption subsidies to retirees' during long periods of expected survival in good health, in contrast to when the program was first introduced in the mid-1930s.

This naturally draws attention to a Diamond-Orszag dictum that it is not necessary to "destroy the program in order to save it" because it provides important social protections. As argued in an earlier chapter, those protections are now considerably diluted. Social Security reforms should aim to gradually eliminate retiree consumption subsidies and retain only genuine protections against longevity risks. Such changes require focusing reforms on the benefit side of the program, together with a transition to a personal retirement saving mechanism within Social Security. Unfortunately, the program's supporters stifle rational debate by constantly repeating the mantra that this sensible approach will "destroy the program."

The liberal approach is rooted in preserving the "guaranteed" status of a base level of Social Security benefits—a principle that the Diamond-Orszag plan largely adheres to. However, it remains doubtful whether Social Security benefits could be considered to be secure and assured when it has no means of effectively saving and investing taxpayer resources to buffer its finances from demographic and economic shocks. Instead, Social Security remains exposed to periodic financial crises that create political pressure to increase payroll taxes to the potential detriment of long-term economic growth.

Diamond and Orszag promote their approach as a balanced division of adjustment costs between tax increases and benefit reductions. The official evaluation of their proposal by Social Security's Office of the Chief Actuary is in terms of the actuarial deficit measure under the Social Security Trustees' intermediate financial projections. But a full evaluation of this reform's key implications requires use of metrics developed earlier in this book. Such an evaluation under DEMSIM's detailed baseline projections would reveal whether the proposal is also balanced along other important dimensions: for example, whether it distributes adjustment burdens across different population groups in a balanced way. In addition, the metrics would reveal how far the proposal shifts the program's finances toward sustainability and not just toward financial solvency during the next 75 years.

Key Elements of the Diamond-Orszag Reform Proposal

The Diamond-Orszag Social Security reform proposal addresses two overall features of socioeconomic evolution in the United States: increasing human longevity that expands future benefit commitments and increases the program's financial shortfalls and increasing inequality as manifested by a historically rising share of workers' earnings exceeding the taxable maximum ceiling. It also addresses one feature of the program's historical operation: the "legacy debt" arising from Social Security's past generosity to early participants.

1. To address increasing longevity, the Diamond-Orszag proposal introduces equal adjustments to benefits and payroll taxes. These adjustments are motivated by the observation that without Social Security an individual would respond to a longer expected life span by reducing consumption while working (to save more), by reducing consumption while retired (to finance a longer expected retirement), and by working more (to accumulate more for consumption during retirement). However, the current Social Security system already accommodates the third provision; hence the reform emphasizes the first two types of adjustments.

    The proposal calls for implementing the adjustments to payroll taxes and benefits taking account of period mortality tables in future years. On the benefit side, beginning in the year 2012, benefit formula factors (90, 32, and 15 percent that are used to convert workers' average indexed monthly earnings [AIMEs] into their primary insurance amount [PIAs]) would be reduced based on a *longevity index*. The first index value is constructed as a ratio of actuarial present values of benefits for workers aged 59 starting in 2009. The numerator of the ratio would be based on the period life table of the prior year minus 3—or 2005. The denominator would be based on the period life table of the current year minus 3—or 2006. The mortality tables are used from the corresponding year's trustees' annual reports of Social Security's trust fund finances and are advanced by one year every year.

One half of the annual change in each year's longevity index would be applied to reduce the PIA factors applicable in that year (reform element 1a). The remaining change would be applied to payroll tax rates for that year, which would be increased by 85 percent of the change in PIA factors (reform element 1b).[2] See appendix 9.1 for more details.

Diamond and Orszag explicitly prefer to use period rather than cohort mortality tables—and their procedure is replicated in the calculations reported below.[3] Note, however, that DEMSIM's mortality rates are distinguished by age, gender, and race, and expected improvements in average mortality rates are likely to slow over time because of an increasing proportion of non-whites in the population (see chapter 5).

Moreover, as appendix 9.1 explains, improvements in longevity imply higher survival rates for both men and women. If survival rates increase proportionally for both genders, average periods of widowhood would increase over time. However, because survivors are generally females with larger benefits during the end of their life spans—based on the larger lifetime earnings of their decedent spouses—mortality improvements would increase the likelihood of survival to periods of high benefits (conditional on age of spouses' death) compared to the typical earner's benefits. This is likely to increase the difference in actuarial present values of benefits under higher relative to lower mortality rates.

2. To counter changes in earnings inequality, the Diamond-Orszag proposal suggests increasing the maximum taxable earnings ceiling until earnings not subject to the payroll taxes are just 13 percent by 2063 (reform element 2). Recall that this element is very similar to one of the Robert M. Ball reform elements, and will likely prove inoperative under DEMSIM because of projected increases in the ratio of taxable-to-total earnings under baseline assumptions (reform element 2). However, the Diamond-Orszag proposal also includes modest benefit reductions for successive cohorts of new retirees whose lifetime earnings are sufficiently high and fall within the highest tier of Social Security's benefit (bend point) formula (reform element 3).[4] This is done to make the system more progressive by imposing larger costs on high-earners and protecting low lifetime earners—those who receive fewer lifetime benefits because of shorter average life spans. As described in chapter 6, DEMSIM's calibrations of mortality rates and labor earnings to U.S. microdata yield a significant positive correlation between lifetime earnings and longevity, making it eminently suitable for evaluating the impact of this reform element under the Diamond-Orszag proposal.

3. The next set of reform elements under the Diamond-Orszag proposal include provisions to pay down the program's "legacy cost"—which arose because of generous benefits awarded to early participants during the first four decades of the program's existence (from 1939, when benefit payments commenced, through about 1980), and which must be paid for by living and future generations collectively. The proposal recommends three reform elements in this context:

    a. Extend Social Security coverage to all workers—thereby moving the system toward universal coverage (reform element 4). This would add several million workers to Social Security's taxpayers and, correspondingly, extend its benefit commitments to them upon their retirement.

    b. Impose a legacy tax on earnings above the current ceiling for payroll taxes (reform element 5). This is motivated by the idea that all earnings, rather than just those below the taxable ceiling, should bear the system's start-up costs—which echoes the motivation under the Ball proposal (chapter 8) for devoting estate taxes to Social Security.

    c. Impose a "residual" legacy charge on future workers and beneficiaries (reform element 6). This element proposes a payroll tax increase on workers after 2023, a benefit reduction for those eligible to collect benefits after 2023, and an increase in the 3 percent surcharge on earnings above the taxable ceiling. All components of the legacy charge would be gradually increased over time to stabilize the size of legacy debt relative to taxable payrolls. The motivation is to impose at least some of the adjustment cost onto living generations rather than push it entirely onto those who will be alive in the distant future.

4. The proposal includes additional provisions such as providing higher benefits to widow(er)s and young survivors (reform element 7) and enhancing the benefits of low-earners (reform element 8). Here, the motivation cited is to strengthen the program's social insurance functions. Current widow(er) benefits constitute a 67 percent replacement rate over the couples' benefit were both spouses still alive. This replacement rate is enhanced for all widow(er)s to 75 percent.[5]

Diamond and Orszag justify these proposals as meeting many objectives: meting out fair treatment to various population groups; eliminating Social Security's long-term (75-year) financial shortfall; avoiding general revenue financing; and protecting the provision of a base level of income "at a time of need" without introducing personal accounts.

The numerical evaluation provided below will reveal if the Diamond-Orszag proposed reforms are, indeed, fair across population groups and whether they would restore the program's finances to long-term solvency and sustainability.

The Impact of the Diamond-Orszag Proposal on Social Security's Aggregate Finances

Appendix 9.1 describes the adjustments made to Social Security Tax and Benefit Calculator (SSTBC) operated under DEMSIM's baseline assumptions to incorporate all eight of the Diamond-Orszag reform elements. These elements are incorporated into the simulation exactly as prescribed under the proposal with just one exception: reform element 3, which requires increasing the taxable earnings ceiling faster during the next 75 years is not needed because DEMSIM's baseline projections already generate an increase in the taxable-to-total earnings ratio beyond the 87 percent threshold prescribed under the proposal. The taxable ceiling is increased, however, to maintain the taxable-to-total earnings ratio above 87 percent in the distant future—years when that ratio declines under DEMSIM's baseline assumptions.

The procedure followed when analyzing the Diamond-Orszag reform proposal is to first implement DEMSIM under baseline assumptions, each time including only one of the eight reform elements. In a final run, all eight reform elements are implemented simultaneously to yield the proposal's total impact including interactions between all reform elements. Such interactions mean that the simple sum of their separate effects on the program's open group imbalances would not add up to their effect under simultaneous implementation. Table 9.1 shows the results.

The first item to note is in the last line of the table, the total impact of the proposal, including interactions between all reform elements, reduces DEMSIM's 75-year imbalance of $7.0 trillion under baseline assumptions—an actuarial imbalance of 3.4 percent of taxable payrolls—to just 1.4 trillion, or 0.7 percent of baseline taxable payrolls. That's a reduction in the actuarial open group imbalance of almost $5.6 trillion—or 80 percent of the original imbalance. The proposal, however, does not fully restore the program to 75-year solvency under DEMSIM's projections—which project a sizable decline in effective labor inputs during future decades and imply considerably larger baseline open group imbalances compared to official projections. Measured in perpetuity, the proposal's impact is even larger—almost 90 percent of Social Security's outstanding actuarial open group imbalance is eliminated.

Examining the impact of individual reform elements shows several features: reform element 1—which addresses financial shortfalls due to increasing human longevity—has a sizable effect that is balanced between

TABLE 9.1 **Impact of the Diamond-Orszag Reform Proposal on Social Security's (OASI) Finances**

| | Post-reform actuarial imbalance | | | | | | Change in actuarial imbalance as a percent of DEMSIM-baseline taxable payrolls | | |
| | Present values in billions of constant 2006 dollars | | | As a percent of DEMSIM-baseline taxable payrolls | | | | | |
Proposed policy change	75-year open group	∞-horizon open group	Closed group	75-year open group	∞-horizon open group	Closed group*	75-year open group	∞-horizon open group	Closed group*
Addressing increasing life expectancy									
1a. Adjust benefits	5,427	9,167	12,543	2.60	3.26	8.62	-0.75	-1.49	-1.12
1b. Adjust revenue	5,427	10,319	13,510	2.60	3.67	9.28	-0.75	-1.08	-0.45
Adjustments for increased inequality									
2. Increase maximum taxable earnings base	6,962	13,239	14,172	3.34	4.71	9.74	-0.01	-0.04	0.00
3. Reduce benefits for high-earners	6,937	13,291	14,122	3.33	4.73	9.70	-0.02	-0.03	-0.03
Adjustments for fairer sharing of legacy costs									
4. Make Social Security coverage universal	6,621	13,258	14,123	3.18	4.72	9.70	-0.17	-0.04	-0.03
5. Legacy tax on earnings over maximum	6,043	12,029	13,460	2.90	4.28	9.25	-0.45	-0.47	-0.49
6. Residual legacy adjustments on taxes and benefits†	4,989	9,577	13,125	2.39	3.41	9.02	-0.96	-1.35	-0.72
Adjustments to strengthen social insurance functions									
7. Widow(er)s given 75% of couple's benefit	7,113	13,605	14,325	3.41	4.84	9.84	0.06	0.09	0.11
8. Low-earner PIA enhancement	7,089	13,514	14,279	3.40	4.81	9.81	0.05	0.05	0.07
Simple sum of all adjustments	728	1,087	10,283	0.35	0.39	7.06	-3.00	-4.37	-2.67
Total effect of implementing all reforms together	1,386	1,610	10,889	0.66	0.57	7.48	-2.69	-4.18	-2.26
Memoranda:									
DEMSIM-baseline imbalance	6,985	13,364	14,172	3.35	4.75	9.74	...	...	...
DEMSIM-baseline taxable payrolls	208,495	281,064	145,572	...	...	...	...	...	...

*Shown as a percent of closed group taxable payrolls.
†Value cumulated with previous row.
Source: Author's calculations.

taxes and benefits. Over the next 75 years, both reform elements 1a and 1b reduce the open group imbalance by 0.75 percentage points of baseline taxable payrolls (from 3.4 percent under the baseline to 2.6 percent). Reform element 1a is also responsible for reducing living generations' net benefits from $14.2 trillion to $12.5 trillion—a difference of $1.7 trillion.

However, reform elements 2 and 3—both of which address the issue of projected increases in inequality—exhibit very small effects on Social Security's open group imbalances over both 75 years and in perpetuity. The reason, as discussed earlier, is that the taxable-to-total earnings ratio as a metric for rising inequality justifies implementation of reform element 2 only during the distant future. And reform element 3, which involves gradually reducing the benefit formula's 15 percent bend point factor to 10 percent, has a very small impact overall because it is the product of three small items: A small change in the bend point factor affecting a small part of earnings of a small segment of the DEMSIM population. It affects the PIAs of only those with AIMEs between the upper bend point and the AIME of a career taxable maximum worker—a small segment of high-earning individuals.

Reform element 4—which extends Social Security's coverage to additional population segments—has a modest impact on 75-year and perpetuity open group imbalances. Elements 5 and 6 make sizable and roughly similar sized contributions toward reducing the 75-year and infinite horizon imbalances. Thus, adding element 6's effect to element 5 doubles element 5's reduction in the open group imbalance ratio from 0.45 percentage points to almost a full percentage point. Cumulatively, these two reform elements reduce the 75-year open group imbalance by $2.0 trillion (from $7.0 trillion under DEMSIM's baseline to $5.0 trillion as shown in row 6 of the table). The reason for their sizable cumulative impact is that the changes apply to all earnings above the taxable maximum, they impose a relatively large legacy surcharge rate of 3 percent on those earnings, and the rate or surcharge is increased in future years. In addition, annually increasing payroll taxes and benefit reductions are levied on current and future participants—measures that magnify their impact considerably. As a result, their impact over the infinite horizon is even larger—a reduction in the imbalance of $3.8 trillion (from $13.4 trillion under the baseline to $9.6 trillion). The three reforms relating to "legacy costs" (rows numbered 4, 5, and 6 in table 9.1) also reduce the closed group imbalance measure by about $1.0 trillion. This constitutes the second largest impact on the closed group imbalance after reform element 1a.

Reform element 7—which increases benefit support for aged widow(er)s—has a small positive impact on open group imbalances because these benefit increases are capped and they apply only during a few terminal years of a person's survivorship. Reform element 8, which enhances the benefits of low-earners, also imposes modest additional costs: increasing the 75-year and perpetuity open group imbalances by just $104 billion and $150 billion, respectively—amounting to 0.06 and 0.05 percent of taxable payrolls.

Another noteworthy effect of the Diamond-Orszag proposal is its impact on the closed group imbalance. The total closed group imbalance under DEMSIM's baseline equals $14.2 trillion—which shows the excess benefits that past and current generations are to receive over and above the present value of their contributions to the program. It includes the sum total of the generous treatment that was provided in the past and would be provided in the future if the program's current rules are sustained during the lifetimes of those alive today. Hence, the closed group imbalance fully measures the size of the "legacy debt" that would be created by maintaining current Social Security rules through the lifetimes of those alive today.

The change in the closed group imbalance shows the extent to which a reform deals with legacy debt. The larger the reduction in the closed group imbalance, the smaller would the imposition of adjustment costs on future generations. Hence, the change in the closed group imbalance relative to that in the open group imbalance is the true test of how "balanced" any reform proposal is.

Reform elements 4, 5, and 6—which are explicitly designed to address the legacy debt issue—together impose a total adjustment cost of $3.9 trillion on current and future generations: reform element 4's contribution in billions of constant 2006 dollars equals $106 billion ($13,364 billion minus $13,258 billion) and those of elements 5 and 6 cumulatively equal $3,787 billion ($13,364 billion minus $9,577 billion). But these reform elements reduce the closed group imbalance by just $1.1 trillion (similar calculations as above using closed group imbalances). Thus, viewed from the metric of the closed group imbalance, living generations would bear a relatively small portion—just 28 percent—of the total adjustment from the reform's legacy debt elements, items 4, 5, and 6.[6] From this perspective, the proposal appears to be not very well balanced. The same remark is applicable when the entire proposal is considered: out of the total adjustment cost imposed by the proposal of $11.8 trillion ($13.4 trillion minus $1.6 trillion), only 28 percent—or $3.3 trillion ($14.2 trillion minus $10.9 trillion)—is imposed on the closed group of past and living generations.

The last column of table 9.1 shows the change in the closed group measure as a ratio of closed group taxable earnings. This is the fraction by which living generations' human capital resources would be reduced as a result of the Diamond-Orszag proposal. When all Diamond-Orszag reforms are implemented together, the reduction equals 2.3 percent.

The message of this section concerns metrics for judging whether a proposal is "balanced." Judgment about this is usually based on how much of its total adjustment arises from tax increases and how much from cuts in scheduled benefits. However, Social Security's financial impact extends throughout workers' lifetimes—from the time of entering the workforce through the ends of their lives. To the extent that workers view Social Security as a substitute for personal retirement saving, cutting future benefits is analogous to increasing current payroll taxes. In that case, basing judgment about "balance" based on the proportion of tax-side versus benefit-side changes is not very useful. For example, a reform may divide its adjustment costs evenly between tax increases and benefit cuts, but if most of those changes are imposed on a particular group—say high-earning white males born after 2050—the proposal would (should) not be considered to be "balanced" in any meaningful sense. A proper perspective on "balance" can only be obtained by judging the extent to which adjustment costs are imposed on various groups. The simplest but nevertheless relevant distinction relates to current versus future generations.

The only caveat to the above argument arises if workers view current payroll deductions for Social Security as pure taxes and not, at least partly, as a substitute for personal savings. In that case, the distinction between tax-side and benefit-side changes retains relevance. Given the evolving shift in the nature of Social Security—away from providing social "insurance" and toward operating as a substitute for personal saving (as argued in chapter 7)—the former perspective appears much more important today. But no analyses to indicate whether reform proposals are balanced on those terms are available from official sources.

Effects on Annual Imbalance Ratios

The Diamond-Orszag proposal's impact on annual imbalance ratios is shown in figure 9.1. It shows that the proposal would increase short-term surpluses and reduce Social Security's annual imbalances from the very beginning. However, its reduction of annual deficits as a percentage of

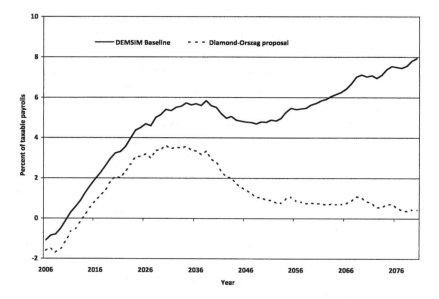

FIGURE 9.1 Annual non-interest imbalance ratios: DEMSIM baseline and Diamond-Orszag reform proposal. *Source*: Author's calculations.

payrolls is relatively small and constant for the next two decades. Large deficit reductions commence only after the mid-2020s. This result is influenced by the elimination under DEMSIM of one of the proposals elements—increasing the taxable earnings ceiling beginning immediately with the objective of increasing the currently depressed ratio of taxable-to-total earnings. Although long-term reductions of annual deficit ratios are significant, the substantial initial bulge in deficits under DEMSIM's baseline projections is largely sustained—with the result that the proposal does not restore Social Security to short-term solvency and sustainability. The program's trust fund becomes exhausted by the year 2035—eight years after the corresponding date under DEMSIM's baseline projections.

Lifetime Net Tax Rate Effects

The unbalanced nature of the Diamond-Orszag reform proposal is also evident in micromeasures—changes in the lifetime net tax rates for particular population groups from implementing the proposal relative to those under DEMSIM's baseline projections. The Diamond-Orszag proposal's adjustments are not imposed on anyone currently retired or approaching retirement—those aged 55 and older in 2005.[7] For affected participants— those younger than age 55 when the reform commences—increasing taxes and benefits gradually implies different lifetime effects for differently situated individuals. Payroll tax increases would affect cohorts close in age to 55 years for only a few years. Thereafter, benefit cuts would impose adjustment costs until death. Younger participants would feel the impact of payroll tax increases for more years and would face deeper benefit cuts because those cuts are scheduled to increase over time.

The effects would be moderated, however, for those belonging to low-earner groups and for women because they are more likely to experience widowhood during retirement. Thus, from a lifetime perspective, the reform elements taken together are unlikely to impose costs in a balanced manner across different population categories.

The first panel of table 9.2 shows lifetime net tax rates under the Diamond-Orszag reform proposal, and the second panel shows changes in those rates compared to DEMSIM baseline assumptions—as shown in panel 11 of table 7.2.

Several properties of lifetime net tax rates under the Diamond-Orszag proposal are evident: panel 2 of the table shows that older participants— those born before 1975—are affected very little by its reforms. These cohorts' lifetime net tax rates increase by 0.4 percentage points of their lifetime earnings. Thus, the proposal effectively protects those aged 30 and older in 2006 from bearing significant adjustment costs.

Lifetime net tax rates increase by about 1 percentage point for people born soon after 1975—those in their twenties and early thirties today. And the increases become progressively larger for later-born generations as shown in panel 2 of the table (see the "All" column). Those to be born during the middle of this century would pay an additional 4.4 percentage points of their lifetime earnings to the government, taking their lifetime net tax rates from about 6.0 percent under the DEMSIM baseline to more than 10.0 percent. This is the natural consequence of the proposal's temporally staggered tax increases and benefit reductions that become larger for later-born generations.

Diamond and Orszag claim that "this approach to financing the legacy debt reflects a reasonable balance between current and distant generations . . . it is meant to keep the full cost of servicing the legacy debt from simply being pushed further into the future for our children and grand children to pay."[8] However, as shown in table 9.2, the Diamond-Orszag

TABLE 9.2 **Effects of the Diamond-Orszag (D-O) Reform Proposal on Selected Population Groups**

Years of Birth	All	Female Non-White E≤Med	Female Non-White E>Med	Female White E≤Med	Female White E>Med	Male Non-White E≤Med	Male Non-White E>Med	Male White E≤Med	Male White E>Med
Panel 1	Traditional Social Security lifetime net tax rates under the D-O proposal								
1946–1960	5.13	4.7	5.5	3.9	5.0	6.6	6.6	6.3	5.8
1961–1975	6.49	6.3	6.6	5.5	6.3	7.6	7.4	7.1	7.0
1976–1990	7.02	7.0	7.0	6.2	6.8	8.1	7.7	7.4	7.4
1991–2005	7.79	7.8	7.8	7.0	7.5	8.9	8.3	8.3	8.1
2006–2020	8.69	8.7	8.7	8.0	8.4	9.5	9.2	9.2	8.9
2021–2035	9.49	9.6	9.3	8.8	9.1	10.3	9.9	9.8	9.7
2036–2050	10.13	10.2	10.0	9.3	9.8	10.9	10.5	10.6	10.4
Panel 2	Percentage point increase in lifetime net tax rates: D-O minus DEMSIM baseline								
1946–1960	0.0	0.1	0.1	0.0	0.1	0.1	0.1	0.0	0.1
1961–1975	0.4	0.4	0.4	0.4	0.4	0.3	0.4	0.3	0.5
1976–1990	0.9	0.9	0.9	0.9	1.0	0.8	0.9	0.7	1.0
1991–2005	1.7	1.6	1.7	1.7	1.7	1.4	1.7	1.4	1.7
2006–2020	2.6	2.6	2.6	2.8	2.7	2.4	2.6	2.4	2.7
2021–2035	3.6	3.5	3.5	3.7	3.6	3.3	3.6	3.4	3.6
2036–2050	4.4	4.3	4.3	4.5	4.4	4.2	4.3	4.3	4.3
Panel 3	Total Social Security wealth as a share of lifetime earnings (*scheduled* benefits, %)								
1946–1960	4.1	5.2	3.5	5.7	4.0	3.2	2.5	3.5	2.8
1961–1975	3.7	4.3	3.4	5.1	3.8	2.9	2.7	3.4	2.9
1976–1990	3.5	3.8	3.4	4.6	3.6	2.7	2.7	3.3	2.8
1991–2005	3.3	3.5	3.1	4.3	3.4	2.4	2.6	3.0	2.7
2006–2020	3.2	3.4	3.0	4.1	3.3	2.6	2.5	2.9	2.7
2021–2035	3.2	3.4	3.0	4.1	3.3	2.6	2.6	3.2	2.7
2036–2050	3.3	3.4	2.9	4.3	3.2	2.7	2.6	3.1	2.8
Panel 4	Total Social Security wealth as a share of lifetime earnings (*payable* benefits, %)								
1946–1960	4.0	5.0	3.4	5.5	3.9	3.1	2.4	3.4	2.7
1961–1975	3.4	3.9	3.1	4.6	3.4	2.7	2.4	3.1	2.7
1976–1990	3.3	3.6	3.2	4.4	3.4	2.5	2.5	3.1	2.6
1991–2005	3.2	3.4	3.0	4.1	3.3	2.3	2.5	2.9	2.6
2006–2020	3.1	3.3	2.9	4.0	3.2	2.5	2.4	2.8	2.6
2021–2035	3.1	3.2	2.9	3.9	3.1	2.5	2.5	3.1	2.6
2036–2050	3.2	3.3	2.8	4.2	3.1	2.6	2.5	3.0	2.7
Panel 5	Percent of Social Security wealth provided by D-O traditional benefits								
1946–1960	100.0	100.0	100.0	100.0	100.0	100.0	100.0	100.0	100.0
1961–1975	100.0	100.0	100.0	100.0	100.0	100.0	100.0	100.0	100.0
1976–1990	100.0	100.0	100.0	100.0	100.0	100.0	100.0	100.0	100.0
1991–2005	100.0	100.0	100.0	100.0	100.0	100.0	100.0	100.0	100.0
2006–2020	100.0	100.0	100.0	100.0	100.0	100.0	100.0	100.0	100.0
2021–2035	100.0	100.0	100.0	100.0	100.0	100.0	100.0	100.0	100.0
2036–2050	100.0	100.0	100.0	100.0	100.0	100.0	100.0	100.0	100.0
Panel 6	D-O: total benefits (traditional *payable*) as a percent of current-law *scheduled* benefits								
1946–1960	96.4	96.8	96.4	98.1	96.3	95.9	95.2	97.8	95.2
1961–1975	86.3	87.1	86.2	87.8	86.7	86.0	85.0	88.3	85.2
1976–1990	85.2	85.9	85.9	86.5	85.7	85.6	84.8	85.5	83.9
1991–2005	83.5	83.9	83.5	84.9	84.0	83.7	83.0	84.2	82.4
2006–2020	81.2	82.3	81.6	82.0	81.5	81.2	80.4	82.0	80.5
2021–2035	79.6	80.2	80.1	80.3	80.0	79.4	78.5	80.6	78.9
2036–2050	80.4	80.9	80.4	81.0	80.9	80.4	79.6	80.6	79.7

Source: Author's calculations.

proposal is anything but balanced with regard to the fiscal treatment of different cohorts as shown by lifetime net tax rate calculations—a metric that is the most meaningful in this context. Furthermore, note that under DEMSIM's calculations, those rates would have to be increased even more because the Diamond-Orszag proposal does not achieve financial solvency for Social Security—whether measured on an annual basis or summarized over 75 years, or in perpetuity.

An increase in future generations' lifetime net tax rates—as under the Diamond-Orszag proposal—is sometimes justified by observing that future generations are likely to be wealthier than current ones and a rising lifetime net tax rate schedule is consistent with a progressive cross-generational tax structure. Proponents of such a policy simply *assume* that future generations will be more productive and enjoy higher earnings and wealth levels. However, imposing a steeply progressive cross-generational Social Security tax schedule may reduce future generations' incentives to acquire skills and remain as productive as today's generations thereby preventing that assumption from being realized. Thus, attempts to impose a lifetime net tax rate schedule as steeply progressive as that under the Diamond-Orszag proposal could lead to a realized cross-generational schedule that is even *more* progressive.[9]

Examining the cells of panel 1 carefully shows that nonwhites and males bear larger lifetime net tax rates compared to whites and females, respectively—explained by shorter longevity and retirement life spans of the former two groups.

Among most white and non-white female cohorts, high lifetime earners bear larger lifetime net tax rates under the Diamond-Orszag reform proposal. This is explained by the proposal's support for survivors, which predominantly turns out to be women. Note that according to panel 1 of table 7.1, low-earning individuals have shorter life spans, and recall that under DEMSIM, males and females sort according to their education levels when marrying. These two features imply that low-earning women would marry earlier-dying husbands and receive greater support from the proposal's increased generosity toward widow(er)s. In addition, low-earning women would gain from the proposal's low-earner PIA enhancement.

Among white and non-white men, however, the opposite is true: low lifetime earners bear larger lifetime net tax rates under the proposal. This is simply explained by the fact that low-earners have shorter lifetimes and collect benefits for fewer years—as table 7.1 shows.

Effects on Retirement Wealth

One of the issues explored in this book is the extent to which Social Security enables people to prepare for retirement without consideration of
past payroll or other taxes that participants may have paid into the system.
The metric of retirement wealth shows the size of Social Security wealth as
a share of lifetime resources as of each DEMSIM individual's year of collecting Social Security benefits. This wealth ratio is calculated as the actuarial present value of Social Security benefits under the reform divided by
lifetime earnings, where both are calculated as of each individual's benefit
collection date.

The metric is shown under two definitions of benefits—those scheduled
under the reform, and those payable under it after imposing an across-the-
board benefit cut to bring total expenditures within available tax revenues
once the trust fund is exhausted. Because traditional payable benefits are
subject to a large degree of (political) risk if a proposal leads the trust fund
to be fully depleted those benefits are discounted at a higher than riskless
rate of interest of 5.0 percent to calculate the retirement wealth metric.

The third and fourth panels of table 9.2 show stable overall Social Security retirement wealth ratios for successive birth cohorts (under the "All"
column) beginning with those born after 1991—today's children and future-born generations. Adults among the current population, however,
enjoy much larger retirement wealth—again the consequence of sparing
most of them from the proposal's adjustment costs.

Examining panel 4 carefully shows that most high lifetime earners have
a smaller share of their lifetime earnings devoted to retirement via Social
Security (under the payable benefits calculation)—which is as expected
because of the progressivity of Social Security's benefits and the ceiling on
income subject to payroll taxes. Panel 4 also shows that whites and women
receive more in retirement support relative to their lifetime earnings compared to non-whites and men, respectively. Again, this is consistent with
their greater longevity (whites and women), lower earnings relative to
benefits (women), and collection of auxiliary benefits (women).

Although Social Security wealth levels computed in this manner reveal average retirement resources contributed by the program as a share
of lifetime earnings, the interest here is to evaluate how each reform increases or reduces retirement wealth compared to current laws. Panel 6
of table 9.2 shows the percentage of current-law scheduled benefits provided by payable benefits under the Diamond-Orszag proposal.[10] Again,
the Diamond-Orszag proposal almost fully preserves the Social Security

Incorporating Diamond-Orszag Reform Elements into DEMSIM

Adjustments for Increasing Longevity

The description of the mortality adjustments used by the Social Security's Office of the Chief Actuary (see Diamond-Orszag 2005, appendix G) makes it clear that the availability of a microsimulation provides considerable advantages. For example, this Diamond-Orszag reform element involves calculating the additional cost of benefit payouts because of increasing longevity. Implementing this requires calculating the ratio of two present values of benefits for the "typical" retiree in each cohort beginning at the normal retirement age. For example, for the cohort aged 59 in 2009—the first cohort for whom the cost factors will be calculated—the ratio's numerator is the actuarial present value of benefits based on the mortality assumptions for 2008 (contained in the Trustees' 2005 Report) and the denominator is the similar calculation based on mortality in 2009 (contained in the Trustees' 2006 Report).

One possible advantage of a microsimulation such as DEMSIM is that it keeps track of the changing composition of the population: For example, the share of the non-white population is projected to increase over time. That means overall mortality reductions are likely to be large during early years when the share of non-whites is low. Average rates of mortality reductions gradually decline in future years as the population share of non-whites—who continue to have higher mortality rates, on av-

retirement resources of today's adults. By the time today's newborns begin to collect Social Security benefits later in this century—by which time all of Diamond-Orszag reform measures would be fully phased in—their Social Security benefits would be about 80 percent as those scheduled under current Social Security laws.

Final Remarks

The net result of the Diamond-Orszag reform proposal under DEMSIM projections is to reduce Social Security's 75-year open group imbalance by about 80 percent and the infinite horizon open group imbalance by almost 90 percent of their baseline values, respectively. However, when measured appropriately, the Diamond-Orszag proposal does not fulfill its important goal of providing a balanced approach to resolving Social Security's financial shortfall. The focus on balancing tax-side and benefit-side reforms ignores the fact that Social Security enforces lifelong participation through payroll taxes and benefits—and any evaluation of whether the distribution of adjustment costs are balanced must be done on a lifetime basis across different population groups, especially across different generations.

The proposal heavily emphasizes tax-side adjustments, protects most current adult generations, and imposes large adjustment costs on today's children and future generations. The authors' justification for this policy is to simply assert that future generations would be better off compared to current ones—an assumption that may not be realized in part because of the much higher lifetime net tax rates imposed on future generations under their reforms.

The Diamond-Orszag proposal delivers sizable reductions in Social Security's open group imbalance ratio—of almost 2.7 percentage points under the 75-year horizon (compared to the current-law ratio of 3.4 percent of payrolls) and more than 4 percentage points under the infinite horizon projection (compared to a 4.8 percent ratio under current laws). But near preservation of current generations' benefits and the steep escalation of lifetime net tax rates on successive future generations means that their proposal reduces the closed group imbalance by just 23 percent.

erage, compared to whites—increases. The procedure used here employs mortality projections by year, age, gender, and race calibrated using data from the National Center for Health Statistics (see appendix 3.1). The two present values of benefits in the ratio described above are calculated as prescribed in Diamond and Orszag (2005).[11]

Using DEMSIM has yet another advantage: For each cohort, the ratio can be calculated using aggregate actuarial present values of benefits across members of that cohort using individual benefit histories derived from a prior implementation of DEMSIM under baseline assumptions. First, that means each individual's benefit receives an equal weight in the calculation—which is consistent with defining the "typical" worker. Second, the increase in the present value of benefits from life-span extension means that *terminal-year* benefits would be extended. This is important for those whose benefits increase upon the death of a spouse, especially if average periods of widowhood increase gradually over time.

The use of microsimulated benefit histories allows the extension of terminal-year benefits throughout each individual's potential lifetime (through age 99 under DEMSIM) when calculating actuarial present values of benefits under alternative mortality rates.

Implementing the mortality adjustment for Diamond-Orszag reforms requires computation of PIA adjustment factors as rolling 75-year averages of the ratios computed above for each cohort (defined by the year in which its members are 59 years old). The results under DEMSIM show that mortality improvements occur rapidly soon after 2009 but the rate of improvement declines over time—confirming the conjecture made above. The 75-year average of the ratios beginning in 2009 equals 0.9930—an improvement by 0.7 percent per year on average. By 2080, however, the 75-year forward average improvement declines to 0.50 percent per year. These ratios can be used directly to construct the PIA and payroll tax adjustment factors—which is yet another advantage of using a microsimulation: unlike the SSOCACT (Social Security Office of the Chief Actuary) method, there is no need to further adjust these factors for scheduled increases in the normal retirement age of each birth cohort because those increases are already incorporated in the individual benefit histories of DEMSIM individuals.

Following the specification in the Diamond-Orszag reform, one half of the implied mortality improvement of 0.7 percent (that is, 0.35 percent) is applied toward reducing PIA bend point values of new retirees beginning in 2012. Again, following the reform's specifications, the adjustment applied to payroll taxes equals 85 percent of the adjustment applied to the bend point factors each year. See Diamond and Orszag (2005) for more details on this calculation procedure.

Adjustments for Rising Inequality

Chapter 8's discussion showed that the ratio of taxable-to-total payrolls is projected to increase under DEMSIM's baseline assumptions. The Diamond-Orszag proposal requires this ratio to reach 87 percent by 2063. However, the ratio already increases to 88 percent by the late 2020s under DEMSIM's baseline assumptions—the result of a declining share of individuals with high labor earnings as the boomers retire. Thus, on this score, the reform element is implemented to just prevent the taxable-to-total earnings ratio from declining beyond the initial 75-year horizon. An appropriate adjustment is applied to the taxable earnings ceiling to maintain the ratio at 87 percent throughout the future.

The second adjustment, which is intended to impose higher costs on higher lifetime earners, is a gradual reduction in the marginal benefits awarded to those to whom the highest bend point in the Social Security's PIA formula is applicable. The 15 percent bend point factor is gradually reduced for new retirees after 2012 to reach 10 percent by 2031 and is maintained at 10 percent thereafter. This adjustment is applied before implementing the PIA factor adjustment for declining mortality as described earlier.

Under the Diamond-Orszag proposal, high-earners' payroll taxes are also increased through the legacy charge—a 3 percent surcharge on payroll taxes on earnings above the taxable maximum ceiling. This legacy charge is to be levied without any concomitant increases in benefits. The legacy charge is further enhanced through a "residual" charge—an additional surcharge, which increases by 0.51 percent each year, to the 3 percent legacy payroll tax rate. The residual charge is also applied to (a) benefits via a reduction in PIA factors by 0.3 percent per year and (b) to the payroll tax rate on earnings below the taxable ceiling via an increase in the tax rate by 0.255 percent per year.

Adjustments to Strengthen Social Insurance Functions

In addition to these changes, the Diamond-Orszag plan increases aged survivor benefits to 75 percent of the benefits that both spouses would have received had the decedent spouse been alive. Implementing this reform element is complicated because it requires first finding the average PIA across all Old Age and Survivor Insurance (OASI) beneficiaries in "current beneficiary status" in each future year—that is, receiving benefits in those years. This calculation is implemented during a prior run of DEMSIM under baseline assumptions. In the next run, the reform element is introduced by calculating the widow(er) benefit enhancement as the smaller of two amounts: (1) 75 percent of the couple's benefit if the spouse were alive (including all benefit reductions or increases for the widow[er]'s retirement age, where applicable) and (2) 75 percent of the couple's benefit if the spouse were alive, assuming the widow(er)'s PIA equals the average PIA across all beneficiaries in current benefit status in the year when the widow is first eligible for this benefit enhancement. It is important to note that it is not just those DEMSIM individuals receiving a widow(er) benefit under the baseline run that gain from this reform element. For example, a survivor with an identical earnings and retirement history as the decedent spouse's would receive no net increase in benefits from entering widowhood compared to her own benefits prior to widowhood. However, under this Diamond-Orszag reform provision, her benefit as a survivor would increase by 50 percent apart from any adjustments for early or late retirement.

The last Diamond-Orszag reform element enhances low-earners' benefits—to provide a boost to those who worked for at least 20 years with average earning at or below that for a minimum wage worker. This element is also incorporated into DEMSIM exactly as described in the report by Social Security's Office of the Chief Actuary and in Diamond and Orszag (2005).

CHAPTER TEN

Centrist Proposal 1 by Representatives Jim Kolbe, Charles Stenholm, and Allen Boyd

"Bipartisan Retirement Security Act"

"Axis of unfunded liabilities . . . Medicare, Medicaid, and . . ."—if that line was not written with Social Security in mind, it should have been.—Allen Boyd

Middle of the Road by Popular Acclaim?

Many Social Security reform proponents have described their approaches as "bipartisan," "balanced," or "centrist."[1] But what constitutes a middle-of-the-road approach, and which proposals should be included under this category? The answer to the first question is quite simple and non-controversial: after defining liberal and conservative approaches and identifying their preferred reform measures, one should label proposals that include elements from both in a reasonably balanced manner as centrist.

Proposals such as those by Robert M. Ball and Peter Diamond and Peter Orszag are described as "liberal" simply because they adhere to the principles and objectives of those on the political left: explicitly, to maintain Social Security's current financing structure as far as possible, to protect the benefits of existing participants—especially of current retirees—and to increase the program's receipts to close future financial shortfalls, in effect, maintaining future participants' benefits at current-law levels. The result of this approach, as seen in chapters 8 and 9, is that an overwhelming share of the program's adjustment costs are imposed on future generations.

Very few liberal proponents of Social Security reform support investments in private capital markets. Among those that support such investments, most emphasize using trust fund surpluses for direct government purchases of private financial securities to increase the program's non-tax income. Under the liberal approach, any increase in Social Security's surpluses intended for such investment should be obtained through payroll tax increases (the "add-on" approach), not through reductions of scheduled Social Security benefits.[2]

In contrast, the conservative approach emphasizes transforming the traditional Social Security system into one that includes personal accounts to promote private ownership of retirement assets, greater individual control over how retirement savings are invested, and increased ability for people to bequeath their retirement savings—features that are not available under the current Social Security system. Under most conservative approaches, Social Security personal accounts would be funded through the diversion ("carve-out") of a portion of existing payroll taxes. This approach implies a gradual move away from the program's current financing structure that channels retirement resources through the government irrespective of whether the introduction of personal accounts improves the system's overall financial solvency or not.

Under the conservative approach, any steps to improve the system's solvency would be implemented through reductions of scheduled benefits of mostly middle and upper wage earners. This could be accomplished either through a larger-than-actuarially-fair benefit offset to compensate the Social Security program for payroll taxes redirected into personal accounts or through progressive reductions of scheduled Social Security benefits by altering the benefit formula.[3]

A centrist approach, then, should combine such liberal and conservative reform features in a roughly balanced manner. It would include the creation of personal accounts via either add-on or carve-out methods (or both), and it must balance Social Security adjustment costs aimed at achieving financial solvency between revenue increases and benefit cuts. But which of several candidate proposals that are advertized by their authors as balanced really deserve the "centrist" label? This poses a conundrum: the question is impossible to answer *before* examining any candidate proposal's effects on the program's taxes and benefits and the nature of proposed personal accounts. However, after detailed examination, it may turn out that the proposal's popular description as "centrist" (or "liberal" or "conservative") is not appropriate because its tax (benefit) measures are considerably weaker than its benefit (tax) measures, and personal accounts appear larger (smaller) than they really are when all features and constraints are considered in full. The approach followed here is to simply select for examination two proposals that are generally accepted as being centrist and, later, two others that are popularly viewed as being conservative. Detailed examination of all of the proposals' features should reveal whether their popular labels are well deserved.

Jim Kolbe, Charles Stenholm, and Allen Boyd

Many Social Security reform proposals include elements consistent with both conservative and liberal principles. Among recent reform proposals—those made during the G. W. Bush administration—the earliest centrist-sounding proposal was put forth by Representatives Jim Kolbe (R-AZ) and Charles Stenholm (D-TX), as the "Twenty-first Century Retirement Act" of 2001. That proposal was later revised into the "Bipartisan Retirement Security Act" in 2004, and still later as the Kolbe-Boyd "Bipartisan Retirement Security Act of 2005."[4]

This proposal, which henceforth will be called Kolbe-Stenholm-Boyd (KSB), seems to satisfy the above mentioned conditions to qualify as a centrist proposal. Lawmakers from both political parties have supported it, and it has been described as a balanced approach to fixing Social Security by prominent scholars. For example, Ed Lorenzen of the Centrist Policy Network—a Washington, DC, think tank—praises the Kolbe-Boyd Social Security reform proposal as a "model of bipartisanship" that provides a "responsible personal accounts plan," "honestly accounts for transition costs," and introduces "progressive benefit changes" to improve the safety-net functions of the system.[5] In public debates, the description of the KSB proposal as centrist, however, is based simply on a listing of its tax- and benefit-side reform elements. To what extent it is actually centrist can be known only after each of its reform elements has been evaluated for its impact on Social Security's financial condition and on taxpayers and beneficiaries of different birth cohorts.

The other "centrist" proposal evaluated (in chapter 11) is that by Jeffrey Liebman, Maya Macguineas, and Andrew Samwick, all of whom have earned strong credentials as academic and policy experts on Social Security's operations and financing. Their proposal also appears as a balanced collection of adjustments to Social Security's revenues and benefits, including personal accounts financed in equal measure by diverting present-law payroll taxes (carve-out financing) and increasing payroll revenues (add-on financing). And, in contrast to the widespread praise of the KSB proposal, it has been strongly *criticized* by both liberals and conservatives.

Features of the Kolbe-Stenholm-Boyd Reform Proposal

The KSB proposal includes 14 reform elements, all of which are evaluated except those pertaining to the Disability Insurance program.[6] The detailed modeling of Social Security's current rules under DEMSIM's Social Security calculator (SSTBC) enables a precise implementation of each reform element as prescribed by the proposal.[7] The KSB proposal's elements include the following:

1. Introduce personal accounts by redirecting 3 percent of the first $10,000 of earnings and 2 percent of earnings beyond $10,000 up to the taxable maximum ceiling into personal accounts from just the employee portion of the payroll tax. Only those younger than age 55 would be affected beginning in 2006. Distributions from such personal accounts would be subject to income taxes. The personal accounts investments would be directed by the individual in a federal individual security account.

   This provision diverts current payroll taxes from the traditional Social Security system and, therefore, would be expected to worsen the traditional program's 75-year and infinite horizon open group imbalances. The income taxation of future personal accounts benefits (in the form of account withdrawals or income from annuities) would provide an offsetting effect. The estimation of revenues from subjecting personal account benefits to income taxes is described later in this chapter.

2. The KSB proposal reduces the 32 percent and 15 percent (the two "upper") primary insurance amount (PIA) factors by 2.5 percent each year between 2013 and 2031. Between 2032 and 2061, all three PIA factors—including the "lowest," 90 percent factor—are reduced by 1.5 percent each year. These factors convert a worker's average indexed earnings into the full retirement benefit— called the Primary Insurance Amount (PIA)—which is then modified depending on whether the worker retires earlier or later than the applicable Social Security's normal retirement age, whether there are "excess earnings" from working while collecting benefits, and so on.

   The PIA factors are designed to introduce progressivity into the calculation of benefits based on past indexed earnings. Those with larger lifetime earnings receive less than proportional increases in retirement benefits compared to those with smaller lifetime earnings. Reducing PIA factors in this manner results in smaller benefits—and the benefit reductions become larger over time for successive retiree cohorts. Reducing during the first few years just the PIA factors applicable to high-earners (the "upper" PIA factors) makes the conversion even more progressive compared to the current benefit formula. And the reductions are cumulative over many decades. Hence, this reform element is likely to reduce the growth of future benefits by a significant amount.

3. Reduce post-retirement cost-of-living adjustments to benefits by 0.4 percentage points annually. This is intended as a permanent reduction in the rate of cost-of-living increases and is to be applied in every future year to the benefits of all except new retirees in the current year.

    The cost-of-living adjustments would affect *current* retirees as well because it commences in 2005. Imposing some of the adjustment cost on current retirees means the adjustments imposed on future generations can be smaller. This reform element distinguishes the Kolbe-Stenholm-Boyd proposal from liberal ones.

4. The KSB proposal would transfer funds from the federal government's general account to Social Security under a specified schedule. The transfer amounts are stated as percentages of annual taxable payrolls beginning with 0.02 percent in 2007 and growing to 0.57 percent in 2065 and thereafter.

    Note that unlike some other plans that are evaluated in later chapters, these transfers are not open-ended. That is, they are not intended to close the program's financial shortfalls "whatever they turn out to be." However, they would clearly extend the system's solvency without any impact on current participants' payroll taxes or benefits. Which groups end up footing the bill depends on how the transfers are financed. The reform proponents envision funding the transfers out of additional non–Social Security revenues to be generated through cost-of-living adjustments in other parts of the federal budget—for example, by slowing the increase in nominal income tax brackets that would generate additional non–Social Security revenues. Needless to say, the distributional effects of this measure are not estimated under DEMSIM.

5. The KSB proposal would begin the increase in the normal retirement age from 66 to 67 in 2013—four years earlier than scheduled under current law. The ultimate normal retirement age remains at 67. This element is also a benefit-side adjustment because actuarial benefit reductions for earlier-than-normal retirement age would apply to earlier retiring cohorts than under current law.

    Note however, that the proposal leaves the ultimate normal retirement age at 67 as under current laws. That means the proposal would do little to restore the program's original role—in the context of chapter 7's discussion.

6. Modify actuarial benefit-reduction and benefit-increase factors for retirement at earlier- and later-than-normal retirement age. The benefit reductions for early retirement apply to workers' own and spousal benefits and are specified under the KSB proposal in a schedule beginning after 2012. If individuals do not adjust the timing of retirement and benefit collection, this reform element would result in cost savings for Social Security.

   This reform element is intended to provide higher marginal increases in benefits to those choosing to remain in the work force for longer and collect benefits later. As such, it will almost surely promote such behavior—implying a feedback effect on participants' timings of retirements and benefit collections. The costs and revenue effects of such behavioral feedbacks, however, would not be visible under DEMSIM because its evaluation is based on a fixed temporal sequence of demographic and economic outcomes, including the timing of retirements. The absence of cost and revenue effects from such feedbacks could lead to a mismeasurement of the total impact of this reform element on Social Security's finances.[8] Calibrating DEMSIM to include such feedback effects, even if it were practical, would require knowledge of labor supply elasticities of individuals nearing retirement under different family configurations.[9]

7. The KSB proposal would adjust PIA levels to reflect changing life expectancy for those newly eligible in 2012 and later. This provision is similar to the first Diamond-Orszag reform element: the PIA would be reduced based on measured changes in remaining "period life expectancy" at age 62. Period age 62 life expectancy three years before the retiree becomes 62 years old is compared with period age 62 life expectancy in 2009 to determine the reduction. That means, if the retiree turns age 62 in 2018, period tables of life expectancy in 2015 and 2009 would be used for the calculations. The amount of the PIA reduction would equal the percentage increase in age 62 life expectancy in 2015 relative to life expectancy in 2009.

8. Increase the number of years used in calculating average indexed monthly earnings. Currently, the 35 years of highest earnings are used. Dividing the sum of indexed earnings during those years, including zeros if those are among highest earnings, by 420—the number of months in 35 years—yields average indexed monthly earnings. This provision would gradually increase the number of years of earnings to eventually include all working years beginning with age 22 in the numerator. And it would increase the number of years in the denominator to 40 by the year 2021.

   This reform element would reduce benefits because increasing the number of years of earnings in the numerator reduces average indexed earnings by bringing in smaller earnings (possibly more years of zero earnings) into the calculation. In addition, the denominator is increased to, again, reduce average indexed monthly earnings.

9. The KSB proposal would redirect revenues from income taxes on Social Security benefits that are currently allocated to the Hospital Insurance program back to Social Security. This would bring in a small amount of additional revenue to Social Security and reduce its open group imbalance.

   This reform element would not directly change anyone's Social Security lifetime net tax rate calculated on the basis of scheduled benefits. It would, however, worsen Medicare's financial status, and the impact on family budgets would depend on which additional adjustments are imposed to offset the financial impact on Medicare.

10. The KSB proposal would establish a minimum PIA for low-earning workers. This provision applies to retired, spousal, and survivor benefits and seeks to protect low-earners' benefits from being reduced significantly by its other reforms. The minimum PIA calculation is applied to those with PIAs that are less than the minimum poverty level of income. However, the minimum PIA applicable to any potential retiree increases the longer that worker's history of labor force participation is. That means those with longer work histories at low earnings would receive better protection. The link to work histories makes this provision consistent with Social Security's philosophy of providing larger retirement income protections to those who choose to remain in the work force for more years.

11. The KSB proposal would increase the taxable earnings ceiling gradually to attain a ratio of taxable-to-total earnings of 87 percent. As mentioned in earlier chapters, it is not necessary to implement any policy change to achieve this objective under DEMSIM: DEMSIM's baseline assumptions already project an increase in the taxable-to-total earnings ratio beyond the target of 87 percent by the mid-2020s. As in the Diamond-Orszag proposal, the only change implemented is to increase the ceiling toward the end of the 75-year horizon (and beyond) to maintain the ratio at or above 87 percent.

12. The KSB proposal would redesign the bend point formula for converting workers' average indexed monthly earnings (AIME) into their primary insurance amounts. Recall that AIME is the monthly average over the highest 35 earnings indexed using the average wage index; bend points are dollar cut-offs that determine segments of AIME that are converted into the PIA and that are increased each year according to growth in economy-wide average wages. For example, the bend points for 2005 were set by the Social Security Administration at $627 and $3,779. The conversion of AIME to PIA is done using fixed percentages called bend point factors—which this KSB reform element would change.

A new, fourth bend point factor would be added to the three existing ones—90, 32, and 15. The new bend point factor would be set to 32 as of 2005, making the new set of bend point percentage factors 90, 32, 32, and 15. The new (second) bend point factor would be associated with a new bend point (dollar amount) that is 192 percent larger than the first, making it equal to $1,204 for 2005.

Because the second bend point factor is identical to the third in 2005, there would be no change in benefits for new retirees in 2005. Beginning in 2006, the second bend point factor is increased by 3.8 percent each year to reach and stabilize at 70 percent by the year 2015. The third bend point factor would be reduced to 20 percent by 2015. The net impact of this reform element would be to make benefits more generous for low-earners and less generous for high-earners. However, if there are many more low-earners—and the earnings distribution becomes significantly skewed toward low-earners in the United States—then this reform element could increase Social Security's open group imbalance. DEMSIM takes changes in the earnings distribution over time into account when estimating this reform element's impact.

13. The KSB proposal would increase widow(er) benefits to equal 75 percent of the benefit that the couple would have received had the decedent spouse survived. This reform element, again, mimics that from the Diamond-Orszag proposal, except that it is made effective in 2007 (instead of 2012 as under Diamond-Orszag). It is implemented accordingly under DEMSIM.

14. The final KSB reform element limits Social Security spousal benefits to constrain the couple's benefits to the benefit of a single worker with lifetime earnings equivalent to that of a worker with career maximum earnings—one who earns at the taxable maximum level during every working year. This measure would reduce disparities in the treatment of single workers versus married single-earner couples (where just one spouse works). Under current rules, the latter family type receives higher benefits per dollar of payroll taxes and reduces the incentives of secondary earners to participate in the work force. Limiting the spousal benefit in this manner would reduce the current disparate treatment of singles and married single-earner couples thereby improving incentives to work.

Effects of Kolbe-Stenholm-Boyd Reforms on Aggregate Social Security Finances

Although the Kolbe-Stenholm-Boyd proposal has the largest number of reform elements, implementing them turned out to be quite straight-forward. Reform elements 1–8, 10, and 12–14 involve applying relatively straightforward parametric changes within SSTBC's computer code. Reform element 9 requires estimating revenues from income taxes on Social Security benefits transferred to the Hospital Insurance program. Fortunately, the Medicare Trustees' Annual Report for 2006 provides projections of revenues from those receipts. The annual ratios of those revenues to projected payroll taxes (exclusive of those transfers) are applied for corresponding years to DEMSIM's simulated payroll tax revenues in each future year. The ratio for years beyond 2080 is assumed to remain at its value for 2080. Finally, reform element 11 is implemented only for maintaining the taxable-to-total earnings ratio above 87 percent in the distant future—years when that ratio gradually declines below the KSB proposal's 87 percent threshold under DEMSIM's baseline assumptions.

Table 10.1 shows results from implementing each element separately. The first reform element involves two steps. First, 3 percent of the first $10,000 of taxable earnings and 2 percent of the remainder of those earnings are diverted to personal accounts. Those funds are accumulated at an assumed rate of return based on a 50–50 stock-bond portfolio of 4.45 percent.[10] At retirement the accumulated funds are used to purchase an annuity—a single-life annuity for single individuals and a joint-life annuity for those who are married in the year of retirement. The annuity calculation is described in detail in appendix 12.1.

The second step of obtaining revenue flows from personal account annuities is implemented by first adding up annuity flows across all individuals in each year after 2006 and applying year-specific revenue ratios to those aggregates. The revenue ratios are calculated from the 2006 Social Security Trustees' report as the ratio of Old Age and Survivor Insurance (OASI) plus Health Insurance revenues from the income taxation of Social Security benefits to total benefits.[11] The Health Insurance program's current revenue share in income taxes on Social Security benefits is included because the KSB proposal requires those revenues to be redirected back to Social Security.

Table 10.1 shows that introducing such personal accounts would, by themselves, increase Social Security's 75-year imbalance by $4.4 trillion—from $7.0 trillion under DEMSIM's baseline to $11.4 trillion (see the second row of table 10.1, which shows the cumulative impact of the introducing personal accounts and subjecting personal accounts benefits to income taxes). The infinite horizon imbalance would increase by $5.8 trillion—from $13.4 trillion to $19.1 trillion. However, the table suggests that this net reduction in the program's revenues would be more than offset by the second reform element (shown in row 3 of the table)—which reduces Social Security benefits by reducing PIA factors (the two upper bend point factors of 15 and 32 percent through 2031 and all bend point factors thereafter through 2061).

Implemented by itself, the second reform element would reduce Social Security open group imbalance by $4.9 trillion within the 75-year time frame (from $7.0 trillion to $2.1 trillion) and by $12.0 trillion (from $13.4 trillion to $1.4 trillion) in perpetuity. Other benefit-side reform elements (specifically, items 3, 5–8, and 14) make those benefit reductions deeper and reinforce the impact of the second reform element to reduce Social Security's financial imbalances—and compensate for the diversion of revenues into personal accounts.

The only benefit-side reform element that *increases* benefits by itself is the introduction of an additional bend point in the PIA formula (reform element 12). This provision increases the benefits of those with low AIMEs and reduces benefits of those with high AIMEs. However, because lifetime earnings are skewed toward the low end of the distribution—that is, a significant number of DEMSIM individuals have relatively low AIMEs—reform element 12 increases benefits, on balance. Notice, however, that its effect is almost fully offset by the proposal's modification of the AIME formula (item 8) by adding additional earning years into the wage-indexed benefit calculation. For many individual with long spells of voluntary or involuntary non-participation in the work force between the ages of 22 and 62, this reform element would increase the number of zeros among maximum earnings that are included in the AIME calculation. In turn, a lower AIME leads to a sizable reduction in retirement and other benefits based on such earnings histories.

The KSB proposal would also increase Social Security's revenues by redirecting revenues currently dedicated to the Hospital Insurance program (item 9) and increase the taxable maximum earnings ceiling (item 11). Under DEMSIM, however, the latter reform is implemented only during the out-years of the 75-year horizon and beyond: DEMSIM's baseline projections already project an increase in the taxable-to-total earnings ratio to levels well above the 87 percent threshold recommended by KSB. Overall, the stand-alone impact of the proposal's revenue increasing elements (items 1b, 4, 9, and 11) are rather weak. Note that item 9 does not increase taxes but simply redirects taxes from the Hospital Insurance program to Social Security. But even when it is included, the total effect of the four revenue-side measures equals $2.2 trillion over 75 years and $3.3 trillion

TABLE 10.1 **Impact of the Kolbe-Stenholm-Boyd Reform Proposal on Social Security's (OASI) Finances**

| | Post-reform actuarial imbalance | | | | | | | | |
| | Present values in billions of constant 2007 dollars | | | As a percent of DEMSIM-baseline taxable payrolls | | | Change in actuarial imbalance as a percent of DEMSIM-baseline taxable payrolls | | |
Proposed Policy Change	75-year open group	∞-horizon open group	Closed group*	75-year open group	∞-horizon open group	Closed group	75-year open group	∞-horizon open group	Closed group*
1. Establish personal accounts									
1a. Redirect payroll tax revenues	11,681	19,720	17,422	5.60	7.02	11.97	2.25	2.26	2.23
1b. Income taxes on personal account benefits†	11,390	19,142	17,120	5.46	6.81	11.76	2.11	2.06	2.03
2. Reduce PIA factors††	2,066	1,413	8,986	0.99	0.50	6.17	−2.36	−4.25	−3.56
3. Reduce COLA by 0.4 percent per year	6,241	12,530	13,402	2.99	4.46	9.21	−0.36	−0.30	−0.53
4. Transfer from general fund to OASI trust fund	6,208	12,625	14,172	2.98	4.49	9.74	−0.37	−0.26	0.00
5. Shorten hiatus in increase in normal retirement age	6,834	13,213	14,022	3.28	4.70	9.63	−0.07	−0.05	−0.10
6. Modify actuarial reduction and increment factors	6,531	12,687	13,749	3.13	4.51	9.44	−0.22	−0.24	−0.29
7. Modify PIA for changes in life-expectancy	5,941	9,250	13,076	2.85	3.29	8.98	−0.50	−1.46	−0.75

8. Cover more than 35 years in AIME calculation	5,220	12,371	2.50	3.75	8.50	−0.85	−1.01	−1.24
9. Redirect benefits tax revenue from HI back to OASI	5,853	14,172	2.81	4.18	9.74	−0.54	−0.57	0.00
10. Establish minimum PIA level	6,986	14,174	3.35	4.76	9.74	0.00	0.00	0.00
11. Increase taxable limit to cover 87 percent of earnings	6,962	14,172	3.34	4.71	9.74	−0.01	−0.04	0.00
12. Redesign the PIA formula (add a new bend point)	8,828	16,041	4.23	5.78	11.02	0.88	1.03	1.28
13. Limit widow(er)s benefits to 75 percent of couple's	7,101	14,312	3.41	4.84	9.83	0.06	0.08	0.10
14. Limit spousal benefits to maximum worker's benefits	6,832	14,018	3.28	4.68	9.63	−0.07	−0.08	−0.11
Simple sum of changes	2,188	9,551	1.05	−0.35	6.56	−2.30	−5.11	−3.17
Total effect of implementing all reforms together	3,369	10,498	1.62	0.66	7.21	−1.73	−4.10	−2.52
Memoranda:								
DEMSIM-baseline imbalance	6,985	14,172	3.35	4.75	9.74	…	…	…
DEMSIM-baseline taxable payrolls	208,495	145,572	…	…	…	…	…	…

*Shown as a percent of closed group taxable payrolls.

†Value cumulated with previous row. Annuities calculated using the same rate of return as applied to personal account contributions.

in perpetuity—far short of the revenue loss from redirecting payroll taxes into personal accounts of $4.7 trillion over 75 years and $6.4 trillion in perpetuity (item 1a compared to DEMSIM baseline imbalances), respectively.

When all KSB reform elements are implemented simultaneously, table 10.1 shows that the 75-year imbalance is reduced by $3.6 trillion—from $7.0 trillion under DEMSIM's baseline to $3.4 trillion. In perpetuity, the imbalance is reduced by a sizable $11.5 trillion—from $13.4 trillion to just $1.8 trillion. That is, most of the proposal's improvement of Social Security's finances would emerge in the distant future—toward the end of the 75-year horizon and later.

Not surprisingly, the imbalance on account of past and living generations—the closed group imbalance—remains relatively high at $10.5 trillion, down by $3.7 trillion from its baseline value of $14.2 trillion. Thus, out of the proposal's total adjustment of $11.5 trillion, living generations contribute $3.7 trillion whereas future generations contribute $7.8 trillion. That is, current generations bear 32 percent of the total adjustment proposed under this reform. In this sense, the program is more "balanced" than the Diamond-Orszag proposal—which imposes only 28 percent of its (albeit slightly larger) total adjustment on current generations. In other words, the Kolbe-Stenholm-Boyd proposal appears to be slightly more fiscally responsible than the Diamond-Orszag proposal because the former makes current generations accountable for a larger share of their net unfunded benefits from the Social Security program under baseline policies.

Table 10.1 shows that the simple sum of all reform elements would result in a sizable cut in the 75-year and infinite horizon open group imbalances. Indeed, the latter would become negative at −$995 billion. However, because the provisions interact with each other when implemented simultaneously—the effects of items 10 and 13 become stronger because they prevent benefits of low lifetime earners and widows from being reduced drastically by the proposal's other reform elements—the joint impact on the 75-year and infinite horizon open group imbalances is smaller.

In terms of ratios to the present value of baseline taxable payrolls under joint implementation of all reform elements, the 75-year open group imbalance that remains unaddressed under the KSB proposal equals 1.6 percent. In perpetuity, the remaining imbalance equals 0.7 percent of taxable payrolls. Both values are larger than the simple sum of the reforms' separate effects of 1.1 percent over 75 years and −0.4 percent in perpetuity.

Table 10.1 also shows the change in the closed group measure as a ratio of closed group taxable earnings. This is the fraction by which living generations' human capital resources would be reduced, on average, as a result of the KSB proposal. When all KSB reforms are implemented together, the reduction equals 2.5 percent (last column of table 10.1)— slightly larger than the corresponding estimate of 2.3 percent under the Diamond-Orszag proposal (see table 9.1).

Effects on Annual Imbalance Ratios

The above evaluation shows that the Kolbe-Stenholm-Boyd proposal significantly reduces Social Security's open group imbalances but does not eliminate them under both the 75-year and infinite projection horizons, though the reduction is larger under the latter horizon. This can also be seen in the proposal's impact on annual imbalance ratios as shown in figure 10.1.

This figure shows that the KSB proposal initially generates larger annual Social Security's deficits through the mid-2020s—the consequence of immediately diverting revenues into personal accounts. As its other reform measures gather strength, annual imbalances under the KSB proposal

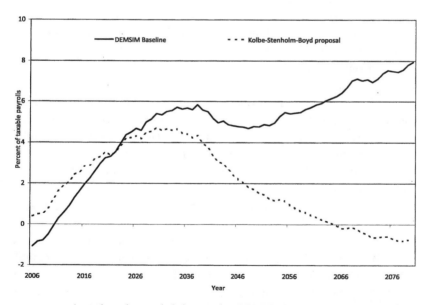

FIGURE 10.1. Annual non-interest imbalance ratios: DEMSIM baseline and Kolbe-Stenholm-Boyd reform proposal. Source: Author's calculations.

gradually become smaller than under DEMSIM's baseline projections. Peak annual imbalances occur during the early 2030s. They decline consistently thereafter, become negative after the year 2065, and remain negative thereafter. The entire positive imbalance under the Kolbe-Stenholm-Boyd Social Security reform proposal arises within the first 75 years. Because of accumulating Social Security surpluses after 2070, the infinite horizon open group imbalance ratio is smaller than the 75-year open group imbalance ratio.

Lifetime Net Tax Rate Effects

How would different population groups fare under the KSB reform proposal? Table 10.2 shows lifetime net tax rates by 15-year birth cohorts, gender, race, and lifetime earnings. It shows lifetime net tax rates for just the traditional Social Security program—not including contributions into and benefits from personal accounts. How those contributions and benefits would be distributed under the KSB proposal is shown in a later segment of table 10.2.

As in table 9.2, the first panel of table 10.2 shows lifetime net tax rates under the KSB proposal when all of its reform elements are implemented simultaneously. Panel 2 of the table shows percentage point differences between the rates of panel 1 and those under DEMSIM's baseline assumptions (panel 11 in table 7.1) for corresponding population groups. As is evident from the differences shown in panel 2, the Kolbe-Stenholm-Boyd proposal reduces lifetime net tax rates for most birth cohorts. The main reason for this result is the diversion of a portion of existing payroll taxes into personal accounts. The other reform elements—cuts in scheduled benefits and increases in the program's receipts—obviously do not fully compensate for diverted payroll taxes for most population groups.

Notice that the KSB proposal is progressive in implementing reductions in average lifetime net tax rates for the traditional Social Security program: within each birth cohort, gender, and race category among those born after 1960, those earning less than median lifetime earnings experience larger percentage point reductions in their average lifetime net tax rates. Most increases (or the absence of change) in average lifetime net tax rates occur in groups with higher-than-median lifetime earnings. In other words, the proposal implements smaller benefit cuts and tax increases for low-earners.

TABLE 10.2 **Effects of Kolbe-Stenholm-Boyd Reforms on Selected Population Groups**

		Female				Male			
		Non-White		White		Non-White		White	
Years of Birth	All	E≤Med	E>Med	E≤Med	E>Med	E≤Med	E>Med	E≤Med	E>Med
Panel 1	Traditional Social Security lifetime net tax rates under the KSB proposal								
1946–1960	5.15	4.6	5.4	4.0	5.1	6.3	6.5	6.2	5.9
1961–1975	5.88	5.5	6.1	4.8	5.9	6.5	6.7	6.4	6.5
1976–1990	5.56	5.4	5.6	4.8	5.5	6.2	6.0	5.8	6.1
1991–2005	5.73	5.6	5.7	5.1	5.7	6.3	6.0	6.1	6.1
2006–2020	5.79	5.7	5.8	5.2	5.7	6.2	6.1	6.1	6.2
2021–2035	5.79	5.7	5.7	5.2	5.7	6.1	6.0	5.9	6.1
2036–2050	5.76	5.7	5.7	5.1	5.7	6.0	6.0	6.0	6.2
Panel 2	Percentage point increase in lifetime net tax rates: KSB minus DEMSIM baseline								
1946–1960	0.1	0.0	0.0	0.0	0.2	-0.2	0.0	-0.1	0.2
1961–1975	-0.2	-0.4	-0.2	-0.3	0.0	-0.8	-0.4	-0.5	0.0
1976–1990	-0.6	-0.7	-0.5	-0.5	-0.3	-1.2	-0.7	-0.8	-0.4
1991–2005	-0.4	-0.6	-0.3	-0.3	-0.1	-1.2	-0.6	-0.8	-0.3
2006–2020	-0.3	-0.4	-0.3	-0.1	0.0	-0.9	-0.5	-0.7	-0.1
2021–2035	-0.1	-0.4	-0.1	0.1	0.1	-0.9	-0.3	-0.5	0.0
2036–2050	0.0	-0.2	0.0	0.3	0.2	-0.7	-0.2	-0.4	0.1
Panel 3	Total Social Security wealth as a share of lifetime earnings (*scheduled* traditional benefits; %)								
1946–1960	4.0	5.1	3.5	5.6	3.8	3.4	2.5	3.6	2.6
1961–1975	3.9	4.6	3.5	5.3	3.7	3.5	2.9	3.8	2.9
1976–1990	3.7	4.2	3.5	4.8	3.5	3.3	2.9	3.8	2.8
1991–2005	3.3	3.6	3.0	4.2	3.1	2.9	2.6	3.3	2.6
2006–2020	3.2	3.5	2.9	4.1	3.0	3.0	2.6	3.2	2.6
2021–2035	3.1	3.4	2.9	3.9	3.0	3.0	2.6	3.4	2.5
2036–2050	3.1	3.5	2.7	4.1	2.9	3.0	2.5	3.3	2.5

TABLE 10.2 (continued)

		Female					Male			
		Non-White		White			Non-White		White	
Years of Birth	All	E≤Med	E>Med	E≤Med	E>Med		E≤Med	E>Med	E≤Med	E>Med
Panel 4										
Total Social Security wealth as a share of lifetime earnings (*payable* traditional benefits, %)										
1946–1960	3.1	3.9	2.7	4.3	2.8		2.6	1.9	2.8	2.1
1961–1975	3.0	3.5	2.7	4.0	2.8		2.7	2.3	2.8	2.2
1976–1990	3.3	3.7	3.1	4.3	3.2		3.0	2.7	3.3	2.6
1991–2005	3.2	3.5	2.9	4.0	3.0		2.9	2.6	3.2	2.5
2006–2020	3.1	3.5	2.9	4.0	3.0		3.0	2.5	3.2	2.5
2021–2035	3.1	3.4	2.8	3.9	2.9		3.0	2.5	3.3	2.5
2036–2050	3.1	3.4	2.7	4.1	2.9		3.0	2.5	3.3	2.5
Panel 5										
Percent of Social Security wealth provided by KSB traditional benefits (*payable* definition)										
1946–1960	94.0	95.2	93.7	96.0	94.7		94.9	91.6	95.0	92.1
1961–1975	78.0	83.8	78.0	84.8	80.0		82.3	75.1	79.7	71.8
1976–1990	65.3	72.4	65.8	74.6	67.0		68.8	62.8	67.8	57.3
1991–2005	60.7	67.5	60.9	70.0	62.3		63.9	58.5	61.7	52.8
2006–2020	61.0	67.5	61.1	69.9	62.4		65.5	57.8	61.7	53.5
2021–2035	61.0	67.1	61.0	69.6	62.3		65.7	58.3	63.0	53.7
2036–2050	61.4	67.4	60.8	70.3	62.4		66.0	58.6	62.4	53.8
Panel 6										
KSB: total benefits (traditional *payable*+IA) as a percent of current law *scheduled* benefits										
1946–1960	73.6	76.9	74.8	75.8	70.0		78.7	72.0	80.1	72.3
1961–1975	74.5	79.4	75.4	77.0	72.1		86.1	78.8	79.4	71.2
1976–1990	83.9	88.1	83.4	84.8	79.8		97.9	86.9	90.2	81.9
1991–2005	81.4	86.2	80.8	81.9	77.0		96.2	83.7	89.6	79.0
2006–2020	80.0	84.3	80.7	81.1	75.1		90.5	83.0	90.1	77.3
2021–2035	78.3	82.8	77.7	79.0	73.9		89.7	78.7	85.8	76.0
2036–2050	77.9	82.1	77.7	78.2	73.9		89.2	78.5	85.3	75.2

Source: Author's calculations.

The second panel of table 10.2 also shows that declines in lifetime net tax rates would become smaller and eventually reverse themselves for successive birth cohorts (looking down each column in panel 2 of the table). The largest reductions traditional Social Security's lifetime net tax rates would be enjoyed by those born in the 1976–90 and 1991–2005 birth cohorts, especially by males with low lifetime earnings. Under the KSB proposal, these two birth cohorts receive an opportunity to redirect their payroll taxes into personal accounts without suffering steep declines in their traditional benefits because changes to traditional scheduled benefits are phased in only gradually. Later-born cohorts, however, receive steeper cuts in scheduled Social Security benefits that, eventually, more than make up for the effect of the diversion of payroll taxes on lifetime net tax rates. The largest impact of cuts in traditional benefits arises for women who receive smaller benefits on their own past earnings and as dependents and survivors under KSB reforms.

A careful look at the second panel of table 10.2 shows that the reductions in the traditional program's lifetime net tax rates are more generous toward non-whites compared to whites, males compared to females, and those with lower lifetime earnings compared to those with higher ones. Again, the smaller reductions in lifetime net tax rates for women compared to men arises from the aforementioned cuts in spousal and survivor benefits because in most families, females are secondary earners and are longer lived than their male spouses.

Evaluating KSB Individual Accounts

Obviously, an evaluation of Kolbe-Stenholm-Boyd reforms would be incomplete without examining the individual accounts component. The proposal describes several rules about how contributions to individual accounts would be invested: mandatory investments by Social Security participants in a federally administered security account that would aggregate transactions with private investment funds, liberalization of portfolio regulations after accumulated funds reach a critical threshold, and so on. These rules imply that account holders would eventually be permitted to hold combinations of stocks and bonds in their individual accounts making the portfolio riskier than holding just government bonds. But riskier portfolios would also earn higher rates of return, on average, than the "riskless" rate earned on an all-government-bond portfolio. Indeed, this

aspect of individual accounts constitutes the chief attraction for many proponents of Social Security private accounts.

Note that the present values of individual account contributions should
not be simply added to lifetime net taxes to re-estimate the lifetime net tax
rates shown in panel 1. Even if they were mandatory, those contributions
are not intended to be viewed as taxes because the accounts are owned
by participants. Moreover, they generate retirement and other benefits
(including any voluntary or involuntary bequests at the end of life) whose
present value would be identical to the present value of individual account contributions. Despite being carved-out of existing payroll taxes,
such individual accounts are a qualitatively different (although an integral)
part of the new Social Security program that would emerge from KSB reforms. An integrated view of both the traditional and individual accounts
sections of the reformed program can be obtained under the retirement
wealth metric discussed below.

Measuring Retirement Wealth under Individual
Accounts Reforms

Many analysts evaluate the effects of the reformed traditional Social Security program separately from the reform's individual accounts component.
In the politically polarized debate on this issue, some analysts go so far as
to ignore the latter—unwilling even to consider individual accounts as an
integral part of the reformed Social Security system. Indeed, some people
view the introduction of individual accounts as tantamount to "destroy-
ing" the existing Social Security system. That view is obviously incorrect
because personal accounts supplement retirement resources provided
by the traditional system and yield other advantages that should not be
ignored.[12]

On the other hand, some analysts habitually extol the benefits of individual accounts exclusively, entirely disregarding the potentially significant improvements in the traditional Social Security program that a
reform proposal may introduce, making the latter a useful complement
to individual accounts—to provide basic retirement security without the
economic distortions and inequities created under the current program.

Because Social Security today could be viewed as a program that, on
balance, acts more as a substitute for personal saving than as an insurance
program, it is important to find out just how much the resulting hybrid of

traditional Social Security and individual accounts would provide by way of retirement resources. In the chapter 9 evaluation of Diamond-Orszag reforms, the impact of Social Security reforms on various population groups' retirement wealth compared post-reform traditional Social Security payable wealth with that based on current-law scheduled benefits. That approach can be easily extended by evaluating Social Security wealth as the sum of the present value of traditional payable benefits and the accumulated value of individual account contributions, both evaluated as of each DEMSIM individual's benefit collection year. The ratio of this wealth to the present value of lifetime earnings—also evaluated as of the benefit collection year—is the retirement wealth metric.

Thus, the numerator of the retirement wealth metric under proposals that create individual accounts includes two elements: the present value of traditional benefits under the proposed reform and the accumulated value of individual account contributions, both evaluated as of each individual's benefit collection year. The traditional Social Security wealth component is calculated as the present value of payable (or scheduled) benefits using a 5.0 percent discount rate. The trust fund is exhausted in the year 2023 when the KSB reform proposal is implemented under DEMSIM. A higher than riskless discount rate is used because lack of program solvency implies uncertainty about how future policy changes would affect benefits. Since each DEMSIM individual's post-reform Social Security benefits terminate upon death, averaging Social Security wealth levels across members within particular population subgroups accounts for mortality risk, making the wealth measure an actuarial average present value of payable Social Security benefits under the KSB proposal.

The second component of the numerator equals the value of individual account contributions accumulated through each DEMSIM individual's benefit collection year. At what rate of return should those contributions be accumulated? Many proponents of Social Security personal accounts suggest using much higher than riskless interest rates—those available on average on private capital investments. But doing so would ignore the risks involved in such investments that could necessitate additional taxpayer costs.

The KSB proposal, for example, prescribes that individual account investment would be managed in a federally administered individual security account similar to the federal employee Thrift Savings Plan. However, when workers' balances in such accounts become larger than a preset threshold, they would be eligible to add any of a range of certified privately administered individual security accounts to their portfolios. With access to broader investment choices, including investments in risky market securities, some individual account holders would do worse than others, and some may suffer losses because of bad investment decisions notwithstanding regulations designed to lower market risks. Given recent evidence about distorted incentive structures, inappropriate regulation, and poor performance of a whole range of financial sector companies—a wide dispersion of investment outcomes despite restricting investments to ex ante "safe" securities is clearly not out of the question.

Moreover, although portfolio restrictions may limit the dispersion of returns across investors at a point in time, market returns may be positively correlated over time. They may remain high for some cohorts during long-lasting economic booms. And they may remain low for others during many years of their lifetimes under long-lasting productivity slowdowns or recessions. Finally, workers could be exposed to market-return volatility just when they wish to withdraw funds or purchase annuities upon retirement.

Would the government offset individual account returns of particular cohorts—especially those who suffer steep losses—by adjusting payroll taxes and benefits under the traditional Social Security system or otherwise providing financial "bailouts?" Increasingly, the answer appears to be in the affirmative: it appears nearly impossible for elected government officials to resist providing such relief—especially if capital market losses are widespread. Such implicit or explicit government guarantees for individual accounts are highly likely—especially within the context of Social Security. The cost of providing such government guarantees—that would ultimately fall on taxpayers—should be subtracted from the expected return on individual account assets before making comparisons between pre- and post-reform Social Security wealth levels.

By how much should private market returns be adjusted in calculating individual account wealth at retirement? The simplest approach is to assume that the cost of providing a full guarantee would equal the cost of eliminating fully the risk of losses on individual account investments. Assuming that capital markets operate efficiently in the long term (a very important assumption) that cost would equal the difference in expected returns on risky individual account investments and the "riskless" rate of return on long-term government bonds. Hence, a conservative, and more appropriate, calculation of individual account wealth at retirement would accumulate account contributions at the riskless rate of return. Data from

Ibbotson Associates on rates of return on the safest long-term financial securities—government bonds—suggest that the riskless rate of return averages about 2.5 percent per year and exhibits very low long-term variability.[13]

However, personal Social Security accounts also confer some advantages to their owners. They enable holders to match investment risks with their preferences, expand portfolio choices, optimize their desired degree of annuitization, better protect benefits from political risks, improve labor market incentives, and so on. Some allowance should be made to reflect that owners reap such advantages from their Social Security personal accounts. These considerations motivate a slight increase in the accumulation rate on personal account contributions. A 3.0 percent rate of return is used in the calculations reported below.[14]

Retirement Wealth under KSB Reforms

Panels 3 and 4 of table 10.2 shows the share of Social Security wealth in lifetime earnings for selected population groups under the KSB proposal. Panel 4 shows that using payable traditional benefits, similar to the Diamond-Orszag proposal, the KSB proposal increases retirement wealth by about 1 percentage point of lifetime earnings for current middle-aged and younger birth cohorts, on average (compare with panel 4 of table 7.2)—similar to the Diamond-Orszag proposal. Moreover, KSB reforms improve the retirement wealth of low lifetime earners to the same degree as under the Diamond-Orszag proposal, despite the latter's stronger benefit enhancements for such groups. A careful visual inspection of the columns in the retirement wealth ratio panels of tables 7.2, 9.2, and 10.2 within each race-gender grouping confirms this claim. This result is the consequence of KSB's progressive implementation of individual accounts: low lifetime earners are allowed to contribute larger payroll tax carve-outs into personal accounts. Furthermore, the KSB proposal implements cuts in scheduled benefits that are also quite progressive. Note that increases in (payable) retirement wealth ratios are sizable even for many of today's older generations—including those born soon after 1960—under the Diamond-Orszag reforms but not under KSB reforms. This is consistent with the results of the previous section that show that the Diamond-Orszag proposal preserves the net benefits of today's generations to a greater extent and that KSB reforms are more fiscally responsible.

Panel 5 of table 10.2 shows the relative size of the two components of Social Security wealth in the numerator of the retirement wealth metric. Because today's middle-aged and older workers are able to participate in individual accounts for only a few years and the KSB proposal's changes to scheduled benefits and taxes are phased in gradually, almost all of their Social Security wealth is comprised of traditional benefits: more than 90 percent for those born during 1946–60 and three quarters for those born during 1961–75. For younger and future generations, however, the contribution of traditional benefits to Social Security wealth is stabilized at about 60 percent across successive birth cohorts. The progressive implementation of KSB individual accounts is evident in panel 5 of table 10.2.

Panel 6 of table 10.2 shows how total Social Security wealth under KSB reforms (under a 3.0 percent rate of return on individual accounts) compares with that based on current-law scheduled benefits. A quick look shows that the KSB proposal would provide *less* retirement wealth compared to current-law scheduled Social Security wealth (in actuarial present value terms) to all birth cohorts, but especially to the baby boomers—those born duing 1946–60). As it happens, baby boomer retirements suffer on both counts under the proposal—their traditional payable benefits become smaller because the trust fund is exhausted sooner (2023) under KSB reforms (in turn, because of carve-out financing of individual accounts) and their individual account contributions accrue returns for only a few years because they would retire soon after the KSB proposal is implemented.

Those born after 1960, however, have more years left before retirement and their individual account accumulations—even at an almost "riskless" rate of return—would grow sufficiently to make their total Social Security wealth (based on traditional payable benefits and individual account accumulations) larger, on average, under the KSB proposal and closer to Social Security wealth based on current-law scheduled benefits. Needless to say, for all of the birth cohorts shown in the table, post-KSB-reform Social Security wealth as defined here is much smaller than Social Security wealth under current-law *scheduled* benefits (compare panel 5 of table 10.2 with panel 5 of table 7.2).

Final Remarks

Individual accounts confer many advantages, but they are conventionally associated with reduced government ability to redistribute resources from richer to poorer families as well as within families depending on survivorship and dependency outcomes. However, evaluation of the KSB reforms in this chapter clearly rebuts the first of these conventional views. Indeed, this proposal increases the retirement wealth of low-earners by more than that of high-earners—and by similar magnitudes as under the Diamond-Orszag proposal.

The other criticism of Social Security personal account reforms—the inability to redistribute within families to counter dependency and survivorship-related financial vulnerabilities—is also not necessarily true. Conventional wisdom backed by empirical evidence suggests that families privately purchase inadequate life insurance to protect secondary earners and non-earning spouses.[15] As a result, the introduction of carve-out individual Social Security accounts may increase financial vulnerability among women who tend to outlive their male spouses. An easy way to avoid such outcomes is to require that contributions into personal accounts be divided—not necessarily equally—between the accounts of both spouses within dual headed families. The KSB proposal, however, does not include such a provision.[16]

Finally, KSB's carve-out Social Security individual accounts would reduce lifetime earnings risk pooling across workers and birth cohorts via the traditional Social Security program. The current Social Security system provides such risk pooling because initial retirement benefits under current Social Security rules are indexed to growth in economy-wide wages from past years. That makes benefits dependent on the productivity and wage growth experiences across population groups widely separated along birth year and other dimensions. However, KSB and other reform proposals include measures that weaken such risk sharing under the traditional Social Security system. Although the results discussed in this chapter help to clarify the effects of KSB reforms on the Social Security's aggregate financial condition and on individuals' lifetime net tax rates and retirement wealth levels, they do not illuminate any aspects of pooling or sharing macroeconomic risks across different population groups via Social Security. However, to the extent that Social Security now operates mostly as a retirement savings substitute, much of the risk-pooling benefits from Social Security may have been offset through changes in private behavior: lower private domestic saving, reduced work effort, less acquisition of human capital, and greater dependence on foreign savings—some of which may be the result of adopting social insurance programs—that may have increased underlying macroeconomic risks, on net, for U.S. residents.[17] Such considerations make it extremely difficult to measure the benefits of risk pooling and risk sharing across generations. Isolating such effects is well beyond the scope of this book.

CHAPTER ELEVEN

Centrist Proposal 2 by Jeffrey Liebman, Maya MacGuineas, and Andrew Samwick

"A Nonpartisan Approach to Reforming Social Security"

The advantages of this plan are straightforward. It achieves sustainable solvency, maintains retirement income levels, and is the most fiscally responsible plan released in recent years.
—Jeffrey Liebman

The second centrist reform proposal that is analyzed here is by Jeffrey Liebman, professor of economics at Harvard's Kennedy School and currently executive associate director at the office of Management and Budget; Maya MacGuineas, director of the Fiscal Policy Program at the New America Foundation and erstwhile advisor to Senator John McCain; and Andrew Samwick, professor of economics at Dartmouth College and erstwhile chief economist with the Bush administration.[1] All three proponents have a long history of academic research in Social Security policy—which lends this Social Security reform proposal considerable gravitas as a potentially carefully crafted policy.

In addition, the affiliation of all of the proposal's authors with Democratic and Republican administrations and policymakers confers on it considerable credibility as a well balanced compromise between opposing perspectives on Social Security's future direction. The authors were reportedly motivated to discover whether a common ground could be found without unduly surrendering the goals of either side—in effect, by adhering to the "principles of compromise without compromising one's principles." Since its release in December 2005, some Social Security analysts, academic economists, and lawmakers have praised it as an example of a reform that would be superior to what is likely to occur under a lop-sided control of Congress and the administration by either party.[2] These observations motivate its inclusion among the two "centrist" plans evaluated in this book.

Similar to some of the reforms evaluated earlier in this book, the Liebman-MacGuineas-Samwick (LMS) reform proposal includes progressive changes to taxes and benefits and prescribes mandatory personal accounts with mandatory conversion of account assets into annuities upon retirement. In addition, the proposal provides many detailed specifications on changes to Social Security benefits and payroll taxes that would arise during any negotiation between liberal and conservative policymakers before reform legislation is finalized—more so than under many other proposals.

The LMS proposal's even-handed approach extends to its personal accounts components as well. Such accounts would be financed out of both "add-on" and "carve-out" methods. As a result, the proposal has been criticized by both liberals and conservatives. Although conservatives applaud carve-out personal accounts, they dislike earmarking any additional resources for Social Security and disagree with the LMS proposal's add-on financing of such accounts. Under their perspective, additional resources for the program in any form would only increase political incentives to provide more generous benefits.

On the other hand, although liberals don't oppose personal accounts with unanimity, they uniformly reject carve-out financed personal accounts because larger short-term Social Security cash flow deficits could jeopardize the continued payment of current benefits and political support for the program in general. It remains to be seen whether the LMS approach would eventually garner enough support among policymakers to deliver a Social Security reform that follows its recommendations closely. The purpose here, however, is to evaluate the LMS proposal's implications under DEMSIM's projections—to assess how far it improves the traditional program's finances, how its costs are distributed across birth cohorts and population groups, and how it affects their total Social Security retirement resources.

Elements of the Liebman-MacGuineas-Samwick Reform Proposal

The LMS plan is made up of four reform elements: It reduces scheduled Social Security benefits by gradually decreasing primary insurance amount

(PIA), or bend point, factors and by increasing retirement ages. Reductions in scheduled benefits are implemented in a progressive manner—"but not so much as to undermine support for the universal social insurance system." The goal of increasing the retirement age is to improve labor market outcomes—by encouraging people to work longer—but also to keep replacement rates high despite the aforementioned cuts in scheduled benefits.

The proposal also increases Social Security's revenues by increasing the taxable labor earnings ceiling. As with reform proposals evaluated earlier, the objective of this measure is to make the program's revenue side more progressive and to restore the ratio of taxable to total income to 90 percent—its value before it began to decline.

The program requires the creation of mandatory personal accounts funded by contributions equal to 3 percent of (pre-reform) Social Security taxable earnings. However, the contributions would initially be funded out of the existing Social Security Trust Fund until it is exhausted—after which it would be partly funded out of new worker contributions and partly out of current payroll taxes.

The LMS proposal's other adjustments provide minimum benefits for low-earners, increase widow(er)'s benefits, reduce spousal benefits, and introduce progressive matches for personal account contributions. It's quite clear that many of these proposals—especially the adjustments to the existing Social Security rules—are similar to those of the Kolbe-Stenholm-Boyd proposal. The distinguishing element in the LMS proposal is their avowed emphasis on sharing the adjustment costs equally between revenue increases and benefit cuts and sharing the funding of personal accounts equally via add-on and carve-out elements.

The sizes of the LMS-proposed adjustments and the structure of the equal-sharing provisions are designed with the Social Security Trustees' current-law projections in mind. Given that the trustees' projections are more optimistic than those of DEMSIM—primarily because of the latter's projection of declining labor quality in the future—reform measures calibrated to official Social Security projections are not likely to balance the program's future costs and revenues. Moreover, analysis of the LMS equal-sharing provisions under DEMSIM will reveal whether they are balanced, especially when one considers revenue- and benefit-side effects in perpetuity. Finally, like the Diamond-Orszag proposal analyzed earlier, the plan may not turn out to be balanced in terms of how adjustment costs are distributed across birth cohorts and across different demographic groups. This chapter uses the metrics described earlier to provide a comprehensive picture of the proposal's financial effects on the Social Security program.

The LMS proposal's approach is to ensure that the current system is preserved (a goal of political liberals) while simultaneously introducing personal accounts (a goal for conservatives). The proposal explicitly intends to maintain the Old Age and Survivor Insurance (OASI) program's benefits at the level allowed under the current payroll tax rate of 10.6 percent. This feature is included to alleviate fears among the program's supporters that any introduction of personal accounts would send the program down "the slippery slope to total privatization."[3]

Under the LMS proposal, the traditional program's benefits would not be allowed to fall below those *payable* under the existing payroll tax rate of 10.6 percent. But the program's benefits would also not be allowed to grow as scheduled under current rules beyond the amount payable out of existing payroll taxes. This is to avoid general revenue transfers that would otherwise become necessary and that would crowd out other federal expenditures, require increases in distortionary taxes, or trigger increased government borrowing. Thus the payroll tax rate of 10.6 percent is preserved throughout the future. But to reduce promised benefits to fit within the *payable* limit, the LMS proposal would reduce scheduled benefits significantly.

Key features of the LMS reform proposal follow:

1. Creation of mandatory Personal Retirement Accounts (PRA) beginning in 2008 for all participants who attain age 55 in 2005 and later. PRAs are funded initially by diverting the Social Security Trust Fund's current annual surpluses—that are today deposited with the Treasury in exchange for non-marketable securities—as long as those surpluses are sufficient to finance required PRA contributions for each worker. When Social Security surpluses are no longer sufficient to finance 1.5 percent of required PRA contributions, trust fund contributions per worker are maintained at 1.5 percent of taxable payrolls with the remainder coming from additional payroll taxes up to 1.5 percent of taxable earnings under current law.

    After a worker becomes eligible for Social Security benefits, distributions from PRAs would only be in the form of an annuity. The LMS proposal requires married couples to purchase joint-and-two-thirds survivor annuities. LMS claim that remaining traditional benefits together with PRA annuities would provide roughly the same level of benefits as scheduled under Social Security's current laws. Whether this claim holds true is examined later in this chapter.

As is well known, allowing participants to choose the fraction of their PRAs to be annuitized is likely to increase the program's cost: those with longer expected retirement life spans would likely choose to annuitize larger fractions of their PRAs, thereby worsening the annuity provider's longevity risk pool and forcing a reduction in annuity interest rates. Such adverse selection would reduce the size of annuity payouts for those who convert PRAs into annuities—that is, those with longer post-retirement life expectancies and, therefore, most in need of retirement support when very old. On the other hand, not allowing participants to choose the share of their PRAs to annuitize penalizes those with shorter expected post-retirement lifetimes—especially minority groups—just as under current Social Security rules.

Trading off these conflicting concerns—perhaps by requiring only partial annuitization to ensure annuities at the poverty level—rather than specifying mandatory full annuitization of PRAs would preserve greater choice in disposing of retirement assets and would be more consistent with a centrist and balanced approach. Another problem with mandatory full annuitization of PRAs is the risk of facing a depressed stock market just when one is about to retire. This risk is especially evident under recent capital market conditions. Partial annuitization or requiring purchases of deferred annuities at the time of making PRA contributions would be more consistent with insuring against sudden adverse capital market conditions.

2. Like the reform proposals evaluated earlier, the LMS proposal also seeks to increase the taxable earnings ceiling in order to increase the taxable-to-total earnings ratio—and as another means of making the system's revenue side less regressive. This ratio equaled 90 percent during the early 1980s but has declined since. Recall from chapter 8 that this ratio equals 85.6 percent in 2006 under DEMSIM's baseline projections—and that DEMSIM's estimate is quite close to the official estimate of 83.3 percent.

But under DEMSIM, the ratio of taxable-to-total payrolls is already scheduled to *increase* under baseline assumptions—to 87 percent in just a few years after 2006 and to remain between 87 and 89 percent throughout the 75-year time horizon after 2006 (see chapter 8's discussion of this result). The LMS proposal, however, targets this ratio to attain 90 percent by 2017—to restore it to its early 1980s value. Achieving that objective requires speeding up only slightly the rate at which the ratio increases under DEMSIM's baseline assumptions. This is implemented by increasing the taxable maximum earnings ceiling—beginning in 2008—by as much as needed to attain the target ratio of taxable-to-total earnings in 2017. Thereafter, the taxable ceiling is increased as and when necessary to maintain the ratio at 90 percent. Note that any increase in taxable earnings from this LMS reform element is not included in the base for calculating the additional 1.5 percent PRA contribution under the first LMS reform element above.

3. The LMS proposal reduces scheduled benefits by even more by bringing forward and extending currently scheduled increases in the normal retirement ages (NRA) of various birth cohorts. The current schedule of increasing the NRAs of successive birth cohorts contains a hiatus: the NRA is scheduled to increase for those attaining age 62 between the years 2000 and 2004; it is maintained at age 66 for those attaining age 62 between 2005 and 2016; and NRA increases resume for those becoming 62 years old between 2017 and 2022—until it reaches age 67 for those reaching age 62 in 2022 and later. The LMS proposal eliminates the hiatus so that the NRA increase continues (by 2 months for every year's advance in the year of attaining age 62) until it reaches age 68 for those becoming 62 years old in 2017.[4]

4. Benefits are reduced in various ways—primarily by reducing the PIA "bend point" factors—90, 32, and 15 percent—gradually beginning in 2008. The 15 percent PIA factor is reduced between 2008 and 2045 by 1.8 percent each year, to end up at 7.5 percent in 2045 and later. That means, highest earners would now receive a much smaller marginal increment in benefits per additional dollar of average indexed earnings. The 32 percent PIA factor is reduced at the same rate beginning in 2013 so that it becomes 16 percent in 2050 and later. Finally, the 90 percent PIA factor is reduced by 0.75 percent per year beginning in 2013 to end up at 67.6 percent for newly eligible beneficiaries in 2050 and later.

These reductions in PIA factors cumulatively result in very significant benefit reductions compared to current-law scheduled benefits. For example, a person beginning benefit collection at the normal retirement age in 2050 would have PIA factors of 67.6, 16.0, and 7.5. Calculations wherein average indexed earnings in constant 2006 dollars are converted into PIAs using the PIA factors applicable in 2007, 2030, and 2050 under the LMS proposal show that new retirees in 2030 with monthly indexed earnings of $2,600 (in constant 2006 dollars) would have their benefits reduced by 20 percent compared to a new retiree with the same real average monthly indexed earnings under current laws.[5] For new retirees in 2050 the benefit reduction would become as large as 37 percent. And benefit cuts are even larger for those with larger average monthly indexed earnings. This makes the program considerably more progressive at high earnings levels compared to current Social Security laws.

According to LMS, this rate of benefit reduction for successive generations of new retirees is structured to match the rate at which those retirees would accumulate assets in Personal Retirement Accounts as proposed by LMS. That means, benefits from the combination of traditional Social Security and PRA annuities would be maintained at about the same level as scheduled under the current Social Security system. Whether this claim is correct is examined below.

Note, however, that under the LMS proposal, PIA factors undergo a reduction phase after which they are stabilized at new, lower levels. The factors are not indexed to, say, human longevity increases in a way that would stabilize aggregate benefits as a share of taxable earnings. The absence of such indexation of benefits has implications for the program's long-term annual imbalances and total present value of financial imbalances—as described below.

5. Other features of the LMS plan: Although the plan specifies other reform elements—such as a low-earner minimum benefit and provision of more generous widow(er) benefits—these reform elements would exert a very small impact on the program's financial imbalance and are not analyzed separately. Further, LMS claim that their plan does not specify any general revenue transfers to Social Security: under official estimates of its effects by the Social Security's Office of the Chief Actuary, the plan was not projected to require general revenue transfers and had among the smallest cumulative deficits when compared to all other reform plans.[6] Under DEMSIM's projections of larger baseline imbalances, however, it is unlikely that such transfers could be avoided—as shown below.

The LMS Proposal's Impact on Social Security's Aggregate Finances

The results from implementing the four reform elements of LMS are shown in table 11.1. As before, this table shows the 75-year and infinite horizon open group imbalances and the closed group imbalance from implementing each reform element separately.

Unlike some other reform proposals—for example, conservative ones that are considered in chapters 12 and 13—the LMS proposal does not include any direct, individual benefit offsets to compensate the traditional Social Security program for lost revenues from introducing PRAs. As a result, introducing PRAs by themselves would substantially increase Social Security's open group imbalances. Row 1 of table 11.1 shows that introducing PRAs as specified by LMS increases the 75-year open group imbalance by $3.1 trillion—from $7.0 trillion under DEMSIM's baseline to $10.0 trillion. And the increase in the infinite horizon imbalance is even

TABLE 11.1 **Impact of the Liebman-MacGuineas-Samwick Reform Proposal on Social Security's (OASI) Finances**

| | Post-reform actuarial imbalance | | | | | | Change in actuarial imbalance as a percent of DEMSIM-baseline taxable payrolls | | |
| | Present values in billions of constant 2006 dollars | | | As a percent of DEMSIM-baseline taxable payrolls | | | | | |
Proposed policy change	75-year open group	∞-horizon open group	Closed group	75-year open group	∞-horizon open group	Closed group*	75-year open group	∞-horizon open group	Closed group*
1. Establish Personal Retirement Accounts	10,048	17,552	16,261	4.82	6.24	11.17	1.47	1.49	1.44
2. Increase taxable earnings limit	6,115	11,772	13,562	2.93	4.19	9.32	-0.42	-0.57	-0.42
3. Shorten hiatus in scheduled increase in NRA	5,270	10,696	12,424	2.53	3.81	8.53	-0.82	-0.95	-1.20
4. Reduce PIA factors beginning in 2008	1,313	3,291	9,293	0.63	1.17	6.38	-2.72	-3.58	-3.35
Simple sum of changes	1,791	3,219	9,024	0.86	1.15	6.20	-2.49	-3.61	-3.54
Total effect of all reforms implemented together	2,120	2,446	9,364	1.02	0.87	6.43	-2.33	-3.88	-3.30
Memoranda:									
DEMSIM-baseline imbalance	6,985	13,364	14,172	3.35	4.75	9.74	...	...	...
DEMSIM-baseline taxable payrolls	208,495	281,064	145,572	...	...	...	...	...	...

* Shown as a percent of closed group taxable payrolls.
Source: Author's calculations.

larger—$4.2 trillion—from the baseline value of $13.4 trillion to $17.6 trillion. One half of this increase accrues to the pocketbooks of living generations: the closed group imbalance increases from $14.2 trillion to $16.3 trillion—an increase of $2.1 trillion—from introducing PRAs.

As expected, the second reform provision of increasing the taxable maximum earnings limit has the smallest offsetting impact to the diversion of payroll taxes into PRAs. Row 2 of table 11.1 shows that the 75-year and infinite horizon actuarial imbalance ratios decline by just 0.4 and 0.6 percentage points, respectively, from this reform element as opposed to much larger declines from the two benefit reduction reform elements as shown in rows 3 and 4 of the table (see the last set of columns in table 11.1, which report changes in imbalance ratios).[7]

Eliminating the hiatus under current laws in advancing the normal retirement age provides a sizable reduction in open group imbalance ratios—which decline by 0.8 percent of baseline taxable payrolls over 75 years and by 1.0 percent over the infinite horizon. But reductions in bend point factors in Social Security's benefit formula exert, by far, the largest impact on its open and closed group imbalances. Again, almost one half of the $10.1 trillion decline in the infinite horizon open group imbalance from this reform element—a decline from the baseline value of $13.4 trillion to $3.3 trillion—is accounted for by a decline in the closed group imbalance from $14.2 trillion to $9.4 trillion.

As expected, LMS reforms do not make Social Security sustainable, and not even financially solvent over 75 years under DEMSIM's projections. A 75-year open group imbalance ratio of 1.0 percentage point remains when all LMS reform elements are implemented together. The infinite horizon open group imbalance ratio is 0.9 percentage points—slightly smaller than the 75-year ratio because LMS benefit cuts become fully effective after the 75th year. Table 11.1 also suggests that there is a fair amount of interaction among various LMS reform elements—one that reinforces the reduction in open group imbalance measures over the longer time horizon. The interaction arises because the two benefit-reduction measures reinforce each other when implemented together and their joint effect is larger than the sum of their separate effects when they are implemented independently.

The reduction in the infinite horizon open group imbalance from jointly implementing all LMS reform elements equals $10.9 trillion—a decline from $13.4 trillion under DEMSIM's baseline to $2.4 trillion. Close to one half —about $4.8 trillion—of this reduction is accounted for by a reduction in the closed group imbalance: the net benefits of past and living generations. Thus, the LMS reform proposal divides its total adjustment roughly equally between living and future generations. That means the authors could extend their claim that the proposal is "balanced" to the generational dimension as well. Indeed, out of those proposals considered so far, the LMS reform proposal is the most aggressive in imposing a substantial fraction—44 percent—of its (sizable) adjustment on today's generations. Nevertheless, under the LMS proposal, the implicit debt to past and living Social Security participants equals $9.4 trillion—the result of excluding older workers and retirees from bearing most of the proposal's adjustment costs.[8]

Effects of the LMS Proposal on Annual Imbalance Ratios

Figure 11.1 compares annual imbalance ratios under the LMS proposal with those under DEMSIM's baseline assumptions and two of the reform proposals evaluated earlier. It shows that the LMS proposal would generate Social Security deficits (positive annual imbalances) during the first 75 years arising from the creation of carve-out PRAs. The deficits are much smaller than under the Kolbe-Stenholm-Boyd proposal because the

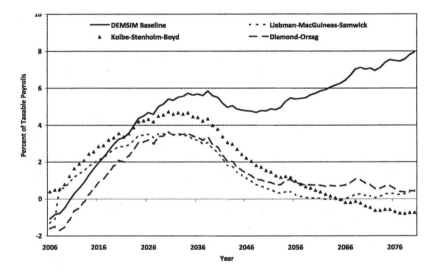

FIGURE 11.1. Annual non-interest imbalance ratios: DEMSIM baseline and Liebman-MacGuineas-Samwick reform proposal. Source: Author's calculations.

LMS carve-out equals just 1.5 percent of taxable earnings compared to the 2–3 percent of taxable payrolls under the former proposal.

Note that figure 11.1 shows LMS annual imbalance ratios trending upward after 2060—a consequence of stabilizing the bend point factors after 2050 rather than indexing them to longevity increases thereafter. This explains why the infinite horizon open group imbalance is larger than the 75-year open group imbalance under LMS reforms—in contrast to KSB reforms (compare with table 10.1).

The LMS Proposal's Impact on Lifetime Net Tax Rates

The foregoing remarks about the LMS proposal pertain only to the traditional system's aggregate financing. How would the proposal's impact be felt across different cohorts and population subgroups? Table 11.2 shows the estimates. As in table 10.2, table 11.2 shows lifetime net tax rates under LMS reforms. When calculating lifetime net tax rates, additional PRA contributions over and above the existing 10.6 percent OASI payroll taxes and the carved-out portion of those payroll taxes are both excluded: these contributions into PRAs are not considered to be taxes because PRAs are owned by workers. Indeed, LMS explicitly state that PRAs are walled off from the federal government (1) to increase the likelihood that PRA contributions would increase national saving—because, unlike trust fund surpluses, they will not be available for financing current government spending—and (2) to help reduce labor market distortions because their owners will not view them as taxes.

Panel 2 of table 11.2 shows the percentage point difference between lifetime net tax rates under LMS reforms and those under the current-law baseline (shown in panel 11 of table 7.2). The "All" column of panel 2 shows that the LMS proposal *increases* lifetime net tax rates, on average, for most younger and future-born cohorts—by between 0.4 and 0.6 percentage points. This result emerges because of sizable reductions in scheduled Social Security benefits specified under the LMS proposal relative to its carve-out PRA funding. Of course, results for particular population groups diverge significantly from the average shown under the "All" column. For example, some birth cohorts of white and non-white males with lower-than-median lifetime earnings would find their lifetime net tax rates unchanged or reduced. This occurs mainly because such groups face relatively small benefit cuts and their benefit collection spans are relatively

TABLE 11.2 **Effects of Liebman-MacGuineas-Samwick (LMS) Reform on Selected Population Groups**

Years of Birth	All	Female				Male			
		Non-White		White		Non-White		White	
		E≤Med	E>Med	E≤Med	E>Med	E≤Med	E>Med	E≤Med	E>Med
Panel 1	Traditional Social Security lifetime net tax rates under the LMS proposal								
1946–1960	5.48	5.1	5.8	4.5	5.3	6.8	6.8	6.6	6.0
1961–1975	6.62	6.4	6.8	5.8	6.5	7.5	7.4	7.2	7.0
1976–1990	6.57	6.4	6.5	5.9	6.4	7.3	7.0	6.9	6.9
1991–2005	6.50	6.4	6.5	5.9	6.4	7.2	6.8	6.9	6.8
2006–2020	6.46	6.3	6.5	5.9	6.3	7.0	6.9	6.8	6.7
2021–2035	6.41	6.4	6.4	5.8	6.2	6.9	6.7	6.6	6.7
2036–2050	6.35	6.3	6.4	5.7	6.2	6.8	6.7	6.6	6.7
Panel 2	Percentage point increase in lifetime net tax rates: LMS minus DEMSIM baseline								
1946–1960	0.4	0.5	0.4	0.5	0.4	0.2	0.3	0.3	0.3
1961–1975	0.5	0.5	0.5	0.7	0.6	0.2	0.3	0.4	0.5
1976–1990	0.5	0.3	0.5	0.7	0.6	-0.1	0.3	0.2	0.5
1991–2005	0.4	0.2	0.4	0.6	0.6	-0.3	0.3	0.0	0.4
2006–2020	0.4	0.2	0.4	0.6	0.7	-0.1	0.3	0.0	0.5
2021–2035	0.5	0.3	0.6	0.7	0.7	0.0	0.4	0.2	0.5
2036–2050	0.6	0.4	0.6	0.8	0.8	0.1	0.5	0.3	0.6
Panel 3	Total Social Security wealth as a share of lifetime earnings (*scheduled* traditional benefits; %)								
1946–1960	3.8	4.8	3.3	5.2	3.6	3.1	2.4	3.2	2.6
1961–1975	3.7	4.3	3.4	4.8	3.6	3.1	2.8	3.4	3.0
1976–1990	3.8	4.3	3.6	4.8	3.7	3.3	3.1	3.8	3.2
1991–2005	3.9	4.2	3.6	4.7	3.8	3.3	3.2	3.8	3.3

2006–2020	3.4	3.8	3.2	3.5	3.8	4.7	3.5	4.2	3.9
2021–2035	3.4	4.0	3.2	3.5	3.7	4.7	3.6	4.2	3.9
2036–2050	3.4	4.0	3.2	3.5	3.7	4.8	3.5	4.2	3.9
Panel 4	Total Social Security wealth as a share of lifetime earnings (*payable* traditional benefits; %)								
1946–1960	2.3	2.9	2.0	2.7	3.2	4.6	2.9	4.3	3.3
1961–1975	2.6	3.0	2.5	2.7	3.2	4.2	3.0	3.7	3.2
1976–1990	3.2	3.7	3.1	3.3	3.7	4.6	3.6	4.1	3.8
1991–2005	3.3	3.8	3.1	3.3	3.7	4.6	3.5	4.1	3.8
2006–2020	3.3	3.7	3.1	3.4	3.6	4.5	3.4	4.1	3.7
2021–2035	3.3	3.8	3.1	3.3	3.6	4.4	3.4	3.9	3.7
2036–2050	3.3	3.8	3.1	3.4	3.5	4.6	3.3	4.0	3.7
Panel 5	Percent of Social Security wealth provided by LMS traditional benefits (*payable* definition)								
1946–1960	92.1	94.8	91.6	94.0	94.6	95.7	93.4	94.6	93.8
1961–1975	71.4	77.3	72.8	79.1	78.5	82.6	76.0	81.5	76.3
1976–1990	55.7	63.1	58.6	62.6	63.6	70.3	61.8	68.1	61.7
1991–2005	52.0	57.1	54.3	57.1	59.0	65.1	57.2	62.5	57.2
2006–2020	52.1	56.2	53.2	58.5	58.7	64.4	56.5	62.1	56.9
2021–2035	52.1	57.2	54.2	58.3	58.5	64.1	56.7	61.5	56.9
2036–2050	52.7	57.1	54.8	59.0	59.0	65.1	56.8	62.2	57.5
Panel 6	LMS: total benefits (traditional *payable* plus IA) as a percent of current law *scheduled* benefits								
1946–1960	82.1	82.1	78.7	79.5	78.9	80.4	80.3	80.8	80.9
1961–1975	85.5	82.6	86.8	83.2	80.7	79.7	82.9	80.7	82.9
1976–1990	102.9	98.8	100.9	102.1	92.8	90.2	95.8	94.3	97.3
1991–2005	105.5	105.4	102.5	106.4	95.2	92.1	98.9	97.7	100.0
2006–2020	101.8	103.9	100.8	99.3	91.9	89.8	96.8	94.9	97.0
2021–2035	98.9	97.9	96.1	97.2	90.1	87.7	93.5	92.9	94.3
2036–2050	98.1	98.2	95.9	97.0	90.0	86.7	93.9	92.5	93.8

Source: Author's calculations.

short, yielding smaller lifetime benefit reductions compared to payroll tax carve-outs during their working lifetimes.

Panel 2 of the table also shows that unlike the KSB reform proposal, the LMS proposal substantially *increases* the lifetime net tax rates of current middle-aged and older generations. These increases arise because LMS-proposed reductions of scheduled benefits and increases in payroll taxes via faster growth in the taxable earnings ceiling begin to outweigh reductions in payroll taxes via carve-out PRAs sufficiently early to affect the net benefits of those alive today. However, the increases in lifetime net tax rates for younger and future generations are much smaller under the LMS proposal compared to the Diamond-Orszag proposal.

Effects of the LMS Reform Proposal on Retirement Wealth

The next questions are the extent to which PRA assets accumulated through the Social Security benefit collection date offset the steep and growing benefit cuts prescribed by the LMS reform proposal; how large are the shares of lifetime earnings devoted to Social Security retirement; and how those shares compare across different population groups. The last three panels of table 11.2 address these questions. Again, these panels are similar to those in table 10.2: only the benefit side is considered in evaluating Social Security's contribution to retirement wealth.

The third and fourth panels of table 11.2 show the retirement wealth metric under LMS scheduled and payable traditional benefits, respectively: the sum of Social Security wealth based on traditional benefits under the LMS proposal and the accumulated value of PRAs by the benefit collection year. Because the LMS proposal does not specify general revenue transfers for financing any transitional financial shortfalls, LMS payable benefits are smaller than LMS scheduled benefits once the Social Security Trust Fund is exhausted. Implementation of the LMS proposal using DEMSIM produces a trust fund exhaustion year of 2026.

Not achieving annual financial solvency, of course, means that post-LMS-reform scheduled benefits are larger than payable benefits. Calculations show that for most population subgroups, differences between LMS scheduled and payable benefits over the next 75 years are much smaller than corresponding differences under current Social Security laws. Nevertheless, post-reform financial insolvency means that traditional benefits could be changed in the future, which justifies using a 5.0 percent annual discount rate (higher than the riskless rate) for calculating present values of traditional benefits. Again, present values of traditional benefits are calculated as of each person's benefit collection year before averaging across members of particular population groups. As noted in chapter 7, the calculated Social Security wealth levels are actuarial calculations that incorporate mortality risks faced by different cohorts and population groups.

Finally, PRA contributions are accumulated using an inflation-adjusted rate of return of 3.0 percent per year—slightly larger than the long-term average rate on very safe financial securities such as long-term government bonds. The higher-than-riskless 3.0 percent accumulation rate is justified by benefits accruing to PRA participants as described in chapter 10: expanded portfolio choices, greater efficiency in consumption and labor market allocations, reduced exposure of retirement assets to political risk, and so on.[9]

Comparing retirement wealth under LMS reforms with that based on current-law scheduled benefits (as represented in panel 6 of table 11.2) shows that the LMS proposal delivers retirement wealth quite close to the current-law scheduled benefits. This is the result of several changes operating simultaneously: reductions in traditional benefits, moderate expansion of the payroll tax base, reductions in payroll taxes from carve-out PRA contributions, and increases in PRA assets from both carve-out and add-on sources. As it happens, the factors making for larger retirement wealth dominate. Indeed, as seen from panel 4 of the table, retirement wealth is stabilized at 3.7 percent of lifetime earnings for future-born cohorts.

Comparing payable retirement wealth under LMS to that under the KSB (panel 4 in table 10.2) and Diamond-Orszag (panel 4 in table 9.2) proposals shows that the former proposal devotes more resources to retirement. This result is, of course, not surprising because, unlike the other two proposals, PRAs under LMS include mandatory add-on financing.

Panel 5 of table 11.2 shows the share of traditional benefits in retirement wealth. It shows that traditional benefits contribute almost entirely to retirement wealth for current older and middle-aged workers. For younger and future-born generations, however, the LMS proposal stabilizes the contribution of traditional benefits at about 55 percent. This is yet another indication of the "balanced" nature of the LMS reform proposal.

Finally, panel 6 shows that retirement wealth under LMS relative to current-law scheduled retirement wealth is roughly comparable across high and low earners—despite the fact that high lifetime earners contribute more into personal accounts than low lifetime earners. This is the result of LMS making progressive reductions of future traditional Social Security benefits.

Summary and Final Remarks

LMS Social Security reforms would implement sizable cuts in current-law scheduled benefits and introduce mandatory personal accounts. However, cuts in scheduled benefits are not linked directly to individual PRA accumulations. Changes to the existing Social Security program and PRA financing are intended to be balanced between tax-side and benefit-side reform elements. However, one of the tax-side reform elements turns out to be weaker than anticipated by the reform's designers—because the ratio of taxable-to-total earnings is projected to increase very close to the LMS target level of 90 percent by 2017. The LMS proposal does not achieve sustainability or 75-year solvency for traditional Social Security. But, overall, it turns out to be reasonably well balanced with regard to the imposition of adjustment costs across living and future generations.

The LMS proposal increases traditional Social Security's lifetime net tax rates for most cohorts and population groups. Moreover, using post-LMS reform traditional payable benefits plus PRA assets accumulated using a conservative real 3.0 percent annual rate of return, the LMS proposal delivers Social Security wealth ratios almost as large as those under current-law scheduled benefits for almost all population groups born after 1975.

One shortcoming of the LMS proposal, however, is the lack of any direct benefit offsets at the individual level that would preserve a close link between payroll tax carve-outs and future benefit reductions. Chapters 12 and 13 explore reform proposals that include individual-level benefit offsets against personal account "carve out" contributions. Another shortcoming of the LMS proposal is the lack of any benefit adjustments linked to future mortality declines. This means lifetime benefits and annual imbalances resume an upward course once all LMS reform element are fully phased in.

Conservative Proposal 1 by the President G. W. Bush Commission to Strengthen Social Security

Model 2

We don't need a special commission to analyze the problem . . . because we already had one, . . . The President's Commission to Strengthen Social Security. . . . It's time to dust off that report, sharpen our policy pencils and get to work on reforming our Social Security system before it's too late. —Edward C. Prescott

Gathering Momentum toward Social Security Individual Accounts

The election of President George W. Bush in the year 2000 was very encouraging for proponents of Social Security privatization.[1] His election campaign was successful despite "touching the third rail" of Social Security reform, including mention of the possibility of introducing personal Social Security retirement accounts.[2] The new administration's emphasis on creating an "ownership society" meshed well with conservatives' long-held desire to transform Social Security—a program that involves high government taxes to finance retirement benefits and one that many conservatives believe should be called "welfare for the middle class"—into a new program whereby individuals would own, control, and dispose of their retirement assets themselves. In many ways this desire to roll back a big government program harks back to the debates prior to the creation of Social Security, when members of the "old right" argued that it would weaken the business sector and reduce the economy's dynamism and growth potential.

The momentum toward greater individual ownership of retirement wealth was already in full swing in the private sector since well before the year 2000. For more than two decades, private employers have been jettisoning defined benefit (DB) pension plans in favor of defined contribution (DC) plans that redirect the choice and responsibility for contributions, portfolio selection, annuitization, and retirement withdrawals in private pension plans from employers to workers.

Assets in DC plans are portable and better suited to a business environment of rapid technological change and labor mobility across jobs and occupations. Moreover, unlike DB annuities, DC assets are better suited for those wishing to leave bequests to their heirs—because they can be safeguarded from federal income taxes. And DC plans allow plan investments to be tailored to match the willingness and ability of their owners, especially younger workers, to trade off safety of principal against the potential for higher investment returns.

For political conservatives, extending these advantages to Social Security is the next logical step. The fact that the program must be reformed—the earlier the better because it faces growing financial shortfalls—provides an opportunity for incorporating into it features similar to those of private DC pensions. Another reason for the strong momentum after the year 2000 toward establishing Social Security personal accounts was that President Clinton's Bipartisan Commission on Entitlement and Tax Reform (Kerrey and Danforth [1994]) also recommended the "exploitation of market investment opportunities" for improving the program's finances, but this could not be pursued when the Clinton administration became mired in the Monica Lewinsky affair. The Clinton commission's recommendations suggested the possibility of bipartisan support in favor of establishing Social Security personal accounts.

One of the Clinton commission's recommendations was to create personal retirement accounts that workers would control and manage. The focus of the Bush administration's Social Security Reform Commission was to finance such accounts by implementing a quid pro quo with the traditional program's future benefit commitments. Workers who choose to participate in the new Social Security individual accounts (IA) system would be allowed to divert a part of their payroll taxes into such accounts, but, in exchange, they would receive reduced future benefits from the traditional program.

The chief justification offered by the Bush administration for this approach was the apparent potential to reap significant investment gains from higher private market returns via personal accounts in contrast to the staid low-single-digit returns on payroll taxes under the traditional system (Moynihan and Parsons [2001]). Unfortunately, conservative promoters of individual accounts did not realize that such a rationale for personal accounts wouldn't work: to the extent that higher *average* returns on private capital investments arise from a risk premium that investors demand, some personal account investors would experience losses and must be made whole in the context of Social Security. Someone must bear the cost of providing such implicit guarantees. If, as intended, everyone participates in the personal accounts program, those costs must fall on the same group of current and future personal account investors. If the market risk premium provides an accurate measure of the underlying risk of losses, subtracting the cost of providing the guarantee on everyone's personal account leaves just the "riskless" rate of return and no more. Thus, although seductive and easy to communicate, higher *average* returns from the risk premium built into capital market returns turn out to be illusory and ill-suited as a fundamental argument for privatizing a fully pay-as-you-go financed Social Security program.[3]

Moreover, to the extent that personal accounts investments are made in "riskless" securities whose returns are also higher than those obtained on payroll taxes via the current Social Security system, this return difference represents the cost of the implicit debt created during Social Security's early years that current and future generations must collectively pay.[4, 5] The charge for servicing the implicit debt, again, leaves the net return from personal accounts equal to that obtained under the current Social Security system on payroll taxes. These are the so-called no free lunch tenets that should be observed when considering Social Security reform alternatives.[6]

As it happened, it proved much more difficult to convince the public about the conservative case for Social Security individual accounts based on the "rate of return advantage" of those accounts. First, financing personal accounts in the manner described earlier would require the creation of large short-term budget deficits from diverting payroll taxes into personal accounts—the quid without an immediate quo of reduced benefit expenditures. Liberal opponents of personal accounts argue that such steep deficits might upset financial markets, raise interest rates, and harm capital formation and economic growth—upsetting the very source of high returns on personal accounts.[7] Second, they suggest that carve-out financed individual accounts would become a separate retirement program, which would make the cost-benefit calculus of the traditional system appear considerably more disadvantaged. That could sap political support for the traditional program and place it on a downhill path to oblivion—ultimately eliminating "valuable social protections" that it provides to low-earners and the middle-class workers.

Third, liberals argue that the large investment gains from carve-out personal accounts that conservatives emphasize would be illusory because the federal government's debt services costs would increase in tandem, implying potentially higher taxes on personal account participants themselves. Finally, the quid pro quo of long-term benefit cuts to pay for diverting current payroll taxes into personal accounts means that such diversions were "just loans" that participants would remain obligated to repay via reduced future benefits even if their personal account investments suffer steep losses.

The public debate during 2005 about the potential benefits from personal accounts was conducted without much empirical support in terms of evaluating their likely impact on different population groups. The scoring of Social Security personal accounts reforms by official budget agencies (the Social Security Administration and the Congressional Budget Office) contain only the impact of the proposals on the program's overall cash flows—the extent of short-term deficits and long-term surpluses within a 75-year projection horizon—a metric well suited to point out the negative government deficit implications of creating carve-out personal accounts but not for indicating any potential long-term benefits.

Excluding from consideration the long-term Social Security surpluses that carve-out personal accounts generate—by adopting a truncated projection horizon—creates a short-term "policy bias" in favor of keeping near-term financial shortfalls low. For example, the G. W. Bush Commission's Model 2—which is evaluated in this chapter—limits personal account contributions to $1,000 per worker as of 2004, with the limit indexed to average wage growth in future years. This limitation on individual account contributions is included to make short-term deficits ("transition costs") low enough to ensure financial solvency over the next 75. Thus, the adoption of a truncated projection horizon seems to have negatively influenced the size of the personal accounts allowed under the G. W. Bush reform proposal.

Although the inconclusive 2005 debate has left the prospects of introducing Social Security personal accounts in limbo, hope has not faded completely for its conservative supporters. The merits and potential mechanisms for adopting personal accounts continue to be discussed behind the scenes. This chapter simply lays out the overall financial implications of a reform proposal that most view as *the* primary conservative plan because it strictly adheres to conservative political principles. That plan is Model 2 described in the final report of the G. W. Bush Commission to Strengthen Social Security, which was published in December 2000. The analysis here reveals Model 2's financial implications for the program's overall finances and for specific population subgroups under DEMSIM's demographic and economic projections. The analysis will show whether Model 2's approach and specifications deliver better results for the program's aggregate finances and for different population groups based on the metrics used in this book.

Reform Elements under Commission Model 2

The Bush Commission's Model 2 is a quintessentially conservative plan and provides a framework for many other conservative Social Security reform proposals by lawmakers, academics, and other Social Security reform advocates. As under the centrist reform proposals evaluated earlier, Model 2 also includes personal accounts. However, unlike centrist proposals, Model 2 does not advocate any payroll or other tax increases and seeks to pay for the costs of diverting Social Security payroll taxes into personal accounts by reducing scheduled Social Security benefits. Also unlike the Liebman-MacGuineas-Samwick plan it does not include any "add-on" financing for personal accounts.

Two hallmarks of Model 2 are, first, that it provides a choice to individuals of remaining within the traditional Social Security system (with all the attendant risks of future tax and benefit changes) or participating in personal accounts by diverting a part of existing payroll taxes as account contributions when working. Second, for those choosing to participate in personal accounts, future benefits are reduced to "offset" the diversion of payroll taxes into personal accounts. Thus, unlike the centrist plans that include personal accounts, the Bush Commission's Model 2 introduces a direct link—on a person-to-person basis—between funding personal accounts and reducing future benefits from the traditional Social Security program.

Potentially, such a link could be established on a dollar-for-dollar basis in present value terms, thereby balancing revenue outflows from the traditional system for financing personal accounts with future cost savings. The evaluation of the traditional program's aggregate long-term finances and the effects on population subgroups under DEMSIM should clarify the size of the imbalance between diverted taxes and future cost savings under Model 2's specifications.

The reform plan under Model 2 of President Bush's Social Security Reform Commission involves several elements, each of which is first incorporated independently into DEMSIM for evaluating its financial implications. Model 2's total impact, including interactions between individual reform elements, is calculated by executing all elements simultaneously. Because Model 2's start date of 2004 falls before DEMSIM's base year of 2006 (and because it is now obsolete), it is pushed ahead to 2009 in the calculations reported below under DEMSIM's projections. All other dates and dollar thresholds specified in Model 2 are correspondingly pushed ahead. For example, Model 2 specifies that personal account contributions would be subject to a maximum of $1,000 in the year 2004, and the contribution limit would be indexed according to the average wage index defined with the base year of 2002. Since personal account contributions are to begin in 2009 under DEMSIM's calculations, the contribution limit in 2009 is set equal to $1,000 times DEMSIM's internally generated average wage index for 2007—calculated with the index's base year set to 2002.[8]

Model 2 of the G. W. Bush Social Security Reform Commission contained several reform elements as described below:

1. Personal Social Security accounts are created by diverting the smaller of two items—(i) 4 percentage points of taxable earnings or (ii) a nominal contribution limit out of payroll taxes calculated as described above. Traditional Social Security's loss from diverted payroll taxes is offset by subtracting a notional annuity value from each IA participant's future annual benefits. The notional annuity is calculated so that its actuarial present discounted value as of the participant's benefit collection year equals the accumulated value of personal account contributions, with the inflation-adjusted accumulation interest rate fixed at 2 percent. Note that the 2 percent interest rate is a parameter specified in the proposal for calculating the notional annuity to be used to offset traditional benefits. The personal account contributions would actually accrue at whatever market returns the account portfolio receives. For married couples, the notional annuity used as the offset is specified as a joint-life annuity with a 67 percent survivor payout rate. Appendix 12.1 describes Model 2's benefit offset calculations in greater detail.

The Bush Commission's final report emphasizes that even under the most conservative estimate of the real return on IA investments—3 percent per year obtainable from investing contributions exclusively in very safe securities—workers could enjoy larger retirement resources available to them by participating in individual accounts. Indeed, the offset rate was set at just 2 percent per year in order to induce a high IA participation rate among workers. However, inducing higher participation in this manner involves a cost—a worsening of the imbalance in the traditional system when its future revenues and expenditures are present valued at a discount rate larger than 2 percent per year. This means that other adjustments to the Social Security's taxes and benefits would have to be larger to balance its aggregate finances over 75 years.

2. Under Model 2, the rate of growth of future benefits under the traditional program would be reduced by lowering bend point percentage factors (90, 32, and 15) by the difference between annual wage growth and consumer price index (CPI-W) growth. As described in chapter 6, these percentage factors convert each worker's average monthly indexed earnings into his or her primary insurance amount—which equals the Social Security retirement benefits if the person retires at his or her normal retirement age.[9]

Under the current Social Security benefit formula, inflation-adjusted benefits grow larger for successive birth cohorts because successive cohorts have higher average real earnings, and both past worker earnings and bend point dollar thresholds are indexed to economy-wide growth in average wages. Reducing bend point factors as described above would reduce benefit growth for successive birth cohorts by (almost) the full amount of the difference between wage growth and inflation (the latter equals the growth of the CPI-W). Because scheduled benefits are reduced under Model 2 by the cumulative amount of this growth rate difference, the gap between post-reform scheduled benefits and those scheduled under current laws would grow larger over time for successive later-born generations.

It should be noted that this reform element does not imply absolute reductions in workers' inflation-adjusted benefits: for example, workers with identical real wage histories would receive the same real Social Security benefits, no matter which cohorts they belong to and when the earnings accrue.[10]

This way of implementing a reduction in future benefit growth has several advantages. First, because reductions are not applied to average indexed monthly wages, the current positive association between the sizes of past wages and benefits is maintained within a given retiree cohort—a desirable feature to preserve incentives to work. Second, because all three bend point percentage factors (90, 32, and 15) are reduced proportionally each year, the same degree

of progressivity is retained in the benefit formula for a given retiree birth cohort as under the existing program. And, third, the shift results in a gradual
reduction of benefits for new retirees each year, implying that younger workers—those with more time to adjust to altered benefit expectations and more
time to accumulate assets via personal accounts—receive larger reductions in
scheduled benefits (over and above their personal account benefit offsets).

3. Model 2 protects low lifetime earners by providing enhanced traditional
   benefits over those resulting from reform element 2. This reform element is
   similar to reform element 6 under the Diamond-Orszag reform proposal (see
   chapter 9).[11] Low-earners' primary insurance amounts are increased by an additional 4.04 percentage points each year beginning in 2014. By 2023, the percentage increase reaches 40.4 percent, where it is maintained in all subsequent
   years.

   This benefit enhancement would be awarded to those with full careers (at
   least 35 years) and who work at the minimum wage throughout. Those who
   work for the same number of years but earn less than the career minimum-
   wage worker would receive the same percentage benefit increase as the career
   minimum-wage worker (as applicable in various years beginning in the year
   2014). Working for a smaller number of years, or working for more than the
   minimum wage would lead to a phaseout of the benefit enhancement.[12] Under
   the phaseout, the percentage factor is gradually reduced for those who work for
   fewer than 35 years during their lifetimes—so that those working for less than
   20 years receive no benefit enhancement. The percentage factor is also reduced
   gradually for those with higher career average earnings than the full-career
   minimum-wage worker—so that it is fully phased out for those with career average earnings that are twice as large as that of the career minimum-wage worker.
   These features imply that larger benefit enhancements are awarded to those
   with longer than 19-year work histories and those with lower lifetime earnings
   than workers earning at twice the minimum wage during their careers.[13]

   This reform element is designed to protect low-income workers from facing poverty during retirement. But it also has a negative implication: the U.S.
   fiscal system is already quite progressive at low income levels.[14] Introducing a
   low-earner benefit enhancement of this type with a phaseout for higher earners would increase the fiscal system's progressivity for low-earners and would
   introduce stronger disincentives to work.

4. Model 2 provides widow(er)s with benefits equal to at least 75 percent of the
   couple's benefit were both spouses still alive. This is similar to reform element
   7 of the Diamond-Orszag proposal (see chapter 9). Under DEMSIM's implementation, however, it is implemented beginning in 2014—five years later than
   specified under the commission's proposal.[15] If the survivor has zero lifetime

earnings, the couple would receive Social Security benefits based on the working spouse's past earnings plus 50 percent of those benefits for the non-working spouse as a dependent—that is, the couple's benefit would equal 150 percent of the worker's own benefit. When the working spouse dies, the surviving non-worker receives 100 percent of the decedent's benefit. Thus, the survivor receives 67 percent of the couple's Social Security benefits (100/150). In a case where both spouses worked with identical earnings, the couple's benefit would equal 200 percent of one worker's own benefit when both are alive during retirement. When one spouse dies, the survivor benefit equals his or her own benefit—100 percent of the decedent's benefit when both were alive, implying a survivor replacement of 50 percent. Increasing that "survivor benefit replacement rate" to 75 percent—regardless of the spouse's earnings history—would provide more generous benefits to survivors—who are predominantly women with relatively sparser earnings histories compared to their male spouses.

It is clear, however, that this reform element discriminates in favor of married survivors: surviving women with full-career earnings histories would receive larger benefits by virtue of having been married relative to unmarried women with similar earnings histories. Thus, if it were implemented, it could prospectively encourage people to marry—which is consistent with conservatives' emphasis on promoting family values. As shown in chapter 9's evaluation of this reform element (with minor differences), its impact is small because it applies only to married couples and to divorcees with at least a 10-year marital history.

5. Finally, Model 2 provides for "transition cost" financing to fill the gap between Social Security's revenues and expenditures once the program's trust fund is fully depleted. It calls for transfers from the Treasury's general account to the Social Security Trust Fund to cover any financial shortfalls that may arise after the earlier described reforms are implemented. Projections under DEMSIM's baseline assumptions will indicate (below) how large the transition cost would be and for how long general fund transfers would be required.

General fund transfers as a means of financing the transition to individual accounts present several problems. First, there are three ways to fund such transfers in the short term, non–Social Security federal spending cuts, increases in non-payroll taxes, and increases in federal debt. Thus, although the proposal does not call for an explicit increase in taxes, specifying general fund transfers leaves the door open for tax increases to be enacted in the future. The label of Model 2 as a "conservative proposal" would be firmer, however, if the proposal identified specific future federal spending cuts to pay for general fund transfers.

Second, specifying general fund transfers introduces (or rather retains) the element of political risk—that the required transfers won't ultimately be made.

This reform element, by itself, does not provide Social Security with a prior claim on general revenues. If the demands of competing federal programs on federal general revenues become large and unavoidable and non-payroll taxes cannot be increased, additional changes to Social Security policies would be required to reduce the program's expenditures. The magnitude of the associated political risk is difficult to assess beyond observing that it would be larger the larger are the transfers projected under the proposal.

It is worth noting that specifying general revenues to cover transition costs makes no difference to the lifetime net tax rate calculation because such transfers are implicitly assumed even when lifetime net tax rates are calculated under DEMSIM's baseline assumptions—which incorporate Social Security's current rules. The rates calculated under Model 2 (and changes in them relative to those under DEMSIM's baseline assumptions) exhibit the distribution of (changes in) payroll tax costs net of (changes in) scheduled post-reform benefits. That is, lifetime net tax rates show the fiscal treatment of selected population groups under given Social Security tax and benefit rules—if those rules are implemented during their lifetimes—irrespective of changes that may be required elsewhere in the federal budget.

Effects of Model 2 on Social Security's Aggregate Finances

The results reported below from implementing Model 2's reform elements assume 100 percent participation in personal accounts by the eligible group—defined as those younger than age 55 in 2007. Table 12.1 shows the effect of each reform element separately. The first two rows—numbered 1a and 1b—summarize the effect of introducing carve-out personal accounts. Note that the figures reported in row 1b are cumulative with those of row 1a. The diversion of payroll taxes into individual accounts and associated benefit offsets together increase the 75-year open group imbalance by about 50 percent from $7.0 trillion under DEMSIM's baseline to $10.5 trillion. The infinite horizon open group imbalance, however, increases by just 18 percent—from $13.4 trillion under the baseline to $15.7 trillion. Thus, under the infinite horizon, DEMSIM's baseline open group imbalance increases by much less than that over 75 years as expected.[16] The imbalances over both horizons—75 years and perpetuity—from introducing individual accounts increase because of the "give-away" from adopting a smaller (2 percent) discount rate to calculate benefit offsets compared to Social Security's Trust Fund interest rate (2.9 percent) used to calculate present values of aggregate payroll taxes and benefit expenditures.

TABLE 12.1 **Impact of the G. W. Bush Commission's Model 2 on Social Security's (OASI) Finances**

	Post-reform actuarial imbalance						Change in actuarial imbalance as a percent of DEMSIM-baseline taxable payrolls		
	Present values in billions of constant 2006 dollars			As a percent of DEMSIM-baseline taxable payrolls					
Proposed policy change	75-year open group	∞-horizon open group	Closed group	75-year open group	∞-horizon open group	Closed group*	75-year open group	∞-horizon open group	Closed group*
Establish personal retirement accounts									
1a. Divert payroll taxes up to wage-indexed limit	13,548	22,924	18,177	6.50	8.16	12.49	3.15	3.40	2.75
1b. Traditional benefits offset at 2% interest rate†	10,528	15,708	15,027	5.05	5.59	10.32	1.70	0.83	0.59
2. CPI-index Social Security benefits	4,031	2,268	11,071	1.93	0.81	7.61	-1.42	-3.95	-2.13
3. Low-earner benefit enhancement	7,063	13,469	14,251	3.39	4.79	9.79	0.04	0.04	0.05
4. Increase widow(er)'s benefit to 75% of couple's	7,116	13,608	14,337	3.41	4.84	9.84	0.06	0.09	0.11
Simple sum of changes	7,783	4,961	12,160	3.73	1.77	8.35	0.38	-2.99	-1.38
Total effect of all reforms implemented together	7,851	5,247	12,233	3.77	1.87	8.40	0.42	-2.89	-1.33
Memoranda:									
DEMSIM-baseline imbalance	6,985	13,364	14,172	3.35	4.75	9.74	...	...	...
DEMSIM-baseline taxable payrolls	208,495	281,064	145,572	...	...	...	...	...	...

*Shown as a percent of closed group taxable payrolls.
†Effect is cumulative with reform element 1a. Individual Account retirement annuities calculated at 3 percent interest rate and subject to income taxes.
Source: Author's calculations.

The increase in the infinite horizon imbalance from impact of introducing personal accounts under Model 2 is much smaller than under the Kolbe-Stenholm-Boyd proposal—wherein it equals about $5.8 trillion (compare the DEMSIM baseline value with that in row 1b in table 10.1). There are two reasons for this. First, Model 2 explicitly links payroll tax diversions with future benefit offsets, whereas the KSB proposal has no such direct linkage. Comparing just payroll tax diversions for the KSB, LMS, and Model 2 shows that Model 2 involves the largest personal accounts (compare open group imbalances in rows 1a in table 10.1, row 1 in table 11.1, and row 1a in table 12.1). This is true notwithstanding the wage-indexed limit on the size of personal accounts under Model 2 (of $1,000 per person per year as of 2004).[17]

As suggested earlier, benefit offsets for carve-out personal account contributions under Model 2 are less than dollar-for-dollar in present value terms: the relatively modest 2 percent rate specified for calculating participants' future benefit offsets is one of Model 2's inducements for greater participation in personal accounts. As row 1b of table 12.1 shows, the cumulative impact of adding benefit offsets to the carve-out personal account contributions does not return the 75-year and infinite horizon open group imbalances back to their DEMSIM baseline levels of $7.0 trillion and $13.4 trillion, respectively—showing that Model 2's personal accounts elements would award additional retirement resources to individual account participants, on net.

In addition to introducing personal accounts and associated individual benefit offsets, Model 2 reduces traditional Social Security benefits by gradually reducing the factors used for converting average wage-indexed labor earnings into benefits. It should be noted that the reduction of bend point factors at the rate of real wage growth applies to *all* beneficiaries, not just to participants in personal accounts. Thus, these additional reductions in scheduled benefits constitute another inducement to participate in personal accounts as a way of compensating for reduced traditional benefits. As seen from row 2 of table 12.1, when introduced independently, Model 2's gradual reduction of bend point factors reduces the 75-year imbalance by $3.0 trillion—from $7.0 trillion under DEMSIM's baseline to $4.0 trillion—or by about 1.4 percent of the present value of taxable payrolls over 75 years.

The reduction in the infinite horizon open group imbalance from indexing benefits to the Consumer Price Index is $11.1 trillion—the difference between $13.4 trillion under DEMSIM's baseline and $2.3 trillion under this reform element. This imbalance reduction is considerably larger because the gap between wage and price indices grows cumulatively very large in the long term.

Each of Model 2's other reform elements—to protect benefits of low lifetime earners and enhance widow(er)s benefits, both of which are also adopted by the Diamond-Orszag proposal—have a very modest impact on the two open group imbalance measures. Hence, Model 2's overall impact on open group imbalances is primarily driven by reductions of scheduled benefits over and above benefit offsets levied against payroll taxes diverted into personal accounts. But these two sources of benefit offsets are insufficient to deliver a smaller open group imbalance when all reform elements are implemented simultaneously. Indeed, full implementation of Model 2 would increase the 75-year open group imbalance by about $0.9 trillion. However, the infinite horizon open group imbalance is reduced by $8.1 trillion—going from $13.4 trillion under DEMSIM's baseline projections to $5.2 trillion. But Model 2's post-reform infinite horizon open group imbalance is significantly larger compared to the KSB ($1.8 trillion) and LMS ($2.4 trillion) reform proposals.

As a share of the present value of taxable payrolls, the 75-year imbalance increases by 0.4 percent and the infinite horizon imbalance decreases by 2.9 percent of the present value of 75-year payrolls. Thus, under DEMSIM's projections, more than 100 percent of Model 2's cost savings emerge *after* the first 75 years after 2006. However, Model 2 also contains a provision for general revenue financing in the amounts needed to ensure that benefits scheduled under it would be fully paid. Thus, calculations of financial shortfalls that ignore this provision (as in table 12.1) reveal the size of the residual adjustment costs explicitly imposed by Model 2 on the rest of the federal government.

Ignoring the general revenue transfer element, Model 2 worsens Social Security's 75-year solvency. Nevertheless it imposes additional costs on today's generations: under it, the closed group imbalance declines by $2.0 trillion—from $14.2 trillion under DEMSIM's baseline to $12.2 trillion—again by considerably less than under most of the other personal accounts reform proposals analyzed earlier.[18]

Thus, Model 2 is similar to the Diamond-Orszag proposal in that it imposes its adjustment cost almost entirely on future generations: just 24 percent of the total change in the infinite horizon open group imbalance is imposed on current generations. On other grounds, it is tempting to say (and many do) that Model 2 is the polar opposite of the Diamond-Orszag proposal. Whereas the latter emphasizes maintaining currently scheduled benefits by increasing taxes on future generations, the former seeks a tax cut of sorts by diverting a portion of payroll taxes into personal accounts and providing a less-than-actuarially-fair benefit offset. However, because Model 2 leaves much larger Social Security imbalances to be met via general revenue transfers—especially during the first 75 years—it leaves the door ajar for significant future (non-payroll) tax increases, which degrades the otherwise clear contrast between the two proposals.

Effects of Model 2 on Social Security's Annual Imbalance Ratios

These features of Model 2 are reflected in the sequence of projected annual imbalance ratios as seen from figure 12.1. Model 2 increases short-term annual imbalances by a considerable amount relative to those under DEMSIM's baseline projections—adding about 2 percentage points to annual Social Security deficits as a share of annual taxable payrolls. Model 2's annual imbalances decline and become smaller than under DEMSIM's baseline projection by the late 2040s. But the long-term reduction in an-

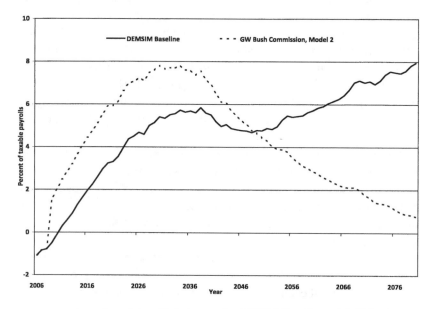

FIGURE 12.1. Annual non-interest imbalance ratios: DEMSIM baseline and G. W. Bush Commission, Model 2. Source: Author's calculations.

nual imbalances, although quite rapid, does not result in imbalance ratios toward the end of the 75-year horizon that are as low as those under the Diamond-Orszag, KSB, and LMS reform proposals—as discussed in greater detail in chapter 14.

Model 2's Impact on Lifetime Net Tax Rates

Table 12.2 shows Model 2's impact on lifetime net tax rates under the traditional system. Obviously, lifetime net tax rates would be reduced by the diversion of payroll taxes into personal accounts, and they would be increased because of future benefit offsets and other changes to scheduled benefits, especially the gradual reduction of bend point factors at the rates of real wage growth.

Panel 1 of table 12.2 shows lifetime net tax rates under Model 2 for selected population groups. And panel 2 shows differences between the rates in panel 1 compared to those under DEMSIM's baseline assumptions (from panel 11 of table 7.1). As noted earlier, lifetime net tax rate calculations do not include general revenue financing as a dedicated revenue source. The rates are calculated based on Model 2's scheduled Social Security taxes and benefits.

Compared to those under current laws, Model 2's lifetime net tax rates are considerably smaller on average—especially for current middle-aged and young workers who are eligible to participate in personal accounts. This is the result of Model 2's benefit offsets that are smaller in present value than the diversions of payroll taxes into personal accounts. Most of the other benefit reductions are phased in gradually—which explains why the differences between lifetime net tax rates under Model 2 and DEMSIM's baseline decline for successive birth cohorts among those born after 1990. Model 2 preserves some of properties of lifetime net tax rates under DEMSIM's baseline assumptions: for example, those rates are smaller for low lifetime earners among today's females, but not so for today's males because of the taxable earnings ceiling is binding for fewer females compared to males.

As panel 2 of the table shows, all cohorts and population subgroups except high earners among baby boomers would face smaller lifetime net tax rates under Model 2. High-earning baby boomers are unable to exploit the advantage of Model 2's low 2 percent benefit offset rate against personal account contributions for very long, but they would be subject to reductions

TABLE 12.2 **Effects of the G. W. Bush Commission's Model 2 on Selected Population Groups**

Years of Birth	All	Female Non-White E≤Med	Female Non-White E>Med	Female White E≤Med	Female White E>Med	Male Non-White E≤Med	Male Non-White E>Med	Male White E≤Med	Male White E>Med
Panel 1	Traditional Social Security lifetime net tax rates under Model 2								
1946–1960	5.00	4.5	5.3	3.8	4.8	6.4	6.5	6.2	5.7
1961–1975	5.94	5.6	6.1	4.9	5.8	6.9	6.9	6.6	6.4
1976–1990	5.32	5.1	5.4	4.5	5.2	6.0	5.9	5.7	5.8
1991–2005	4.78	4.6	4.9	4.1	4.7	5.4	5.2	5.1	5.2
2006–2020	4.72	4.6	4.8	4.2	4.6	5.1	5.1	5.1	5.0
2021–2035	4.82	4.8	4.8	4.4	4.7	5.2	5.0	5.1	5.1
2036–2050	4.97	4.9	4.9	4.6	4.8	5.2	5.1	5.3	5.2
Panel 2	Percentage point increase in lifetime net tax rates: Model 2 minus DEMSIM baseline								
1946–1960	–0.1	–0.1	0.0	–0.2	0.0	–0.2	0.0	–0.1	0.0
1961–1975	–0.2	–0.3	–0.1	–0.2	0.0	–0.4	–0.2	–0.3	–0.1
1976–1990	–0.8	–1.0	–0.7	–0.7	–0.6	–1.4	–0.9	–0.9	–0.7
1991–2005	–1.4	–1.6	–1.2	–1.3	–1.1	–2.1	–1.4	–1.8	–1.2
2006–2020	–1.3	–1.5	–1.2	–1.1	–1.0	–2.0	–1.6	–1.7	–1.3
2021–2035	–1.1	–1.3	–1.0	–0.8	–0.9	–1.8	–1.3	–1.3	–1.1
2036–2050	–0.8	–1.0	–0.8	–0.2	–0.6	–1.5	–1.1	–1.1	–0.9
Panel 3	Total Social Security wealth as a share of lifetime earnings (*scheduled* traditional benefits; %)								
1946–1960	4.1	5.3	3.6	5.8	4.0	3.4	2.6	3.6	2.8
1961–1975	3.9	4.5	3.5	5.2	3.8	3.2	2.8	3.6	3.0
1976–1990	3.8	4.3	3.5	4.9	3.7	3.4	3.0	3.8	3.1
1991–2005	3.8	4.2	3.4	4.7	3.6	3.3	3.0	3.7	3.1

2006–2020	3.6	4.0	3.2	3.4	3.4	2.9	3.6	3.1
2021–2035	3.4	3.7	3.1	3.2	3.2	2.8	3.5	2.9
2036–2050	3.1	3.4	2.8	3.0	2.9	2.6	3.3	2.7

Panel 4

Total Social Security wealth as a share of lifetime earnings (*payable* traditional benefits; %)*

1946–1960	2.6	3.3	2.2	2.0	2.4	1.5	2.3	1.8
1961–1975	2.4	2.8	2.2	2.0	2.3	1.8	2.2	1.8
1976–1990	2.9	3.3	2.8	2.7	2.9	2.4	2.9	2.4
1991–2005	3.3	3.6	3.0	3.0	3.2	2.7	3.3	2.8
2006–2020	3.4	3.7	3.1	3.2	3.3	2.8	3.4	2.9
2021–2035	3.3	3.6	3.0	3.1	3.2	2.8	3.5	2.9
2036–2050	3.1	3.4	2.8	3.0	2.9	2.6	3.3	2.7

Panel 5

Percent of Social Security wealth provided by Model 2 traditional benefits (*payable* definition)

1946–1960	94.7	94.4	94.0	93.9	95.1	92.3	95.3	94.0
1961–1975	73.8	76.1	72.1	74.9	75.9	70.4	73.4	70.9
1976–1990	52.8	57.2	52.2	51.7	56.0	49.9	51.5	47.7
1991–2005	41.8	47.3	40.9	41.6	45.1	38.7	39.5	35.5
2006–2020	38.2	45.8	38.1	41.7	41.2	34.2	36.5	30.7
2021–2035	35.7	43.1	35.3	39.4	38.1	31.9	36.0	27.9
2036–2050	32.0	40.2	30.9	36.5	34.1	28.1	32.0	23.7

Panel 6

Model 2: total benefits (traditional *payable* plus IA) as a percent of current law *scheduled* benefits

1946–1960	61.2	61.3	60.3	58.6	59.2	57.2	64.6	61.9
1961–1975	59.3	59.5	60.3	60.5	58.4	61.3	60.7	59.3
1976–1990	75.4	74.3	74.7	80.9	72.7	77.7	76.8	77.7
1991–2005	85.6	84.2	84.3	93.8	81.5	88.4	90.4	88.9
2006–2020	87.8	86.3	87.4	92.2	83.3	92.9	93.9	91.3
2021–2035	84.8	84.1	83.8	89.5	80.9	86.7	87.6	88.3
2036–2050	78.7	78.5	78.8	83.9	75.3	81.0	83.1	81.8

* The payable benefits definition ignores Model 2's general revenue transfers provision.
Source: Author's calculations.

in scheduled benefits from lower future bend point factors—especially high-earners who already face low benefit replacement rates (the 15 percent primary insurance amount [PIA] bend point).

The largest reductions in lifetime net tax rates under Model 2 would occur for the 1991–2005 birth cohort. This birth cohort is relatively young and would be able to divert a larger portion of its lifetime payroll taxes into personal accounts and reap a commensurately larger advantage from the low benefit offset discount rate. In addition, relative to later born individuals, reductions in bend point factors for primary insurance amount calculations (because of Model 2's shift to price indexing) would still not fully negate the advantage of the low benefit offset rate.

Those born toward the middle of this century and later, however, would experience smaller reductions in Social Security lifetime net tax rates under Model 2 compared to under current laws because of the increasing impact of future reductions of bend point factors (numbers under the "All" column of panel 2 become less negative for successive birth cohorts). Panel 2 shows that, in general, low lifetime earners receive larger reductions of lifetime net tax rates compared to high-earners but that advantage becomes smaller for later-born cohorts. This occurs because of the declining share of traditional Social Security benefits in total Social Security benefits for later-born cohorts under Model 2—as discussed below.

Model 2's Impact on Retirement Wealth

Model 2 includes an open-ended general revenue financing provision. Despite that provision, Social Security does not have a prior claim on federal general revenues because other federal programs are also supported by those revenues. Thus, Model 2's retirement wealth ratios are also shown under both scheduled and payable definitions. Under the latter, the general revenue financing provision is ignored, and an across-the-board benefit reduction is imposed when the traditional program's trust fund income falls short of Model 2's scheduled benefits expenditures. The trust fund exhaustion date under Model 2 is 2019.

Model 2 generates very large Social Security cash flow deficits for several decades when the general revenue financing constraint is ignored and implies substantial political risk about whether those general fund transfers would be sustained. Therefore, present values as of each person's benefit collection year of Model 2's scheduled and payable traditional benefits are calculated under a 5 percent inflation adjusted annual discount rate.

Panels 3 and 4 of Table 12.2 report total Social security wealth ratios for Model 2 under the two alternative definitions of traditional Social Security benefits. The numerators of the retirement wealth ratios equal the discounted value of traditional Social Security benefits—scheduled and payable, respectively—plus personal account balances accumulated through the benefit collection year using a 3 percent inflation adjusted annual rate of return. And the denominators equal the accumulated value of labor earnings through the benefit collection year using a 5 percent annual inflation adjusted rate of interest.

Comparing panels 3 and 4 of table 12.2 with their counterparts in table 11.2 shows that Social Security's contribution to retirement assets as a share of lifetime earnings would be substantially smaller under Model 2 compared to those under the LMS proposal. This is not surprising given the LMS proposal's prescription of add-on financing for personal accounts. For current workers (those born before 1990), retirement wealth under Model 2 is also smaller than under the Diamond-Orszag proposal (compare with table 9.2). All retirement wealth under the latter proposal is made up of traditional (payable) benefits. Model 2's restriction of personal account contributions to $1,000 in 2004—with the nominal limit wage-indexed thereafter—means that many of today's participants would not be able to significantly offset Model 2's reductions of traditional benefits through returns on personal accounts.

Under Model 2, the share of lifetime earnings devoted to retirement via Social Security (under the "payable" definition) increases for younger and future-born generations for a while, but declines for those born toward the middle of the century. This occurs because, although personal accounts grow larger at the same rate as successive cohorts' earnings, future reductions in scheduled benefits over and above offsets against payroll tax diversions into personal accounts reduce total Social Security wealth relative to labor earnings. It should be noted that the wealth accumulation rate used here is very conservative—just 3 percent per year compared to the calculations of many other analysts. Even under this relatively low interest rate (which implies very conservative and low-risk personal account portfolios), Model 2's retirement resource shares of lifetime earnings for today's children and future generations are at levels comparable to those of the Diamond-Orszag proposal.

The fifth panel of table 12.2 shows the contribution of post-reform traditional benefits to total Social Security wealth. As expected, those shares decline for successive birth cohorts among today's adult generations. For those born after 1990, the shares fall below 50 percent, and personal accounts begin to increasingly dominate the provision of retirement wealth. This is in contrast to the personal account proposals of earlier chapters wherein traditional benefits contribute at least 50 percent to total Social Security retirement wealth.

The final panel of table 12.2 compares "payable" retirement wealth from adopting Model 2 to that under current-law scheduled benefits. The key result here is that Model 2's Social Security wealth levels would eventually increase to about four-fifths of those under current-law scheduled benefits for younger population subgroups and that Model 2 entails significant sacrifices from current older workers (those born before 1960) and small sacrifices from current middle-aged workers (those born between 1976 and 1990). Model 2 protects only those aged 55 and older as of 2007 (as it is implemented under DEMSIM) compared to current-law benefits. Those slightly younger than this threshold would not benefit significantly from IA participation under Model 2 but would be exposed to benefit reductions from its other reform elements.

Summary and Final Remarks

Many people view Model 2 as the quintessentially conservative plan, and its provisions have been mimicked by many other Social Security reform proposals—including liberal ones. Its reform elements—not including the general revenue funding provision—create substantial open group imbalances, implying significant financing burden on the general government budget for several decades. Indeed, the 75-year open group imbalance becomes larger under Model 2 because of sizable increases in annual imbalances during that period. This is as expected under a personal accounts reform that excludes add-on financing, does not increase the program's dedicated revenues, and trades off payroll tax diversions against future benefit reductions on a person-to-person basis on terms favorable to personal account participants, on net.

However, Model 2 reduces lifetime net tax rates under the traditional Social Security program for most birth cohorts (among those analyzed here). Model 2's lifetime net tax rates are considerably smaller than those under the Diamond-Orszag, KSB, and LMS reform proposals. Model 2's retirement wealth ratios for young future generations are commensurate with those under the Diamond-Orszag and KSB reform proposals but smaller than those under the LMS proposal. However, Model 2 reduces the retirement wealth ratios of successive cohorts—implying deep cuts in future benefits and increasingly heavier reliance on personal accounts resources for younger and future generations.

Model 2 contains strong inducements to participate in personal accounts, and one would conjecture that most people would participate were the proposal adopted. However, high-earning baby boomers would bear the same lifetime net tax rates, and today's older and middle-aged workers could experience either no change or a net reduction in retirement resources under Model 2 compared to those under current-law scheduled benefits. These two considerations may explain the lukewarm political support that President Bush's Social Security reform proposals received.

Benefit Offset Calculation under
G. W. Bush Commission Model 2

The notional annuity used for offsetting traditional Social Security benefits is derived by first calculating the value, A, of lifetime personal account contributions as of the end of the year before the benefit collection year, $\tau - 1$, accumulated at an interest rate of 2 percent per year—the "benefit offset discount rate." The actuarially fair notional annuity is calculated so that its present value as of the beginning of the benefit collection year τ equals A.

In the following description, the primary and secondary annuitants are denoted by superscripts p and s, respectively. Let x^p represent the value of annual notional annuity payouts. For computation purposes the last period of payouts is assumed to be T^p, the year in which primary annuitant is aged 115. Let $A^p_{\tau-1}$ represent the value of assets to be annuitized—handed over to the insurer at the end of year $\tau - 1$. Annuity payouts begin at the end of the year τ—the benefit collection year.

Set λ to 1 if it is a joint-life annuity, 0 if it is a single-life annuity. The secondary annuitant would (notionally) receive an annuity payout of $\lambda\theta x^p$, where $0 \le \theta \le 1$, is the survivor's "replacement rate." According to Model 2's specifications, θ is set to 0.67. Let $\pi^p_{a,\tau}$ represent the probability that the primary annuitant, who is of age a at the beginning of year τ, will die before the year ends. Let the corresponding conditional survival probability be $\emptyset^p_{a,\tau} = 1 - \pi^p_{a,\tau}$.

Finally, let, $R = 1 / [(1 + g)(1 + \psi) / (1 + i)]$, where g is the real annual growth rate of the yearly payout, ψ is the annual inflation rate, and i is the annual *nominal* interest rate. To calculate the benefit offset, the notional annuity is calculated as a fixed inflation-adjusted payment through time—that is, g is set equal to 0. Thus, R is an annual real interest (or discount) factor—which is calibrated under Model 2's specifications to equal to 1 / 1.02.

In this example, the primary annuitant is assumed to be aged a, and the secondary annuitant aged b, in the benefit collection year, τ. The present value as of year τ of the secondary annuitant's payout—payable only if he or she survives the primary annuitant—can be expressed in the following manner:

$$\lambda\theta x^P \left\{ R\phi^s_{b,\tau}\pi^P_{a,\tau} + R^2\phi^s_{b,\tau}\,\phi^s_{b+1,\tau+1}\,(\pi^P_{a,\tau} + \phi^P_{a,\tau}\pi^P_{a+1,\tau+1}) + \right.$$
$$\left. R^3\phi^s_{b,\tau}\phi^s_{b+1,\tau+1}\,\phi^s_{b+2,\tau+2}(\pi^P_{a,\tau} + \phi^P_{a,\tau}\pi^P_{a+1,\tau+1} + \phi^P_{a,\tau}\phi^P_{a+1,\tau+1}\pi^P_{a+2,\tau+2}) + \ldots \right\}. \quad (1)$$

In expression (1), the first term within curly brackets equals the discount factor applying to the survivor's payout at the end of year τ. In this term, the discount factor, R, is qualified by the probability, $\phi^s_{b,\tau}$, that the secondary annuitant survives through the end of year τ and collects the payout but the primary annuitant dies, with probability $\pi^P_{a,\tau}$, before the end of year $\tau - 1$. The second term in curly brackets equals the discount factor applicable to the survivor's payout in year $\tau + 1$. Here, the discount factor, R^2, is multiplied by the probability that the secondary annuitant's survives through the end of year $\tau + 1$, while the primary annuitant could die before the end of either year τ or year $\tau + 1$, and so on, for the rest of the terms in equation (1). Collecting the terms involving $\pi^P_{a,\tau}$ in each of these expressions yields the expression

$$R\pi^P_{a,\tau}\left\{ \phi^s_{b,\tau} + R\phi^s_{b,\tau}\phi^s_{b+1,\tau+1} + R^2\phi^s_{b,\tau}\phi^s_{b+1,\tau+1}\,\phi^s_{b+2,\tau+2} + \cdots \right\}. \quad (2)$$

Next, collecting the terms involving $\phi^P_{a,\tau}\pi^P_{a+1,\tau+1}$ yields the expression

$$R^2\phi^s_{b,\tau}\,\phi^P_{a,\tau}\pi^P_{a+1,\tau+1}\left\{ \phi^s_{b+1,\tau+1}\,R\phi^s_{b+1,\tau+1}\,\phi^s_{b+2,\tau+2} + R^2\phi^s_{b+1,\tau+1}\,\phi^s_{b+2,\tau+2}\,\phi^s_{b+3,\tau+3} + \cdots \right\}. \quad (3)$$

Taking the sum of the series indicated by expressions (2) and (3) yields the expression

$$\sum_{j=\tau}^{T^s} R^{j-\tau+1}\left\{ \prod_{u=\tau+1}^{j} \phi^s_{b+u-(\tau+1),u-1}\phi^P_{a+u-(\tau+1),u-1} \right\}\pi^P_{a+j-\tau,j}\sum_{u=j}^{T^s} R^{u-j}\prod_{v=j}^{u}\phi^s_{b+v-\tau,v}. \quad (4)$$

Hence, the actuarial present value of the notional annuity equals

$$A^p_{\tau-1}$$

$$= x^p \left\{ \sum_{j=\tau}^{T^p} R^{j-\tau+1} \prod_{u=\tau}^{j} \phi^p_{a+u-\tau,u} \right. \tag{5}$$

$$\left. + \lambda\theta \sum_{j=\tau}^{T^s} R^{j-\tau+1} \left[\prod_{u=\tau+1}^{j} \phi^s_{b+u-(\tau+1),u-1} \phi^p_{a+u-(\tau+1),u-1} \right] \pi^p_{a+j-\tau,j} \sum_{u=j}^{T^s} R^{u-j} \prod_{v=j}^{u} \phi^s_{b+v-\tau,v} \right\}.$$

In equation (5), the first term within curly brackets shows the discount factor applicable to the primary annuitant—the sum of the probabilities of dying in periods between τ and T^p. The second term is the discount factor derived in expression (4). Knowing mortality rates, the discount rate, and $A^p_{\tau-1}$ the actuarially fair annuity value, x^p, can be calculated by dividing $A^p_{\tau-1}$ by the discount factor shown within the curly brackets in equation (5). This annuity calculation method (using discount rates as appropriate) is also employed for evaluating the KSB and LMS reform proposals—as indicated in chapters 10 and 11.

Under DEMSIM's calculation procedure, each spouse of a married family is treated symmetrically: First, the male spouse is considered as the primary annuitant for whom payroll taxes, personal account contributions, and Social Security benefits are calculated. Those items enable calculations of $A^p_{\tau-1}$ and x^p as described above. The male spouse's traditional Social Security benefits derived after applying all other reform elements of Model 2 are offset (reduced) by x^p in each year beginning with the benefit collection year. Next, the female spouse is considered as the primary annuitant, and the entire process is repeated.

If a spouse has only zeros in his or her earnings history and receives all Social Security benefits as a dependent or a survivor, personal account accumulations are zero and no benefit offset is applicable. That is, dependent and survivor benefits are based on the earning spouse's primary insurance amount including applicable reductions for age or increases for delayed retirement. Benefit offsets are applicable against dependent and survivor benefits (but not against child benefits) only when the spouse has a positive earnings history and is deemed to have participated in Model 2's personal account program.

CHAPTER THIRTEEN

Conservative Proposal 2 by Representative Paul Ryan

"Social Security Personal Savings Guarantee and Prosperity Act"

Many will disagree with this approach. But it is my sincere hope that it will spur Congress to move beyond simply rehashing the problem—to the politically difficult, but critical task of debating, and implementing actual solutions. —Paul D. Ryan

Congressman Ryan has a long history of active participation and leadership on entitlement reform.[1] His message on Social Security reform—as displayed on his official Web site—recognizes that although Social Security provides an important safety net for millions of Americans, it faces a bleak financial future with "a $4.6 trillion deficit over the next 75 years."[2] The Web site recognizes that Social Security's financial shortfalls are only a part of wider budget problems facing the federal government—most of them emerging from the prospective aging of the U.S. population.

Congressman Ryan's latest initiative is a comprehensive reform of the budget process within which he pledges to preserve the current Social Security safety net and to ensure its continued solvency for future generations. The Ryan Social Security reform proposal is contained within "A Roadmap for America's Future"—a comprehensive guide to addressing the "interrelated crises in health care, entitlement spending, the outdated Federal tax code, and our growing debt."[3]

The Ryan Social Security reform proposal builds on the G. W. Bush Commission's framework. The Ryan proposal preserves Social Security's current rules and operation for those aged 55 and older as of 2009. Younger and future generations are given the option to participate in a Personal

Security Account (PSA) system—funded by diverting up to one third of their payroll taxes. PSA participants' would be guaranteed to receive total Social Security benefits (gross of PSA payouts) that are at least as large as benefits under the reformed traditional system.

Thus, outcomes regarding the roles of the traditional and privatized systems under the Ryan proposal would depend on how much traditional benefits are reduced. The proposal could end up eventually eliminating the traditional program and replacing it with a fully privatized system if the reformed program's benefits are reduced to zero. And the deeper the reductions in the traditional program's benefits, the weaker would become the benefit guarantee associated with PSA participation. However, if the traditional program's benefits remain sizable, the Ryan reform proposal offers younger and future Social Security beneficiaries the opportunity to obtain the upside from private capital market returns while limiting the downside from participating in PSAs. The implication of this, of course, is that taxpayers would bear the downside risk of poor market performance of PSA investments. Again, this constitutes an inducement for younger individuals to participate in PSAs because, unless one is sure of being a low-earning individual with close-to-zero income tax liabilities throughout one's lifetime, non-participation in PSAs would mean exclusively bearing the downside risk as a taxpayer.

Determining the expected taxpayer cost of such a Social Security benefit guarantee is difficult at best. The magnitude of the risks involved depends on the fraction among eligible workers who choose to participate in PSAs, their portfolio choices, and on the future distributions of private investment returns—all of which are difficult to estimate and project. The PSA portfolio choices of participants are especially difficult to predict in a system where extra-normal returns from choosing risky portfolios accrue to participants but losses from exposure to market risks are socialized via a benefit guarantee. Indeed, moral hazard effects associated with such guarantees would be expected to promote riskier PSA portfolio choices, increasing the chance of losses and, therefore, the expected taxpayer costs of such benefit guarantees.

The evaluation undertaken here is to assume a particular PSA participation rate (one of 100 percent, 67 percent, and 33 percent), project baseline revenues and costs under the reformed traditional system, and estimate accumulations in PSAs by participants' benefit collection dates under *average* (risky and riskless) investment returns in a manner similar to that of earlier chapters. It should be noted, however, that the evaluation of the Ryan proposal remains incomplete in the absence of a full and proper pricing of the benefit guarantee included in it.[4]

The Ryan Proposal's Social Security Reform Elements

The Ryan reform proposal includes modifications to the existing system's taxes and benefits and introduces Personal Security Accounts. The proposal is viewed as a "conservative proposal" because it includes large personal accounts funded in a carve-out manner and it pays for the ensuing transition cost mostly from future adjustments to participants' benefits. However, it includes an expansion of the payroll tax base in a way that not only increases workers' payroll taxes, it also makes the benefit guarantee larger because the tax base broadening is permitted to trigger additional benefits. Its proposed modifications to the current program are described first, followed by a description of the Personal Security Accounts system.

1. As under the G. W. Bush Commission's Model 2 evaluated in the previous chapter, the Ryan proposal also modifies the existing Social Security benefit formula to reduce the growth of current-law scheduled benefits of successive *high-earner* cohorts. As is well known, each successive cohort of workers receives higher inflation-adjusted benefits than earlier cohorts because the current Social Security benefit formula scales up benefits according to (1) workers' earnings histories—which increase, on average, for each successive cohort of retirees— and (2) to economy-wide growth of average wages. Appendix 13.1 describes the details of how this reform element is implemented.

    Applying the so-called progressive Consumer Price Index (CPI-W) indexing to scheduled benefit growth, the Ryan proposal reduces the benefit growth of successive future cohorts—but only for high lifetime earners. Benefit growth for successive cohorts of low lifetime earners is preserved as under current laws.

    Indexing benefits to the CPI reduces benefit growth for successive birth cohorts of higher earners in a graduated way. Successive cohorts of those with average wages a little higher than a certain threshold (as specified under the Ryan proposal) would experience only a slight reduction in their inflation-adjusted benefit growth compared to earlier cohorts. The reduction in benefit growth becomes larger the higher are lifetime earnings—so that successive cohorts with lifetime average wages equal to those earning at the Social Security taxable maximum earnings each year (or more) would enjoy *zero* real benefit growth compared to earlier cohorts.

Under current laws, high lifetime earners receive larger benefits within a given birth cohort, although progressivity in the benefit formula implies that benefits are larger by less than in proportion to differences in lifetime earnings. Naturally, if benefit growth of successive cohorts of high lifetime earners is reduced whereas benefit growth of low lifetime earners is preserved, the *benefits* of the former must eventually become equal to those of the latter for some future birth cohort. At that time, the degree of progressivity in benefits would be at its most extreme: among the cohort of new retirees at that time, everyone's benefits would be the same regardless of differences in their lifetime earnings.

The Ryan proposal does not specifically address what would happen to the benefit growth of high-earners after this point in time: would it continue to be lower than the benefit growth of low-earners (which would reverse the current positive association of earnings and benefits), or would benefit growth for high-earners revert back to benefit growth under current laws? The latter is assumed in the calculations reported below—implying that after benefit equality is achieved between high- and low-earners' benefits, benefit growth would be restored for successive cohorts of high lifetime earners—so that everyone's benefits keep pace with growth in average wages. The main point, however, is that this Ryan reform element eventually equalizes the Social Security benefits of all workers. Under DEMSIM's baseline projections, benefit equality would be achieved well after the next 75 years—sometime toward the middle of the 22nd century.

2. The second Ryan reform element provides additional benefits for full-career minimum-wage workers in the same manner as the G. W. Bush Commission's Model 2. The additions to benefits are gradually phased out as lifetime earnings increase and are eliminated for workers earning more than twice the minimum wage during their full careers. The additions are also phased out for those with shorter work histories—the number of years of labor force participation under Social Security–covered occupations. The only difference from the G. W. Bush Commission's Model 2 is that the federal minimum-wage level under the Ryan proposal equals that scheduled under current law for 2009—$7.25 per hour—instead of $5.15 per hour as under Model 2. The other details of this provision are the same as those described in the corresponding provision of Model 2 in chapter 12.

3. Recognizing that Social Security's long-term financial shortfalls arise from a gradual projected increase in the population's average age caused by the expected increases in future human longevity, the Ryan proposal modifies currently scheduled changes to Social Security's normal retirement age (NRA). It brings forward by one year the transition of the NRA age from 66 to 67:

under the proposal those who attain age 62 in 2021, rather than 2022, would have a normal retirement age of 67. For those attaining age 62 in 2022 and later, the NRA would keep pace with increasing human longevity: the proposal specifies that the rate of advancement in NRA should keep constant the ratio of expected years of survival after NRA to the working lifespan before NRA, calculated as NRA minus age 20.

As described in chapter 4, DEMSIM keeps track of future changes in the demographic composition of the population. Projected higher fertility rates relative to mortality rates among non-whites compared to whites implies a long-term increase in the share of non-whites in the population. However, persistently higher mortality rates among non-whites also means that the rate mortality improvement would slow over time.

To implement the Ryan proposal's indexation of NRA to longevity increases, the average maximum age of life, A^{max}, is calculated for each 10-year birth cohort in DEMSIM's projected population beginning with those attaining age 62 between 2022 and 2031. According to the Ryan proposal, the ratio, r, to be maintained for later cohorts at the same level as that calculated for the cohort aged 62 in 2022 can be expressed as $r = [A^{max} - NRA] / [NRA - 20]$. The values are NRA = 67 and DEMSIM's estimated $A^{max} = 78.6$ imply $r = 0.248$ for the cohort aged 62 in 2022. Taking the projected average A^{max} values for future 10-year birth cohorts, it is easy to invert the equation for r given above to obtain the required NRA for each cohort. Figure 13.1 shows the values of the NRA calculated in this manner for each future 10-year birth cohort. As expected, it shows that, under DEMSIM's projections, NRA indexed to longevity improvements increases during future decades but the rate of increase declines over time.

4. The next Ryan reform element levies payroll taxes on currently payroll-tax-exempt employer-provided group health insurance benefits beginning in the year 2010. This reform element increases the payroll tax base for both the employer and employee shares of the payroll tax for each covered worker receiving employment based group health insurance benefits. This measure increases both workers' payroll taxes and their future benefits from the expanded definition of earnings used in the Social Security benefit formula—up to the taxable maximum. The taxable maximum earnings are not increased under the Ryan proposal, however.

Although conservatives generally reject tax increases for fixing Social Security's finances, this particular tax increase on workers is justified as a restoration of the original intent of the payroll tax. This tax was first levied on total worker pay at a time when the distinction between wages and total compensation was negligibly small. Group health benefits as a share of wages and salaries amounted

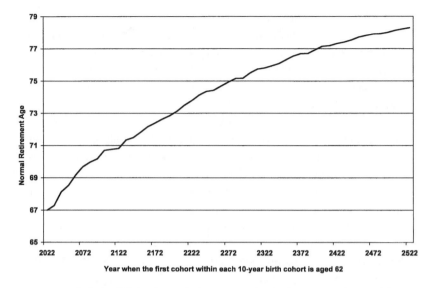

FIGURE 13.1. Indexing NRA to longevity increases under the Ryan reform proposal. Source: Author's calculations.

to merely one third of 1 percent in 1948—the earliest available estimate.[5] Nontaxed benefits in employment contracts have since increased considerably as employers sought to minimize employment costs and employees to maximize total after-tax compensation. As a result, the share of group health benefits in total compensation exceeds 10 percent today.

Clearly, this Ryan reform element detracts from the conservative nature of the Ryan reform proposal, especially because—as discussed below—it constitutes a large increase in payroll taxes.[6] However, chapter 12's analysis of the Bush Commission's Model 2 proposal revealed large increases in Social Security annual imbalances during initial decades because Social Security's revenue loss from carving-out personal accounts from existing payroll taxes remains uncompensated for many decades into the future. As will become clear later in this chapter, the Ryan Social Security reform proposal reduces Social Security's 75-year open group imbalance, much of it because of this tax increase.

Estimates from the 2006 Current Population Survey of the Census Bureau suggest that between one quarter and one third of middle-aged workers are covered under employer-provided group health insurance. This Ryan reform element is implemented by constructing relative profiles of group health insurance coverage by race, gender, and age for 2006 using the Current Population's March Supplement files. These profiles are combined with population data from the National Center for Health Statistics by race, gender, and age and used to distribute the 2006 national aggregate employer expenditures on employee group health insurance to obtain per-capita values of group health benefits by race, gender, and age for 2006. Values of group health insurance benefits for future years are projected by assuming that health care costs will continue to grow faster than worker incomes per capita—by 2.3 percentage points per year through the year 2080, after which the health care growth rate wedge is set to zero.[7] DEMSIM's internally generated average wage index is augmented each year by this growth rate differential to obtain DEMSIM's estimate of per capita growth in health care expenditures. Values of group health benefits projected in this manner by demographic category are added to individuals' simulated earnings over their lifetimes (only when earnings are positive) to form the expanded definition of payroll taxable earnings under the Ryan proposal.

5. The Ryan Social Security reform proposal could not be included among conservative proposals unless it advocated the creation of carve-out individual accounts—which it does by way of its Personal Saving Accounts reform element. Under the proposal, PSAs are to begin operation in 2011 for those aged 55 as of 2009 and younger generations on a voluntary basis. Participants' payroll taxes would be diverted into PSAs according to a gradually escalating schedule: Between 2011 and 2020, the diverted percentage would be 2 percent out of the first $10,000 of taxable earnings and 1 percent of taxable earnings above that limit. Between 2021 and 2030, the percentages diverted would be 4 and 2 percent, respectively, and so on, until in 2041 and later, the percentages would be 8 and 4, respectively. The $10,000 threshold as of 2011, would be indexed to the growth in economy-wide average wages. Thus, the Ryan proposal contains the largest personal accounts system of all those analyzed in this book, perhaps the largest of all Social Security reforms ever proposed.

   Although carve-out financed PSAs would involve large revenue shortfalls for the traditional Social Security program initially, the Ryan proposal makes up for this by including a benefit offset for PSA participants. Their future benefits from the traditional system would be reduced, with the amount of reduction determined by applying a ratio to traditional (post-reform) benefits. The ratio would be calculated as (a) the accumulated value of actual PSA contribution through retirement divided by (b) the accumulated value of notional PSA contributions as if PSAs were available throughout the worker's lifetime and the contribution rates were 8 and 4 percent (as discussed above and applicable after the year 2041). Under (b), the contribution threshold of $10,000 would be indexed to average wage growth for years *before* the first year of actual contributions—2011. The ratio from this offset formula would be less than

1.0 for those collecting benefits before 2041, and it would increase gradually for successive new-retiree cohorts until it reaches 1.0 for those beginning benefit collection in 2041 and later. These retiree cohorts would, therefore, surrender their entire traditional benefits from participating in PSAs—except when PSA accumulations turn out to be too small to provide even post-reform scheduled Social Security benefits. In such cases, the Ryan proposal provides a Social Security benefit guarantee to top off any shortfalls from PSA annuities in during retirement.

6. Other provisions: The Ryan proposal also contains provisions to safeguard PSA accumulations from premature withdrawals; to allow access to a broader category of investment options once PSAs invested in relatively safe securities reach a minimum threshold value; to mandate annuitization of PSAs upon retirement to provide retirement income at least as large as post-reform scheduled Social Security benefits; to provide general revenue transfers to ensure the program's cash-flow solvency on a year-to-year basis; and to require that payroll taxes be reduced in future years when scheduled rates imply long-range program surpluses. Finally, post-retirement withdrawals and annuities from PSAs would not be subject to income taxes under the Ryan reform proposal.

Effects of the Ryan Proposal on Social Security's Aggregate Finances

Results from implementing each of the Ryan reforms using DEMSIM are shown in table 13.1. The diversion of a part of payroll taxes into personal accounts generates a large increase in Social Security's open group imbalances—of about 3 percent of the present value of baseline taxable earnings over a 75-year horizon and 3.5 percent over the infinite horizon (the "Changes" columns for row 5a in the table). The low-earner benefit enhancement (row 2 of the table) also increases the program's imbalances, but its impact is considerably smaller—merely 0.04 percent as a share of the present value of pre-reform taxable earnings over both 75 years and the infinite horizon.

Subjecting employer-provided group health benefits to payroll taxes reduces Social Security's open group imbalances by a relatively small amount—by 0.82 percentage points of pre-reform taxable payrolls over 75 years and by 0.6 percentage points in perpetuity. Employer group health care coverage, which constitutes about 10 percent of workers' compensation today, is assumed to expand more rapidly compared to worker pay-

TABLE 13.1 **Impact of the Ryan Proposal on Social Security's (OASI) Finances**

Proposed policy change	Post-reform actuarial imbalance			As a percent of DEMSIM-baseline taxable payrolls			Change in actuarial imbalance as a percent of DEMSIM-baseline taxable payrolls		
	Present values in billions of constant 2006 dollars								
	75-year open group	∞-horizon open group	Closed group	75-year open group	∞-horizon open group	Closed group*	75-year open group	∞-horizon open group	Closed group*
1. Progressive CPI-indexing of benefits	5,199	8,148	12,257	2.49	2.90	8.42	−0.86	−1.86	−1.32
2. Low-earner benefit enhancement	7,068	13,476	14,256	3.39	4.79	9.79	0.04	0.04	0.06
3. Index the normal retirement age to longevity	6,144	9,143	15,439	2.95	3.25	10.61	−0.40	−1.50	0.87
4. Subject group health benefits to payroll taxes	5,277	11,673	13,739	2.53	4.15	9.44	−0.82	−0.60	−0.30
5a. Divert payroll taxes (PSA)	13,269	23,193	17,466	6.36	8.25	12.00	3.01	3.50	2.26
5b. Benefit offset[†]	7,463	3,240	11,299	3.58	1.15	7.76	0.23	−3.60	−1.97
Simple sum of changes	3,211	−7,776	10,302	1.54	−2.77	7.08	−1.81	−7.52	−2.66
Total effect of all reforms together—100% PSA participation	4,661	−983	9,152	2.24	−0.35	6.29	−1.11	−5.10	−3.45
Total effect of all reforms together—67% PSA participation	3,940	−401	9,686	1.89	−0.14	6.65	−1.46	−4.90	−3.08
Total effect of all reforms together—33% PSA participation	3,238	189	10,225	1.55	0.07	7.02	−1.80	−4.69	−2.71
Memoranda:									
DEMSIM-baseline imbalance	6,985	13,364	14,172	3.35	4.75	9.74	...	...	...
DEMSIM-baseline taxable payrolls	208,495	281,064	145,572	...	...	...	...	...	...

* Shown as a percent of DEMSIM-baseline open minus closed group present value of payrolls. That is, the denominator equals future generations' payrolls.
† Effect is cumulative with reform element 5a.
Source: Author's calculations.

rolls through 2080, after which this growth differential is reduced to zero. Subjecting such worker compensation to payroll taxes, however, may reduce its future growth as employment contracts are adjusted by shifting to other forms of non-taxed compensation. As a result, the estimate shown in table 13.1 may overstate the revenue impact of this reform element.[8]

Indexing traditional Social Security benefits of new retirees to CPI in a progressive manner—as described in appendix 13.1—has a sizable impact on the program's open group imbalances (shown in row 1 of the table). The imbalance is reduced by 0.86 percent of the present value of baseline taxable earnings over 75 years and by 1.86 percent in perpetuity. The larger percentage over the longer horizon shows this reform element's effect of cumulatively larger reductions in the scheduled benefits of successive birth cohorts over time.

Now for the bottom line: When implemented together and when 100 percent participation in Ryan PSAs is assumed, the five Ryan reform elements reduce the 75-year imbalance as a share of baseline taxable payrolls from 3.35 percent to 2.24 percent, or by 1.11 percentage points, a moderate but not negligible amount. Recall that under Model 2 of the G. W. Bush Commission, the 75-year imbalance *increased* by 0.38 percentage points of pre-reform taxable payrolls (see the 75-year "Changes" column in table 12.1 for the case where all Model 2 reforms are implemented together). Moreover, the Ryan reform proposal would fully eliminate the infinite horizon open group imbalance. Under 100 percent participation in PSAs, the infinite horizon imbalance becomes −0.35 percent of taxable payrolls. As can be seen from row 5b of table 13.1, the chief reason for this is the eventual elimination of traditional benefits of PSA participants from the benefit offset, which, cumulatively with payroll tax diversion into personal accounts, contributes the largest reduction in the infinite horizon open group imbalance.

Table 13.1 also shows how the five Ryan reform elements interact when all are implemented together assuming a 100 percent PSA participation rate. Simply adding the effects of all changes implemented independently would result in a substantial reduction in open group imbalances. However, with 100 percent participation in PSAs, which eliminates traditional benefits in the long term, the effects of some of the benefit-side reform elements—such as progressive CPI indexing of benefits and longevity-indexed increases in normal retirement ages—are dominated by the effects of PSA-related elements.[9]

The interaction between PSA benefit offsets and other Ryan reform elements becomes more interesting when one considers a less than 100 percent PSA participation rate. Of course, for PSA non-participants, traditional benefits would be reduced from progressive CPI indexing and increases in the normal-retirement-age as scheduled under the Ryan proposal. And their benefits would become larger because of the extension of the payroll tax base to employer-provided group health benefits: the latter increases worker's payroll taxes but also qualifies those among PSA non-participants who receive employer group health benefits for additional traditional Social Security benefits. Thereby, it also increases the size of the benefit guarantee for PSA participants.[10]

Such interactions among the Ryan reform elements mean that the impact of the proposal on the traditional system's open group imbalances depends upon the rate of PSA participation. A less than 100 percent participation rate would result in smaller payroll tax diversions into personal accounts, but also smaller future benefit offsets. That means other benefit-side reform elements would have a larger impact because they would determine PSA non-participants' benefits. Whether the open group imbalances would increase or decrease depends on the relative strength of these partially counterbalancing benefit-side changes.

Table 13.1 also shows total effects from implementing all reform elements together but assuming less than 100 percent PSA participation. To simplify the calculations, partial PSA participation is implemented by allowing each person a one-time and irrevocable decision about whether to participate.[11] When the participation rate is assumed to be two thirds, the 75-year open group imbalance as share of baseline taxable payrolls becomes *smaller* (1.89 percent) compared to that under 100 percent PSA participation (2.24 percent). However, the infinite horizon open group imbalance share in baseline taxable payrolls *increases* to −0.14 percent compared to −0.35 percent under 100 percent PSA participation. With the PSA participation rate set at one third, the 75-year and infinite horizon imbalance ratios become 1.55 percent and 0.07 percent, respectively.

These results are easy to explain: a smaller PSA participation rate reduces the outflow of payroll taxes from the traditional system and reduces the open group imbalance over 75 years. But smaller PSA participation rates also reduce benefit offsets over the long term. With more people remaining under the traditional program, the Ryan non-PSA benefit-side reforms receive more play. However, the traditional benefits of PSA non-participants do not decline sufficiently to fully neutralize the lost long-term savings in terms of benefit offsets of those switching from participation to non-participation. Hence, the infinite horizon imbalance increases with smaller PSA participation rates. Traditional benefits do not decline sufficiently because of low-earner benefit enhancement and expanded traditional benefits from extending the payroll tax base to employer health insurance benefits. This result, again, points to the insufficiency of truncated measures of the program's finances. In general, reforms to the program's taxes and benefits shift the time profile of net costs, and truncating the projection horizon at 75 years yields incomplete information about a reform's full, long-term impact on the program's financial condition.

Table 13.1 also shows that the Ryan reform proposal is similar to the KSB proposal in its distribution of adjustment costs on current and future generations. Under 100 percent PSA participation, $5.0 trillion of the $14.3 trillion change in the infinite horizon imbalance—or 35 percent—is imposed on current generations by way of expanding the payroll tax base and reducing traditional benefits. Nevertheless, under the proposal, past and living generations would receive more than $9.0 trillion in excess benefits over their payroll taxes—the result of protecting those aged 55 and older (as of 2009) from most of the reform's adjustments.[12]

The additional cost, relative to DEMSIM's current-law baseline, that is imposed on future generations as a whole equals $9.3 trillion—an increase in their total cost of participating in Social Security from $0.8 trillion under DEMSIM's current-law baseline to $10.1 trillion.[13] Future generations' total cost under the Ryan proposal of $10.1 trillion compares favorably with DEMSIM's baseline closed group imbalance of $14.2 trillion. However, a part of the traditional Social Security system's adjustment costs on both living and future generations would be made up from PSA accumulations as described below.

Transition Costs under the Ryan Reform Proposal

As noted earlier, the cost of transitioning to a PSA system under the Ryan proposal would depend on the PSA participation rate. However, as figure 13.2 shows, transition costs turn out to be not too different during the next few decades compared to DEMSIM baseline annual shortfalls under current laws—no matter how high or low PSA participation rates are. That's because PSA contributions are increased gradually over the next three decades rather than introduced at once (as under Model 2). Although lower participation rates reduce payroll tax diversions into PSAs, non-participants' benefits are also reduced from other benefit-side reforms. After about the mid-2040s, however, the PSA participation rate

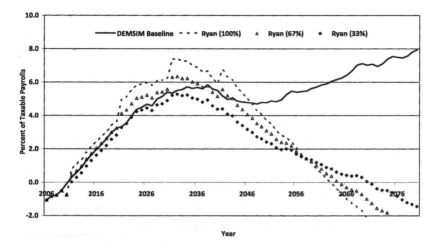

FIGURE 13.2. Annual non-interest imbalance ratios: DEMSIM baseline and Ryan proposal under selected PSA participation rates. Source: Author's calculations.

has a large impact on the rate at which annual imbalances decline. Higher PSA participation means sharper future benefit reductions, on average (from benefit offsets), leading to faster accumulations of the traditional program's surpluses. In general, a larger PSA participation rate leads to larger short-term deficits and to larger long-term surpluses, which emerge sooner.

Although it is difficult to estimate the likely degree of PSA participation under the Ryan proposal, calculations using DEMSIM show that it avoids Model 2's large short-term increases in annual imbalance ratios compared to DEMSIM's baseline—even under a 100 percent PSA participation rate. Because initial annual imbalances are smaller under the Ryan proposal, long-term imbalances are also smaller (or more negative) under it compared to under Model 2.

Effects of the Ryan Proposal on Lifetime Net Tax Rates

The Ryan proposal increases Social Security revenues by subjecting employer-provided group health benefits to payroll taxes, but it also diverts a significant portion of payroll taxes into PSAs. It reduces the traditional program's benefits by introducing progressive CPI indexing for high lifetime earners, and it increases traditional benefits for low-earners.

These changes would be expected to have countervailing influences on participants' lifetime net tax rates. As it happens, the net impact is to increase the traditional program's lifetime net tax rates for most birth cohorts. Panel 1 of table 13.2 shows lifetime net tax rates under the Ryan proposal across various population groups, and panel 2 compares them to those under DEMSIM's baseline assumptions.

The table shows that lifetime net tax rates are higher under the Ryan proposal compared to DEMSIM's baseline for most population groups and the rates increase, on average (see the "All" column), for successive birth cohorts. Apparently, the balance between payroll tax diversions to PSAs and future benefit reductions increasingly swings in favor of the latter: Recall, that the Ryan offset method eliminates all traditional benefits for PSA participants who enter the workforce after 2041. That means, payroll tax rates should be close to the limit given by the current statutory Old Age and Survivor Insurance (OASI) payroll tax rate of 10.6 percent minus about 4 percentage points for personal account contributions—or 6.6 percent. Recall, however, that payroll tax increases from extending the tax base to employer health insurance benefits continues for later generations—implying that for those not subject to the payroll tax ceiling, lifetime net tax rates could exceed 6.6 percent of payrolls—as table 13.2 shows.

Panel 2 of table 13.2 also shows that the increases in lifetime net tax rates are regressive—those with less-than-median lifetime earnings would receive larger increases (or smaller reductions) in lifetime net tax rates under the traditional system. Social Security's ceiling on taxable earnings is responsible for this result: diverting a given percentage of taxable earnings into PSAs represents a smaller share of total earnings for the higher-earning group.

Effects on Retirement Wealth

The effects of Ryan reforms on Social Security retirement wealth ratios is shown in panels 3 and 4 of table 13.2. This is the retirement wealth metric. As before, the first column shows averages for selected population groups of total Social Security wealth as shares of lifetime earnings. Total wealth includes traditional benefits payable under the Ryan reform plan plus individual account wealth from contributions accumulated through the year of benefit collection assuming a 3 percent annual rate of return—one involving very low market risk over investment horizons as long as normal adult working lifetimes.[14] The totals shown assume 100 percent participation in PSAs.

Similar to the G. W. Bush Commission's Model 2 analyzed in chapter 12, the Ryan proposal explicitly provides for general revenue transfers to Social Security to tide over any emerging financial shortfalls. However, retirement wealth ratios using traditional payable benefits are calculated by ignoring that provision. As was done for proposals evaluated earlier, a 5 percent (higher than riskless) discount rate is used to calculate traditional Social Security wealth levels as of the benefit collection year because the Ryan proposal entails general fund transfers after 2030. Indeed, DEMSIM's projections show that required general revenue transfers would be quite large during the first few decades after the proposal is implemented, and it remains uncertain if the federal government would be willing to sustain such large transfers in preference to other policies for restoring balance in the traditional program's finances.

Restricting eligibility to PSAs to those aged 55 in 2009 and younger cohorts means that only the young among baby boomers would invest their earnings in PSAs. The percentage of lifetime earnings that could potentially be invested in PSAs increases for those born later. It should be noted that although table 13.2 is calculated under the assumption of 100 percent participation in PSAs, it could be interpreted as showing per capita estimates for those who participate even if the overall participation rate were less than 100 percent. Panels 3 and 4 show that the fraction of lifetime resources devoted to Social Security is larger (under both definitions) for those born before 1976—because their traditional benefits remain high—but declines to about 3 percent of lifetime earnings for today's younger and future generations. Unlike Model 2, wherein retirement wealth ratios decline very gradually, the wealth ratios are stabilized at about 3.0 percent under the Ryan reform proposal as soon as for those born after 1990.

Panels 3 and 4 of table 13.2 show that under the Ryan proposal, early-born low-earners have a larger share of their lifetime earnings devoted to retirement wealth—reflecting the progressive implementation of CPI indexing. Later-born low-earners also have larger retirement wealth ratios because of the progressive structure of PSA contributions. In addition, women receive larger traditional Social Security benefits in present value because of their longer retirement life spans, Finally, early-born non-whites have smaller retirement wealth ratios—presumably reflecting their shorter average lifespans.

TABLE 13.2 **Effects of the Ryan Social Security Reform Proposal on Selected Population Groups**

| | | Female | | | | Male | | | |
| | | Non-White | | White | | Non-White | | White | |
Years of Birth	All	E≤Med	E>Med	E≤Med	E>Med	E≤Med	E>Med	E≤Med	E>Med
Panel 1	Traditional Social Security lifetime net tax rates under the Ryan proposal								
1946–1960	5.22	4.8	5.5	4.2	5.0	6.7	6.6	6.4	5.8
1961–1975	6.56	6.4	6.6	5.8	6.3	7.5	7.3	7.2	6.8
1976–1990	6.97	7.1	6.8	6.6	6.7	7.8	7.2	7.5	7.0
1991–2005	6.83	7.0	6.5	6.8	6.5	7.4	6.7	7.5	6.7
2006–2020	6.51	6.7	6.2	6.6	6.1	6.9	6.3	7.1	6.3
2021–2035	6.52	6.8	6.1	6.7	6.1	6.9	6.2	7.2	6.3
2036–2050	6.77	7.0	6.2	7.0	6.2	7.2	6.4	7.6	6.5
Panel 2	Percentage point increase in lifetime net tax rates: Ryan minus DEMSIM baseline								
1946–1960	0.1	0.2	0.1	0.2	0.1	0.2	0.1	0.1	0.1
1961–1975	0.5	0.5	0.4	0.7	0.5	0.2	0.2	0.4	0.3
1976–1990	0.9	1.0	0.8	1.4	0.9	0.4	0.5	0.9	0.6
1991–2005	0.7	0.8	0.5	1.4	0.7	-0.1	0.1	0.6	0.3
2006–2020	0.5	0.6	0.1	1.3	0.5	-0.2	-0.3	0.3	0.0
2021–2035	0.6	0.7	0.3	1.5	0.5	-0.1	-0.1	0.8	0.1
2036–2050	1.0	1.1	0.4	2.2	0.7	0.5	0.2	1.2	0.5
Panel 3	Social Security wealth as a share of lifetime earnings (*scheduled* traditional benefits; %)								
1946–1960	4.0	5.1	3.5	5.5	3.9	3.2	2.5	3.4	2.8
1961–1975	3.6	4.2	3.3	4.7	3.5	3.1	2.7	3.4	2.9
1976–1990	3.2	3.6	3.0	4.0	3.0	2.8	2.5	3.3	2.6
1991–2005	2.9	3.2	2.7	3.4	2.7	2.8	2.5	3.1	2.6
2006–2020	2.9	3.2	2.7	3.2	2.6	3.0	2.5	3.3	2.7
2021–2035	3.0	3.3	2.7	3.3	2.7	3.1	2.6	3.5	2.8
2036–2050	3.1	3.4	2.7	3.3	2.7	3.1	2.6	3.7	2.9

Panel 4

Social Security wealth as a share of lifetime earnings (*payable* traditional benefits; %)*

1946–1960	3.0	3.8	2.6	4.0	2.8	2.3	1.7	2.7	2.1
1961–1975	2.3	2.7	2.1	3.0	2.3	2.0	1.7	2.2	1.8
1976–1990	2.7	3.1	2.6	3.4	2.7	2.5	2.3	2.7	2.3
1991–2005	2.9	3.2	2.7	3.4	2.7	2.8	2.4	3.1	2.5
2006–2020	2.9	3.2	2.7	3.2	2.6	3.0	2.5	3.3	2.7
2021–2035	3.0	3.3	2.7	3.3	2.7	3.1	2.6	3.5	2.8
2036–2050	3.1	3.4	2.7	3.3	2.7	3.1	2.6	3.7	2.9

Panel 5

Percent of Social Security wealth provided by Ryan traditional benefits (*payable* definition)

1946–1960	98.0	98.0	97.9	98.5	98.2	97.8	97.0	98.4	97.7
1961–1975	82.4	85.1	81.5	85.9	84.2	84.6	79.9	84.2	79.3
1976–1990	57.4	63.8	57.7	65.0	60.6	61.3	55.7	59.6	50.7
1991–2005	29.3	34.6	27.5	36.4	31.3	33.6	25.8	30.5	24.3
2006–2020	6.7	9.0	6.7	9.3	6.9	8.3	5.4	7.0	5.1
2021–2035	0.1	0.1	0.0	0.1	0.1	0.1	0.1	0.1	0.1
2036–2050	0.0	0.0	0.0	0.0	0.0	0.0	0.0	0.0	0.0

Panel 6

Ryan: total benefits (traditional *payable* plus PSA) as a percent of current-law *scheduled* benefits

1946–1960	98.3	97.7	98.9	97.3	98.0	99.4	100.0	98.6	98.9
1961–1975	91.1	92.1	92.6	89.4	90.3	97.0	94.4	96.4	92.6
1976–1990	81.7	81.7	79.8	77.3	76.8	90.2	83.6	87.6	84.7
1991–2005	76.8	73.6	75.4	67.0	70.1	87.6	80.8	85.2	83.4
2006–2020	76.2	70.1	75.3	63.0	67.2	80.9	84.1	89.0	85.2
2021–2035	77.3	72.4	74.8	63.1	68.0	82.5	82.0	87.2	87.2
2036–2050	78.2	73.2	76.6	62.9	69.0	84.1	82.6	92.1	88.1

*The payable benefits definition ignores the Ryan proposal's general revenue transfers provision.
Source: Author's calculations.

For each population subgroup, the fifth panel of table 13.2 shows the share of traditional Social Security wealth in total Social Security wealth as defined earlier. It shows the share to be almost 100 percent for the baby boomers (those born during 1946–60), but the shares decline consistently for later-born cohorts until it reaches zero for those born after 2020. Corresponding to the steep reduction in the share of traditional benefits under the Ryan proposal is a steep increase in the share of individual accounts: the share of Social Security wealth generated from individual accounts increases from close to zero for older living workers to 100 percent for those born after 2020. This stands in contrast to other reform proposals: for example, the LMS and KSB proposals maintain the share of traditional benefits above 50 percent for successive future generations (see panels 5 of tables 10.2 and 11.2).[15] The choice here depends on how one views the balance between traditional and personal account benefits. Conservatives who favor the eventual elimination of traditional benefits would prefer the Ryan proposal over the LMS and KSB proposals. Whatever the preference, the introduction of personal accounts should not be viewed as a "destruction" of the Social Security system. As argued in chapter 7, a gradual dilution of the insurance aspects of Social Security is already progressing even under the existing system.

The last panel of table 13.2 shows total (traditional payable plus PSA) wealth under the Ryan proposal as a percentage of Social Security scheduled wealth under current laws. The percentages are comparable to those under the reform proposals evaluated in earlier chapters except for the LMS proposal, where the values are much larger. Most proposals with individual accounts trade-off traditional benefits for largers shares of individual account wealth. That trade-off is at its most extreme under the Ryan reform. Like most other reform proposals (except the LMS proposal) the Ryan proposal eventually restores about 80 percent of current-law scheduled benefits. However, its transition to a larger share of individual accounts wealth may trigger other beneficial changes—say to retirement and saving incentives—that are beyond the scope of this book's analytical framework.

Guaranteed Benefits under the Ryan Proposal

How large are guaranteed benefits under the Ryan proposal, and how do they compare with those scheduled under current laws and under the Ryan reforms? Table 13.3 examines these questions. The first panel of table 13.3 shows average Social Security wealth for various population subgroups based on traditional benefits at retirement with all Ryan benefit-side reforms activated except for participation in PSAs and the associated benefit offsets. This panel's wealth estimates should be interpreted as based on Ryan-guaranteed lifetime benefit amounts. These figures show present values of minimum post-reform scheduled benefits (annuities) that PSA participants of specific population groups would receive (in principle) if their PSA accumulations through their benefit collection years turn out to be insufficient to purchase annuities of like amounts.[16] Under the Ryan reform proposal, any shortfall in the PSA annuity (with all PSA assets annuitized) compared to the guaranteed benefit level would be made up by the federal government each year. Again, however, because required general-revenue transfers (transition costs) are quite large under the Ryan proposal, such guaranteed traditional benefits are also discounted at a higher-than-riskless rate of interest—5 percent per year—when calculating present values.[17]

Panel 2 of table 13.3 shows Ryan-guaranteed retirement wealth minus Social Security wealth based on current-law *payable* benefits—both calculated using an inflation-adjusted annual interest rate of 5.0 percent. Social Security wealth levels based on current-law payable benefits are taken from table 7.2, panel 2. Panel 2 of table 13.3 shows that Ryan-guaranteed Social Security wealth levels are larger than current-law payable levels for almost all population groups shown. In part, this result occurs because the Ryan proposal increases traditional benefits by expanding the payroll tax base as described earlier. However, the excess of guaranteed wealth levels over current-law payable levels declines for later-born cohorts as the benefit cuts applicable to PSA non-participants become more stringent over time.

The third panel of table 13.3 shows Ryan guaranteed retirement wealth minus of that implied by current-law *scheduled* benefits—again, with both benefit flows discounted at a 5 percent rate. The latter wealth amounts are taken from table 7.2, panel 1. Here, the differences are negative in all but one of the cells, indicating that Ryan guaranteed benefits would be almost always less than benefits scheduled under current laws. The values become more negative for later-born cohorts indicating that growth over time of Ryan guaranteed benefits is slower relative to that of current-law scheduled benefits. The differences are more negative for those with larger- compared to smaller-than-median lifetime earnings and also for whites compared to non-whites among various population subgroups.

TABLE 13.3 Retirement Wealth Levels Under Ryan Guaranteed, Ryan Scheduled, and Current Law: Thousands of Constant 2006 Dollars by 15-Year Birth Cohorts, Gender, Race, and Lifetime Earnings (E)

Years of Birth	All	Female				Male			
		Non-White		White		Non-White		White	
		E≤Med	E>Med	E≤Med	E>Med	E≤Med	E>Med	E≤Med	E>Med
Panel 2									
Ryan-*guaranteed* Social Security wealth levels (r=5%)									
1946–1960	175.7	116.0	199.7	153.6	238.5	88.8	183.1	101.9	212.2
1961–1975	172.7	109.7	203.6	146.7	231.3	99.9	206.4	109.3	213.1
1976–1990	185.0	119.6	220.9	161.3	249.3	112.9	230.1	129.5	221.0
1991–2005	196.0	134.6	225.1	176.8	254.1	130.3	241.2	137.5	233.0
2006–2020	208.4	147.1	233.0	198.4	266.7	156.0	242.1	153.1	237.6
2021–2035	222.7	160.7	253.4	219.7	270.8	173.7	265.0	181.4	244.1
2036–2050	235.7	178.9	257.6	238.7	284.8	190.9	271.8	196.5	250.4
Panel 3									
Ryan-*guaranteed* minus current-law-*payable* Social Security wealth levels (r=5%)									
1946–1960	28.3	20.3	32.5	24.0	43.0	17.2	39.8	14.5	32.1
1961–1975	48.4	32.1	57.0	40.1	63.8	31.0	61.1	34.9	58.5
1976–1990	44.4	34.9	50.3	42.0	56.0	36.5	55.9	39.3	45.7
1991–2005	47.2	41.6	50.9	49.6	53.6	47.2	53.7	44.6	43.9
2006–2020	48.5	44.0	46.1	63.8	47.7	54.5	46.2	55.9	34.3
2021–2035	44.8	49.9	39.0	69.0	33.5	60.0	30.8	60.1	21.5
2036–2050	30.3	48.2	21.5	55.1	15.2	59.6	3.5	62.4	-3.3

Panel 4	Ryan-*guaranteed* minus current-law-*scheduled* (r=5%) Social Security wealth levels								
1946–1960	–2.5	–0.8	–4.7	–4.7	–3.3	–0.6	0.1	–0.5	–1.3
1961–1975	–9.3	–4.0	–11.4	–9.5	–14.2	–1.3	–7.2	1.0	–12.9
1976–1990	–27.9	–8.5	–38.9	–19.7	–45.9	–3.0	–35.8	–5.5	–43.2
1991–2005	–48.9	–18.7	–63.7	–33.1	–77.7	–7.4	–71.5	–13.3	–76.4
2006–2020	–72.4	–33.9	–96.1	–38.6	–119.7	–23.2	–104.3	–16.0	–118.1
2021–2035	–101.8	–41.4	–137.9	–55.1	–162.5	–34.2	–163.7	–38.9	–161.5
2036–2050	–139.9	–60.1	–174.2	–97.0	–208.0	–49.2	–218.9	–48.9	–213.7

Panel 4	Ryan-*guaranteed* (r=5%) minus Ryan *scheduled* (r=5%) and minus accumulated PSA (r=3%)								
1946–1960	0.5	1.9	–2.5	–0.5	1.6	–0.1	0.2	0.9	1.0
1961–1975	5.5	5.0	4.5	7.1	9.6	1.7	4.7	4.9	3.9
1976–1990	11.1	14.9	13.7	21.4	22.8	8.4	7.7	11.2	–2.7
1991–2005	7.8	21.8	7.5	36.2	21.6	9.8	–11.4	9.1	–25.1
2006–2020	–5.7	20.2	–14.7	49.1	7.1	11.1	–49.4	2.7	–65.6
2021–2035	–28.3	14.4	–39.4	46.1	–23.6	2.1	–86.6	–10.8	–109.7
2036–2050	–58.0	3.8	–73.2	27.5	–55.1	–11.0	–133.4	–29.6	–158.6

Source: Author's calculations.

Finally, the fourth panel of table 13.3 shows Ryan-guaranteed Social Security wealth minus the sum of (a) Ryan Social Security wealth under scheduled benefits (scheduled post-reform traditional benefits with benefit offsets assuming PSA participation discounted at a 5 percent annual rate of interest) and (b) the value of PSAs at benefit collection date (PSA contributions accumulated at a 3 percent annual interest rate). These estimates are generally positive for today's workers but become smaller and eventually negative for younger and future ones—indicating that Ryan-guaranteed benefits (which are the same as those scheduled for PSA non-participants under the reforms) dominate those obtainable from PSA participation for the baby boomers, gen-Xers, and, indeed, most of those born as late as in 2005. For future-born generations, however, the Ryan reform promises to deliver substantial additional benefits from PSA participation compared to Ryan-guaranteed levels, on average.

If, on average, Social Security wealth from non-participation in PSAs exceeds that obtainable from participation (which happens when the estimates in panel 4 are positive), people in corresponding population groups would avoid participation in Ryan PSAs. If the estimates are negative, PSA participation during the person's remaining lifetime is financially beneficial and members of such groups would choose to participate in PSAs. Thus, panel 4 provides a rough guide about which population groups would choose to participate in Ryan PSAs and which not. Indeed, panel 4 suggests that participation is relatively unlikely among those alive today.

Summary and Final Remarks

The Ryan reform proposal is considered by most analysts to be one of the most conservative of Social Security reform proposals because of its emphasis on creating large, carve-out personal accounts. However, it also includes a payroll tax increase by extending the payroll tax base to employer-provided group health insurance benefits. This reform element is justified as restoring the original intent of the program of financing benefits out of dedicated taxes on employees' total pay or compensation—which did not deviate by much from wages when Social Security was created in 1935. Although this element detracts from the proposal's conservative credentials, it helps to avoid large annual Social Security imbalances during the short term—as under Model 2, for example.

The Ryan proposal's extension of the payroll tax base to employer-provided group health insurance benefits also triggers additional future benefits. This feature makes the Ryan proposal's benefit guarantee more generous. The benefit guarantee is also more generous because the progressive CPI indexing of benefits and indexation of the normal retirement age to longevity increases—measures that, once they are fully factored into the program, are mostly effective for PSA non-participants—do not reduce benefits as rapidly as benefit offsets imposed on PSA participants.

The traditional program's financial projections under the Ryan proposal are heavily dependent on the degree of participation in PSAs. The generosity of benefit guarantees is meant to encourage PSA participation. But for current generations, especially those who have only a few years remaining before retiring, it may act as a deterrent because net benefits from non-participation would exceed those from participation in PSAs. Although, the PSA participation rate that the reform would elicit is difficult to estimate, DEMSIM calculations suggest that those rates would be low rather than high.

The Ryan proposal, like most others with personal accounts, must deal with a basic conflict: providing generous benefit guarantees reduces PSA participation, but cutting guaranteed benefits is politically unpopular because it is viewed as exposing participants to private market risks. However, the calculations show that even under low-risk investment strategies, almost all participants would come out ahead under the Ryan plan compared to the current system's *payable* benefit levels—if they participate in PSA's.

Progressive CPI Indexing Social Security Benefits under the Ryan Reform Proposal

This Ryan reform element intends to reduce growth in scheduled benefits by more for those with high lifetime earnings. Recall that a worker's average monthly indexed earnings are calculated by applying the average wage index to past earnings to place them on par with the most recent economy-wide average wage level. Successive retiree cohorts receive higher real benefits because (1) their own wages are higher than those of earlier retirees and (2) average economy-wide wages increase over time—at a rate faster than price inflation, on average.

Each worker's average monthly indexed earnings are converted into a primary insurance amount—which equals the Social Security retirement benefit if the worker decides to begin collecting benefits at his or her normal retirement age. The conversion is done by applying bend point factors to different segments of the worker's average monthly indexed earnings, where the segments are defined by specific dollar thresholds called bend points. The bend point factors are progressive: They yield a conversion ratio of 90 percent of average indexed earnings up to the first bend point, 32 percent up to the second bend point, and 15 percent of average monthly indexed earnings beyond the second bend point. Bend point values for 2008 are set by the Social Security Administration at $711 and $4,288, and they are scheduled to grow at the same rate as the average wage level.

The Ryan proposal would introduce a new bend point between the two existing ones beginning in 2016. It would gradually and proportionately reduce the 32 and 15 percent bend point factors in future years.[18] These cuts in the upper bend point factors would reduce the future Social Security benefits of higher lifetime earners but leave currently scheduled benefit growth undiminished for low lifetime earners—those for whom average monthly indexed earnings is smaller than the new bend point value. The reduction in bend point factors is designed so that even among those affected, those with lower average monthly indexed earnings would receive smaller reductions in scheduled Social Security benefits. The Ryan proposal applies this change in the benefit formula to reduce scheduled retirement and aged survivor benefits but not benefits of surviving children and parents with children in care (called mother/father benefits in appendix 6.1).

Note that this reform element makes the distribution of future Social Security benefits even more progressive than it is under current laws— that is, until the two upper bend point factors of 32 and 15 percent are reduced to zero. Thereafter, to maintain benefit growth for career-maximum earners at the inflation rate, the upper two bend points would have to become negative. But the proposal specifies that they be limited from below to zero.

Key Conclusions about Social Security's Financial Condition and Reform Alternatives

The Value Added from Microsimulations

The reader may have earlier wondered why one should bother to re-implement the calculations of Social Security's Trustees and actuaries who examine, analyze, and publish reams of statistics each year on that program's operations, financial condition, and reform options. There are two reasons. First, DEMSIM shows that constructing Social Security's financial projections gains from modeling key aspects of the economy and demographics, including interactions among them, at the individual and family level. Indeed, DEMSIM confirms the view emphasized repeatedly by the Social Security Advisory Board's Technical Panel on Assumptions and Methods.[1] For example, the 2007 Technical Panel writes:[2]

> Many of this panel's methodological recommendations—transparency, the use of micro-simulation and stochastic analyses, specifying and estimating inter-actions, employing additional data—are not new. Previous Technical Panels and other experts have made similar recommendations. . . . The actuaries have made some progress on many of these fronts. There are reasons to be impatient, however. New computing power, new sources of data, and new estimating techniques should allow OCACT to make faster progress in advancing their models and methods. Indeed, others . . . are exploiting these developments and creating the means to analyze the system and its response to change. Only by

aggressively deploying new data and techniques and by making the process more transparent can OCACT and the Trustees remain the definitive source-of-record for this information.[3]

Second, official evaluations of Social Security reforms focus on the program's solvency over a limited 75-year time horizon without (a) fully revealing their likely impact on different population groups via lifetime actuarial measures and (b) employing sufficient metrics that enable a proper comparative analysis across policy alternatives.

This book's analysis uses an independent methodology and reaches different conclusions from official ones about Social Security's financial condition and the impact of reform options. Its methods are consistent with current Actuarial Standards of Practice. ASOP's guidelines recognize that "actuarial practice involves the identification, measurement, and management of contingent future events in environments that rarely, if ever, emerge exactly as projected. . . . Two actuaries could follow generally accepted practice, both using reasonable methods and assumptions, and reach appropriate results that could be substantially different."[4]

ASOP guidelines on social insurance also suggest that when measuring future financial flows, especially receipts, for a program such as Social Security, proper consideration should be given to "the actual past experience of the social insurance program, over both short- and long-range periods, also taking into account relevant factors that *may create material differences in future experience*" (emphasis added).

Incorporating information from a microsimulation such as DEMSIM reveals forces built into the current U.S. population and economy that are likely to create such a material difference—in particular, the interaction between labor force participation rates, earnings distributions, life-cycle earnings abilities, and changing distributions of the population by age, gender, race, education, and other characteristics. Such interactions produce a significantly different time profile of Social Security's financial imbalances compared to official ones.

This book presents estimates of Social Security's finances under static demographic and economic projections. A reexamination may be warranted after incorporating modifications to DEMSIM's modeling—for example, by calibrating behavioral responses by individuals to changes in future Social Security policies. The analysis presented here is only the first step toward providing a more comprehensive framework for analyzing the effects of government programs.

The rest of this chapter summarizes the findings of earlier chapters by condensing key estimates under alternative reforms to draw broad conclusions about available policy choices.

Aggregate Measures and Micromeasures

Several alternative measures are traditionally used to evaluate Social Security's financial condition. Studies on the accuracy and consistency of alternative measures in reflecting the program's overall financial condition point to two aggregate estimates—the infinite horizon open and closed group actuarial imbalance measures of the system's finances.[5] However, in order to provide a reference point to official reports of the program's financial condition, this book also reports 75-year open group imbalances (in dollars and as a ratio to the 75-year present value of taxable payrolls) and annual imbalance ratios over the next 75 years.

The distributional implications of Social Security's current payroll tax and benefit rules and those under alternative reforms are measured in several ways. The lifetime net tax rate measure shows the share of lifetime earnings that must be surrendered, on net, by people in various demographic and economic categories for participating in Social Security. This tax could be interpreted as a pure tax, a charge for retirement income insurance, or as a load factor for substituting government in place of private retirement saving. It does not use the income replacement rate metric because, under current demographic realities, the program appears to operate more as a substitute for personal retirement saving than as an insurance against income loss because of old age. That's because survival to ages well beyond the program's statutory retirement ages are now much more common and expected compared to when the program was first started.

The lifetime net tax rate is supplemented with another distributional metric: the retirement wealth ratio that shows share of lifetime earnings devoted to accumulating Social Security wealth. The latter is defined as the actuarial present value of Social Security benefits plus the accumulated value of any personal account assets as of the benefit collection date. This metric measures each population groups Social Security's wealth without considering past payroll tax payments. This metric is important because there is independent interest in knowing the extent to which Social Security supplements private sources of retirement support.

Aggregate imbalance measures and micromeasures together provide as comprehensive view of how current laws and alternative reforms would affect Social Security's finances and the budgets of various population groups. For example, they show whether the adjustment costs are "balanced" across current and future generations and across people with different characteristics. This is distinct from the conventional notion of balance in policymaking that focuses on the relative prevalence of tax-side versus benefit-side elements contained in a reform proposal.

Social Security's Financial Condition under DEMSIM's Baseline Assumptions

The principle findings of DEMSIM are that projected growth in Social Security's tax base could turn out to be much slower compared to standard economic assumptions made by various official agencies that evaluate the program's financial condition. The reason is that during the next few decades, today's most experienced and highest earning cohorts—the baby boomers—will be replaced by a smaller cohort of Generation-X members. This transition directly implies a decline in aggregate labor inputs. Other changes to the U.S. population's demographic and economic attributes are also likely to slow the growth of future payrolls.

The method used by DEMSIM to track the growth of aggregate payrolls utilizes Jorgenson et al.'s (2007) method of decomposing total output growth into various components including growth in technology, the total capital stock, and aggregate labor inputs. Technological growth is projected based on the historical average rate as estimated by Jorgenson et al. Growth in the capital stock is calibrated using microdata information on the net worth of individuals by gender and age. And each year's aggregate labor input equals the product of the number of workers and their quality. Labor quality estimates take into account evolving demographic patterns by carrying forward the momentum of demographic and economic forces that are built into the current U.S. population.

DEMSIM incorporates a very detailed calibration of U.S. economic and demographic variables. The simulated distributions of all relevant variables—for both the initial 1970 population and its transitions across subsequent years through 2006—are validated against information from microdata surveys. This exercise shows a close match between simulated and actual distributions to provide confidence that forward simulation of the underlying transition rules would properly capture the trends and in-teractions between all variables. It would also reveal the likely course of the population's size; its distribution by age, gender, race, and education; and trends in family formation and dissolution, racial composition, acqui-sition of education, labor force participation, retirement, and so on.

The simulation is augmented by "driver" regressions of labor quality on individuals' demographic and economic characteristics. These regres-sions are integrated into the demographic transition described earlier to generate estimates of annual aggregate "effective labor inputs," which, in turn, form the basis for projecting future aggregate payrolls, payroll taxes, and Social Security benefits. DEMSIM's results show that aggregate effec-tive labor inputs are likely to decline in the future and impose a drag on labor productivity growth from projected increases in multifactor produc-tivity and the capital stock.

DEMSIM is further augmented by a Social Security benefit calculator—SSTBC—that takes account of even the most esoteric features of the Social Security benefit formula, including calculations of spousal and de-pendent child and survivor benefits, early retirement reductions, delayed retirement credits, re-computations for additional years of earnings after initial benefit collection, divorcee benefits, benefits based on old-law for-mulae, benefits for parents with children in care, and so on.

DEMSIM's simulation can be continued as far into the future as neces-sary to produce estimates of Social Security's long-term financial imbal-ances under its current laws. Note that estimates based on forces built into the population are useful because those forces—especially trends in the population's composition by age, gender, and race that influence other characteristics and the interactions between them—are likely to be sus-tained far into the future. The main results on Social Security's projected financial imbalances can be summarized as follows:

1. The program's 75-year open group imbalance—the present value of annual deficits (receipts excluding interest income minus expenditures) between 2006 and 2080 plus the accumulated value of the Old Age and Survivor Insurance (OASI) trust fund as of the beginning of 2006—equals $7.0 trillion in constant 2006 dollars.

2. The program's infinite horizon open group imbalance—the same calculation as under (1) in perpetuity—equals $13.4 trillion.

3. A sizable percentage of the program's total (infinite horizon open group) imbal-ance arises within the next 75 years ($7.0 trillion divided by $13.4 trillion, or 52

percent) under DEMSIM. The Social Security Trustees, unfortunately, do not publish this estimate for the OASI program.

4. Calculating the financial imbalance over the closed group of past and current participants aged 15 and older yields $14.2 trillion—which is larger than its infinite horizon open group imbalance. Subtracting the closed group imbalance from the open group value of $13.4 trillion yields −$0.8 trillion—the amount that future generations are scheduled to receive from the program under current Social Security policies in present value as of 2006 (the negative value means that future generations would pay, on net, $0.8 trillion to Social Security).

5. Social Security's current rules (scheduled benefits and taxes) would impose life-time net tax rates of 5.1 percent for those born before 1960, remaining steady at 6.1 percent for those born between 1961 and 2020, and declining for those born still later. Lifetime net tax rates average as high as 7.5 percent for some population groups—for example, today's non-white male children who would earn less than median lifetime earnings during their careers. And those born between 2036 and 2050 would experience lifetime net tax rates averaging 5.8 percent. The decline in the lifetime net tax rates of later cohorts under current laws arises from their lengthier projected retirement spans. Lifetime net tax rates are not necessarily progressive for all groups when the calculation is based on individuals' total rather than just taxable earnings. Only high-earning white females have larger lifetime net tax rates compared to low-earning ones. That occurs because of marital sorting: white women tend to marry white men—who earn more on average—and the surviving female spouses receive significant dependent and survivor benefits based on their spouses' earnings records.

6. The range for Social Security's open group financial imbalance ratios under optimistic and pessimistic economic and demographic assumptions—including variations in the rates of labor force participation, education acquisition, fertility, mortality, immigration, productivity, inflation, and capital accumulation—is quite wide. Over the 75-year horizon, imbalance ratios range from 0.4 percent to 7.0 percent. Under infinite horizon calculations, they range from 2.0 percent to 8.5 percent. Closed group imbalances range from 4.3 percent to 19.5 percent of closed group payrolls.

A final remark on long-term imbalance measures concerns their interpretation. A simple way to think about the baseline infinite horizon open group imbalances is that they represent the amount of funds that must be available to the government, invested at interest, in order to maintain existing Social Security policies unchanged. Under normal conditions, those

imbalances grow larger over time both in dollar terms and as ratios of
the pool of resources out of which they must be paid—the present values
of future payrolls or total national output. For example, at a 2.9 percent
interest rate, the $13.4 trillion infinite horizon imbalance as of 2006 would
grow to $13.8 trillion in one year, and so on, if Social Security policies and
economic and demographic projections remain unchanged. Because total
payrolls grow at the annual rate of productivity growth—discovered to be
0.71 percent per year under DEMSIM—the present value of taxable payrolls of $281.1 trillion as of 2006 (see table 6.1) would grow to $283.1 trillion by 2007. That implies the ratio of the imbalance to the present value
of payrolls would become larger over time: compared to its 2006 value of
13,364 / 281,064 = 0.0475, or 4.75 percent, its value would become 13,752 /
283,060 = 0.0486, or 4.86 percent. Such calculations tell us how rapidly
Social Security's unfunded payment obligations are escalating over time
relative to the resources available to pay for them.

The ratio of the 75-year open group imbalance to the present value of
taxable payrolls over the same period has a similar interpretation. The
increase in this ratio with the passage of time, however, is likely to be
even more rapid because, under current laws and projections, each new
estimate of the 75-year open group imbalance incorporates the financial
shortfall from one additional (terminal) year that is included within the
75-year time horizon.

Effects under Liberal, Centrist, and Conservative Reform Proposals

The major objective of the book is to evaluate alternative approaches to
reforming Social Security. Six reform proposals are selected from among
scores developed over the years by many eminent policymakers, academicians, and Social Security analysts. The criterion for choosing among the
proposals is admittedly quite crude—judging whether reform proposals
represent liberal, centrist, and conservative approaches based on whether
they are sponsored and supported by liberal, conservative, or avowedly
centrist policy proponents. That judgment usually boils down to examining whether the proposals contain predominantly tax-side or benefit-side
reform elements or a "balanced" combination of both.

As argued earlier, Social Security now operates mostly as a substitute
for personal retirement saving rather than as insurance against the loss of

retirement assets or income during old age under today's economic and demographic environment. To the extent that people view it as such, and to the extent that they compensate for retirement saving via Social Security by reducing personal saving, whether the program's existing imbalances are closed using tax-side or benefit-side reform elements appears rather moot: both types of reforms would be perceived as a "tax" increase by those who are affected.[6] Hence, judgment about which set of reforms would be preferable should rest on more neutral measures, such as lifetime net tax rates: how alternative reform proposals would change those rates, how they are distributed across different population groups, and whether any alternative saving mechanisms are created should be considered when judging the proposals' merits and demerits. The remainder of this chapter presents information collected from earlier ones to provide a comparative analysis of the reform proposals evaluated in this book.

Comparison Based on Aggregate Measures

As noted in chapter 8, DEMSIM projects an increase in the ratio of taxable to total earnings in future years. Recall that DEMSIM's estimate of this ratio—85.6 percent—is quite close to the official estimate of 83.3 percent. Rising age-earning profiles imply that secular movements in the population's age distribution—especially baby boomer retirements—are likely to generate low-frequency movements in the taxable-to-total earnings ratio. In 2006, the boomers' age range of 42 through 60 spanned the range of highest life-cycle labor earning years. As the boomers retire and are replaced by relatively smaller-sized cohorts, the relative weight on experienced high-earning workers will decline causing the taxable-to-total earnings ratio to increase. DEMSIM projects this ratio to increase to 88 percent by the mid-2020s and remain around that value throughout the 75-year horizon.

The projection of a rising ratio of taxable-to-total earnings under DEMSIM considerably weakens the leverage of reform proposals that call for accelerating the currently scheduled annual increases in maximum taxable earnings to achieve a higher target ratio by a certain future year. Projected increases in the ratio under DEMSIM's baseline mean that very little additional growth of the taxable earnings ceiling is required to achieve such target ratios. Hence, such a reform is likely to generate very little additional Social Security revenues, near-term surpluses, and reductions in the program's financial imbalance.

In particular, this feature of DEMSIM leads to the spectacular failure of the Robert M. Ball proposal, which critically depends on a sizable boost to Social Security's trust fund from this and other policies in order to gain from higher returns by investing the trust fund in private capital markets. As figure 8.2 and table 14.1 show, the Ball proposal does not make much difference to Social Security's future annual imbalances relative to those under DEMSIM's baseline.

Table 14.1 shows four important metrics based on the open and closed group imbalances reported in earlier chapters. The information is presented as ratios to Social Security's 75-year and infinite horizon open group imbalances under DEMSIM's baseline projections. For proposals that create personal accounts, the results shown assume 100 percent participation in those accounts (participation is mandatory under the LMS proposal for people aged 55 and younger in 2005).

1. The first column of table 14.1 shows shares of the baseline 75-year imbalance that would be resolved by each of six reform. The Diamond-Orszag proposal eliminates the largest share, and the LMS proposal comes in second. The former proposal wins this contest because of its relatively steep tax increases, especially on high lifetime earners and especially on future generations. In contrast, the G. W. Bush Commission's Model 2 *increases* the 75-year imbalance from the introduction of personal accounts. In general, reforms that create exclusively "carve-out" personal accounts—the KSB, Model 2, and Ryan proposals—reduce the 75-year open group imbalance by much less in present value terms.

2. The second column of the table shows the share of the infinite horizon open group liability that is resolved. In this case, the Ryan proposal delivers the largest effect—by creating large personal accounts together with steep benefit cuts that become increasingly binding over the long term. Indeed, assuming 100 percent participation in personal accounts, traditional Social Security benefits would eventually be eliminated as a direct program cost with only a notional calculation used for determining payouts under the proposal's benefit guarantee. Three of the proposals—Diamond-Orszag, KSB, and LMS—resolve more than 80 percent, and Model 2 resolves about 60 percent of DEMSIM's baseline infinite horizon imbalance.

3. The third column of table 14.1 shows the fraction of the change in the infinite horizon open group imbalance that is resolved within the first 75 years. This

TABLE 14.1 **The Effects of Alternative Reform Proposals on Social Security's Aggregate Finances**

Reform Proposal	Percent of 75-year imbalance resolved	Percent of infinite horizon imbalance resolved	Change in 75-year imbalance / Infinite horizon imbalance (percent)	Change in closed group Imbalance / Baseline closed group imbalance (percent)
Ball	16.6	14.6	8.7	0.9
Diamond-Orszag	80.2	88.0	41.9	23.2
Kolbe-Stenholm-Boyd	51.8	86.2	27.1	25.9
Liebman-MacGuineas-Samwick	69.6	81.7	36.4	33.9
G. W. Bush Commission—Model 2	−12.4	60.7	−6.5	13.7
Paul Ryan (100% PSA participation)	33.3	107.4	17.4	35.4

Source: Author's calculations.

metric shows how rapidly the total fiscal imbalance is resolved under various reform proposals. The Diamond-Orszag proposal wins this contest; the LMS proposal comes in as a close second; and the poorest (and negative) performance is by Model 2.

4. The final metric shown in the table is the ratio of the closed group imbalance to DEMSIM's baseline closed group imbalance. It shows the share of the | "give-away" to today's and earlier generations under current Social Security policies that each proposal would eliminate. This is a measure of how much fiscal responsibility each proposal would impose on today's voters. Note that although the Diamond-Orszag proposal resolves the largest fraction of the total infinite horizon imbalance within the first 75 years, it imposes much of that adjustment on future generations among those alive during the first 75 years after 2006. That explains why it trails the LMS proposal under the closed group metric. Even the KSB proposal imposes a larger fraction of the cost on current generations despite resolving a relatively small share of the total imbalance within the first 75 years compared to the Diamond-Orszag proposal. Overall, the Ryan proposal would be the most fiscally responsible of all were it able to deliver 100 percent participation in personal accounts. Assuming 67 (or 33) percent personal accounts participation under the Ryan proposal, however, would make the LMS proposal (wherein participation is mandatory for those aged 55 and younger in 2005) the most fiscally responsible proposal.

Annual Imbalance Ratios

The preferred metric of many Social Security analysts is simply the program's annual imbalance ratios—the shortfall of annual non-interest receipts to annual taxable payrolls. This metric has the advantage of showing the timing of future shortfalls, but it does not show the total size of the program's financial imbalances under given policies because of its finite horizon, nor does it show the distributional effects of alternative reforms. Figure 14.1 shows annual imbalance ratios for all six of the reform proposals evaluated in this book using DEMSIM.

The Ball, Diamond-Orszag, and Ryan proposals increase the program's short-term surpluses. The Ryan proposal does so for a very brief period as a result of extending the payroll tax base to employer group health benefits. The remaining proposals increase Social Security's short-term deficits from carve-out financing of personal accounts. Model 2 and Ryan proposals increase short-term deficits beyond those under current laws

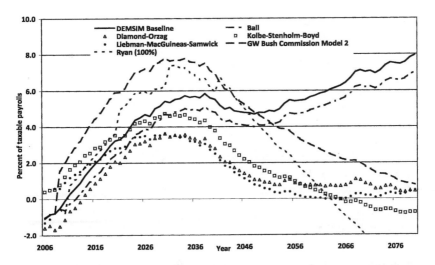

FIGURE 14.1. Annual imbalance ratios: DEMSIM baseline and alternative reform proposals.
Source: Author's calculations.

through the mid-2040s. However, the Ryan plan would generate the largest Social Security deficit reversals during the latter half of the 21st century and beyond.

During the medium term, the largest reduction in annual financial imbalances occurs under the Diamond-Orszag proposal with the LMS reform not far behind. Indeed, annual imbalance ratio profiles for LMS and Diamond-Orszag reforms lie very close to each other. Exclusively reporting annual imbalance ratios, however, would not communicate to policymakers and the public extensive differences between the two proposals, both in the aggregate and at the level of detailed population groupings. In particular, annual imbalance ratios alone would not reflect the vast differences in the two proposals' adjustment cost allocations—broadly across current and future generations, and according to gender, race, lifetime incomes, and so on.

Based on figure 14.1, it is easy to place the Ryan and Ball proposals as polar opposites. Assuming 100 percent participation in personal accounts, the former eventually eliminates the traditional system—although its traditional benefits remain relevant for calculating guaranteed benefit levels to personal account participants. In contrast, the latter preserves the current program's structure and operations by bringing additional revenues to pay for the program's benefit obligations. However, the Ball proposal's reform elements fail to operate as envisioned because key revenue-increasing elements are not projected under DEMSIM to increase the program's receipts by much. Model 2, by far, creates the largest short-term Social Security deficits, is unsuccessful in reducing them significantly within 75 years, and lags behind all others in addressing the program's financial problems.[7]

Lifetime Net Tax Rate, Personal Accounts, and Retirement Wealth

Table 14.2 collects the "All" columns from earlier tables to report lifetime net tax rates and Social Security retirement wealth provided under five of the reform proposals examined here. The Ball proposal is excluded from table 14.2. To reiterate, the numerator in a lifetime net tax rate (panel 1 of the table) equals net taxes—individual payroll taxes minus traditional benefits in each year—discounted back to that individual's age 18. The denominator equals that individual's lifetime earnings discounted back to the same age. A 5 percent rate of discount is used for all elements in the numerator and denominator, and the ratios are averaged over members of each 15-year birth cohort.

Retirement wealth ratios are calculated by accumulating personal account contributions (where applicable) at a "riskless" 3.0 percent rate of interest through the person's year of benefit collection. That accumulated amount is added to the present value of the person's traditional *payable* benefits under each reform as of the benefit collection year using a 5.0 percent discount rate. The denominator is the accumulated value of labor earnings calculated as of the benefit collection year using a 5 percent interest rate.

The third panel of table 14.2 shows average shares of traditional benefits in total retirement wealth as of the benefit collection year. And the fourth panel of the table shows total post-reform retirement wealth—including traditional benefits and individual accounts valued as of the benefit collection year—as a share of retirement wealth based on traditional scheduled benefits.

In these calculations, a 3.0 percent personal account accumulation rate is used so that personal account wealth levels do not include any compensation for investment risk. Moreover, because none of the reform proposals fully eliminate Social Security's financial imbalance and would require

TABLE 14.2 **Lifetime Net Tax Rates, Personal Account Sizes, and Total Social Security Wealth at Retirement Under Various Reform Proposals**

Birth Cohort	DEMSIM Baseline	DO	KSB	LMS	Model 2	Ryan
Panel 1	Lifetime net tax rate (%)					
1946–1960	5.1	5.1	5.2	5.5	5.0	5.2
1961–1975	6.1	6.5	5.9	6.6	5.9	6.6
1976–1990	6.1	7.0	5.6	6.6	5.3	7.0
1991–2005	6.1	7.8	5.7	6.5	4.8	6.8
2006–2020	6.1	8.7	5.8	6.5	4.7	6.5
2021–2035	5.9	9.5	5.8	6.4	4.8	6.5
2036–2050	5.8	10.1	5.8	6.4	5.0	6.8
Panel 2	Total Social Security (payable+IA) wealth as a share of lifetime earnings (%)*					
1946–1960	3.4	4.0	3.1	3.3	2.6	3.0
1961–1975	2.7	3.4	3.0	3.2	2.4	2.3
1976–1990	2.6	3.3	3.3	3.8	2.9	2.7
1991–2005	2.3	3.2	3.2	3.8	3.3	2.9
2006–2020	2.2	3.1	3.1	3.7	3.4	2.9
2021–2035	2.1	3.1	3.1	3.7	3.3	3.0
2036–2050	2.1	3.2	3.1	3.7	3.1	3.1
Panel 3	Share of traditional benefits in Social Security wealth (%)*					
1946–1960	100.0	100.0	94.0	93.8	94.7	98.0
1961–1975	100.0	100.0	78.0	76.3	73.8	82.4
1976–1990	100.0	100.0	65.3	61.7	52.8	57.4
1991–2005	100.0	100.0	60.7	57.2	41.8	29.3
2006–2020	100.0	100.0	61.0	56.9	38.2	6.7
2021–2035	100.0	100.0	61.0	56.9	35.7	0.1
2036–2050	100.0	100.0	61.4	57.5	32.0	0.0
Panel 4	Post-reform total *payable* retirement wealth as a share of current law *scheduled* benefit (%)*					
1946–1960	82.7	96.4	73.6	80.9	61.2	98.3
1961–1975	68.3	86.3	74.5	82.9	59.3	91.9
1976–1990	66.0	85.2	83.9	97.3	75.4	81.7
1991–2005	60.7	83.5	81.4	100.0	85.6	76.8
2006–2020	56.9	81.2	80.0	97.0	87.8	76.2
2021–2035	54.8	79.6	78.3	94.3	84.8	77.3
2036–2050	54.7	80.4	77.9	93.8	78.7	78.2

* Percent as of each person's benefit collection year. Assumes 100 percent personal accounts participation under KSB, LMS, Model 2, and Ryan reform proposals.
Source: Author's calculations.

large general revenue transfers to finance transition costs, projected traditional benefits are discounted using a 5.0 percent interest rate to reflect post-reform policy uncertainty.

Table 14.2 shows that the Diamond-Orszag plan would increase average lifetime net tax rates for all except the baby boomers. And the rates would escalate to more than 10 percent of lifetime earnings for those born toward the middle of this century. Panel 4 of the table shows that the Ryan and Diamond-Orszag proposals provide almost identical total Social Security resources at retirement. Under the latter proposal traditional benefits—exclusively in the form of government annuities—are provided, but they require steep tax increases in lifetime net tax rates. Under the latter, traditional benefits are eventually eliminated (except for benefit guarantee purposes), individual account benefits of similar dollar amounts (and also quite secure) are provided but under much smaller increases in lifetime net tax rates on future generations.

Panel 2 of table 14.2 shows that among all proposals involving personal accounts the LMS reform proposal provides the largest retirement wealth ratios. This is not surprising because this proposal requires additional deposits into its personal accounts beyond the OASI payroll tax rate of 10.6 percent on taxable earnings. Despite its larger retirement wealth ratios, the LMS proposal's lifetime net tax rates are generally smaller than those under the Ryan proposal. The reason is the Ryan proposal's payroll tax levy on employer health insurance benefits—which are not invested in personal accounts—and steep cuts in traditional benefits that increase lifetime net tax rates.

The third panel of table 14.2 shows the share of traditional benefits in total retirement wealth that different proposals would establish. It shows alternatives between the two extremes of 100 percent traditional benefits throughout under the Diamond-Orszag proposal to phasing out traditional benefits entirely under the Ryan proposal assuming 100 percent participation in personal accounts. Preferences over the composition of total Social Security wealth are driven by the advantages of each. Whereas traditional benefits would be suitable for fulfilling social insurance functions, a dilution of those functions under current demographic and economic realities weakens the case for continuing them as under the current system.

Social Security's Insurance "Beyond the Veil of Ignorance" under Alternative Reforms

The third and fourth panels of table 14.2 are based on *average* contributions of Social Security to retirement wealth. This metric does not address the question about underlying within-cohort variability in Social Security wealth levels under the different proposals. One way to examine this would be to calculate the variability of wealth levels for each population subgroup separately and compare it to variability under baseline assumptions.

Because panel 3's Social Security wealth levels are based on personal account contributions accumulated at (almost) the risk free rate, any potential for significant within group variability in Social Security wealth from volatile market returns may be considered to be almost fully eliminated. Thus the major source of within-cohort variation is underlying differences in earnings that trigger differences in personal account contributions. And differences in life-cycle earnings, in turn, are based on differences in life-cycle demographic and economic transitions. Although underlying earnings differences are identical for all columns in panel 2 of table 14.2, the various reform elements included under each proposal may increase or reduce within-cohort variation in Social Security wealth levels.

However, simply examining the variability of Social Security retirement wealth would not take account of cross-cohort variability in payroll taxes and personal account contributions. A more comprehensive approach would be to measure Social Security's effect on lifetime income uncertainty "beyond the veil of ignorance"—that is, uncertainty about lifetime income at the beginning of each individual's career.[8] This effect can be estimated by comparing within-cohort income variability with and without Social Security's taxes and benefits under current rules and under alternative reforms. In this case, labor earnings without Social Security are defined as pre-tax labor earnings grossed up for the employer's share of payroll taxes—the earnings that would in principle be established under labor market equilibrium in the absence of Social Security, all other things equal.

Table 14.3 shows the percentage *reduction* in the standard deviation of lifetime earnings—that is, labor earnings grossed up for employer payroll taxes—from Social Security's taxes, benefits, and personal accounts provisions as applicable under DEMSIM's baseline and alternative reforms. The table shows one minus the ratio of the standard deviations of lifetime income calculated with and without Social Security—including and excluding, respectively, any personal accounts contributions and benefits—times 100. The denominator of the ratio has the variance of (grossed-up) lifetime earnings, and the numerator has the variance of those lifetime earnings minus lifetime Social Security payroll taxes (including employer and employee payroll taxes and personal account contributions) plus lifetime traditional Social Security and personal account benefits.[9] Again, the term "lifetime" indicates that present values of earnings, taxes, personal

TABLE 14.3 **Reduction in Lifetime Income Uncertainty Under DEMSIM Baseline and Alternative Reform Proposals (%)**

Birth cohort	Baseline	DO	KSB	LMS	Model 2	Ryan
Earnings – payroll taxes – IA contributions*						
1946–1960	11.9	12.0	12.0	12.1	11.9	11.8
1961–1975	15.2	15.7	15.9	16.7	15.7	15.7
1976–1990	15.4	16.3	16.8	18.6	16.7	16.8
1991–2005	15.4	16.8	16.9	19.0	17.5	17.9
2006–2020	15.6	17.6	17.1	19.2	18.2	19.1
2021–2035	15.5	18.2	17.0	19.1	18.2	19.4
2036–2050	15.3	18.7	16.9	18.9	18.0	19.3
Earnings – payroll taxes + traditional payable benefits						
1946–1960	9.5	9.8	10.1	9.8	9.6	9.4
1961–1975	12.8	12.6	13.3	13.0	12.3	12.4
1976–1990	13.1	13.1	12.9	13.1	12.2	13.0
1991–2005	13.1	13.6	12.9	13.1	12.0	13.0
2006–2020	13.4	14.4	13.0	13.2	12.1	12.9
2021–2035	13.3	14.9	12.9	13.1	12.1	12.8
2036–2050	13.1	15.4	12.9	13.1	12.2	12.7

* IA contributions subtracted only for KSB, LMS, Model 2, and Ryan reform proposal.
Source: Author's calculations.

account contributions, and benefits as of each person's benefit collection year are being used in the calculation.

Note that in arriving at the ratio described above, grossed-up lifetime earnings are modified in two ways: taxes and personal account contributions are subtracted, and traditional and personal account benefits are added. It would be useful to know how the ratio changes when just taxes and personal account contributions are subtracted—an intermediate step that would separately identify variance reduction from just the tax component. Variance reductions from just taxes and contributions are shown in the top panel of table 14.3. The lower panel shows the total reduction in variance from all Social Security transactions. The calculations are shown for all except the Robert M. Ball reform proposal.

The first panel of table 14.3 shows that under DEMSIM's baseline, taxes and personal account contributions reduce the variability of lifetime earnings by slightly more than 15 percent for all cohorts except the baby boomers—for whom the reduction is about 12 percent. The second panel of the table shows that adding the present value of Social Security benefits increases the variability of lifetime income slightly—by about 2 percentage points for most birth cohorts. This benefit-side "offset" to the tax-side reduction in lifetime (net) earnings variability occurs because under Social Security's current laws, benefits are positively related to earnings and, therefore, reinforce the variability of earnings across members of a given birth cohort. Overall, the Social Security program would reduce the variability of gross lifetime earnings by about 13 percent for younger and future generations. Note that all of the reduction in lifetime earnings variation arises from levying payroll taxes. This is as expected under a proportional tax on (almost) the entire payroll base. And Social Security benefits offset only a small fraction of the payroll-tax-induced reduction of the earnings variation because although benefits are linked to each person's career earnings, they are perturbed by various eligibility rules, early retirement reductions, delayed retirement credits, dependent and survivor benefits, and so on, which appear to be negatively correlated to lifetime earnings variations.

Similar remarks apply to earnings variance reductions under the Diamond-Orszag reforms—except that tax-induced reductions and benefit-induced offsets are both larger. Note that increasing lifetime net tax rates for successive cohorts leads to progressively larger reductions in lifetime net earnings variability. Higher payroll taxes and surcharges on high-earners generate most of the action under the Diamond-Orszag reform proposal. The second panel of table 14.3 shows that the total reduction in lifetime earnings variations are not much larger compared to the current system: Diamond-Orszag reforms do not provide much additional lifetime income insurance.

The story is different under the four remaining reform proposals, all of which introduce personal accounts. Under all proposals, tax-induced reductions in earnings variability are about the same or slightly larger than under the Diamond-Orszag proposal. That is because these proposals include a slightly larger reduction in grossed-up earnings, via payroll taxes plus personal account contributions. Indeed, such reductions in grossed-up earnings are the largest under the Ryan reform element especially for future-born generations. In addition, recall that the Ryan proposal contains a significant revenue-increasing element that extends the payroll tax base to employer-provided group health insurance benefits.

The second panel of table 14.3 shows that under the four proposals with individual accounts, benefit-side offsets of tax-side reductions to earnings variability are much larger than under the Diamond-Orszag proposal. That's because carve-out financing of individual account contributions restores more fully the positive linkage between earnings, taxes, and benefits: individual account benefits redound to the contributors rather than being redistributed to others as under current laws and under the Diamond-Orszag proposal. It's not surprising, therefore, that the benefit-side offsets to reduced earnings variability are largest under the Ryan proposal, which includes the largest carve-out personal accounts.

Thus, the provision of lifetime earnings insurance "beyond the veil" via reductions in income uncertainty is mostly achieved by payroll taxes and personal account contributions. The Diamond-Orszag proposal seeks to increase such tax-side redistributions by increasing taxes on high-earners and by maintaining weak benefit-side offsets of such redistributions. In contrast, the LMS and KSB proposals maintain the overall reduction in lifetime earnings variability at current-law levels whereas the Model 2 and Ryan proposals generate slightly smaller reductions in lifetime earnings variability compared to current laws.

As expected, the overall reduction in lifetime earnings variability is highest under the Diamond-Orszag proposal and least under the Model 2 and Ryan proposals. Note, however, that obtaining additional insurance against lifetime earnings uncertainty when entering adulthood—as under the Diamond-Orszag proposal—is unlikely to be costless: weakening linkages between work effort and its rewards by levying higher taxes and redistributing benefits to support relatively less productive workers and dependents is likely to reduce economic efficiency over time. Estimating magnitude of this "feedback" effect remains outside the scope of this book.

The final observation is that the differences across all the proposals in their total reductions of lifetime income variability are quite small. It does not appear that these differences provide a strong case for or against any particular reform proposal.

Final Remarks

Social Security is in much deeper financial trouble than official score-keeping agencies are suggesting by ignoring the implications of current economic and demographic forces on the evolution of effective labor inputs. Official analysts also do not provide information about the impact of reforms using appropriate long-term macro- and micromeasures of the program's financial prospects and effects on particular population groups. Indeed, de-emphasizing long-term measures provides fodder to proponents of the status quo on Social Security. Focus on short-term measures also helps to hide the program's full costs, providing leverage to those arguing for maintaining it in its current structure, size, and financing mechanisms: they suggest that the program's financial troubles are small and may be non-existent, especially if official estimates are based on pessimistic projections. DEMSIM's exploration of Social Security's financial outlook suggests, to the contrary, that official projections are too optimistic because they do not fully incorporate key demographic and economic forces built into the current population and economy.

Tables 14.1 through 14.3 present information about how the various reforms considered herein would implement broad trade-offs when resolving outstanding Social Security imbalances: (1) distribute adjustment costs over time and across generations, (2) distribute adjustment costs across particular types of people within particular birth cohorts, (3) contribute toward the retirement wealth of various population groups, and (4) enhance or degrade Social Security's insurance provision against lifetime income uncertainty.

The lesson that has been learned is that we cannot escape the "legacy costs" from the past. The lesson that remains elusive is that postponing decisions about how to pay those costs—by allowing financial imbalances to build during the lifetimes of current generations—is equivalent to providing additional "legacies" that will prove even more costly for future citizens to resolve.

Unfortunately, because Social Security's financial status and reform options are not officially evaluated under the metrics used in this book, policymakers and the public do not have ways to appropriately assess how alternative reforms would work and the public policy discourse on Social Security appears to be poorly informed. Hopefully, this book's analysis will improve the quality of the Social Security reform dialogue.

Acknowledgments

I would like to thank the Cato Institute, the Earhart Foundation, and the Searle Freedom Trust for research support. I am grateful to Dale Jorgenson and Kevin Stiroh for providing key time series on multifactor productivity and capital inputs; Felicitie Bell of the Social Security Administration for providing demographic files from the 2006 Annual Report of the Social Security Trustees; Social Security Administration staff for answering several questions and providing details about the Social Security Trustees' financial projections; Angela Erickson and Joanne Fung for excellent research assistance; Kent Smetters for moral support; Andrew Biggs, Andrew Rettenmaier, John Samples, Tom Saving, seminar participants at the Congressional Budget Office and the Federal Reserve Bank of New York, and two anonymous referees for very helpful comments; Peter Van Doren for valuable discussions and comments on each chapter as work on this book progressed; and David Pervin, Carissa Vandarian, and Mark Reschke of the University of Chicago Press staff for excellent editorial support. Finally, I owe a large debt of gratitude to my wife, Anjali, for putting up with endless hours of my working on a laptop on many an evening and weekend. Any and all errors are solely attributable to me.

Notes

Chapter One

1. For instance, Fortune Online reported in June 2007 that Senators Charles Rangel and Jim McCreary were "joined in secrecy on a project that just about everyone else in Washington considers doomed to failure." See Easton (2007).

2. See Solvency Memoranda, Social Security Administration, available at www.ssa.gov/OACT/solvency/index.html.

3. The Social Security Advisory Board's 2003 Technical Panel on Assumptions and Methods (Social Security Advisory Board 2003) made similar remarks about longer term measures of Social Security's financial condition. The 2007 Advisory Board, however, recommends de-emphasizing longer term measures because of the uncertainty associated with financial projections extended to distant years. See Social Security Advisory Board (2007).

4. Another key problem from adopting short time horizon for measuring Social Security's financial condition arises with respect to interpreting the effects of changing key economic assumptions underlying future projections—such as whether faster wage growth would improve or worsen the system's finances. For a description of the problems with traditional finite-horizon measures of Social Security's finances, see Gokhale and Smetters (2006) and Biggs and Gokhale (2007).

5. This is just an illustrative example and does not represent the reasons why earnings abilities are projected to decline over time under DEMSIM. A more detailed explanation is provided in later chapters where DEMSIM's features are described.

6. By "fiscal treatment" is meant the per-person lifetime cost imposed on a group by way of payroll taxes net of per-capita lifetime Social Security benefits. Calculating this net cost as a ratio of the group's per capita average lifetime earnings provides a sense of the cost relative to lifetime resources. The "lifetime net tax rate" metric used in this book to assess Social Security's fiscal treatment of various population groups is discussed in greater detail in chapter 7.

7. This book's estimates are limited to the Old Age and Survivors Insurance (OASI) program.

8. The "entitlement" to benefits exists until Congress changes Social Security laws. But this is not the same as a right to receive payments of particular amounts at particular times backed by a legally enforceable contract between the federal government and participating workers. See U.S. Supreme Court (1960).

9. Medicare Part A—the program that pays for inpatient hospital charges—is an exception because it is also fully financed out of dedicated payroll taxes. However, overwhelming portions of Medicare Parts B and D (the outpatient and doctor services program and the prescription drug program, respectively) are financed out of general revenues. That probably makes the link between Medicare's portion of payroll taxes and entitlement to Medicare as a whole less strong.

10. A search on Google of the phrase "Social Security financial problems" found more than 36 million sites. Searching for "Social Security has no financial problems" produced more than 18 million sites. The phrase "Social Security has huge financial problems" generated about 1.3 million sites.

11. For example, if all inputs—capital and quality-adjusted labor—are doubled, output should also double at a minimum. If output increases by more than proportionately compared to the increase in inputs, it means that the additional capital-labor input embodies better multifactor technology—that is, technology pertaining to the joint operation of capital and labor. (Note that better worker skills are already captured through the quality-adjusted labor input measure.)

12. The usefulness of this approach is further illustrated in chapter 6.

13. Indeed, reporting this measure over 5, 10, 25, and 50 years would show the time pattern of accruing future shortfalls. However, this book also reports annual imbalance ratios to preserve comparability with official reporting. Open group measures are reported only over 75 years and in perpetuity.

14. Some analysts believe that estimates beyond the 75th year require non-policy-related projections—about economic and demographic factors—that are too uncertain to justify extending the projection horizon beyond the 75th year. First, the projection exercise is not intended to forecast future events but only to indicate the "best estimate" of the future implications of continuing current policies. Truncating the projection at the 75th year is equivalent to implicitly assuming that it is zero thereafter—which likely introduces a larger estimation error. Second, projections of taxes and benefits after the 75th year would be determined by the population's characteristics as they evolve under specific "best guess" assumptions and rules. Those rules are meant to capture the momentum of forces driving the evolution of population characteristics. Then, *conditional on population attributes projected for the 75th year*, continuation of the "best guess" assumptions and rules appears to be the more natural way to extend the projections than to simply truncate them at the 75th year.

15. The debate was conducted between Senator Arthur Vandenburg (R-OH), who was against accumulating a large Social Security Fund, and President Franklin

Delano Roosevelt and his advisors Edwin Witte and Arthur Altmeyer, who wanted to pre-fund accrued Social Security benefits.

16. Under a pay-as-you-go system, each beneficiary generation receives all of the payroll taxes of the working generation as benefits. Even if payroll tax rates and benefit replacement rates (the ratio of benefits to pre-retirement earnings) are fixed, each generation of Social Security participants receives a positive rate of return on payroll taxes if the sum of population and productivity growth rates are positive. Positive population growth and increasing worker productivity mean that more revenues are available to be distributed over time to each beneficiary cohort than the payroll taxes of the beneficiary generation.

17. See Smetters (2004) and Nataraj and Shoven (2004) on this point.

18. It should be noted that the closed group unfunded obligation measure is not the same as the "accrued" obligation measure. The latter includes only future benefits of current retirees and workers that are accrued on the basis of their past payroll taxes. Instead, the closed group measure also includes future payroll taxes of current workers and the future benefits that would accrue (under current laws) on the basis of those taxes.

19. These figures are as reported in Social Security Board of Trustees (2008). The future generations' net figure includes a rounding error.

20. Note that this interpretation of the closed group measure—as the amount of debt current generations would bequeath to future ones—imposes a policy change after current generations have passed away to eliminate the open group imbalance. That is, it imposes a zero open group imbalance. This "bequest of debt" interpretation of the closed group measure requires the future policy change mentioned in the text—one that, by definition, is disallowed when calculating future generations' net benefits/taxes under current laws as the difference between the open and closed group measures.

21. Some analysts carry the argument further: levying a higher tax rate on future GDP seems appropriate because GDP will be larger in the future—which is consistent with maintaining a progressive tax system wherein higher earners bear higher tax rates. But this argument is based on the *assumption* of a higher future GDP that may not be realized—if only because expectations of higher future tax rates reduce economic incentives and chokes off GDP growth.

22. The official estimate is 34 percent—the ratio of the present value of pre-76th year Social Security financial shortfall ($4.6 trillion) to the total present value of the program's shortfall in perpetuity ($13.4 trillion)—according to the Social Security Board of Trustees (2006), but it is based on the Old Age, Survivors, and Disability Program.

23. Note that measures based only on lifetime payroll taxes and benefits—ones that do not incorporate lifetime earnings—are inadequate because they do not show how progressive Social Security's fiscal treatment is across high and low lifetime earners. Progressive fiscal treatment under Social Security would imply smaller Social Security lifetime net tax rates for low lifetime earners compared to high-earners.

24. Lifetime net tax rates for later-born cohorts are available but are not shown for lack of space. Moreover, extending the display through the 2036–50 birth-cohort proved adequate for revealing trends for those born even later.

Chapter 2

1. A "distribution" refers to the shares of the population with different values of the characteristic being examined. For example, the race characteristic has two values, white and non-white. The race distribution refers to the share of whites and non-whites in the population. A "conditional distribution" refers to a distribution whose shares depend on the value of a prior characteristic. For example, the education distribution may depend on the race attribute. The shares of people with and without a college degree may depend on whether they are white or non-white. Thus, the distribution of the education characteristic would have as many segments as the number of values in the prior (or "conditioning") characteristic(s).

2. Notable exceptions are mortality, fertility, and net immigration rates. For these three items, the information derived from microdata surveys are adjusted to be consistent with projections of the Social Security Administration.

3. Note that despite its obvious complexity, the approach to analyzing Social Security reform options as described so far remains a "partial" one. The future economic choices of individuals and families that comprise the simulated econ-omy—that is, their labor force participation, education acquisition, earnings, and so on—mostly follow rules built into the terminal year of the historical simulation. Future policy changes that would affect those choices are obviously not included in the projected simulation. More specifically, the projected simulation does not allow individuals and families to respond (say, by changing their labor force participation rates, family formation and dissolution behavior, and acquisition of education) to future changes in Social Security's tax and benefit rules. Adding this feature re-quires introducing behavioral rules into individual economic choices. Such a "be-havioral" simulation is not attempted here.

4. The demographic features of DEMSIM are calibrated to the Current Popula-tion Surveys beginning in the late 1960s. The CPS sample targets the civilian non-institutional population. Its samples do not include people who are in jail and those military families and households that contain zero civilian adults. However, these sample omissions are unlikely to result in any notable errors in the quality of the simulated population with respect to its representativeness of the U.S. population. The Current Population Survey is widely considered to be the most suitable micro-data source for the construction of a microsimulation such as DEMSIM.

5. Income taxes levied on Social Security benefits ("benefit taxes") are a rev-enue source for Social Security. That makes asset income, income from private defined benefit pensions and annuities, and taxable withdrawals from defined con-

tribution pension plans during retirement relevant for simulating Social Security's total revenues. The 2007 Annual Report of Social Security's Trustees projects that the ratio of benefit taxes to Social Security's payroll taxes will increase from 3.2 percent in 2007 to 9.3 percent by 2085. The demographic and labor earnings simulation described in the text does not simulate non–Social Security income during retirement. The officially estimated year-specific ratios of benefit taxes to payroll taxes are used to derive total simulated Social Security revenues after payroll tax revenues have been simulated by applying the payroll tax rate to each person's simulated gross labor earnings. See Social Security Board of Trustees (2007).

6. Data from each year's March supplement of the CPS are used.

7. Most computer software packages provide random number generators using the uniform distribution within the range [0.0, 1.0]. Every time that it is invoked, the generator returns a number between 0.0 and 1.0 (inclusively) such that all real numbers (with a pre-specified accuracy) within that interval have an equal chance of being picked. A sequence of successive calls to such generators delivers a sequence of random real numbers between 0.0 and 1.0.

8. The driver values are not shown on figure 2.1 with a high degree of accuracy because of the lack of space. However, the driver values for all attributes are calculated to be accurate to at least five decimal places.

9. The male adult is assumed to be the family head of a dual-headed (married) family.

10. To keep the discussion simple, only univariate comparisons of the attributes listed in the text are shown. More detailed conditional averages and frequency distributions also exhibit reasonably good matches between the CPS and simulated populations.

Chapter 3

1. For years prior to 2004, mortality rates by race, gender, and age from the National Center for Health Statistics are used in simulating mortality. For 2004 and later, the NCHS mortality rates are projected by using mortality rate projections by gender and age obtained from the Social Security Administration. For both races (white and non-white), the NCHS mortality rates are reduced for each future year by the same percentage as the reduction in the Social Security Trustees' mortality rate for the given gender and age.

2. The implementation of mortality could end up designating all the adults of a family as deceased, leaving the children designated as orphaned. In such cases, the eldest orphan child is designated as the head. Orphaned individuals do not interact with any others until they become 18 years old and split off to form their own "non-family" units that are eligible to marry, enter the labor force, and earn income. In each year, surviving orphans' aged 17 and younger advance in their years

of education according to applicable probabilities conditional on race, gender, and age.

3. Some demographers believe that decompositions by race of NCHS mortality rates are not reliable. Biases in these rates could arise from reporting inconsistencies, imputations without adequate validation, and allocations of decedents to racial categories based on regional rather than genealogical information. The extent of such errors remains unknown. However, under the methodology adopted in this book (and perhaps in general), not distinguishing such parameters by race could potentially introduce a larger error in projecting demographic and economic trends compared to distinguishing mortality rates by just age and gender.

4. See statistics at DivorceMagazine.com, available at http://www.divorcemag .com/statistics/statsUS.shtml.

5. Another reason for future changes in labor force affiliations is future changes in government tax and transfer policies. However, this simulation exercise is intended to reveal the trends and implications of current demographic and economic forces independent of future policy changes.

6. The Social Security' Trustees assume a constant number of net immigrants in future years, implying a gradually declining ratio of net immigrants to the total population.

7. CPS data on each individual's age between 1988 and 2001 extends through the "90 and older" category. Post-2001, the age variable extends through the "80 and older" category.

8. The frequency of marriages increases with the number of tries for each male with alternative female partners. This number is calibrated to deliver a close match of the number of "non-family" individuals in the simulated population with that observed in the Current Population Survey in various years.

9. Reporting of detailed marriage and divorce statistics were suspended during the 1990s and comprehensive male marriage probabilities are available only through the year 1988. See http://www.cdc.gov/nchs/pressroom/96facts/mardiv. htm.

10. This number is generated simply by taking the $P(union)$ and dividing it by 20. The same principles for $P(union)$ are applied in determining if there should be a marriage or not.

Chapter 4

1. More than 60 percent of the elderly now live alone compared to 25 percent in the 1940s. See Borsch-Supan et al. (1992).

2. Immigration counts are projected to remain steady throughout the future. This assumption is the same as that made by Social Security's trustees. See Social Security Board of Trustees (2006).

3. See Costa and Kahn (2008).

4. The trend toward an increasingly non-white population is difficult to reverse given the population structure already in place in 2006. Using mortality, fertility, and net immigration assumptions (consistent in the aggregate with the Social Security Trustees' assumptions, but distinguished by age, gender, education, and race as described earlier in the text) the share of non-whites in the population increases from 17 percent today to 29 percent by the year 2100. However, beginning in 2006, if the generally lower fertility rates by age and education applicable to white women are also applied to non-white women, the population share of non-whites in the year 2100 changes by very little: it increases to about 26 percent.

5. Note that transition rates between non-participation, full-time, and part-time labor force participation are conditional on education. DEMSIM assumes that the systematic differences among white and non-white male labor force transition rates by education—that imply lower rates of labor force participation by non-white males—would be maintained in the future. Hence, despite achieving parity on education levels with whites, non-whites are projected to continue working less and an increase in their population share over time would imply declining labor force participation rates overall.

6. Although some individuals would be assigned children's benefits based on their parents' eligibility, these beneficiaries are very small in number (very few females give birth in the late-40s and, hence, very few have eligible dependent children when they and their spouses are collecting retirement benefits). Hence child beneficiaries are ignored when calculating the worker-to-beneficiary ratio.

7. The official ratio is taken as that for OASDI rather than OASI because eventually all DI beneficiaries receive benefits from the OASI trust fund.

8. The crude fertility and mortality rates refer to the number of births and deaths, respectively, per 1,000 of the existing population. The projection is taken forward for 500 years beginning in 1970 to allow a sufficient number of future years over which to discount Social Security's financial aggregates. Discounting future flows over such a long time usually ensures that present values converge to finite aggregates—effectively yielding "infinite horizon" estimates of items such as present values of revenues, expenditures, and program shortfalls (see text box 1 in chapter 1).

9. The estimated population for 2006 of 298.2 million divided by the population for 1970 of 205.1 yields 1.454. See the Census Bureau's information on historical and projected populations, available at http://www.census.gov/prod/2005pubs/06statab/pop.pdf.

10. The reported terminal values of crude fertility and mortality rates are averages over the last 50 years of the projected simulation.

11. The federal Disability Insurance program is not included in this book's analysis.

Chapter 5

1. For example, see Kydland and Prescott (1993) and references therein.

2. The wage growth adjustment applied to individual annual PSID earnings is equivalent to using a wage growth index to deflate annual nomimal earnings. This adjustment is necessary to place all labor earnings on an equal footing before deriving the relationship between workers' "core labor inputs" and their demographic and economic attributes. See note 19 for more details.

3. Maintaining consistency among variable definitions required restricting PSID data to the years between 1971 and 1993.

4. CPS reported "wages and salaries" are multiplied by CPS "person weights"—provided in each year of the survey's March supplement—before adding them up. The weights represent the number of times that a CPS sample person's combination of attributes is closely approximated within the total U.S. population. This adjustment converts the CPS sample into a nationally representative sample. Despite implementing this step, however, CPS aggregate labor earnings underestimates those reported by the Bureau of Economic Analysis as part of the National Income and Product Accounts. See also the Economic Report of the President (2008), table B29.

5. This regression is implemented on values of the joint index for years between 1982–2006. Earlier years are excluded to ensure that an extrapolation of the influence of productivity and inflation factors on nominal wage growth is based on relatively recent data—and to restrict the time series to a period of relatively stable inflation after the early 1980s.

6. The calculation $[(1.0386 / 1.0299) - 1] \times 100$ yields 0.85 percent.

7. For a discussion of prospective improvements in U.S. educational attainments, see Ellwood (2001).

8. See Kirkegaard (2007) who predicts an accelerating broad-based skills shortage among younger workers in the United States, which will be felt increasingly acutely as the baby boomers begin to exit the work force.

9. See Goldin and Katz (2007).

10. For example, only a third of women participated in the labor force during the 1950s, whereas their participation rate was close to 60 percent during 1990s. Estimates by Fullerton (1999) suggest that the rate would remain stable at about 60 percent during future years.

11. Net national saving is calculated by substracting capital depreciation from gross saving. It is customary to divide the nation's net saving into that of households, firms, and the government. This projection exercise assumes that saving by firms is internalized by households and that the government's net debt (debt held by the public) results from additions to the economy's capital stock.

12. Although the evidence suggests that most bequests are involuntary (for example, see Gan et al. [2004]), the nature of bequest motives are not relevant to the method used in this book for projecting the capital stock.

13. For years before 2006, capital stock index values are taken from Jorgenson et al. The capital stock index for the year 2006 is normalized to 1. Index values for 2006 and later are based on the procedure described here. First, age- and gender-specific relative values of individual net worth are derived from the latest available microdata: the Federal Reserve's 2004 Survey of Consumer Finances (SCF). This survey asks participants to account for their asset holdings in great detail and compiles a comprehensive and representative picture of households' total (financial and tangible) assets and liabilities. The SCF data are first allocated to household heads and spouses and averaged separately by age and gender for those aged between 18 and 90. The profiles are smoothed using a third order polynomial regression in age to yield two profiles of net worth holdings by age (through DEMSIM's maximum age of 99)—one for each gender. For each DEMSIM individual in 2004, the corresponding relative profile value is aggregated into an aggregate savings variable. In each successive year, aggregate savings derived in this manner are multiplied by a per capita labor productivity growth index. This latter index is derived as the ratio of per-capita labor earnings in year t to per capita labor earnings in year $t - 1$. Thus, the total capital stock grows at a rate equal to the product of population and productivity growth rates. In addition, its growth reflects the changing age and gender composition of the population.

14. Although foreign capital inflows could affect the rate of growth of the capital stock, such inflows cannot remain positive indefinitely. Lacking a method for modeling and predicting such flows, they are not included in the method for projecting the future capital stock. Although capital flows into the United States have been sizable during the last two decades, U.S. net investment position was just $2.5 trillion as of year-end 2005—a second order of magnitude compared to total household net worth of $51.7 trillion at the same point in time.

15. The calculations are not exact because of rounding errors.

16. The growth rates cited in the text under DEMSIM's baseline assumptions are in real terms. In nominal terms, the aggregate composite productivity factor grows at 4.38 percent per year. Applying the growth rate of aggregate "effective labor inputs" during the same period of -0.31 percent per year yields nominal aggregate productivity growth of 4.05 (=1.0438 / 1.0031) percent per year. Next, applying the projected average growth of the worker-population through 2080 of 0.32 percent per year yields a growth rate of nominal productivity per worker of 3.72 (=1.0405 / 1.0032) percent per year. Finally, applying the assumed future inflation rate of 2.99 percent per year generates growth in real labor productivity of 0.71 (=1.0372 / 1.0299) percent per year.

17. The level shift factor is calculated for every DEMSIM-simulated person born between 1909 and 1951 (between the ages of 61 and 19 in 1970) as follows: Take the mean earnings profile of figure A5.3 and select the segment corresponding to the late career ages of the person under consideration (age in 1970 through the year when the person achieves age 70). Calculate a factor (A) that when applied to the mean earnings segment minimizes the sum of squared differences between it and the person's earnings simulated by DEMSIM for years 1970 and later. Next take a randomly selected earnings record from the public-use file from among those born in the same year. Select the segment corresponding to the person's early (pre-1970) career. Calculate a second factor (B) that when applied to the early career mean earnings segment minimizes the sum of squared differences between it and the public-use file's early career earnings segment. The level shift factor mentioned in the text is A / B. Application of the level shift factor to the early career segment of the selected public-use file earnings record yields the imputation for the person's early career earnings history. This procedure adjusts the early career record's earnings to be level-consistent with DEMSIM's simulated late career earnings. Note that this way of imputing pre-1970 earnings retains patterns of year-to-year changes in earnings that may be associated with macro-business cycles in the economy before 1970.

18. Naturally, the share of output received by owners of capital equals $(1 - \alpha)$, but this amount is not calculated because it is not relevant for determining Social Security's finances.

19. The construction of ln Z_{it} flushes out the impact of inflation and the two productivity factors, lnA_t and αlnK_t, on wages. The remainder is simply the logarithm of the contribution of labor quality to wages. This method of isolating labor's contribution to wages is simply a method of estimating a broad concept of "human capital" that each worker brings to the production process. Because that term has a specific technical meaning, it is simply called a worker's "core labor input" in this book. Another way of viewing the construction of ln Z_t is that it places wages earned in different periods "on par" with each other—similar to the process of "wage indexing" past worker earnings in Social Security's primary insurance amount computation. It enables pooling PSID's cross-section and time-series data to estimate the regression specified in equation (6).

20. Because a worker's effective labor input is determined by applying the PSID-based earnings regression coefficients to the worker's demographic and economic attributes, those coefficients could alternatively be called "core labor input aggregators."

21. Note that the distribution of regression errors has a mean of zero by construction. However, in order to avoid drawing errors for low-earners from errors applicable at higher earnings levels and to minimize the measurement-error-induced bias in the estimation, a segmented bootstrap method is employed. Under this method, the perturbation error terms are selected from the distribution of

sampling errors within a limited range of PSID earnings levels close to the predicted earnings level for the worker in question.

22. See Jorgenson et al. (2007). Dale Jorgenson and Kevin Stiroh provided to the author the annual series of multifactor productivity and capital inputs estimated in that study.

Chapter 6

1. See Social Security Advisory Board (2007).

2. The employee share is only one-half that rate, or 5.3 percent of gross taxable wages, the remainder being paid by the employer. For calculating payroll tax revenues, however, it suffices to simply apply a 10.6 percent payroll tax rate to gross employee wages up to each year's applicable taxable earnings ceiling.

3. Annual adjustment factors for 2006 and later years are calculated as the ratio of covered workers to the total population of working aged adults, both of which are available on a single-year basis from the Social Security Administration under its low-, intermediate-, and high-cost economic and demographic assumptions. Using official demographic projections for this calculation is defensible because DEMSIM's *demographic* projections are not very different from those of the Social Security Trustees (see chapters 3 and 4). The ratio for 2080—the terminal year of the Social Security Administration's projections—is applied for years after 2080. The year-specific adjustment factors are applied to aggregate revenue projections, not to the payroll taxes of simulated individuals.

4. Tests across all of the cases studied show that SSTBC's Primary Insurance Amount values are within 0.21 percent of those obtained from ANYPIA. Retirement benefit values are within 0.82 percent. A table of test results from the two calculators is available from the author upon request.

5. The calculations assume that the year of collection is the same as the last year with positive earnings or age 70, whichever is smaller, but not less than age 62.

6. Analysts criticize this approach as not conveying important information about the probability of alternative outcomes. That would be feasible under a microsimulation such as DEMSIM after incorporating a joint probability distribution across all key assumptions. Estimating this joint distribution is difficult and time consuming, and such an experiment is not attempted here.

7. DEMSIM-SSTBC simulated estimate of Social Security benefits for 2006 are 4 percent smaller than official benefit estimates. The simulated estimate of Social Security revenues are 6 percent larger than official revenue estimates (after adjusting for taxes on Social Security benefits).

8. Since each additional unit of capital growth is assumed to contribute 0.42 units to output and wage growth under baseline assumptions, it is straightforward to calculate that capital would have to grow by an *additional* 0.74 percentage points

per year—that is, in addition to its average projected growth of 1.19 percent per year—to fully offset the decline in total effective labor inputs at the rate of 0.31 percent per year: $1.0031(1/0.42) = 1.0074$.

9. See Social Security Board of Trustees (2006), table IV.B5.

10. In the case of full-time labor force participation and education acquisition rates, annual transition probabilities are increased by 2.5 percent of baseline values. For example, if the probability of transiting from part-time to full-time work at any age is p, that probability is increased to $p \times 1.025$, subject to the constraint that it cannot be larger than 1. As another example, the probabilities of acquiring an additional year of education after high school is increased in the same manner by 2.5 percent subject to a maximum of 1.0 (which turns out never to be binding). For immigration, mortality, and fertility rates, the age, gender, race, and education specific rates (as applicable) are increased by 5 percent. The faster fertility and immigration rates dominate the effect of higher mortality rates and the total simulated population increases over time.

One might question why a uniform change of 2.5 percent is applied to the transition probabilities of education acquisition and labor force participation whereas a 5 percentage point variation is applied to mortality, fertility, and immigration rates. For labor force participation rates, microdata sample averages and standard deviations of transition probabilities for three 8-year periods—1970–77, 1978–85, and 1986–93—were calculated separately for males and females. Those calculations indicated that although within-period standard deviations of transition probabilities are quite large, cross-period standard deviations of mean transition probabilities are 2.2 percentage points for males and 3.4 percentage points for females—which suggests that using a 2.5 percentage point variation to calibrate DEMSIM's optimistic and pessimistic scenarios is not inappropriate. Similar calculations based on microdata-based age, race, and prior education level specific probabilities of acquiring an additional year of education also supported using a 2.5 percentage point variation for education acquisition rates. The larger (and uniform) 5 percentage point variation used for mortality, fertility, and immigration rates turns out to be insufficient to replicate the Social Security Trustees' alternative population paths. Matching those paths would require a much larger percentage point variation for all three items. However, implementing DEMSIM's pessimistic scenario using a sufficiently large variation on mortality, fertility, and immigration rate to replicate the trustees' lower population growth path generates an unsustainable population trajectory beyond the 75-year horizon. Using a 5 percentage point variation is (close to) the largest such variation consistent with a sustainable population path over the long term under DEMSIM. In the interest of maintaining symmetry across the optimistic and pessimistic assumption changes, a 5 percent variation is also adopted for DEMSIM's optimistic case.

11. The official annual deficit ratio for 2080 is reported in the 2006 Annual Report of Social Security's Trustees—see Social Security Board of Trustees (2006).

Annual payroll tax and benefits projections are provided by the Social Security's Office of the Chief Actuary. Official projections of annual taxable payrolls are taken from the Social Security Administration's Web site for the 2006 Annual Report (tables by single year): http://www.socialsecurity.gov/OACT/TR/TR06/lr6F6.html.

12. See Biggs and Gokhale (2007).

13. The 2008 Technical Panel on Assumptions and Methods of the Social Security Advisory Board, in contrast, recommends greater emphasis on short horizon measures. The main argument used to support such a recommendation is that estimates about future outcomes grow more uncertain the longer the horizon. The problem with this view is that it confuses forecasts about the future with projections under given assumptions. The exercise here is not to predict the future accurately but to accurately examine the implications of continuing demographic and economic evolution along trends observed historically, including their projected interactions over time. Clearly, those trends cannot be "forecast" with high accuracy, but an analysis of their long-term implications under given assumptions (derived from historical data and trends) could nevertheless contain information that is relevant and useful for policymaking. Indeed, if a finding that current trends imply unsustainable Social Security policies were to trigger policy changes and changes in private individuals' economic choices, the projection under earlier policy and behavioral assumptions would, by construction, be rendered obsolete. But this does not imply that the earlier projection was useless. Judgment about its usefulness should be based not on whether the distant future is very accurately "forecastable" but on whether it improves the policymaking process by providing complete and consistent information about future outcomes under existing policies.

14. Chapter 1 contains brief descriptions of these measures. They are defined in detail in Gokhale and Smetters (2003), which also describes their importance for analyzing Social Security's financial condition and for fully understanding the effects of alternative reforms. The infinite horizon open group measure is simply the present value difference between Social Security's projected revenues and benefits minus the value of Treasury securities in the program's trust fund at the beginning of the first year (2006). The closed group measure is the same calculation implemented for Social Security participants alive in 2006.

15. The results are based on running DEMSIM's calculations for 400 years after 2006. Under baseline assumptions, the difference between the present value of annual financial shortfalls over 350 years and 400 years is only 0.3 percent. This difference is deemed small enough to justify interpreting present values of annual shortfalls and payrolls calculated over the next 400 years as good approximations to infinite horizon estimates.

16. The trustees report an infinite horizon open group imbalance of $13.4 trillion, but it includes the Disability program. See Social Security Board of Trustees (2006), table IV.B7.

17. It is not directly clear from Social Security Trustees' reports whether official projections incorporate potential interactions by race (in addition to age and gender) between mortality, fertility, and immigration, when projecting future rates for each. A phone conversation with a senior actuary from the Social Security Administration revealed that future projections of such rates do *not* take into account any interactions on account of the population's evolving demographic and economic characteristics. The conversation identified this to be true especially for the race variable—primarily because the program's rules are blind to race distinctions. The Social Security Trustees' approach appears to be to simply project future mortality, fertility, and other rates based on incoming (historical) data on those variables. For mortality rates, for example, incoming data is distinguished by disease factors that are influenced by the current changes in the population's racial composition. It is obviously very difficult to incorporate interactions between several demographic and economic drivers when making future projections unless an explicit and sufficiently detailed microsimulation approach is adopted. But that means even key interactions with potentially significant effects on the program's finances would be ignored. The quite likely slower decline in future U.S. mortality rates from a rising share of non-whites in the population because of their higher fertility rates appears to be a case in point.

18. For example, see Goss (1999).

19. The description of the SSTBC in this appendix is based on a prior published version © Alan J. Auerbach and Ronald D. Lee 2001 (see Caldwell et al. 2001). It is reproduced here with updates with the permission of Cambridge University Press.

20. Examples of non-covered work are certain categories of federal, state, and local workers with alternative pension systems, college students with stipend income, and service personnel in religious institutions. Wages of election workers, household employees, and the self-employed are exempt from Social Security payroll taxes up to specific dollar amounts. DEMSIM's financial projections for Social Security include adjustments for employment in non-covered occupations.

21. The Social Security Handbook is available on the Social Security Administration's Web site, http://www.socialsecurity.gov/op_home/handbook/handbook.html.

Chapter 7

1. The option to claim benefits as early as age 62 was introduced in 1961. The associated actuarial reduction of benefits was not introduced until much later.

2. According to national U.S. mortality statistics, the likelihood at age 20 of surviving through age 65 was 60 percent during the early 1930s. As of 2003, it was 84 percent. These probabilities are calculated for all races across 34 death registration

states in the United States. For the underlying data, see table 10 in National Vital Statistics Report (2006). Table 11 of the same report indicates that life expectancy at age 20 extended through age 66 during the early 1930s. During the early 2000s, however, it extends through age 76 for men and age 81 for women.

3. The Social Security earnings test reduces benefits if a worker earns more than a certain amount between age 62 and his or her normal retirement age. The rules governing Social Security's earnings test are available at http://www.ssa.gov/OACT/COLA/rtea.html.

4. Gruber and Wise (1999) document the strong positive association between statutory retirement ages and early retirement in many developed nations.

5. Indeed, studies on fertility and saving behavior suggest that generous entitlement programs with low retirement eligibility and high replacement rates may also promote lower fertility when young and continued high consumption during retirement. See Boldrin et al. (2005) and Gokhale et al. (1996).

6. Other likely effects are greater use of market and non-market insurance arrangements for elder- and long-term care.

7. Actuarial calculations incorporate adjustments for mortality risk.

8. In this context, the alternative measure of the ratio of the present value of benefits to the present value of taxes appears to be inferior to the lifetime net tax rate. The former measure would work well if payroll taxes were strictly proportional to earnings. But the ceiling on taxable earnings means that the former ratio does not fully reflect the system's overall progressivity. Another shortcoming of that ratio arises in terms of comparing the effects of alternative reforms that involve changing both the numerator and denominator.

9. In the denominator of the lifetime net tax rate metric, one could either use pre-tax labor earnings or gross up those earnings with the employer's share of the payroll tax. The problem with the latter method is that some reforms may involve a different amount of employer payroll taxes and a varying denominator would not permit fair comparisons across different reform proposals. Hence, the denominator used to calculate lifetime net tax rates is simply pre-tax labor earnings.

10. Some have argued that Social Security benefits should be discounted at a lower rate than payroll taxes because of declining marginal utility of benefits relative to taxes. These considerations are as yet unsettled and are beyond the scope of this book. For related discussions, see Liu et al. (2007).

11. Issues about the appropriate discount rate to use for the numerator—especially when individual accounts are created—are discussed in more detail in chapter 10. In this case, the estimate of Social Security wealth in the numerator includes the present value of traditional benefits discounted at a 5.0 percent interest rate and the value of individual account contributions accumulated at a 3.0 percent rate of return. The denominator is calculated by accumulating earnings at a 5.0 percent discount rate. The ratio shows the share of lifetime earnings devoted to retirement consumption via Social Security. That share would obviously be different (larger)

if a 3.0 percent discount rate were used to calculate the denominator. However, the size of the denominator and the resulting value of the ratio of Social Security wealth to lifetime earnings are themselves not as important as the percentage change in the ratio under alternative reforms. That percentage change depends only on the numerator because the denominator remains fixed given that simulated earnings and the interest rate chosen for calculating the denominator are both identical under DEMSIM's baseline assumptions and under alternative reforms.

12. For example, the Congressional Budget Office has rejected "dynamic scoring" when evaluating the impact of tax law changes.

13. The average age at death is not the same as life expectancy at birth reported for the birth cohort in question. Life expectancy at birth statistics generally assume constant health and nutrition of the cohort's population as of its birth year—the so-called period life expectancy. Improvements in these factors as the cohort ages mean that its members would experience higher average ages of death compared to its life expectancy at birth. In addition, the numbers are likely to be somewhat higher for the baby boomers among DEMSIM's simulated cohorts because DEMSIM's calculations are based on the age distribution of those who survived through first year of the simulation—1970.

14. The Centers for Disease Control, the National Center for Health Statistics, and Census Bureau information on mortality suggest similar relative differences across race and gender. To the author's knowledge, no independent statistics are available on mortality rates across low and high career earners.

15. The age of retirement need not be the same as the age of first collecting Social Security benefits.

16. However, under a given age-earnings profile and given the length of the total life span, shorter retirement spans—and, therefore, longer work spans—have an ambiguous impact on OASI lifetime net tax rates. Although a longer work span implies a higher present value of lifetime earnings in the denominator, which reduces the lifetime net tax rate, it also means a higher present value of payroll taxes in the numerator, which increases the lifetime net tax rate.

17. Panel 7 of table 7.1 excludes years of retirement—those after the last year with positive earnings.

18. Average education for the 1946–60 and 1961–75 cohorts is calculated only for those surviving through 1970—the first year of DEMSIM's historical simulation. Hence, average values for these two birth cohorts do not include those who died prior to 1970 without necessarily attaining their normal potential years of education.

19. The projected decline in effective labor inputs described in chapter 5 occurs despite constancy of average educational achievement over time. It can be attributed to other social and economic factors such as the changing frequencies of marriage and divorce, increasing shares of non-families in the population, changing

racial composition of the population, and changing patterns of labor force participation across full- and part-time work.

20. Panel 1 of table 7.1 shows that males with larger than median earnings comprise one third of the overall DEMSIM sample. The denominator of the lifetime
net tax rate is total labor earnings and not taxable earnings. The result that lifetime
net tax rates are smaller for high-earning males might be reversed if the latter were
used in the denominator. For a discussion of alternative measures for evaluating
Social Security's overall progressivity, see Coronado et al. (2000).

21. For instance, Erik Hurst (2008) shows that some households who arrive at
retirement with too little wealth to sustain consumption at the same rate as during
working years did so in part because they followed myopic consumption behavior
during their working years. The study finds that this behavior is not the result of
binding liquidity constraints while working. According to the study, about 20 percent
of households do not appear to follow permanent income consumption rules when
working. Lusardi (2002) documents that about one third of households nearing retirement report having "hardly thought" about retirement. These households have
much lower wealth levels than those who report thinking a lot about retirement.

22. In subsequent chapters that evaluate individual account Social Security reforms, the numerator is augmented by the accumulated value of individual account
contributions through the first year of collecting traditional benefits. That accumulated value is calculated using an inflation-adjusted rate of return of 3.0 percent per
year. The rationale for doing so is described in later chapters.

Part 2

1. For a more detailed discussion about this claim, see Gokhale and Smetters
(2003).

2. All official analyzes of Social Security reform proposals—by the trustees,
the Congressional Budget Office, Office of Management and Budget, Department
of Treasury, and the Government Accountability Office—are also limited to assessing only first order effects of reforms on the program's future revenues and
expenditures.

Chapter 8

1. For the quote used as an epigraph for this chapter, see the October 29, 2007,
Washington Post article, available at http://www.washingtonpost.com/wp_dyn/
content/article/2007/10/28/AR2007102801150.html.

2. See Social Security Administration (2003 and 2005a).

3. The goal is expressed in terms of bringing Social Security's finances "well within close actuarial balance." The close actuarial balance measure examines whether income and costs are within 5 percentage points of each other over the next 75 years when measured as a share of the payroll tax base. This is taken as an indication of the program's financial solvency within the context of uncertain future projections.

4. The 2008 Social Security Trustees' annual report states that the ratio declined by an average of 0.3 percent per year between 1983 and 2006. This is quite understandably the result of baby boomers moving into their highest earning life-cycle phase. Hereafter, however, the ratio would be expected to increase if the boomers leave the workforce as expected. The trustees' intermediate assumptions, however, extrapolate the past decline through the year 2017 and maintain it unchanged thereafter at its 2017 value of 82.9 percent. See chapter V, section C, subsection 3, of "Taxable Payroll and Payroll Tax Revenue," in Social Security Board of Trustees (2008). The author thanks Andrew Biggs for providing the information for this note.

5. Rising inequality in the long term is not surprising under DEMSIM wherein demographic projections under baseline assumptions generate long-term declines in labor quality and effective labor inputs. When the share of the population with attributes associated with relatively lower rates of education and labor force participation, and so on, increases while the earnings premium on education remains high, earnings disparities in the population as a whole would naturally grow larger over time.

6. The taxable earnings ceiling limits the exposure of high earnings to payroll taxes to avoid extending Social Security benefits to high-earners. However, the taxable ceiling indirectly influences the degree of retirement wealth—an issue dealt with in later chapters. It also influences the persistence of retirement wealth inequality across family dynasties. The latter effect arises because the taxable ceiling makes retirement wealth and bequest distributions even more skewed than the distribution of earnings as shown in Gokhale and Kotlikoff (2002b). Eliminating the earning's ceiling would eliminate these effects of Social Security and make the distribution of retirement wealth less unequal over time.

Chapter 9

1. For the quote used as an epigraph for this chapter, see Diamond and Orszag (2005), 253, n. 13.

2. This is because the cost of benefits to new beneficiaries over 75 years equals 85 percent of the 75-year cost of benefits in total.

3. Period mortality tables list current mortality rates by age. Cohort mortality tables list anticipated mortality rates for each birth cohort. Naturally, with improv-

ing longevity, the actuarial present value of a given dollar stream through one's lifetime (Social Security benefits, for example) computed using the former would yield a smaller value compared to one computed using the latter.

4. For more details, see the description in appendix 6.1 of how each person's Primary Insurance Amount—the full benefit if first collection is at normal (or full) retirement age—is calculated.

5. A more detailed explanation is provided in chapter 12 in connection with the conservative reform proposal by President G. W. Bush's Social Security reform plan—which was proposed earlier than the Diamond-Orszag plan.

6. This percentage equals the sum of changes in the closed group imbalance divided by the sum of changes in the infinite horizon open group imbalance, with the sums taken over rows 4 and 6 in table 9.1.

7. See the introduction in Diamond and Orszag (2005), 8.

8. See the introduction in Diamond and Orszag (2005), 5.

9. Studies show that higher taxes to finance generous social insurance programs in Europe are the chief factor underlying the decline in European living standards during the past three decades despite access to technologies and labor productivity that are similar to those in the United States. The reason cited in the studies is the negative impact of higher taxes on work efforts through earlier retirements, longer vacations, and lower incentives to acquire education and skills. See Prescott (2004a) and Jacobs (2008).

10. The fifth panel of table 9.2 shows the fraction of Social Security retirement wealth contributed by traditional Social Security benefits. All of the numbers equal 100 percent because the Diamond-Orszag proposal does not include the creation of any alternative source of Social Security retirement wealth, such as personal accounts.

11. For more details, see the description in appendix G in Diamond and Orszag (2005).

Chapter 10

1. For the quote used as an epigraph for this chapter, see Hickey (2003).

2. Some also support redemption of Treasury securities held in the Social Security Trust Fund for investing the proceeds in private capital markets.

3. As will become clear in later chapters, some conservative personal account proposals that include direct benefit offsets at the individual level propose smaller than actuarially fair benefit offsets in order to induce worker participation in personal accounts.

4. See U.S. Congress (2001, 2004, and 2005).

5. See http://www.centristpolicynetwork.org/pages_2005_02/2_Kolbe-Boyd .html.

6. Adjustments to OASI benefits resulting from prior disability periods are also not included in the analysis.

7. This description of reform elements is based on Social Security Administration's Office of the Chief Actuary's solvency memorandum on the Kolbe-Boyd (2005) reform proposal. See Social Security Administration (2005b).

8. The revenue feedback effects are also not included in the official scoring of reform proposals by the Social Security Administration's Office of the Chief Actuary. See Social Security Administration (2005b).

9. Although there is a large literature on labor supply responses to wage and tax, there appears to be little consensus among economists about the sign and size of the response both within and across periods as after-tax wages fluctuate. In general, estimates of labor supply responses to (compensated) changes in take-home pay tend to range between very low to moderate-sized (MaCurdy [1981]; Altonji [1986]; Ziliak and Kniesner [1999] French [2004]). Most economists agree, however, that labor supply responses to tax changes are larger among secondary earners within families (Congressional Budget Office [1996]).

10. The rate of return assumed is the same as that used by Social Security's Office of the Chief Actuary (SSOCACT)—4.45 percent per year, which is based on a 6.5 percent rate of return on stocks, a 3 percent rate of return on bonds, and a 0.3 percent administrative charge. This calculation is used only for estimating the revenue flow from income taxes on annuities on the same basis as the SSOCACT calculations.

11. This admittedly shorthand manner of estimating revenues from the income taxation of benefits has the advantage of being anchored to total benefit expenditures. To the extent that personal accounts provide marginal additions to retirement benefits, the increase in income tax revenues as a fraction of those benefits may be larger under a progressive income tax system than the average ratio of such federal receipts to total Social Security benefits, other things equal. However, this source of estimation error is unlikely to be large because other KSB reforms would reduce traditional Social Security benefits.

12. The New America Foundation in Washington, DC, once held a panel discussion on Social Security reforms involving individual accounts, but specifically prohibited panel participants from speaking about any beneficial aspects of individual accounts themselves!

13. See table 2-1 in Ibbotson Associates (2008). Calculated as geometric means, annual total returns on long-term government bonds between 1926 and 2007 averaged 5.5 percent whereas inflation averaged 3.0 percent. Curiously, the average annual total return on long-term corporate bonds is reported as 5.8 percent, and the standard deviation of returns on corporate bonds is *smaller* than that on government bonds.

14. Geanakoplos et al. (1999) suggest that a 20 percent premium on the riskless rate would be appropriate. Applying that premium on the riskless rate of 2.5 percent yields 3.0 percent as the appropriate interest rate to use for calculating Social

Security wealth from individual accounts. This rate is considerably smaller than conventional average annual rates of return of 5 percent or more per year in inflation-adjusted terms on private capital portfolios involving moderate risk levels.

15. See Bernheim et al. (2003).

16. This omission is not necessarily a serious shortcoming of the Kolbe-Stenholm-Boyd proposal because mandatory sharing of personal account contributions between married couples could be offset via changes in the allocation and sharing of other private assets.

17. For an analysis of the impact of government entitlement programs on national saving, see Gokhale et al. 1996.

Chapter 11

1. For the quote used as an epigraph for this chapter, see "Samwick Coauthors Social Security Reform Plan," available at http://www.dartmouth.edu/~vox/0506/0109/security.html.

2. For example, see praise for the plan by economist-blogger Brad DeLong, at http://www.j-bradford-delong.net/movable_type/2005–3_archives/001792.html.

3. Under LMS's description (Liebman et al. [2005]), the proposal encompasses the entire 12.4 percent payroll tax, which includes the Disability Insurance program. Here, however, the discussion is restricted to the OASI program.

4. The LMS proposal also increases the earliest eligibility age—currently 62. The ultimate increase is by three years—to 65—at the rate of two months per year for those born in 1955 and later. This transition would take 18 years, but it would have no impact on lifetime benefits and the present value of the program's total future benefit expenditures because retiring earlier than at one's normal retirement age results in actuarially fair benefit reductions. Hence, this feature is not modeled under DEMSIM.

5. Of course, average monthly indexed earnings for retirees in 2030 would be higher than those of today's retirees, but the objective here is to compare PIA reductions for given values of average monthly indexed earnings.

6. See Liebman et al. (2005) and Social Security Administration (2005c).

7. Under official Social Security's Office of the Chief Actuary (SSOCACT) scoring of the LMS proposal (Social Security Administration [2005c]), this reform element reduces the 75-year open group imbalance by 1 percentage point of taxable payrolls. Note that SSOCACT's estimate of the present value of taxable payrolls is much larger than DEMSIM's estimate because of the persistent decline in aggregate effective labor inputs under the latter.

8. However, older workers would not be protected from higher payroll taxes as a result of increasing the taxable earnings ceiling.

9. See Geanakoplos et al. (1999).

Chapter 12

1. For the quote used as an epigraph for this chapter, see Prescott (2004b).

2. A few of President G. W. Bush's 2000 election campaign ads contained the question, "Shouldn't our grandchildren find Social Security secure?" and the statement, "Social Security needs improvement." However, the Republican National Committee's ads during that campaign season explicitly mentioned that G. W. Bush had a "bipartisan plan" to "strengthen and improve" Social Security that "provides younger workers a choice to invest a small part of their Social Security in sound investments that they control for higher returns." See the campaign archives of the Political Communication Lab, available at www.pcl.stanfort.edu /campaign.

3. Sounder arguments for introducing personal Social Security accounts lie in the program's undesirable economic effects of labor market distortions, inducements to consume more and save less, unintended intergenerational wealth transfers, and loss of intergenerational economic mobility that have been documented by scholars too numerous to cite here, and that probably outweigh Social Security's now diluted social insurance advantages.

4. Historically, real returns on "riskless" government bonds have averaged 2.5 percent per year, whereas calculations of internal rates of return on payroll taxes show annual real returns of about 1.0–1.5 percent. See Ibbotson Associates (2008) and Leimer (1991).

5. Older workers among early participants in Social Security were awarded benefits without having paid commensurate payroll taxes when working. The cost of those generous benefits represents the implicit debt which must be serviced by current and future generations. One indication of the implicit debt is that the cumulative accruing liabilities of Social Security to current retirees and workers far exceed its available assets in terms of past trust fund surpluses plus projected payroll taxes of the same group of beneficiaries. This is the closed group obligation measure discussed in the text.

6. For a full discussion of Social Security rate of return issues see, Geanakoploset al. (1999). Readers may wonder why retirement wealth ratios reported in this book are calculated using a 3.0 percent accumulation rate for personal account contributions rather than an even lower interest rate commensurate with Social Security's internal rate of return under current laws. Using a 3.0 percent rate is justified because it is consistent with accounting for the cost of providing a guaranteed level of Social Security wealth via personal accounts. However, personal accounts are only one component of reforms that include them. Other changes to current Social Security taxes and benefits are likely to deliver smaller-than-3-percent overall post reform internal rates of return for different population groups.

7. Ironically, events of 2007 and 2008 have reversed the causality: it was upset financial markets that triggered massive government bailouts of financial, auto, and insurance industry giants—and forced large increases in government deficits and debt.

8. The contribution limit for 2009 equals $1,000 \times (AW_{2007}/AW_{2002})$, where AW_t stands for the average wage in year t. Across multiple DEMSIM runs, the contribution limit for 2009 equals $1,200, on average.

9. As another example of the Social Security benefit formula, consider that a worker's past earnings refer to those beginning at age 22 through the year before the worker decides to first collect Social Security benefits. Earnings are first indexed using average wages where the index is constructed by dividing the historical series of average wages by those for the year when the worker turns age 60. The worker's non-indexed nominal earnings, if any, are used from years after the worker turns 60. From the resulting (partially) indexed earnings series, the 35 highest values are selected (including zeros if the worker had no earnings in some years) and their sum is divided by 420—the number of months in 35 years—to yield average indexed monthly earnings (AIME). The conversion of AIME into the PIA uses *bend points*—which are dollar thresholds that increase at the rate of growth of annual wages and are declared each year by the Social Security Administration—and the *bend point factors* mentioned in the text. For example, the bend points for the year 2006 equal $711 and $4,288. These values would be used to calculate the PIA for workers beginning their Social Security benefit collection in 2008. If a worker's average indexed monthly wage equals $5,000, the PIA would be calculated as $711 \times **0.90** + ($4,288 − $711) \times **0.32** + ($5,000 − $4,288) \times **0.15** = $1,891 per month, where the items in boldface type are the bend point factors mentioned in the main text. Note that if AIME were less than $4,288, the third term would not apply and the second term would have the AIME value instead of $4,288 in it, and so on.

10. Of course, the later that a worker with given real lifetime earnings is born, the lower would be his or her position in the distribution of lifetime earnings and post-reform Social Security benefits among that birth cohort.

11. Note that the G. W. Bush Social Security Commission's proposal was published first—in 2001—much earlier than Diamond-Orszag proposal that was published in 2003.

12. For example, the full (year-specific) percentage increase is applied to those with the same average monthly indexed earnings as that of a 35-year (career) minimum-wage worker in the year 2000. Such a hypothetical worker would have worked for 2,000 hours per year throughout a 35-year career at the minimum wage of $5.15 per hour. The worker would therefore have an annual wage in the year 2000 of $5.15 × 2,000 = $10,300. In years after 2000, workers' annual wages are indexed by DEMSIM's internally generated average wage index.

13. The implementation of the low-earner benefit enhancement follows exactly the details specified in the memorandum by Social Security's Office of the Chief Actuary, included in Moynihan and Parsons (2001).

14. See Gokhale et al. (2002c).

15. Under the Diamond-Orszag proposal, this reform element is implemented beginning in 2012.

16. The 75-year time horizon excludes benefit offsets beyond the 75th year that would be levied against a portion of payroll taxes diverted to personal accounts before the 75th year.

17. According to the designers of Model 2, the limit on personal account contributions was imposed to ensure that the transition cost would not become too large. This limit would become binding on many middle- and upper-earners, preventing them from accumulating substantial assets in their personal accounts.

18. If participation in personal accounts were assumed to be less than 100 percent, living generations would bear larger adjustment costs. This follows from the fact that the discount rate applied to calculate benefit offsets against diverted payroll taxes is very low—just 2.0 percent. Non-participation in personal accounts by some current workers would increase their adjustment costs because they would not gain from the higher than 2 percent (3 percent "riskless") return on personal account contributions but would still be subject to reduced future Social Security benefits on account of reduced bend point factors. Since Model 2 contains multiple incentives and no disincentives to participate in personal accounts, it seems most appropriate to assume a participation rate of 100 percent among those eligible for personal accounts.

Chapter 13

1. For the quote used as an epigraph for this chapter, see Ryan (2008a).

2. See http://www.house.gov/ryan/issuepapers/socialsecurityissuepaper.html.

3. See Ryan (2008b).

4. See Biggs et al. (2009) for one method of pricing such benefit guarantees.

5. Estimate based on the National Income and Product Accounts, tables 2.2A, 2.2B, and 7.8, of the Bureau of Economic Analysis, available at http://www.bea .gov.

6. The base broadening itself would not be opposed by conservatives if it were done in a revenue-neutral manner. Indeed, conservatives are likely to welcome a revenue-neutral broadening of the payroll tax base as that would level the playing field across different types of wage compensations and reduce economic distortions.

7. The historical differential in the growth rate of health care costs per capita is imposed through 2080 and then reduced to zero. The historical growth rate differential is estimated as the difference between GDP growth per capita since 1982 and growth per capita in employer group health expenditures since 1982 using data from Bureau of Economic Analysis (see note 4 above).

8. In conformity with the "no-feedback effect" analytical constraint described in chapter 6, no attempt is made to estimate the size of the private sector's adjustment to employment contracts after subjecting employer-provided group health benefits to payroll taxes.

9. Those two reforms remain relevant because of the Ryan benefit guarantee — as discussed below.

10. Another channel for these reform elements to interact is via the Ryan benefit guarantee. Although benefit offsets mean that benefits are eliminated for those entering the workforce after 2040, changes to traditional benefits remain relevant for PSA participants for calculating benefit guarantee payouts contingent on the performance of PSAs: where PSA accumulations are insufficient to purchase annuities equal to post-Ryan-reform traditional benefits, a government annuity payout to restore total (PSA plus government annuity) Social Security benefits equal to non-PSA-participants' traditional benefits would be awarded. The present value cost of such contingent benefit guarantees is not included in the calculations reported here.

11. Although the Ryan reform proposal allows participants unlimited freedom to switch between participation and non-participation throughout their lifetimes, implementing partial participation experiments as described in the text should make no material difference to results on the program's aggregate finances.

12. Older workers' group health benefits' would become subject to payroll taxes under the Ryan reform proposal.

13. Future generations net benefits under DEMSIM's current-law baseline equals the difference between the open group imbalance of $13.4 trillion and the closed group imbalance of $14.2 trillion — or –$0.8 trillion.

14. A higher (5 percent) rate of return would, of course, yield larger total Social Security wealth estimates at retirement but would imply higher risk in PSA portfolios with attendant costs of guaranteeing such a high rate of return. See the discussion of this issue in chapter 10.

15. The share of traditional benefits in total Social Security wealth under Model 2 declines to about 30 percent for the 2036–50 birth cohorts, but it is on a declining trend and could become close to zero for those born later in this century.

16. Although Social Security is designed to be gender- and race-blind in its benefit determination, in principle, each worker's labor earnings history would be available for benefit computations under non-PSA Ryan reform elements. The values in panel 1 of table 13.3 show actuarial present values of benefits that members of different population groups would be guaranteed to receive. The present values in constant 2006 dollars that are shown in panel 1 include the effects of differential survival rates applicable to particular population groups.

17. Note that a 5 percent discount rate is used notwithstanding the fact that the Ryan proposal eventually eliminates the infinite horizon open group imbalance. That alone is not sufficient to eliminate uncertainty about future taxes benefits because of sizable general government transfers required to finance the substantial transition costs under the Ryan proposal.

18. The new bend point is set by adding 28.6 percent of the difference between the two bend points to the first bend point — determined so that 30 percent of workers would have average monthly indexed earnings below the new bend point.

Chapter 14

1. This panel is convened every four years and includes distinguished academicians and other analysts, demographers, and statisticians; members examine and make recommendations about the assumptions and methods adopted by the program's trustees when analyzing the program's current operations and future financial prospects.

2. See the 2007 report of the Technical Panel on Assumptions and Methods to the Social Security Advisory Board, available at http://www.ssab.gov/documents/2007_Technical_Panel_Report.PDF.

3. See Social Security Advisory Board (2007).

4. See Actuarial Standards Board (2008), paragraphs 3.1.5 and 3.1.6.

5. See Gokhale and Smetters (2006).

6. Unfortunately, even the most comprehensive of polls on Social Security (by National Public Radio, the Kaiser Family Foundation, and the Kennedy School of Government) do not ask about how people think of the Social Security program and whether they would have saved more out of their incomes in its absence. Studies of consumer behavior suggest that a vast majority of people are rational in choosing how much to consume and save—taking into account benefits they would receive during retirement from public programs like Social Security and Medicare. For example, see Erik Hurst (2008).

7. It could be argued, in fairness, that Model 2's proponents envisioned the expansion of personal accounts to accelerate after the proposal was enacted with more adjustments to be implemented down the road.

8. The term "beyond the veil of ignorance" is used to describe an investigative method devised by John Rawls. It connotes the fundamental uncertainty—prior to being born—about the multitude of demographic and economic outcomes that a person possesses and experiences during one's lifetime. Social Security may mitigate such uncertainty regarding lifetime earnings outcomes by redistributing income or wealth from those who turn out to have high earnings to those with lower earnings.

9. As in earlier chapters, this discussion focuses on payable traditional benefits under various reforms. The objective is to examine the implications of treating individuals under the tighter of benefit- and tax-side constraints under alternative Social Security reform proposals.

References

Actuarial Standards Board. 2008. *Introduction to the Actuarial Standards of Practice*, Document No. 096, adopted in December 2004. Washington, DC: ASB.

Altonji, Joseph G. 1986. "Intertemporal Substitution in Labor Supply: Evidence from Micro Data." *Journal of Political Economy* 94 (3, pt. 2): S176–S215.

Ball, Robert M. 2007. "Meeting Social Security's Long-Range Shortfall: A Golden Opportunity for the New Congress," available at http://robertmball.org.

Bernheim, B. Douglas, Katherine Grace Carman, Jagadeesh Gokhale, and Laurence J. Kotlikoff. 2003. "The Mismatch between Life Insurance Holdings and Financial Vulnerabilities: Evidence from the Survey of Consumer Finances." *American Economic Review* 93 (1): 354–65.

Biggs, Andrew G., Clark Burdick, and Kent Smetters. 2009. "Pricing Personal Account Benefit Guarantees: A Simplified Approach." In *Social Security Policy in a Changing Environment*. Chicago: University of Chicago Press.

Biggs, Andrew G., and Jagadeesh Gokhale. 2007. "Wage Growth and the Measurement of Social Security's Financial Condition." In *Government Spending on the Elderly*, ed. Dimitri B. Papadimitriou. New York: Palgrave, Macmillan.

Board of Governors of the Federal Reserve System. 2004. *Survey of Consumer Finances*. Washington, DC: Board of Governors of the Federal Reserve System.

Boldrin, Michele, Mariachristina DeNardi, and Larry E. Jones. 2005. "Fertility and Social Security." National Bureau of Economic Research, Working Paper No. 11146.

Borsch-Supan, Axel, Jagadeesh Gokhale, Laurence J. Kotlikoff, and John N. Morris. 1992. "The Provision of Time to the Elderly by Their Children." In *Topics in the Economics of Aging*, ed. David A. Wise. Chicago: National Bureau of Economic Research/University of Chicago Press.

Bureau of Economic Analysis. 2007. *National Income and Product Account*. Washington, DC: BLS.

Caldwell, Steven, Alla Gantman, Jagadeesh Gokhale, Thomas Johnson, and Laurence J. Kotlikoff. 2001. "Projecting Social Security's Finances and Its Treatment of Postwar Americans." Chapter 8 in *Demographic Change and Fiscal Policy*, ed. by Alan J. Auerbach and Ronald D. Lee, 297–385. New York: Cambridge University Press.

Congressional Budget Office. 1996. "Labor Supply and Taxes." CBO memorandum, January.

———. 2002. "Federal Budget Estimating." Statement of Dan L. Crippen, before the Subcommittee on Legislative and Budget Process Committee on Rules, U.S. House Of Representatives, May 9.

———. 2008. "Updated Long-Term Projections for Social Security." CBO paper, August.

Coronado, Julia Lynn, Don Fullerton, and Thomas W. Glass. 2000. "The Progressivity of Social Security." National Bureau of Economic Research, Working Paper No. W7520.

Costa, Dora, and Matthew Kahn. 2008. *Heroes and Cowards: The Social Face of War.* Princeton, NJ: Princeton University Press.

Diamond, Peter, A., and Peter R. Orszag. 2004. *Saving Social Security: A Balanced Approach,* Washington, DC: Brookings Institution Press.

Dupuy, Arnaud, and Philip Marey. 2008. "Shifts and Twists in the Relative Productivity of Skilled Labor: Reconciling Accelerated SBTC with the Productivity Slowdown." *Journal of Macroeconomics* 30 (2): 718–35.

Easton, Nina. 2007.. "A Political Odd Couple Tackles Social Security." Fortune Online, July 19, available at http://money.cnn.com/2007/06/07/magazines/fortune/easton_powerplay_social.fortune/index.htm?postversion=2007060816.

Economic Report of the President. 2008. Washington, DC: U.S. Government Printing Office.

Ellwood, David T. 2001. "The Sputtering Labor-Force of the of the 21st Century: Can Social Policy Help?" National Bureau of Economic Research, Working Paper No. 8321, June.

French, Eric. 2004. "The Labor Supply Response to (Mismeasured but) Predictable Wage Changes." *Review of Economics and Statistics* 86 (2): 602–13.

Fullerton, Howard N., Jr. 1999. "Labor Force Participation: 75 Years of Change 1950–98 and 1999–2025." *Monthly Labor Review* 122, no. 12 (December).

Gan, Li, Guan Gong, Michael Hurd, and Daniel McFadden. (2004). "Subjective Mortality Risk and Bequests." National Bureau of Economic Research, Working Paper No. 10789.

Geanakoplos, John, Olivia S. Mitchell, and Stephen P. Zeldes. 1999. "*Social Security Money's Worth,*" *Prospects for Social Security Reform,* ed. Olivia Mitchell, Robert J. Myres, and Howard Young. Philadelphia: University of Pennsylvania Press.

Gokhale, Jagadeesh, (2005) "The Case for (Carve Out) Personal Accounts." Techcentralstation.org, available at http://www.cato.org/pub_display.php?pub_id=3978.

Gokhale, Jagadeesh, and Laurence J. Kotlikoff. 2002a. "Social Security's Treatment of Postwar Americans: How Bad Can It Get." In *Distributional Aspects of Social Security and Social Security Reform,* ed. Martin Feldstein and Jeffrey B. Liebman. Chicago: National Bureau of Economic Research/University of Chicago Press.

———. 2002b. "The Impact of Social Security and Other Factors on the Distribution of Wealth." In *Distributional Aspects of Social Security and Social Security*

Reform, ed. Martin Feldstein and Jeffrey B. Liebman. Chicago: National Bureau of Economic Research/University of Chicago Press.

Gokhale, Jagadeesh, Laurence J. Kotlikoff, and John Sabelhaus. 1996. "Understanding the Postwar Decline in Saving: A Cohort Analysis." *Brookings Papers on Economic Activity,* Winter, 315–407.

Gokhale, Jagadeesh, Laurence J. Kotlikoff, and Alexi Sluchynsky. 2002c. "Does It Pay to Work?" National Bureau of Economic Research, Working Paper No. 9095.

Gokhale, Jagadeesh, and Kent A. Smetters. 2003. *Fiscal and Generational Imbalances: New Measures for New Budget Priorities.* Washington, DC: AEI Press.

———. 2006. "Measuring Social Security's Financial Outlook within an Aging Society." *Dædalus,* Winter, 91–104.

Goldin, Claudia, and Lawrence Katz. 2007. "The Race between Education and Technology: The Evolution of U.S. Educational Wage Differentials, 1890–2005." National Bureau of Economic Research, Working Paper No. 12984.

Goss, Stephen C. 1999. "Measuring Solvency in the Social Security System." In *Prospects for Social Security Reform,* ed. Olivia S. Mitchell, Robert J. Myres, and Howard Young. Philadelphia: University of Pennsylvania Press.

Gruber, Jonathan, Kevin Milligan, and David A. Wise (2009). "Social Security Programs and Retirement Around the World: The Relationship to Youth Employment, Introduction and Summary." National Bureau of Economic Research, Working Paper No. 14647.

Gruber, Jonathan, and David Wise. 1999. *Social Security and Retirement around the World.* Chicago: University of Chicago Press.

Hickey, Jennifer G. 2003. "Could the Buck Stop Here?" *Insight on the News,* February 18.

Hurst, Erik. 2008. "Grasshoppers, Ants, and Pre-Retirement Wealth: A Test of Permanent Income Consumers." Michigan Retirement Research Center, Working Paper No. 2004–088.

Ibbotson Associates (2008). *Ibbotson SBBI 2008 Classic Yearbook: Market Results for Stocks, Bonds, Bills, and Inflation 1926–2007.* Chicago: Morningstar Inc.

Internal Revenue Service, Statistics of Income Division. 2007. "Tax Statistics: Estate Tax Returns Filed for 2004 Decedents Values for Tax Purposes, by Tax Status and Size of Gross Estate," available at http://www.irs.gov/taxstats/indtaxstats/article/0,,id=96442,00.html#3.

Jacobs, Bas. 2008. "Is Prescott Right? Welfare State Policies and the Incentives to Work, Learn and Retire." CESifo Working Paper No. 2277, April.

Jorgenson, Dale W., Mun Ho, and Kevin Stiroh. 2007. "A Retrospective Look at the U.S. Productivity Growth Resurgence." Federal Reserve Bank of New York, Staff Report No. 277.

Kabe, Tetsuo. 2007. "Japan." In *International Perspectives on Social Security Reform,* ed. Rudolph G. Penner. Washington, DC: Urban Institute Press.

Kerrey, Robert J., and John C. Danforth. 1994. Bipartisan Commission on Entitlement and Tax Reform, Final Report, December, available at http://www.ssa.gov/history/reports/KerreyDanforth/KerreyDanforth.html.

Kirkegaard, Jacob Funk. 2007. *Accelerating Decline in America's High-Skilled Workforce: Implications for Immigration Policy*. Washington, DC: Peterson Institute for International Economics.

Kydland, Finn E., and Edward C. Prescott. 1993. "Cyclical Movements of the Labor Input and Its Implicit Wage." Federal Reserve Bank of Cleveland, *Economic Review* 29 (2): 12–23.

Leimer, Dean R. 1991. "Cohort-Specific Measures of Lifetime Net Social Security Transfers." Office of Research and Statistics, Working Paper No. 59, Social Security Administration, Washington, DC.

Liebman, Jeffery, Maya MacGuineas, and Andrew Samwick. 2005. "Nonpartisan Social Security Reform Plan," December, available at http://www.newamerica.net/files/archive/Doc_file_2757.pdf.

Liu, Liqun, Andrew Rettenmaier, and Thomas R. Saving. 2007. "Valuing Intergenerational Transfers: What's Social Security Worth?" Unpublished manuscript, Texas A&M University and National Center for Policy Analysis.

Lusardi, Annamaria. 2002. "Explaining Why So Many Households Do Not Save." Photocopy, Dartmouth College.

MaCurdy, Thomas E. 1981. "An Empirical Model of Labor Supply in a Life-Cycle Setting." *Journal of Political Economy* 89 (6): 1059–85.

Moore, Stephen, and Peter Ferrara. 2005. "Senate Social Security Sellout?" National Review Online, available at http://www.nationalreview.com/moore/moore.asp.

Moynihan, Daniel P., and Richard Parsons. 2001. *Strengthening Social Security and Creating Personal Wealth for All Americans*. Final Report of the President's Commission to Strengthen Social Security, December, available at http://www.csss.gov/reports.

Nataraj, Sita, and John Shoven. 2004. "Has the Unified Budget Undermined the Federal Government Trust Funds?" National Bureau of Economic Research, Working Paper No. 10953.

National Vital Statistics Report. 2006. Volume 54, No. 14, April 19, available at http://www.cdc.gov/nchs/data/nvsr/nvsr54/nvsr54_14.pdf.

Prescott, Edward C. 2004a. "Why Do Americans Work So Much More than Europeans?" *Federal Reserve Bank of Minneapolis Quarterly Review* 28 (1): 2–13.

———. 2004b. "Why Does the Government Patronize Us?" *Wall Street Journal*, November 11, 2004.

Ryan, Paul D. 2008a. "How to Tackle the Entitlement Crisis." *Wall Street Journal*, May 21, 2008, A19.

———. 2008b. "A Roadmap for America's Future," available at http://www.house.gov/budget_republicans/entitlement/roadmap_detailed_entirereport.pdf.

Smetters, Kent A. 1999. "Thinking about Social Security's Trust Fund." In *Prospects for Social Security Reform*, ed. Olivia S. Mitchell, Robert Myres, and Howard Young, Philadelphia: University of Pennsylvania Press.

———. 2004. "Is the Social Security Trust Fund a Store of Value." *American Economic Review, Papers and Proceedings* 94 (2): 176–81.

Social Security Administration. 2003. "Estimated OASDI Financial Effects for Two Provisions That Would Improve Social Security Financing Plus a Balancing Tax Rate Increase." Office of the Chief Actuary, SSA, Washington, DC, October.

———. 2005a. "Estimated OASDI Financial Effects for a Proposal with Six Provisions That Would Improve Social Security Financing." Office of the Chief Actuary, SSA, Washington, DC, April.

———. 2005b. "Estimated Financial Effects of the 'Bipartisan Retirement Security Act of 2005.'" Office of the Chief Actuary, SSA, Washington, DC, November.

———. 2005c. "Estimated Financial Effects of the 'Nonpartisan Approach to Reforming Social Security.'" Office of the Chief Actuary, SSA, Washington, DC, November.

Social Security Advisory Board. 2003. Report of the Technical Panel on Assumptions and Methods. Social Security Advisory Board, Washington, DC.

———. 2007. Report of the Technical Panel on Assumptions and Methods. Social Security Advisory Board, Washington, DC.

Social Security Board of Trustees. 2006. *The 2006 Annual Report of the Board of Trustees of the Old Age and Survivors Insurance, and Federal Disability Insurance Trust Funds.* Washington, DC: Social Security Board of Trustees.

———. 2007. *The 2007 Annual Report of the Board of Trustees of the Old Age and Survivors Insurance, and Federal Disability Insurance Trust Funds.* Washington, DC: Social Security Board of Trustees.

———. 2008. *The 2008 Annual Report of the Board of Trustees of the Old Age and Survivors Insurance, and Federal Disability Insurance Trust Funds.* Washington, DC: Social Security Board of Trustees.

U.S. Census Bureau and Bureau of Labor Statistics. 1968–2006. Current Population Survey, March and June supplements.

U.S. Congress. 2001. "The 21st Century Retirement Security Act." *House Resolution 2771*, 107th Congress of the United States.

———. 2004. "The Bipartisan Retirement Security Act." *House Resolution 3821*, 108th Congress of the United States.

———. 2005. "The Bipartisan Retirement Security Act." *House Resolution 440*, 109th Congress of the United States.

U.S. Supreme Court. 1960. *Flemming v. Nestor*, 363 U.S. 603, No. 54, argued February 24, 1960; verdict: June 20, 1960, 169 F. Supp. 922, reversed.

Ziliak, James P., and Thomas J. Kniesner. 1999. "Estimating Life Cycle Labor Supply Tax Effects." *Journal of Political Economy* 107 (2): 326–59.

Index

accrued obligation measure, 319n18
Actuarial Standards of Practice (ASOP),
295
add-on personal accounts, 149, 150, 205,
207, 230, 231, 243, 263, 264
adjustment costs, 33, 297, 313; under Bush
Commission Model 2 reform proposal,
33, 257–58, 340n18; under Diamond-
Orszag reform proposal, 33, 185, 192–93,
195, 198–99; under Kolbe-Stenholm-
Boyd reform proposal, 33, 204, 205;
under Liebman-MacGuineas-Samwick
reform proposal, 33, 231, 238, 244; under
Ryan reform proposal, 33, 280
adjustment factors, annual, 327n3
age, 12–13, 48–49, 59–61, 78–80. See also life
expectancy; retirement age
aggregate finances: Ball reform proposal's
effects on, 175–80, 303; Bush Commission Model 2 reform proposal's effects
on, 254–58, 303; Diamond-Orszag
reform proposal's effects on, 189–93,
303; Kolbe-Stenholm-Boyd reform
proposal's effects on, 211–13, 303;
Liebman-MacGuineas-Samwick reform
proposal's effects on, 235–38, 303; Ryan
reform proposal's effects on, 276–80
AIME. See average indexed monthly earnings (AIME)
Altmeyer, Arthur, 319n15
Altonji, Joseph G., 336n9
annual adjustment factors, 327n3
annual benefit statements, 14–15
annual deficit ratio, 127, 128

annual imbalance ratios, 20, 170, 296, 304–6;
under Ball reform proposal, 179–80, 302,
304–5, 306; under Bush Commission
Model 2 reform proposal, 258–59, 304–5,
306; under Diamond-Orszag reform
proposal, 193–94, 238, 304–5; under
Kolbe-Stenholm-Boyd reform proposal,
217–18, 238–39, 305; under Liebman-
MacGuineas-Samwick reform proposal,
238–39, 305; under Ryan reform proposal, 280–81, 304–5
ANYPIA, 117, 118
ASOP. See Actuarial Standards of Practice
(ASOP)
attributes: age, 12–13, 48–49, 59–61, 78–80;
conditioning, 40–43, 49–51; distribution
of, 36–37, 320n1; divorce, 12, 54–55, 68;
education (see education); effect on
lifetime net tax rate, 149, 153–61; effect
on retirement wealth, 151; family type,
12, 41–45, 59–60, 78–80, 96; fertility
(see fertility); gender (see gender); immigration, 58, 72–76, 125, 126; of initial
population, 1970, 36, 38–46; interaction
between demographic and economic
variables, 5, 11–13, 19–20, 27, 37–38,
87; and labor earnings, 12, 29, 87–104,
110–15; labor force participation, 12,
55–58, 69–71, 81–84, 125, 126; and labor
inputs, 96–97, 123, 125, 132; marriage,
12, 53–55, 66–68, 159–60; mortality (see
mortality); in projected simulation,
77–86; race (see race)
Auerbach, Alan J., 330n19

average indexed monthly earnings (AIME): under Bush Commission Model 2 reform proposal, 251, 339n9; under Kolbe-Stenholm-Boyd reform proposal, 209–11, 213

baby boomers: under Bush Commission Model 2 reform proposal, 259–62; children of, 61; definition of, 42; under Kolbe-Stenholm-Boyd reform proposal, 226; lifetime net tax rate, 32, 160; mortality rate of, 84–86; postponement of retirement, 98, 123; in projected simulation, 77–78; retirement of, 15, 82, 99–101, 123, 301; under Ryan reform proposal, 283; savings of, 99–100; taxable-to-total payrolls ratio, 175, 180–81, 334n4
Ball, Robert M., 167, 173
Ball reform proposal, 32–35, 173–83, 204; annual imbalance ratios, 179–80, 302, 304–5, 306; earnings ceiling, 174, 177, 187; estate tax, 174, 177–78, 181, 182–83; impact on Social Security aggregate finances, 175–80, 303; key elements of, 174–75; open group imbalance, 33; taxable-to-total payrolls ratio, 174, 175–77, 180–81; trust fund, 174–75, 178–79, 181, 302
baseline assumptions, 30, 120–25, 127, 152, 297–300; Ball reform proposal, 175–81; Bush Commission Model 2 reform proposal, 254–65; Diamond-Orszag reform proposal, 189–93; Kolbe-Stenholm-Boyd reform proposal, 211–17; Liebman-MacGuineas-Samwick reform proposal, 235–44; Ryan reform proposal, 276–91
bend points, 135, 138, 140; under Bush Commission Model 2 reform proposal, 251, 256, 259, 262, 339n9; under Diamond-Orszag reform proposal, 191, 201–2; under Kolbe-Stenholm-Boyd reform proposal, 210, 211, 213; under Liebman-MacGuineas-Samwick reform proposal, 231, 234, 237, 239; under Ryan reform proposal, 292–93
Benefit and Earnings Public-Use File, 102–3
benefit offset calculations for Bush Commission Model 2 reform proposal, 250, 266–68

benefit recomputation, 137–38
benefit reductions: under Bush Commission Model 2 reform proposal, 251–52, 256–57; under Liebman-MacGuineas-Samwick reform proposal, 230–31, 234–35, 237, 244; under Ryan reform proposal, 271–72, 286, 292–93
benefits: benefit taxes to payroll taxes ratio, 320n5; calculations for projected simulation, 118–19; guaranteed, 286–90, 291; and lifetime net tax rate, 152–53; linkage to payroll taxes, 14–15; payable (see payable benefits); scheduled (see scheduled benefits); to taxes ratio, 331n8. See also Social Security Tax and Benefit Calculator (SSTBC)
Bernheim, B. Douglas, 337n15
Biggs, Andrew G., 317n4, 329n12, 340n4
Boldrin, Michele, 331n5
Borsch-Supan, Axel, 322n1
Boyd, Allen, 204. See also Kolbe-Stenholm-Boyd reform proposal
Bureau of Economic Analysis: National Income and Product Accounts (NIPA), 95
Bureau of Labor Statistics: Consumer Price Index (CPI-W), 90, 92, 95–96
Bush, George W., 9, 10, 338n12
Bush Commission Model 2 reform proposal, 32–35, 245–68; adjustment costs, 33, 257–58, 340n18; annual imbalance ratios, 258–59, 304–5, 306; average indexed monthly earnings (AIME), 251, 339n9; benefit offset calculations, 250, 266–68; benefit reductions, 251–52, 256–57; closed group imbalances, 255–57; effects on Social Security's aggregate finances, 254–58, 303; elements of, 249–54; general fund transfer, 253–54; individual accounts, 248–51, 254–56, 264, 265, 307; lifetime earnings variability, 312; lifetime net tax rates, 254, 259–62, 307; low-earner benefits, 252, 257; open group imbalances, 33, 254–58, 264, 302–3; Primary Insurance Amount (PIA), 251, 339n9; retirement wealth, 262–64, 265, 283, 307; widow(er)'s benefits, 252–53, 257

capital stock, 19, 122–23; capital stock index, 89, 92; foreign capital inflows, 325n14; in projected simulation, 99–101 carve-out personal accounts, 32, 149–50; under Bush Commission Model 2 reform proposal, 248, 254, 256, 302, 304; under Kolbe-Stenholm-Boyd reform proposal, 205, 207, 226, 227, 302, 311–12; under Liebman-MacGuineas-Samwick reform proposal, 230, 231, 239, 242, 243; under Ryan reform proposal, 271, 275, 290, 302, 304

CBO. See Congressional Budget Office (CBO)

cell-based methodology, 3–4, 11–13

Census data, 37, 64–65, 72–76

centrist reform proposals, 32, 205–6. See also Kolbe-Stenholm-Boyd reform proposal; Liebman-MacGuineas-Samwick reform proposal

characteristics. See attributes

child dependent benefits, 138–39

Clinton, Bill: Bipartisan Commission on Entitlement and Tax Reform, 246; Social Security reform commission, 10

closed group imbalances, 23–25, 30–31, 124, 130–32, 169–70, 299, 319n18, 319n20, 329n14; under Ball reform proposal, 33; under Bush Commission Model 2 reform proposal, 255–57; under Diamond-Orszag reform proposal, 33, 191–93, 199, 303–4; under Kolbe-Stenholm-Boyd reform proposal, 214–16, 303–4; under Liebman-MacGuineas-Samwick reform proposal, 236–38, 303–4; under Ryan reform proposal, 33, 277, 303–4

computation years, 135, 141

conditional distribution of attributes, 36–37

conditioning attributes, 40–43, 49–51

Congressional Budget Office (CBO), 25; microsimulation for, 3–4, 5; scoring of reform proposals, 6

conservative reform proposals, 32, 205. See also Bush Commission Model 2 reform proposal; Ryan reform proposal

Consumer Price Index (CPI), 15, 271, 281, 283, 292–93

Consumer Price Index (CPI-W), 90, 92, 95–96

core labor inputs, 87, 89, 92–93, 96–97, 107, 111–15

Costa, Dora, 80, 323n3

cost-of-living adjustments, 208

covered worker, 22, 82–83, 273

Current Population Survey (CPS), 37; labor earnings, 324n4; match with DEMSIM, 28, 37–38, 41–46, 47, 320n4; age, 59–60; education, 49–50; family type, 41–45, 59–60; labor earnings distributions, 88, 93–95; labor force participation, 56, 57; marriage, 55; use of to calibrate demographic features of initial population, 39

Danforth, John C., 246

delayed retirement, 98, 137

DeLong, Brad, 337n2

Demographic and Economic Microsimulation (DEMSIM). See DEMSIM

demographic transition, 1971–2006, 28, 36–38; age, 48–49, 59–61; annual transitions, 47–48; divorce, 54–55, 68; education, 49–51; family type, 59–60; fertility, 51–53, 64–65; immigration, 58, 72–76; labor earnings, 92–96, 105–9; labor force participation, 55–58, 69–71; marriage, 53–55, 66–68; mortality, 48–49, 62–63; validation of, 58–61, 297–98

DEMSIM: baseline assumptions (see baseline assumptions); demographic transition, 1971–2006 (see demographic transition, 1971–2006); evaluation of reform proposals, 169–72, 300–313; initial population, 1970 (see initial population, 1970); interaction between demographic and economic variables, 5, 11–13, 19–20, 27, 37, 87; labor earnings (see labor earnings); lifetime net tax rate, 153–61; match with CPS population, 28, 37–38, 41–46, 47, 320n4; age, 59–60; education, 49–50; family type, 41–45, 59–60; labor earnings distribution, 93–95; labor force participation, 56, 57; marriage, 55; optimistic assumption, 120, 124, 125–26, 127, 128; pessimistic assumption, 120, 126–28; projected simulation (see projected simulation); random numbers, 38, 39–41; retirement wealth ratios, 162–64; usefulness of, 4–7, 11, 294–95. See also microsimulations

Diamond, Peter A., 154, 184

Diamond-Orszag (DO) reform proposal, 32–35, 184–203, 204; adjustment costs, 33, 185, 192–93, 195, 198–99; annual imbalance ratios, 193–94, 238, 304–5;

Diamond-Orszag (DO) reform proposal
  (*cont.*)
  benefit reductions for wealthy, 187;
  closed group imbalances, 33, 191–93,
  199, 303–4; earnings ceiling, 187, 202;
  impact on Social Security's aggregate
  finances, 189–93, 303; key elements of,
  186–88; legacy cost, 188, 191–92, 202;
  life expectancy, 186–87, 189–91, 200–202;
  lifetime earnings variability, 311–12;
  lifetime net tax rate, 194–97, 307; open
  group imbalances, 33, 189–91, 199,
  302–3, 304; retirement wealth, 198–99,
  263–64, 307, 308; taxable-to-total earnings ratio, 191, 202; widow(er)s and
  survivor benefits, 188, 192, 201–3
Disability Insurance (DI), 116–17
distribution of attributes, 36–37, 320n1
diversity, 80–81, 323n4. *See also* race
divorce, 12, 54–55, 68
driver parameters, 38–41
Dupuy, Arnaud, 97

early retirement, 136, 143–44, 155
earnings ceiling, 117–18, 189, 301, 334n6;
  under Ball reform proposal, 174, 177,
  187; under Diamond-Orszag reform
  proposal, 187, 202; under Kolbe-
  Stenholm-Boyd reform proposal, 210;
  under Liebman-MacGuineas-Samwick
  reform proposal, 231, 233, 237
earnings record, 103, 135, 136, 137, 138, 326
earnings test, 137
Easton, Nina, 317n1
education, 12, 125, 126; as a conditioning
  attribute, 49–51; in demographic transition, 1971–2006, 49–51; and gender,
  82, 323n5; and labor earnings, 97; and
  lifetime net tax rates, 159; in projected
  simulation, 81–82; and race, 81, 82, 159,
  323n5; transition probabilities, 328n10
effective labor inputs, 12, 29, 88–91, 92,
  95–102, 105–9, 110–12, 120, 122–23,
  125–28, 132, 298
elapsed years, 135, 141
Ellwood, David T., 324n7
estate tax under Ball reform proposal, 174,
  177–78, 181, 182–83
evolution of population. *See* demographic
  transition, 1971–2006
expectations, public, 13–15

family maximum benefit level, 138
family type, 12, 41–45, 59–60, 78–80, 96. *See
  also* marriage
father/mother benefits, 139, 140
Federal Reserve: Survey of Consumer
  Finances, 89, 182–83, 325n13
feedback effects. *See* second order effects
fertility, 12, 125, 126; crude rate, 323n8; in
  demographic transition, 1971–2006,
  51–53, 64–65; projection through 2469,
  84–86; and race, 80, 81, 273, 323n4;
  variation rate, 328n10
first eligibility, 135
fiscal treatment, definition of, 317n6
fiscal treatment of population groups,
  26–27, 31–32, 145–65
French, Eric, 336n9
Fullerton, Howard N., Jr., 324n10
fully insured status, 135

Gan, Li, 325n12
Geanakoplos, John, 336n14, 337n9, 338n6
gender, 12–13, 27; and education, 82,
  323n5; and labor force participation,
  81–82, 98; and lifetime net tax rate, 32,
  153–61, 197, 218–21, 239–42, 259–62,
  284–85; and marriage, 160; and mortality, 154–58; and retirement wealth,
  163–64, 198, 219–20, 240–41, 260–61,
  284–85
general fund transfer: under Bush Commission Model 2 reform proposal, 253–54;
  under Kolbe-Stenholm-Boyd reform
  proposal, 208
Gokhale, Jagadeesh, 317n4, 329n12, 329n14,
  331n5, 333n1, 334n6, 337n17, 339n14,
  342n5
Goldin, Claudia, 97, 324n9
Goss, Stephen C., 330n18
gross domestic product (GDP), growth in,
  26, 319n21
group health insurance, 273–75, 276, 290–91,
  308
Gruber, Jonathan, 143, 331n4
guaranteed benefits, 286–90, 291

health insurance, group. *See* group health
  insurance
Hickey, Jennifer G., 335n1
high-cost assumption, 119–20
Hospital Insurance program, 210, 213–16

human capital input. *See* labor inputs
Hurst, Eric, 333n21, 342n6

Ibbotson Associates, 225, 338n4
immigration, 125, 126; in demographic
  transition, 1971–2006, 58, 72–76; in
  projected simulation, 80–81; projection
  through 2469, 84–86; variation rate,
  328n10
implicit debt, 16, 247, 338n5
income replacement. *See* replacement rate
individual accounts, 149–50, 170–71, 205,
  302, 306–8, 309; add-on, 149, 150, 205,
  207, 230, 231, 243, 263, 264; under Bush
  Commission Model 2 reform proposal,
  248–51, 254–56, 264, 265, 307; carve-
  out (*see* carve-out personal accounts);
  debates about, 245–49; under Kolbe-
  Stenholm-Boyd reform proposal,
  207, 212–13, 221–27, 256, 307; under
  Liebman-MacGuineas-Samwick reform
  proposal, 230, 231, 232–33, 239–44,
  256, 307; portfolios, 221–23, 223–24,
  225, 243, 246–47, 270; rates of return,
  225, 336nn13–14; under Ryan reform
  proposal, 269–71, 275–76, 307, 308
individual equity objective, 14
inequality, 186, 187, 191, 202
inflation and labor earnings, 90, 95–96
information: for decision making on reform
  options, 6–7; restriction of, 6
initial population, 1970, 28, 36–46; attributes
  of, 36, 38–46; driver parameters, 38–41;
  labor earnings, 88, 91–92, 102–3, 105–9,
  110–12
intermediate-cost assumption, 119–20,
  121–25
internal rate of return, 146

Jacobs, Bas, 335n9
Japan, 101
Jorgenson, Dale W., 89, 90, 95, 297, 325n13,
  327n22

Kabe, Tetsuo, 101
Kahn, Matthew, 323n3
Katz, Lawrence, 97, 324n9
Kerrey, Robert J., 246
Kirkegaard, Jacob Funk, 97
Kniesner, Thomas J., 336n9
Kolbe, Jim, 206

Kolbe-Stenholm-Boyd (KSB) reform proposal, 32–35, 206–28; adjustment costs,
  33, 204, 205; AIME calculation, 209–11;
  annual imbalance ratios, 217–18, 238–39,
  305; average indexed monthly earnings
  (AIME), 213; closed group imbalances,
  214–16, 303–4; cost-of-living adjustments, 208; earnings ceiling, 210; effects
  on Social Security's aggregate finances,
  211–13, 303; features of, 207–11; general
  fund transfer, 208; Hospital Insurance
  program, 210, 213–16; individual accounts, 207, 212–13, 221–27, 256, 307;
  life expectancy, 209; lifetime earnings
  variability, 312; lifetime net tax rate,
  218–21, 307; open group imbalances,
  33, 213–16, 302–3; primary insurance
  amount (PIA), 207–8, 209, 210, 213;
  retirement age, 208–9; retirement
  wealth, 222–26, 307; spousal benefits,
  211; taxable-to-total earnings ratio, 210;
  widow(er) benefits, 211
Kotlikoff, Laurence J., 334n6
Kydland, Finn E., 324n1

labor earnings: and attributes, 12, 29,
  87–104, 110–15; core labor inputs,
  87, 89, 92–93, 96–97, 107, 111–15; for
  demographic transition, 1971–2006,
  92–96, 105–9; distribution of, 93–95; and
  education, 97; effective labor inputs, 12,
  29, 88–91, 92, 95–102, 105–9, 110–12,
  120, 122–23, 125–28, 132, 298; inflation, 90, 95–96; for initial population,
  1970, 88, 91–92, 102–3, 105–9, 110–12;
  multifactor productivity parameter, 90,
  92, 95; physical capital inputs, 89–90, 95;
  for projected simulation, 18–20, 96–102,
  105–9, 120, 122–23, 125–28; taxable-to-
  total earnings ratio, 174, 175–77, 180–81,
  187, 189, 191. *See also* lifetime earnings
labor force participation, 12, 125, 126; in
  demographic transition, 1971–2006,
  55–58, 69–71; and gender, 81–82, 98; in
  projected simulation, 81–84; and race,
  81–82, 323n5; transition probabilities,
  328n10
labor inputs: core, 87, 89, 92–93, 96–97,
  107, 111–15; effective, 12, 19, 29, 88–91,
  92, 95–102, 105–9, 110–12, 120, 122–23,
  125–28, 132, 298

labor productivity, 19, 29, 80, 101, 126, 298
labor quality, 88–91, 95, 101, 298. *See also*
    labor inputs
labor quantity, 88–91, 95. *See also* labor
    inputs
Lee, Ronald D., 330n19
legacy costs, 188, 191–92, 195, 202, 313
Leimer, Dean R., 338n4
level shift factor, 326n17
liberal reform proposals, 32, 204–5. *See also*
    Ball reform proposal; Diamond-Orszag
    reform proposal
Liebman, Jeffrey, 206, 229
Liebman-MacGuineas-Samwick (LMS)
    reform proposal, 32–35, 206–7, 229–44;
    adjustment costs, 33, 231, 238, 244; an-
    nual imbalance ratios, 238–39, 305; ben-
    efit reduction, 230–31, 234–35, 237, 244;
    closed group imbalances, 236–38, 303–4;
    earnings ceiling, 231, 233, 237; elements
    of, 230–35; impact on Social Security's
    aggregate finances, 235–38, 303; individ-
    ual accounts, 230, 231, 232–33, 239–44,
    256, 307; lifetime earnings variability,
    312; lifetime net tax rates, 239–42, 307,
    308; low-earner benefits, 231, 235; open
    group imbalances, 33, 235–38, 302–3,
    304; Primary Insurance Amount (PIA),
    230–31, 234–35; retirement age, 231, 234,
    237, 337n4; retirement wealth, 242–44,
    307, 308; spousal benefits, 231; taxable-
    to-total earnings ratio, 233, 244;
    widow(er)'s benefits, 231, 235
life expectancy, 13, 27, 142–43, 168, 330n2,
    332n13; in Diamond-Orszag reform
    proposal, 186–87, 189–91, 200–202; in
    Kolbe-Stenholm-Boyd reform proposal,
    209; in Ryan reform proposal, 272–73.
    See also mortality
lifetime earnings: and lifetime net tax rate,
    153–61; and marriage, 159–60; and
    retirement wealth, 163–64; variability in,
    7, 309–12. *See also* labor earnings
lifetime net tax rates, 6, 13, 27, 31–32, 145,
    146–61, 170, 296, 299, 306–8; allocation
    of payroll taxes and benefits, 152–53; un-
    der Bush Commission Model 2 reform
    proposal, 254, 259–62, 307; under
    Diamond-Orszag reform proposal,

194–97, 307; effect of attributes on, 149,
    153–61; under Kolbe-Stenholm-Boyd
    reform proposal, 218–21, 307; under
    Liebman-MacGuineas-Samwick reform
    proposal, 239–42, 307, 308; pre-tax labor
    earnings denominator, 331n9; under
    Ryan reform proposal, 281–82, 307, 308
Liu, Liqun, 331n10
longevity. *See* life expectancy
Lorenzen, Ed, 206
low-cost assumption, 119–20
low-earner benefits: under Bush Commis-
    sion Model 2 reform proposal, 252, 257;
    under Liebman-MacGuineas-Samwick
    reform proposal, 231, 235; under Ryan
    reform proposal, 272
Lusardi, Annamaria, 333n21

MacGuineas, Maya, 206, 229. *See also*
    Liebman-MacGuineas-Samwick reform
    proposal
MaCurdy, Thomas E., 336n9
Marey, Philip, 97
marriage, 12; in demographic transition,
    1971–2006, 53–55, 66–68; and gender,
    160; and lifetime earnings, 159–60; and
    lifetime net tax rate, 159–60; and race,
    159–60. *See also* family type
McCreary, Jim, 317n1
Medicare, 9, 210, 318n9
men. *See* gender
micromeasures, 31, 142–65, 194, 296–97
microsimulations: for Congressional Budget
    Office (CBO), 3–4, 5; in current use, 2–5;
    by private institutions, 4–5; usefulness
    of, 2, 12. *See also* DEMSIM
Model 2. *See* Bush Commission Model 2
    reform proposal
mortality, 12, 125, 126, 145, 321n1; crude
    rate, 323n8; in demographic transition,
    1971–2006, 48–49, 62–63; and gender,
    154–58; life expectancy, 13, 23, 142–43,
    168, 186–87, 189–91, 200–202, 209,
    272–73, 330n2, 332n13; and lifetime net
    tax rate, 153–58; projection through
    2469, 84–86; and race, 129, 154–58,
    200–201, 273, 322n3, 330n17; variation
    rate, 328n10
Moynihan, Daniel P., 247, 339n13

multifactor productivity, 19, 90, 92, 95, 99, 101, 105, 108, 120, 122–23, 125, 126, 298

Nataraj, Sita, 319n17
National Center for Health Statistics (NCHS): divorce rates, 68; marriage and divorce, 66–68; mortality rates, 48–49, 62–63, 321n1
National Income and Product Accounts (NIPA), 95
net national savings, 99, 324n11
NIPA. *See* National Income and Product Accounts (NIPA)
no free lunch constraints, 170–71, 247

OASDI. *See* Old Age, Survivors, and Disability Insurance (OASDI)
Obama, Barack, 9, 10
Old Age, Survivors, and Disability Insurance (OASDI), 116–17
Old Age and Survivors Insurance (OASI). *See* Social Security
open group imbalances, 20–21, 24–25, 124, 128–32, 169–70; under Ball reform proposal, 33; under Bush Commission Model 2 reform proposal, 33, 254–58, 264, 302–3; under Diamond-Orszag reform proposal, 33, 189–91, 199, 302–3, 304; infinite horizon, 20–21, 25, 30–31, 33, 296, 298–300, 302–4, 304, 329n14; under Kolbe-Stenholm-Boyd reform proposal, 33, 213–16, 302–3; under Liebman-MacGuineas-Samwick reform proposal, 33, 235–38, 302–3, 304; under Ryan reform proposal, 33, 276–79, 302–3; 75-year, 21, 30–31, 33, 296, 298–300, 302–3
optimistic assumption, 120, 124, 125–26, 127, 128
orphans, 321n2
Orszag, Peter R., 154, 184. *See also* Diamond-Orszag reform proposal

Panel Study of Income Dynamics (PSID), 28, 37; divorce, 54, 67; labor earnings, 38, 88, 91–93; labor force status, 69–71
Parsons, Richard, 247, 339n13
Paulson, Henry, 9
payable benefits, 137, 162–63, 306, 310; under Bush Commission Model 2 reform

proposal, 263; under Diamond-Orszag reform proposal, 196, 198–99; under Kolbe-Stenholm-Boyd reform proposal, 223, 226; under Liebman-MacGuineas-Samwick reform proposal, 242, 244; under Ryan reform proposal, 283, 285, 287, 290
pay-as-you-go, 22–23, 319n16
payroll taxes, 117–18; to benefit taxes ratio, 320n5; and lifetime net tax rate, 152; linkage to benefits, 14–15; taxable earnings ceilings (*see* earnings ceiling)
personal accounts. *See* individual accounts
Personal Security Account (PSA). *See* individual accounts
pessimistic assumption, 120, 126–28
physical capital inputs, 89–90, 95. *See also* capital stock
population, evolution of. *See* demographic transition, 1971–2006
population, initial. *See* initial population, 1970
population, projected size of, 84–86
portfolios: choice of, 221–22, 225, 243, 246–47, 270; restriction of, 223–24
pre-funding benefits, 22
Prescott, Edward C., 245, 324n1, 335n9, 338n1
present value calculations, 17–18
Primary Insurance Amount (PIA), 135–36, 140; under Bush Commission Model 2 reform proposal, 251, 339n9; under Kolbe-Stenholm-Boyd reform proposal, 207–8, 209, 210, 213; under Liebman-MacGuineas-Samwick reform proposal, 230–31, 234–35
private pensions, 246
productivity, labor. *See* labor productivity
productivity, multifactor. *See* multifactor productivity
projected simulation, 28–29, 37, 77–86; age distribution by family type, 78–80; annual deficit ratio, 127, 128; baseline assumptions (*see* baseline assumptions); benefit calculations, 118–19; capital stock in, 99–101; education in, 81–82; evolution of demographic and economic attributes, 80–81; fertility in, 80, 81; fiscal treatment of population groups, 145–65; immigration in, 80–81;

projected simulation (*cont.*)
  labor earnings, 18–20, 96–102, 105–9,
    120, 122–23, 125–28, 132; labor force
    participation, 81–84; and lifetime net tax
    rate, 153–61; long-range (through 2469),
    84–86; optimistic assumption, 120, 124,
    125–26, 127, 128; payroll tax revenues,
    118; pessimistic assumption, 120, 126–28;
    retirement wealth ratios, 162–64; short-
    falls, 168–69
PSID. *See* Panel Study of Income Dynamics
    (PSID)
public expectations, 13–15
public goods, 14, 16, 22

race, 12, 80–81; and education, 81, 82, 159,
    323n5; and fertility, 80, 81, 273, 323n4;
    and labor force participation, 81–82,
    323n5; and lifetime net tax rate, 153–61,
    197, 218–21, 239–42, 259–62, 284–85; and
    marriage, 159–60; and mortality, 129,
    154–58, 200–201, 273, 322n3, 330n17;
    and retirement wealth, 163–64, 198,
    219–20, 240–41, 260–61, 284–85. *See also*
    diversity
random numbers, 38, 39–41, 321n7
Rangel, Charles, 317n1
rates of return for individual accounts, 225,
    336nn13–14
Rawls, John, 342n8
reciprocal changes, 170–71
redistribution, 6, 227
reform proposals, 9–11; centrist, 32, 205–6
    (*see also* Kolbe-Stenholm-Boyd reform
    proposal; Liebman-MacGuineas-
    Samwick reform proposal); conserva-
    tive, 32, 205 (*see also* Bush Commission
    Model 2 reform proposal; Ryan reform
    proposal); impact of, 169–72; informa-
    tion needs for decision making, 6–7;
    liberal, 32, 204–5 (*see also* Ball reform
    proposal; Diamond-Orszag reform
    proposal); scoring of, 5–6, 11–13; second
    order effects, 151–52, 171–72, 209,
    320n3; selection of, 169, 300
reforms of 1983, 22, 23
re-indexing method, 141
replacement rate, 6–7, 13, 31, 142, 145, 151
retirement, early, 136, 143–44, 155
retirement, postponement of, 98, 137

retirement age, 142–44; under Kolbe-
    Stenholm-Boyd reform proposal, 208–9;
    under Liebman-MacGuineas-Samwick
    reform proposal, 231, 234, 237; under
    Ryan reform proposal, 272–73
retirement wealth, 7, 145, 150–51, 162–64,
    170, 296, 306–8, 308–12, 334n6, 338n6;
    under Bush Commission Model 2
    reform proposal, 262–64, 265, 283, 307,
    308; under Diamond-Orszag reform pro-
    posal, 198–99, 263–64, 307, 308; under
    Kolbe-Stenholm-Boyd reform proposal,
    222–26, 307, 308; under Liebman-
    MacGuineas-Samwick reform proposal,
    242–44, 307, 308; private pensions, 246;
    under Ryan reform proposal, 282–86,
    307, 308
revenues. *See* payroll taxes
Roosevelt, Franklin Delano, 319n15
Ryan, Paul D., 269
Ryan reform proposal, 32–35, 269–93;
    adjustment costs of, 33, 280; annual
    imbalance ratios, 280–81, 304–5; benefit
    guarantee, 341n10; benefit reduction,
    271–72, 286, 292–93; closed group
    imbalances, 33, 277, 303–4; Consumer
    Price Index (CPI), 271, 281, 283,
    292–93; effects on Social Security's
    aggregate finances, 276–80, 303; group
    health insurance, 273–75, 276, 290–91,
    308; guaranteed benefits, 286–90, 291;
    individual accounts, 269–71, 275–76, 307,
    308; lifetime earnings variability, 311–12;
    lifetime net tax rates, 281–82, 307; low-
    earner benefits, 272; open group imbal-
    ances, 33, 276–79, 302–3; retirement age,
    272–73; retirement wealth, 282–86, 307,
    308; transition costs under, 280–81

Samwick, Andrew, 206, 229. *See also*
    Liebman-MacGuineas-Samwick reform
    proposal
saving behavior, 144, 168, 300–301
savings, net national, 99, 324n11
scheduled benefits, 149, 162–63, 170, 205,
    299, 306; under Ball reform proposal,
    179; under Bush Commission Model 2
    reform proposal, 251, 252, 256, 257, 259,
    261–62, 263, 264, 265; under Diamond-
    Orszag reform proposal, 193, 196, 199,

258; under Kolbe-Stenholm-Boyd reform proposal, 210, 218, 220–21, 223, 225, 226; under Liebman-MacGuineas-Samwick reform proposal, 231, 232, 234, 239, 242, 243, 244; under Ryan reform proposal, 271, 278, 285, 286, 287, 292
second order effects, 151–52, 171–72, 209, 320n3
Shoven, John, 319n17
skills, 97. *See also* education
Smetters, Kent A., 317n4, 319n17, 329n14, 333n1, 342n5
social adequacy objective, 14
social insurance, 6, 27, 144, 168, 188, 202–3, 208, 227, 295
Social Security: advantages and disadvantages of, 167–68, 335n9, 338n3; aggregate finances (*see* aggregate finances); benefit calculations, 118–19; as an entitlement, 14, 318n8; future finances of, 15–18, 29–30, 116–33, 168–69; government obligations, 13–15; high-cost assumption, 119–20; individual equity objective, 14; intermediate-cost assumption, 119–20, 121–25; low-cost assumption, 119–20; public expectations, 13–15; social adequacy objective, 14; as a substitute for personal retirement saving, 31, 168, 300–301; tax calculations, 117–18; worker-to-beneficiary ratio, 82–84, 121
Social Security Administration (SSA), 37; annual benefit statements, 14–15; ANYPIA, 117, 118; Benefit and Earnings Public-Use File, 102–3; mortality rates, 48–49, 62; projection methodology, 3
Social Security Advisory Board: Technical Panel on Assumptions and Methods, 3, 12, 61, 294–95, 317n3
Social Security Board of Trustees: annual reports, 1–2, 4, 15–16, 30; cell-based methodology, 3–4, 11–13
Social Security's Office of the Chief Actuary (SSOCACT), scoring of reform proposals, 5–6, 11–13, 337n7
Social Security Tax and Benefit Calculator (SSTBC), 29–30, 83, 86, 117, 134–41, 145–46, 189, 207, 298; benefit recomputations, 137–38; delayed retirement, 137;

early retirement, 136; earnings test, 137; insured status, 135; Primary Insurance Amount (PIA), 135–36, 140; re-indexing method, 141; retirement benefits, 136; spousal and child dependent benefits, 138–39; survivor benefits, 139–40, 141; testing of, 118–19; wage-indexing method, 140–41
Solow growth model framework, 19, 88–91, 105
spousal benefits, 138–39, 211, 231. *See also* widow(er)'s benefits
SSA. *See* Social Security Administration (SSA)
SSTBC. *See* Social Security Tax and Benefit Calculator (SSTBC)
Stenholm, Charles, 206. *See also* Kolbe-Stenholm-Boyd reform proposal
stimulus programs, 9, 10
Stiroh, Kevin, 327n22
Survey of Consumer Finances (SCF), 89, 182–83
survivor benefits, 27, 139–40, 141, 188, 201–3. *See also* widow(er)'s benefits

taxable-to-total earnings ratio, 301, 334n4; under Ball reform proposal, 174, 175–77, 180–81; under Diamond-Orszag reform proposal, 187, 189, 191, 202; under Kolbe-Stenholm-Boyd reform proposal, 210; under Liebman-MacGuineas-Samwick reform proposal, 233, 244
taxes, payroll. *See* payroll taxes
Technical Panel on Assumptions and Methods, 3, 12, 61, 294–95
time horizons, 5, 11, 124, 128–29, 169–70, 298–300, 317n4, 318, 329n13
transition probabilities, 328n10
trust fund: under Ball reform proposal, 174–75, 178–79, 181, 302; exhaustion of, 1, 16, 198, 223; proposal to invest in equities, 174–75, 178–79, 181; surplus, 22–23, 26; use of to fund non–Social Security government expenditure, 22

uncertainty, income, 7, 75, 309–13, 342n8
University of Michigan, Panel Study of Income Dynamics (PSID). *See* Panel Study of Income Dynamics (PSID)

Vandenburg, Arthur, 318n15
variance: of lifetime earnings, 309–12;
    reduction, 310–11

wage-indexing method, 140–41
wealth tax rate, 146
widow(er)'s benefits, 201–3; under Bush
    Commission Model 2 reform proposal,
    252–53, 257; under Diamond-Orszag
    reform proposal, 188, 192; under
    Kolbe-Stenholm-Boyd reform proposal,

211; under Liebman-MacGuineas-
    Samwick reform proposal, 231, 235.
    See also spousal benefits; survivor
    benefits
Wise, David, 331n4
Witte, Edwin, 319n15
women. *See* gender
worker-to-beneficiary ratio, 82–84, 87–88,
    121, 126–28

Ziliak, James P., 336n9